Rural Life and Rural Church

Rural Life and Rural Church

Theological and empirical perspectives

Edited by

Leslie J. Francis
and
Mandy Robbins

Published by Equinox Publishing Ltd.
UK: Unit S3, Kelham House, 3 Lancaster Street, Sheffield, S3 8AF
USA: ISD, 70 Enterprise Drive, Bristol, CT 06010

www.equinoxpub.com

First published 2012

ISBN: 978-1-84553-983-2 (hardback)
ISBN: 978-1-84553-984-9 (paperback)

British Library Cataloguing-in-Publication Data

A catalogue record for this book is available from the British Library.

Library of Congress Cataloging-in-Publication Data

Rural life and rural church: theological and empirical perspectives/edited by Leslie J. Francis and Mandy Robbins.
    p. cm.
  Includes bibliographical references and indexes.
  ISBN 978-1-84553-983-2 (hb)—ISBN 978-1-84553-984-9 (pb)
  1. Rural churches—Great Britain. I. Francis, Leslie J. II. Robbins, Mandy.
  BR747.R87 2012
  253.0941'091734—dc23

                              2011026704

Typeset by SJI Services, New Delhi
Printed and bound in the UK by MPG Books Group

CONTENTS

Preface   ix

Foreword by The Bishop of Shrewsbury,
The Rt Revd Mark Rylands   xi

1. Introduction: shaping rural theology   1
   Leslie J. Francis

PART 1. PERSPECTIVES FROM THE BIBLE

2. Israelite wisdom and pastoral theology in the rural church   8
   Gareth Lloyd Jones

3. The invisible countryside of the New Testament   22
   William A. Strange

4. Sheep and goats: pastoral imagery in the Bible and today   33
   Richard T. France

PART 2. PERSPECTIVES FROM ORDINARY THEOLOGY

5. Ordinary theology for rural theology and rural ministry   42
   Jeff Astley

6. The kneelers are most impressive: reflections on reading a
   visitors' book   52
   Norman Morris and Lewis Burton

7. Ordinary prayer and the rural church: an empirical study of
   prayer cards   64
   Tania ap Siôn

PART 3. THEOLOGICAL AND SOCIOLOGICAL PERSPECTIVES

8. Encountering New Age spirituality: opportunities and
   challenges for the rural church   82
   John Drane

9. God in creation: a reflection on Jürgen Moltmann's theology   94
    William K. Kay

10. Belonging to rural church and society: theological and
    sociological perspectives   105
    David S. Walker

PART 4. HISTORICAL PERSPECTIVES

11. Blackshawhead: a local case history in rural church
    categorization   120
    Lewis Burton

12. Is the rural church different? The special case of confirmation 131
    David W. Lankshear

13. Rural Anglicanism: one face or many?   145
    Carol Roberts

14. Pastoral fragments: discovered remnants of a rural past   161
    Trevor Kerry

PART 5. LISTENING TO VISITORS

15. I was glad: listening to visitors to country churches   180
    Keith Littler, Leslie J. Francis and Jeremy Martineau

16. Sacred place and pilgrimage: modern visitors to the shrine
    of St Melangell   188
    Michael Keulemans and Lewis Burton

17. Visitor experiences of St Davids Cathedral: the two worlds
    of pilgrims and secular tourists   201
    *Emyr Williams, Leslie J. Francis, Mandy Robbins and
    Jennie Annis*

PART 6. LISTENING TO THE COMMUNITY

18. Social capital generated by two rural churches: the role of
    individual believers   216
    Keith Ineson and Lewis Burton

19. Local festivals in two Pennine villages: the reactions of the
    local Methodist church congregations   229
    Sue Pegg and Lewis Burton

20. Extended communion: a second best option for rural
Anglicanism? 242
Stella Mills

PART 7. LISTENING TO CHURCHGOERS

21. All types are called, but some are more likely to respond: the
psychological type profile of rural Anglican churchgoers in
Wales 258
*Leslie J. Francis, Mandy Robbins, Angela Williams and
Rhys Williams*

22. The social significance of Harvest Festivals in the countryside:
an empirical enquiry among those who attend 266
David S. Walker

23. Psychological type profile of volunteer workers in a rural
Christian charity shop 281
Leslie J. Francis and Sue Pegg

PART 8. LISTENING TO CHURCH LEADERS

24. Deployment of the churches' ministry: Anglicans and
Methodists in a rural diocese 286
Lewis Burton

25. Views on baptism and confirmation in the Church in Wales:
are rural clergy different? 299
Keith Littler

26. Children and communion: listening to churchwardens in
rural and urban Wales 305
Ann Howells and Keith Littler

PART 9. SATISFACTION AND STRESS IN MINISTRY

27. Burnout and the practice of ministry among rural clergy:
looking for the hidden signs 316
Christopher J. F. Rutledge

28. How happy are rural Anglican clergy? 325
Christine E. Brewster

29. Perceptions of stress on those in rural ministry: listening to
    church leaders   337
    Paul Rolph and Jenny Rolph

    Contributors   347

    Sources   350

    Subject Index   353

    Name Index   363

PREFACE

In 2002 we welcomed the invitation from the Rural Theology Association to serve as founding editors of the new peer-review journal, *Rural Theology*. At the close of the decade we decided to stand back and to review the articles that had been published in the journal by that stage. We were impressed by the range, by the originality, and by the contribution already made to serious reflection on the life, ministry, and mission of the rural church.

As we reviewed the material, we also recognized that clear themes and clear patterns were emerging from these original articles. We recognized, too, that the cumulative impact of the individual contributions could be enhanced by drawing them together within a thematic structure and by offering them to a wider audience through a reader on *Rural Life and Rural Church*.

There has been a close association between the development of this reader and the Doctor of Ministry programme offered by Glyndŵr University in association with the St Mary's Centre and the Centre for Studies in Rural Ministry. On the one hand, some of the articles have emerged as the direct result of MA dissertations, DMin dissertations and research conducted by faculty in association with course participants. On the other hand, the journal has served as a core resource for the programme to provide models for the development of the research-based reflective practice to which the programme is committed.

We have only been able to produce this reader because of the work of many colleagues. We wish therefore to thank the authors who have submitted material to *Rural Theology*, our colleagues on the editorial board, those who have accepted invitations to peer review material, and those who worked with us on the production of the journal and this reader. Throughout the production of the journal a team of four colleagues have worked with us on copyediting, proofreading and checking the text: Lewis Burton, Stephen Cope, Keith Littler, and Jeremy

Martineau. Susan Thomas prepared the first editions of the journal for printing and Diane Drayson has checked the final manuscript.

In 2010 *Rural Theology* joined the growing family of Equinox journals and this reader was located within the Equinox list. We are grateful to Janet Joyce for the support, encouragement and opportunities that she has offered through Equinox Publishing.

Further information about the initiatives underpinning this reader can be found on the following websites: Rural Theology Association, Equinox Publishing, and Centre for Studies in Rural Ministry.

Leslie J. Francis
Mandy Robbins

FOREWORD

It was a sunny summer morning before breakfast. Wandering in the meadows up on Dartmoor, I saw a Copper, a Blue, a Marbled White, a Comma, a Clouded Yellow and a Fritillary - all in the space of half an hour. The experience took me straight back to my childhood and memories of my father who taught me to spot and catch butterflies. Twenty-nine years a country parson in South Cheshire, I'll never forget the picture of his study as I showed a wedding couple in for marriage preparation. In the far corner, between the window and the bookshelves, were butterfly nets with boxes on the floor full of chloroformed butterflies waiting to be set. A fishing rod leant against the filing cabinet with an open spool reel and trout flies resting on top of the banns of marriage book. Behind an armchair, beer was brewing; and next to the beer was a large planter pot, full of moist dark peaty soil, growing mushrooms. To a boy brought up in a rural rectory, it seemed like an Aladdin's cave – I enjoyed drifting in there when Dad was out visiting.

Rural ministry has, at times, been viewed in the Church of England as a 'second class' ministry – a place for those without the courage or ability to cope with the cutting edge of a deprived urban estate or the demands of a large town church. This is, obviously, a warped view from which I was fortunately spared by the example of my father and his ministry. A countryman at heart, living and understanding the lives of his parishioners - 3000 souls and many more cattle, pigs and sheep - his was a big God who created the universe yet also cares deeply for each part of his creation. My father opened my eyes to the beauty and diversity of God's world, the hidden crosses borne quietly by many in the countryside and, thereby, the virtue and integrity of a vocation to a rural Cure. He helped me see its many opportunities for reaching every area of community life with the Gospel and the imperative for Christian witness to embody the good news with a seamless join between life and lip.

Added to this rural upbringing, 11 years in Cheshire and Somerset serving as a rural multi-church minister, until recently in Devon as Canon Missioner and now in Shropshire as Bishop of Shrewsbury, I have become more alert to the opportunities for rural ministry and mission as well as aware of the challenges faced by village churches. As incumbent, Canon Missioner, and now as Bishop, I recognize and welcome the energy, skill and commitment of the clergy and lay people who are living and proclaiming the Gospel of Christ within the rural parishes of England and Wales.

Serving as Chair of the Rural Theology Association (RTA), I have appreciated the significant contribution made by that organization over three decades to the life of the rural church. The RTA has done much to raise the profile of the distinctiveness of rural life, of rural ministry, and to raise the level of debate concerning rural theology. The newsletter and the journal of the RTA have been crucial to achieving these ends.

In this, I believe we owe a particular debt of gratitude to Professor Leslie Francis who, over this period, has persistently critiqued and championed ministry in rural areas. His scholarship, quiet determination and enthusiasm for the promotion of Christianity in the countryside has infected and affected thousands of people. Indeed, 'The School of Francis' – Leslie and his disciples – has given both academic credibility and global reach to rural theology and mission.

When in 2002 the RTA launched the new peer-reviewed journal, *Rural Theology*, it provided a forum for international, inter-disciplinary, and inter-denominational debate designed to attract the best quality research and scholarship relevant to the ministry and mission of the rural church. The present book demonstrates just how much the founding editors and editorial board of *Rural Theology* have achieved in a short space of time.

Rural Life and Rural Church serves as a reader drawing together key articles published during the first decade of the new journal. The skilful organization of these articles within nine focused sections provides an excellent and authoritative account of current research, research that needs to be taken seriously by all who are shaping the future of our rural churches, both ordained and lay. Here is material that will help us cherish the virtue and integrity of our calling; a calling that originated in a small countryside mission beside Lake Galilee.

Mark Rylands
Bishop of Shrewsbury

Chapter 1

INTRODUCTION: SHAPING RURAL THEOLOGY

Leslie J. Francis

Abstract – This article situates the notion of rural theology within the broader framework of contemporary concern with contextual theologies. Then it identifies the contours of rural theology that give shape to the present volume: perspectives from the Bible, perspectives from ordinary theology, theological and sociological perspectives, historical perspectives, listening to visitors, listening to the community, listening to churchgoers, listening to church leaders, and satisfaction and stress in ministry.

Introduction

Theology is a discipline shaped more by its subject matter than by the methods with which the subject matter is approached. Theologians (ordinary theologians as much as professional theologians) are concerned with the study of discourse about God and with all that purports to reveal knowledge of God or to be concerned with the experience of God.

Throughout the twentieth century Christian theology became increasingly aware of the importance of perspective in informing and shaping the theological exercise. Contextual theology recognizes that the same subject matter may be viewed from different perspectives and that such perspectival viewing can generate authentic and legitimate insights into the subject matter that grasps the theologian's attention – the study of discourse about God. Liberation theology reflects on the insights of those who see God and hear God speak from the perspective of the oppressed. Feminist theology reflects on the insights of those who see God and hear God speak from the perspective of women. Black theology reflects on the insights of those who see God and hear God speak from the perspective of people of colour. Such perspectives are not in competition, but are complementary as the whole people of God talk about the things of God, as the whole people of God share their insights into the revelation of God.

Rural theology

It is within such a context that the notion of rural theology is properly located. There is no one thing that is rural theology, but there is a distinctive perspective from which rural theology regards the study of God, the revelation of God, the knowledge of God, the experience of God. Like other contextual theologies, rural theology does not exist for its own benefit, for its own salvation. Rural theology is not an isolationist movement, not an escape into a rural retreat. Rural theology exists to serve the whole people of God, the whole Church of God, and to interact with the whole of the theology faculty. There are some key insights of a theological nature that may perchance best be glimpsed within the rural context.

The branch of rural theology represented by the present collection of essays was originally nurtured by a small group of pioneering Anglican clergy serving in England in the late 1970s. Neither they, nor the tradition to which they gave rise, were constrained by being Anglican, being English, or being ordained. The vision was properly ecumenical, international, and interdisciplinary, a vision to be caught by the whole people of God, lay and ordained, a vision to inspire ordinary theologians as much as professional theologians. It was to stimulate such a vision that the Rural Theology Association was formed.

In 2002 the Rural Theology Association launched its new journal *Rural Theology* to stimulate its mission of encouraging and disseminating this form of contextual theology. During the first eight years of its life the journal has helped to scope the field of rural theology in a novel and purposive way. The present volume has been designed to draw together and to coordinate that field in a coherent fashion.

Contours of rural theology

Although theology is a discipline shaped more by its subject matter than by the methods with which the subject matter is approached, the discipline is best recognized in the public sphere by the distinctive ways in which theologians go about their business. The framework adopted by this volume is one formed precisely by the approach taken by different writers to give contours to the field of rural theology.

The first section, *Perspectives from the Bible*, is shaped by theological voices grounded in the text of scripture. Gareth Lloyd Jones employs his insights into the Hebrew scriptures to argue that pastoral theology proclaimed from rural pulpits and practised in rural ministry may be disloyal to the biblical roots if inadequate attention is given to the perspective of the Israelite Wisdom tradition. William A. Strange, working as a scholar of the New Testament, explores the clear contrast between the treatment of the countryside in Paul (for whom rural concerns emerge only as the source for occasional metaphors) and the Synoptic gospels (in which agrarian life is portrayed unselfconsciously but in sympathetic detail). Richard T. France draws on themes from both the Old Testament and the New Testament to explore pastoral imagery in the Bible and today.

The second section, *Perspectives from ordinary theology*, draws on a new and innovative voice within theology to demonstrate the application and relevance of this method. Jeff Astley, with whom this method originates in a seminal book published in 2002, describes and defends the notion of a non-technical 'ordinary theology', and argues for its role as an originating source for both academic theology and official ecclesiastical theology. He then identifies rural ministry as a context in which ordinary theology may be discerned most clearly and explored most successfully. Astley's category of rural theology is then set to work in the following pair of essays. Norman Morris and Lewis Burton read the ordinary theology that emerges from the visitors' book in one rural church. Tania ap Siôn reads the ordinary theology that emerges from just over one thousand prayer cards left in another rural church. The visitors' book and the prayer board provide powerful insights into the ordinary theology of those who use them.

The third section, *Theological and sociological perspectives*, demonstrates how practical theology within a rural context is informed by both disciplines. Three practical theologians develop three distinctive themes. John Drane reviews the rise of New Age spiritualities and argues that the Church has resources, particularly in its rural manifestations, that can begin to address the concerns of today's spiritual searchers. William K. Kay draws on Jürgen Moltmann's book, *God in Creation* (concerned with the totality of the relationship between God and the created order), as a stimulus to reflection on a theology of the environment and a theology of the rural church. Using both theological and sociological theory, David S. Walker develops a fourfold model of belonging (to activities, to people, to events, and to places) and applies this model to investigate how the ministry of the parish church relates to those who would define themselves as belonging with it.

The fourth section, *Historical perspectives*, demonstrates the role of historical enquiry in shaping rural theology. Lewis Burton undertakes a local case history in rural church categorization by profiling Blackshawhead in West Yorkshire, and draws attention to the value of the study of the local church for more general issues in rural theology. David W. Lankshear draws on the nationally published statistics of confirmation candidates in the Church of England between 1950 and 1999 to test the thesis that the rural church is different. Carol Roberts also draws on the nationally published statistics to test the thesis that there is a coherent picture across the Church of England. She concludes that, as autonomous administrative units, the dioceses may have considerable say in their destinies through diocesan policies. She prefers to speak, therefore, of the many faces of Rural Anglicanism, rather than in terms of one Rural Anglicanism. In a very different kind of historical study, Trevor Kerry records the discovery of pages from an unpublished manuscript of an autobiography by Jean Blathwayt, daughter of the rector of Melbury Osmund, the Revd Francis Blathwayt, who held the living from 1916 until 1929.

The fifth section, *Listening to visitors*, turns attention to the perspectives of empirical theology that have been especially fostered by the journal *Rural Theology*. Three groups of empirical theologians illustrate the key ministry and mission of the rural church among those who are passing through. Keith Littler, Leslie J. Francis and Jeremy Martineau analyse qualitative data provided by 765 visitors and discover how their data provide a valuable guide to visitors' views about the provisions churches should make for visitors and tourists. Michael Keulemans and Lewis Burton analyse the responses of 107 visitor to the shrine of St Melangell at Pennant Melangell in Wales, and discover that many visitors today are aware of sacred place and can be described as being on pilgrimage. Emyr Williams, Leslie J. Francis, Mandy Robbins and Jennie Annis analyse the response of 514 visitors to St Davids Cathedral in West Wales. The data demonstrated clear differences between the experience of pilgrims (defined as visitors who attend church services weekly) and the experiences of secular tourists (defined as visitors who never attend church services).

The sixth section, *Listening to the community*, employs empirical techniques to explore three areas of concern for rural ministry and mission. Keith Ineson and Lewis Burton demonstrate the contribution of rural churchgoers to the social capital of their own church-related community (bonding social capital) and to the social capital of the wider community (bridging social capital). Sue Pegg and Lewis Burton examine the reaction of two Pennine village churches to a local festival in their communities (the Jazz Festival and the Moonraker Festival). They found that both festivals had potential for outreach. Stella Mills examines the responses to extended communion within a rural Anglican benefice.

The seventh section, *Listening to churchgoers*, employs empirical techniques within the context of congregational studies. Leslie J. Francis, Mandy Robbins, Angela Williams and Rhys Williams demonstrate that, although all are called, some people are more likely to join the village church. Alongside the more visible demographic bias in terms of sex and age, they draw attention to the less visible bias in terms of psychological type. Some psychological types clearly found it more difficult to fit into the village church. David S. Walker draws attention to the social significance of Harvest Festivals in the countryside by profiling the diverse characteristics of those who attend. Leslie J. Francis and Sue Pegg draw attention to the distinctive ministry of rural Christian charity shops among the volunteer workers.

The eighth section, *Listening to church leaders*, employs empirical techniques within the context of clergy studies. Lewis Burton discusses a survey among clergy in pastoral appointments in the Diocese of York and similarly employed ministers in the York and Hull Methodist district, and documents the differences in pastoral practice and the contrasting provisions of ministry to rural churches offered by these two denominations. Keith Littler discusses a survey among Church in Wales stipendiary parochial clergy concerning various aspects of baptism and confirmation, and demonstrates that rural clergy are more community orientated and probably more sensitive to the conservative view of parishioners. Ann Howells and Keith Littler compare two surveys contrasting the views of clergy and churchwardens on the issue of children receiving communion before confirmation. Churchwardens emerge as notably less supportive than clergy.

The final section, *Satisfaction and stress in ministry*, profiles an issue of growing practical concern within rural churches as the nature of ministry changes in response to declining congregations, declining financial resources, and fewer stipendiary clergy. Drawing on a sample of 318 rural Anglican clergy who completed a modified form of the Maslach Burnout Inventory, Christopher J. F. Routledge concludes that an unacceptably high number of rural clergy show signs of emotional exhaustion from their ministry and that burnout is reflected in many subtle ways in the practice of ministry. Working within the framework of positive psychology, Christine E. Brewster draws on a sample of 722 Anglican clergy working with at least three rural churches who completed the Oxford Happiness Questionnaire. She concludes that while the majority of these clergy experience moderately high levels of happiness in their work environment, the benefits of this positive affect are diminished by the enormous demands placed on them by multi-parish benefices. Paul Rolph and Jenny Rolph complete this section by examining the perceptions of eleven senior church leaders on the nature and extent of stress among rural clergy.

Conclusion

In 1990 the report of the Archbishops' Commission on Rural Areas, *Faith in the Countryside*, was quite hard pressed to identify a discrete body of knowledge that could be identified as *rural theology*. Taken together, the nine sections in the present volume illustrate just how far the journal of the Rural Theology Association has now helped to establish the contours of a form of contextual theology that can be properly styled *rural theology*. Building on these foundations, the Rural Theology Association, the Arthur Rank Centre, and the Centre for Studies in Rural Ministry are now strongly placed to enhance the self-awareness and self-confidence of ordinary theologians and professional theologians engaged in rural theology, with consequent strengthening of the mission and of the ministry of the rural church, well beyond the confines of Anglicanism and well beyond the confines of England and Wales. That small group of pioneering Anglican clergy serving in England in the late 1970s whose vision established the Rural Theology Association have indeed achieved a great deal.

Part 1

PERSPECTIVES FROM THE BIBLE

Chapter 2

ISRAELITE WISDOM AND PASTORAL THEOLOGY IN THE RURAL CHURCH

Gareth Lloyd Jones*

Abstract – This article argues that pastoral theology proclaimed from rural pulpits and practised in rural ministry may be disloyal to its biblical roots if inadequate attention is given to the distinctive perspective of the Israelite Wisdom tradition. A review of recent significant development in our understanding of this particular biblical tradition is followed by an examination of a prominent aspect of Hebrew Wisdom, namely its anthropocentricity. Attention will be drawn to the literature's key themes including human concerns, human responsibility, human authority, and human limitations.

Introduction

Traditionally the writings ascribed to Israel's sages have included five books: Proverbs, Job and Ecclesiastes in the canon of the Old Testament, and the Wisdom of Solomon and the Wisdom of Ben Sira (Ecclesiasticus) in the Apocrypha. When considering this literature, it is useful to make a distinction between books of a prudential nature, which contain practical advice on how to succeed in life (Proverbs and parts of the Wisdom of Ben Sira), and those of a reflective kind, where the authors probe the meaning of existence and question the accepted order (Job and Ecclesiastes).

Though scholars have recently extended the scope of Israelite Wisdom, having detected the influence of the sages in other parts of

* The Revd Professor Gareth Lloyd Jones is Professor Emeritus of Theology and Religious Studies in the University of Wales, Bangor. *Address for correspondence*: Department of Theology and Religious Studies, University of Wales, Bangor, New Arts Building, Bangor, Gwynedd, LL57 2DG. E-mail: rss402@bangor.ac.uk

the Old Testament such as Genesis, Deuteronomy, and 2 Samuel, this development does not concern us here. The primary focus of this article is on the recognized Wisdom books, and specifically on the Book of Proverbs with its essentially prudential message and optimistic outlook. But before we examine this element in the teaching of the sages, let us note the reception given to the Wisdom tradition in general within Christian scholarly circles during the past half-century.

Deficient theology

Until well into the 1960s the emphasis in biblical scholarship was on the Law and the Prophets. Though the Wisdom literature was a recognized part of the canon, its theological relevance was considered to be marginal. It was regarded as a foreign body within the Old Testament. G.E. Wright, a prominent figure in the Biblical Theology Movement, admitted that 'in any outline of biblical theology, the proper place to treat the Wisdom Literature is something of a problem' (Wright, 1952, p. 115, n.1). A similar claim was made over thirty years later by H.G. Reventlow (1985, p. 184) in whose opinion 'the integration of wisdom into Old Testament theology is an unresolved task that remains for the future'. What accounts for this negative view of Wisdom and for the indifference to it exhibited by many biblical scholars?

The primary reason is the reluctance of the sages to mention 'the mighty acts of God'. During the early part of the twentieth century, theologians concluded that the Old Testament bore witness to a God who acted within the day-to-day life of a particular nation in order to save humanity. Consider the main themes of the Pentateuch, all of which are presented as historical events: the promise to Abraham, the Exodus, the making of the covenant, and the wilderness wanderings. These traditions were thought to be the raw materials of an Old Testament theology. The belief that God is revealed within the historical order as a redeemer was at the heart of Israelite religion. As in the New Testament, history was the arena of divine action; hence the term 'salvation-history'.

When judged according to such a scheme, the canonical Wisdom books appear to be theologically deficient. The wise do not mention liberation, election, covenant, for example; they address human beings irrespective of their nationality. For them, authoritative truth is not based on revelation but on observation and experience. The essence of religion is not temple-worship but right living. It is difficult, therefore, to find any correlation between Wisdom and the central ideas of the

Old Testament. Its teachings are theologically incompatible with those of the Torah and the prophetic books. They are difficult to fit into any theology which is dominated by the concept of a God who acts on behalf of a chosen people.

Because it did not conform to a view of God's revelatory actions, the Wisdom literature was considered to be utilitarian and worldly with little or no theological depth. This led Wright to the conclusion that the book of Proverbs 'remains near the pagan source of wisdom in which society and the Divine work in history played no real role' (Wright, 1952, p. 104). Furthermore it was perceived to have 'a strongly secular flavour' and to be 'only loosely connected with religious faith' (Eichrodt, 1967, II, p. 81). When the sages are compared with the prophets they come out a poor second.

Given that their theology has been regarded as deficient by leading and influential theologians, perhaps it is not surprising that the common lectionary contains very few readings from the canonical Wisdom literature for Sundays and Holy Days.

A reappraisal

It can now be confidently stated that such negativity belongs to a previous generation. Today we witness a positive attitude toward the Wisdom literature. Current scholarship is at pains to revise past opinion and emphasize the distinctiveness of Wisdom within the religion of Israel. There can be no doubt that 'the wisdom literature has moved toward the centre of interest of Old Testament scholars during the past quarter of a century' (Emerton, 1979, p. 214). For any evaluation of the theological significance of the Old Testament, the words of the wise have become an element of the first importance. This reappraisal has opened up a dimension of Israelite life and thought which has never before been fully understood nor adequately appreciated.

The reason for this re-evaluation of the theological significance of Wisdom is that the emphasis once placed on 'the God who acts in history' has been greatly reduced. Philosophical critique has played a major part in this. For example, Maurice Wiles has pointed out that the concept of a God who is revealed within the historical order is not as distinctive a characteristic of Old Testament thought as is often supposed. If the core of Israel's theology is to be found in God's action, then a substantial part of the canon must be regarded as having only an ancillary role to play in the nation's religious tradition. To say the least, 'one finds it a little difficult to know what to do with the Wisdom literature' (Wiles, 1986, p. 1).

But philosophy is not the only contributor to the qualification of the emphasis on the 'mighty acts' of God and to the subsequent reappraisal of Wisdom. The contemporary secular worldview is another. Most people do not regard God as the proximate source of all that happens. The notion that he is the direct cause of every occurrence is alien to them. When we hear of a pedestrian killed by a hit-and-run driver, we do not believe that the accident is an act of God. Amos's conviction that the Lord actively punishes a corrupt political system, either through natural catastrophes or by enemy action (Amos 3:6), finds little favour today. Though some see the destruction of the Twin Towers on 11 September 2001 as divine punishment of a corrupt culture, the vast majority of us take responsibility for the consequences of our actions without any reference to a divine agency. The idea of a wrathful deity who acts within history to strike down those who displease him seems closer to pagan mythology than to the Judaeo-Christian tradition. Does the God of Israel, asks Wiles, 'like Zeus, send out thunderbolts in his displeasure?' (Wiles, 1986, p. 1). Today we think in terms of autonomy rather than theonomy, of the secular rather than the sacred.

For some people the word 'secular' has negative connotations in that it means 'irreligious', and is therefore an inappropriate term to describe Israelite thought. But in his pioneering study of the theological legitimacy of the secular experience, Harvey Cox distinguishes between secular-*ization* and secular*ism*. Secularization has a positive meaning in that it refers to 'the discovery by man that he has been left with the world on his hands, that he can no longer blame fortune or the furies for what he does with it. Secularization is man turning his attention away from worlds beyond and toward this world and this time (*saeculum* = "this present age")'. It is a 'historical process, almost certainly irreversible, in which society and culture are delivered from tutelage to religious control'. Its children are pluralism and tolerance which 'represent a society's unwill-ingness to enforce any particular worldview on its citizens' (Cox, 1965, pp. 2–3).

Secularism, however, has negative connotations. It is 'the name for an ideology, a new closed worldview which functions very much like a new religion .... Like any other 'ism', it menaces the openness and freedom secularization has produced' (Cox, 1965, pp. 20–21). So when Eichrodt describes Wisdom as having 'a strongly secular flavour', he is referring to secularization not secularism. He might claim, as others would, that the teachings of the sages 'were essentially common sense as opposed to having their starting point in religious ideas about God' (Dell, 2000, p. 29).

Theological anthropology

In his reappraisal of the significance of the Wisdom tradition R.E. Murphy summarizes the central message or 'kerygma' of the book of Proverbs in one word: 'life' (Murphy, 1966, p. 3). It is noteworthy how often the word is used:

> Heed admonition and you are on the road to life (10:17).
> A soothing word is a tree of life (15:4).
> He who perseveres in right conduct and loyalty finds life (21:21).

In this context 'life' does not mean longevity or survival. Rather it implies peace, security, wellbeing, material needs, human rights, friends, family, health. It includes 'all these things' promised by Jesus in Matthew 6:33, things which allow people to live to their full potential.

Because it is chiefly concerned with the human quest for prosperity and wholeness, and lacks a readily identifiable theological core, the Wisdom literature has been regarded as markedly anthropocentric in character. The various definitions given to the teaching of the sages highlight this description. It has been described as: 'an approach to reality', 'the ability to cope', 'non-revelatory speech'. In the words of G. von Rad, 'Israel understood "wisdom" as a practical knowledge of the laws of life and of the world, based upon experience' (von Rad, 1962, I, p 418). Three characteristics of the literature witness to its anthropocentricity.

First, *the focus on the individual.* The advice given by the wise is sometimes in the form of an instruction extending over several verses, but more often in the form of a proverb. It is always the fruit of observation, for observation is the quintessence of proverb-making. A word of wisdom is often prefaced by 'I saw' or 'I saw and took note'. It is clear from the advice given that the sages had every person's welfare at heart. Various types of individuals receive close attention in an effort to provide direction for those who seek it. There is an emphasis on character so that specific virtues and vices are identified. The drunkard, the sluggard and the scoundrel are condemned and mocked.

> Wine is an insolent fellow, and strong drink a brawler, and no one addicted to their company is wise (20:1; cf. 23:29-35).
> A door turns on its hinges, a sluggard on his bed (26:14; cf. 24:30-34).

A scoundrel rakes up evil gossip, it is like scorching fire on his lips (16:27; cf. 6:12-19).

Genuine friendship is extolled and three of its characteristics emphasized: constancy, 'A friend shows his friendship at all times' (17:17); candour, 'Open reproof is better than love concealed' (It is better to correct people openly than let them think that you do not care for them at all, 27:5); counsel, 'As iron sharpens iron so one person sharpens the wits of another' (27:17). These are but a few of the many examples of the sages' interest in the individual.

Second, *the insignificance of history.* We have already noted that the canonical Wisdom books are devoid of any reference to Israelite history. Not a word is said about the nation's glorious past. The liberation from Egypt, the conquest of Canaan, the achievements of King David, are all passed over in silence. In the rest of the Old Testament these are the bricks and mortar of the theology, for they reveal God at work in the world. The sages knew their history, but they chose to ignore it because their message was centred on humanity not on God.

Third, *the universality of wisdom.* Because the literature is intended for and applied to everyone, the particularism which stressed that Israel was God's chosen people is deliberately ignored. So there is no mention of the priesthood, the temple, or Jerusalem. The only concession the author of Proverbs makes to his Israelite background is the use of the word 'Yahweh'. If this proper name were to be replaced with 'God', the book would be as relevant to Muslims and Buddhists as it is to Jews and Christians. The sage's parish is the world. His viewpoint is ecumenical. His message is for everyone, regardless of creed, colour or country. Everything concerned with humanity is within his sphere of interest. This characteristic has been partly responsible for the general appeal of his teachings down the ages.

However, the view that the anthropocentric framework is primary does not mean that Wisdom totally lacks a religious dimension. While it is true to say that the focus of the sages is on humanity, that 'man is at stage-centre in OT wisdom literature' (Towner, 1977, p .138), it is not true to say that God is absent. We will have occasion to explore further the theocentric aspect as we consider the features which flow from the theological anthropology of the wise.

Human concerns

It is not for nothing that Wisdom has been termed 'the humanism of the Ancient East'. The authors of Proverbs, for example, display an altruism which implies a critique of society not unlike that found in the prophetic books. Because they believe in everyone's inalienable right to enjoy the good life, which is God's gift, they regard the ideal person as one who condemns avarice and oppression, and cares for the underprivileged:

> Whoever despises the hungry does wrong, but happy are they who are generous to the poor (14:21).
> Do not move an ancient boundary stone, or encroach on the land of the fatherless (23:10).
> If a king steadfastly deals out justice to the weak his throne will be secure for ever (29:14).

The authors have a lively social conscience. They make it clear that concern for the needy is not an optional activity but a basic human requirement. The litmus test for any community is the way it treats those who live a marginal existence.

Because they did not disparage the things of this world, but placed great emphasis on mundane matters, it is not surprising that the sages have been considered secular and materialistic. But in attempting to safeguard people's welfare and stress the importance of life on earth, they provide an important contrast to another way of regarding human existence, namely that of life as a pilgrimage. The nomadic image is one of the individual as a pilgrim 'who nightly pitches his moving tent a day's march nearer home'. The people of God have no lasting city here on earth but 'are seekers after the city which is to come' (Hebrews 13:14). They live in the hope of a blessed future. The Christian is properly warned against any over-attachment to the things of this world and offered a life which is eternal and transcendent. The ultimate goal is deferred.

While this image contains a profound truth, like all images it can be misleading if taken in isolation. It has led many Christians to look to the future at the expense of the present, a viewpoint reflected in some popular hymns.

> Through the night of doubt and sorrow
> Onward goes the pilgrim band,
> Singing songs of expectation,
> Marching to the promised land.

This hymn was sung with great gusto in Victorian England while ten-year-old boys were sent down the mines and their parents sweated for a pittance 'in those dark, satanic mills'. Faced with social deprivation, the established Church did little to remedy the situation; it merely talked about a promised land where all would be well. And although the fact was never emphasized, everyone knew that the only way to get there was via the cemetery. The American plantation owner had similar ideas. In order to keep his slaves quiet he taught them to sing:

> This world is not my home, I'm just a-passin' thru.

While keeping alive the dream of heaven, Christians have been justly criticized for aiding and abetting those who promote the conditions of hell. A pilgrim theology may be true to one aspect of biblical teaching, but it has been the source of considerable indifference in the Church. Because it devalues and fails to influence the present it is open to judgement.

Returning to the Wisdom literature, we see a totally different emphasis. There is no talk here of a deferred goal, but a concern for the quality of life. Whatever does not contribute to wholeness and wellbeing is characterized as death. The rewards of sensible living are not extrinsic to life in the world, but part of it. Fullness of life for the human community should be a present reality, not the end-point of history. The sage is concerned not with how things will work out in the long run, but how they actually are in the short run.

Such a this-worldly emphasis is surely not alien to the Christian, for Christianity has been described as the most materialistic of all religions. By sharing our nature God demonstrated that human life matters. Flesh became the vehicle of salvation; matter became the means of revelation. The Church, however, has tended to reject Christian materialism in favour of an other-worldly spirituality, pilgrim theology, in which matter becomes second-rate. It has regarded a concern for material things as reprehensible and concentrated largely on the spiritual. But when William Booth went into the slums of 'darkest England' in the nineteenth century, he said that he brought with him three things: soup, soap and salvation. And he added, 'in that order'. Israel's sages would have said 'Amen' to that.

Human responsibility

We have noted that the dominant model in Old Testament theology for decades was that of salvation-history, with its focus on the God who redeemed his people. The Exodus story stressed the ability of God to liberate those who could do nothing to save themselves from the callous regime of the Pharaoh. It was a theology for the powerless, which was cherished and remembered by Israel whenever the chips were down (for example, during the Babylonian Exile) because it offered hope in a seemingly hopeless situation.

This concept of God at work in history intervening against hostile forces, doing for the community of faith what it could not do itself, found expression in the liberation theology of the mid-twentieth century. It was accepted as an appropriate model for the world's marginal and oppressed people. But how appropriate is it for theological reflection in a prosperous western country? In an affluent society, talk of liberation from bondage and deliverance from oppression, in a physical sense, can seem hollow and hypocritical.

If such a model does not have an immediate appeal, it might be worth pondering an alternative found in the Wisdom literature. Assuming that the earliest Israelite sages were active during the age of David and Solomon, they were living in a period of expansion, wealth and military might. The nation had never had it so good. As the wise reflected on this new-found prosperity, they attempted to fashion a theology which would speak to their contemporaries. This was not salvation-history. They did not picture God as intervening to save a dejected people, but rather as the creator and sustainer of life on earth. In this ordered universe human beings stand alongside the Creator as vice-regents or trusted servants. They are created in his image and have been given the responsibility for shaping their own destiny.

Such a view of human nature is clearly optimistic. It claims that humans do have the ability to cope with life's problems, though traditional Christian theology rejects this. The Church has put much liturgical energy into the confession of sin; an essential part of worship is a declaration of how bad and inadequate we are. The sages advocate a change of emphasis:

> The man of Proverbs is not the servile, self-abasing figure often urged by our one-sided reading of scripture in later Augustinian-Lutheran theological traditions. Rather he is an able, self-reliant, caring, involved, strong person who has a significant influence over the course of his own life and over the lives of his fellows .... Proverbs is not atheism .... It does not speak of the death of God, but it has no patience for a god who only saves sinners and judges sins. The God affirmed here trusts man, believes in him, risks his world with him, and stays with him in his failures (Brueggemann, 1972, p. 118).

To the powerful and the prosperous the sages preach a theology of responsibility. Human beings are accountable for their own destiny. They are able to make choices, and they should make them responsibly. The problem most people live with is not guilt or inadequacy, but the threat of chaos, a threat exacerbated by human irresponsibility.

All too often we plead our human nature as an excuse for our failings: 'I'm only human after all.' But the wise reject such an excuse. They maintain that it is precisely because we are human that we should accept the responsibility we have over the created order. There are many things which are not beyond the wit of human beings if they will but take their responsibilities seriously.

But such responsible citizenship will not be achieved without effort. It will depend on character formation; hence the constant emphasis on discipline and education. The Book of Proverbs is essentially pedagogic. In chapters 1–9 attention is focused on the family as the ideal environment for character-forming. Children sit silently at the feet of their parents: 'My son, observe your father's commands and do not abandon the teaching of your mother' (6:20). It is only after they have been schooled in discernment and communal virtues that individuals will contribute effectively to society. Although, as we have noted above, the sages consistently direct their instruction at the individual, they do not lose sight of the importance of the community. The primary duty of every person is to contribute responsibly and to the best of his or her ability to the society of which they are part.

Human authority

When the prophets were confronted with injustice in society, they spoke out in God's name. Their pronouncements were made on the highest authority: 'Thus says the Lord.' When, after the Exile, the priests sought to re-establish temple worship, they invoked the authority of Moses to whom they attributed the ritual laws of the Pentateuch. During the crisis of the fifth century Ezra tried to enforce the Jewish way of life by appealing to the authority of the written law.

But the sages follow none of these methods. They do not base their authority on spiritual experiences, the words of an infallible leader, or an inspired text. They make no dogmatic assertions which claim enduring validity. Instead of a structural form of authority, they adopt one which is based on experience, on the way things are:

Kindness brings its own reward; cruelty earns trouble for itself (11:17).
The way of righteousness leads to life, but there is a well-worn path to death (12:28).
An evil messenger causes trouble, but a trusty envoy brings healing (13:17).
A mild answer turns away anger, but a sharp word makes tempers rise (15:1).

The method of the Wisdom teachers was to observe, and from their observations to make certain deductions about human behaviour which should be regarded as authoritative. Things are so, not because someone says that they are, but because experience has proved them to be so. Because proverbs and aphorisms are deliberately written for ordinary people, they contain no theorizing or philosophizing. The authors appeal to the reader to note the consequences of certain actions because, for them, the appeal to experience is far more compelling and authoritative than a discussion of abstract ideas.

This understanding of authority is not without its attraction. Today structural authority is being questioned in all segments of society. There was a time when people took notice of authoritative pronouncements made by the major Churches on ethical and doctrinal issues. Few pay attention to them anymore. Those in positions of authority, in both Church and state, are not heeded in the way they once were. Their words, though they come from the top, do not command immediate, automatic, and universal attention. Those who wish to make an impact on society must now earn the right to be heard. In this situation the way of the wise may have something to commend it.

Much is made in certain quarters, and rightly so, of the role of the professing Christian as a counsellor, as one who is prepared and able to give guidance to others. Some counsellors provide weighty answers to the problems posed, answers which are hallowed by tradition, dictated by the Church, or found in the scriptures. Such a method, to my mind, may well produce negative results. Personally I have found that those people who have a prepacked answer to every difficulty have been of far less help to me than those who appear to do no more than make me think things out for myself. Those with a ready-made answer are only waiting for me to stop talking so that they can get me cleared up and put right. Those without one are more ready to listen and explore patiently what course of action should be taken. Israel's sages would have approved of such a non-directive method.

Human limitations

'The fear of the Lord is the foundation of knowledge' (1:7). This saying, described as the motto of the sages and the theological foundation of the Wisdom tradition, is the first actual proverb in the Book of Proverbs. It demonstrates that despite their consuming interest in matters of daily life, the authors believe that there is more to Wisdom than simply the ability to cope. Despite their emphasis on responsibility and their appeal for common sense, they are fully aware of the limits of human capability. They demonstrate this awareness in two ways.

First, they point out that there is an *incalculable element* in life which cannot easily be explained or dismissed. There is a realm of unpredictability which is beyond the control of even the wisest individual. It is here that the sage sees the hand of God. If a person wishes to be counted as wise, he should always reckon with God as a limiting factor in all things:

> Someone may plan his journey by his own wit, but it is the Lord who guides his steps (16:9).
> The human mind may be full of schemes, but it is the Lord's purpose that will prevail (19:21).
> A horse may be made ready for the day of battle, but victory rests with the Lord (21:31).

Commenting on the last of these verses, G. von Rad writes:

> The aim of this sentence is to put a stop to the erroneous concept that a guarantee of success was to be found simply in practising human wisdom and in making preparations. Man must always keep himself open to the activity of God, an activity which completely escapes all calculation, for between the putting into practice of the most reliable wisdom and that which actually takes place, there always lies a great unknown. (von Rad, 1972, p. 101)

Humans must always be open to this incalculable element in life, for despite its importance, wisdom is no guarantee of success.

Second, they believe that there is an *order to life*. This fixed order, found in the consistency and constancy of the natural world and in the instincts of animals, points to God as creator and preserver. Within this ordered world boundaries exist which no power can move. The successful farmer is the one who follows the annual cycle of seedtime and harvest, whereas 'the lazy man who does not plough in autumn looks for a crop at harvest and gets nothing' (20:4). Israel's kings had to learn that injustice and oppression were unacceptable, not because they were proscribed by a person or a book, but because they violated the created order. Living within limits may appear to be a negative experience but the sages regard boundaries as beneficial. For them they witness to God's providential care guarding humanity against its own follies.

So despite its consuming interest in the world and in human behaviour, the Wisdom literature contains more theology than many exegetes are prepared to admit. To quote von Rad again:

> Given the world in which they found themselves, the teachers considered it appropriate to speak at great length of valid rules and orders, even feeling obliged to include human activity as a factor. On the other hand, they regarded themselves equally justified in drawing attention from time to time to the hand of God intervening directly in human life. (von Rad, 1972, p. 105)

Conclusion

I conclude with an appeal that we do not neglect the message of Israel's sages in our preaching, teaching, and counselling. Let us keep in mind their concern for life and their belief in human dignity. What part can the Christian play in the fight against 'all that kills abundant living'? Let us remember their emphasis on responsibility, on the fact that humans are trusted creatures working in partnership with God. Where does the Christian stand on the vital question of ecology? Let us not dismiss their appeal to the authority of experience. In the counselling situation, in the face of human need, how do we provide constructive answers to those who seek help? Let us take to heart their recognition that whatever their capabilities, human beings are not the masters of all things. There is a limit to human potential. What convictions about the Lord of life can we share with others?

The theological anthropology of the sages cannot be promoted as *the* hermeneutical key for unlocking the Bible. But because it is a recognized element within the biblical tradition and contributes to the richness of the scriptures, it can legitimately be called upon to provide an alternative to a theology based on salvation-history.

Acknowledgement

Unless otherwise stated, biblical quotations are from the Book of Proverbs. The version used is the Revised English Bible 1989.

References

Brueggemann, W. (1972). *In man we trust: The neglected side of biblical faith.* Richmond, Virginia: John Knox Press.

Cox, H. (1965). *The secular city.* London: SCM.

Dell, K. (2000). *'Get wisdom, get insight': An introduction to Israel's wisdom literature.* London: Darton, Longman and Todd.

Eichrodt, W. (1967). *Theology of the Old Testament II.* London: SCM.

Emerton, J. (1979). Wisdom. In G. W. Anderson (Ed.), *Tradition and Interpretation* (pp. 214–237). Oxford: Oxford University Press.

Murphy, R. E. (1966). The kerygma of the Book of Proverbs. *Interpretation, 20,* 3–14.

Reventlow, H. G. (1985). *Problems of Old Testament Theology in the Twentieth Century.* Philadelphia: Fortress.

Towner, W. S. (1977). The renewed authority of Old Testament wisdom for contemporary faith. In G. W. Coats and B. O. Long (Eds.), *Canon and Authority* (pp. 132–147). Philadelphia, Pennsylvania: Fortress.

von Rad, G. (1962). *Old Testament Theology I.* Edinburgh: Oliver and Boyd.

Wiles, M. (1986). *God's action in the world.* London: SCM.

Wright, G. E. (1952). *God who acts.* London: SCM.

Chapter 3

THE INVISIBLE COUNTRYSIDE OF THE
NEW TESTAMENT

William A. Strange*

Abstract – There is a clear contrast in the New Testament between the treatment of the countryside in Paul (for whom rural concerns emerge only as the source for occasional metaphors) and the Synoptic gospels (in which agrarian life is portrayed unselfconsciously but in sympathetic detail). This article explores rural imagery and the depiction of the countryside in the Synoptics. This article also seeks to explain the process by which the countryside became invisible to Paul by observing the shift from the mainly rural context of Jesus' first followers to the urban context of Paul's mission. It notes the significance of Luke's transition from a Synoptic to a Pauline perspective between the gospel and Acts. It reflects on issues of urban power and rural powerlessness in the first and twenty-first centuries.

What about the countryside, Paul?

[24]Five times I received at the hands of the Jews the forty lashes less one. [25]Three times I was beaten with rods. Once I was stoned. Three times I was shipwrecked; a night and a day I was adrift at sea; [26]on frequent journeys, in danger from rivers, danger from robbers, danger from my own people, danger from Gentiles, danger in the city, danger in the wilderness, danger at sea, danger from false brothers (2 Corinthians 11:24-26, ESV).

For the benefit of his wayward friends in Corinth, Paul surveyed in 2 Corinthians all the things which had caused him distress or which had

*   The Ven. Dr William A. Strange is Archdeacon of Cardigan. *Address for correspondence*: The Vicarage, Cwmann, Lampeter, SA48 8DU.
    E-mail: archdeacon.cardigan@churchinwales.org.uk

brought him shame in his work as a servant of Christ. It led him to write of dangers from human beings and of perils within the natural world.

The dangers from human beings were comprehensive enough. Paul had experienced hostility from his own people (verses 24–25) and from Gentiles (verse 26). He had even experienced hostility from within the community of the churches ('false brothers', verse 26). The danger from Gentiles included no doubt the robbers also mentioned in verse 26. Some historians have seen the first two centuries of the Christian era as the halcyon days for travellers in the Roman Empire, when there was little to fear from robbers (Casson, 1974, p. 122). Paul's experience as a traveller was clearly different.

Dangers within the natural world were an added dimension to his troubles. He mentions the sea, where his experience included surviving three shipwrecks (presumably different incidents from the one narrated by Luke in Acts 27:39-44) and he returns to the particular perils of the sea in verse 26. On land, rivers receive a special mention (verse 26), and if Paul was in the habit of travelling in wintertime or in spring through mountainous terrain such as that of Asia Minor, we can see why rivers should have caused him difficulties.

But as Paul turns from physical to human geography, his perception is interesting and telling: 'danger in the city, danger in the wilderness' (verse 26). Why is there nothing in Paul's consciousness between the city and the desert? Why has the countryside become invisible?

We should note that the Greek word *polis* (usually translated 'city') referred to more than what a modern English speaker would mean by 'city'. The *polis* was the basic unit of political organization in the Greek world. The fact that English has based its adjective 'political' on the word *polis* is some indication of that fact. The *polis* was the ruling centre of a district and the term could also refer to the territory ruled from that centre. It implied a certain organization with institutions which distinguished this central settlement from its subordinate satellites. Sometimes, and perhaps rather loosely, quite a small settlement could be referred to as a *polis* (Matthew 2:23). There were gradations of status between cities and, according to Luke, Paul could claim that his home of Tarsus was 'no obscure city' (Acts 21:39). When he placed 'city' and 'wilderness' in opposition, Paul seems to have had in mind the wilderness as a place which was dangerous because it was empty of people and the city as a place which was dangerous because it was full of networks of power which could turn against him.

A glance at Paul's writings confirms that this duality of 'city-wilderness' is not merely a rhetorical flourish. Paul's work lay almost entirely within the cities of that great mission field which he described as stretching 'from Jerusalem all the way round to Illyricum' (Romans 15:19). We can deduce this both from the fact that his letters to churches are characteristically addressed to Christian groups in cities, and from the numerous internal references to city-based congregations. Possible exceptions to the rule that Paul's letters are addressed to cities might be Galatians and the opening section of 2 Corinthians, both of which are addressed to whole provinces (Galatia: Galatians 1:2; Achaia: 2 Corinthians 1:1). It is possible that he was writing these letters to congregations in villages or rural settlements: certainly on occasion Paul can speak of the churches in provinces rather than individual cities (Romans 15:26; 16:19, 2 Corinthians 9:3, Galatians 1:22, 1 Thessalonians 1:7-8, 14). But even if there were congregations in small rural settlements, Paul seems to have taken no real interest in them. He never mentions any minor settlement specifically, and the only particular places he names are cities (Rome, Jerusalem, Cenchreae, Corinth, Troas, Damascus, Antioch, Ephesus, Philippi, Thessalonica). In Galatians and in 2 Corinthians, it would be most consistent with Paul's normal practice if he envisaged the letters going to the cities in Galatia and Achaia respectively.

The story-line of Acts shows Paul travelling from city to city, with little of interest between the gates of one city and those of the next. The only exception to this is the scene toward the end of Paul's ministry when, shipwrecked on Malta, the apostle finds himself ministering on the country estate of the 'chief man' of the island (Acts 28:7-10). Luke is often criticized in contemporary scholarship for his failure to give us the authentic Paul in the pages of his Acts of the Apostles. But nothing could be more authentically Pauline than Luke's narrative line which focuses almost exclusively on urban contexts as though everything lying in between were merely empty space.

The visible countryside of the gospels

Which one of you who has a sheep … ? (Matthew 12:11, see also Luke 15.4).

In the context of the gospels this is a natural question. Those who heard Jesus' parables could take sheep ownership as a matter of course. But it would be a very unexpected question in one of Paul's letters, or for that matter in one of the speeches of Acts. The readers of Paul's letters might be surprised if he had asked them a rhetorical question which assumed that they kept sheep. The people who read Paul's letters were not livestock owners, but in contrast Jesus in the Synoptic gospels draws on farming and rural imagery, and not merely as metaphor but as part of the experience he shares with his hearers.

In the gospels the countryside plays a major role: it is more carefully observed and described than in Acts and the letters; it is the setting for some significant events; and the life of the countryside provides some of the most vivid imagery to be found in the gospels.

The 'wilderness' makes its appearance in the gospels, as it does in Paul's catalogue of suffering. In the gospels, as in Paul, the 'deserted places' can stand in contrast to the cities (Mark 1:45). It is the setting in which John the Baptist preached (Mark 1:4 and parallels) and to which the Spirit drove Jesus for his temptation (Mark 1:12 and parallels). Shepherds might use the 'wilderness' (*erēmos*) to look after their sheep (Luke 15:4: 'wilderness' NRSV, 'open country' in the ESV and NIV). Jesus used the 'deserted place' for creative solitude (Matthew 14:13).

But the gospels describe a whole world which lies between the wilderness and the city. They have a far clearer focus on rural conditions than either the letters or Acts. The gospels do not work with the simple 'city-wilderness' contrast which Paul draws in 2 Corinthians 11. 'Cities' are contrasted with other forms of settlement: small towns or villages (*kōmai*: Matthew 9:35; 10:11, Luke 8:1; 13:22, John 11:1, and one reference in Acts 8:25); and hamlets or individual farms (*agroi*, lit. 'fields', Mark 5:14; 6:36, Luke 8:34, 9:12). Mark once places all three types of settlement in a descending order of size (Mark 6:56). The Greek *kōmē* (singular) perhaps corresponds to the Hebrew *kefar*, used in rabbinic sources to describe nucleated settlements in general, and *agroi* to the Hebrew *'ir*, which referred to isolated farms or villas (Applebaum, 1977, pp. 363–364).

Recent work on the society and economy of Galilee in Jesus' day has revealed the significance of Sepphoris and Tiberias as major urban settlements and economic centres. The reader of the New Testament would be aware of the existence of Tiberias (mentioned three times in John, twice in the phrase 'the sea of Tiberias', John 6:1 and 21:1, 'Tiberias' alone in John 6:23). But from this sparse data the reader would not guess that it was Herod's capital from 25AD and a significant urban centre. The silence of the gospels on the subject of Sepphoris is even more remarkable. The city of Sepphoris was known as 'the ornament of Galilee'. It was the main administrative and commercial centre of Galilee while Jesus was growing up, and remained a major centre even after the founding of Tiberias. Even more remarkably Sepphoris lay only six miles from Nazareth, so it was the obvious market centre to which artisans, such as Jesus' family appear to have been, would have made their way to sell their wares or their skills. But there is no reference in any of the gospels to Jesus visiting either Sepphoris or Tiberias.

Scholars can only speculate about the reason for the striking absence of the main urban centres of Galilee from Jesus' itinerary as the gospels record it. Jesus may have avoided them because of their presumed Gentile populations (especially in the case of Tiberias), but Jesus entered Gentile communities on other occasions (for example Mark 7:24, 31). Tiberias as Herod's capital may have been too politically dangerous, but the example of John the Baptist must have demonstrated that Herod's arm was as powerful outside Tiberias as within it. Whatever the reason, the absence of the main cities of Galilee from the gospel record is another indicator of the essentially non-urban backdrop of Jesus' ministry.

While the gospels pass over the cities of Galilee in silence, the Palestinian landscape appears in the gospels in some detail, as do the occupations of agriculturalists. These details are found mainly in the imagery of Jesus' teaching, but there are some narrative details too: for instance, Mark notes the 'green grass' on which the five thousand people sat (Mark 6:39, also John 6:10), and he also envisages Jesus' ministry encompassing everyone in the whole 'region' of Gennesaret and being exercised in rural as well as urban contexts (Mark 6:53-56).

The countryside as a significant setting in the gospels

Significant events in the gospels are not confined to urban settings. Things happen in the countryside as well as the towns. The shepherds to whom the angels announce the Messiah's birth are given a rather vague location by Luke (*en tē chōra tē autē*: 'in that country') but are clearly away from any human settlement (Luke 2:8). Jesus and his followers have one of their most important debates with the Pharisees as they are passing through an arable field (*dia tōn sporimōn*, Mark 2:23 and parallels). The exorcism of the demon-possessed man in the 'country of the Gerasenes' (no urban-dweller) evidently took place in a location which was outside a city, though close enough to be the site of its tombs. The herdsmen carried the news of his deliverance to the countryside (*eis tous agrous*) as well as to their city (Mark 5:1-20 and parallels). The feeding miracles take place well away from human habitation, in the type of wilderness setting which recalls the feeding of Israel in the desert (Mark 6:30-44 and parallels, Mark 8:1-10 and parallel in Matthew 15:32-9). The story-line in the Synoptic gospels, unlike that of Acts, does not simply pass from one city to another. It is rooted in the countryside of Palestine – and this is no less true in the case of Luke, who will change to a more urban focus in Acts, than it is of Matthew and Mark.

These observations are less true of John. The fourth gospel tends to localize action more specifically in particular 'cities', and even names the Sea of Galilee after its most significant city: the Sea of Tiberias (John 6:1) as the Greek traveller Pausanias did. John includes the feeding of the five thousand, but does not emphasize the emptiness or loneliness of the place where the feeding miracle takes place, only that it was on a mountain (John 6:3), and that the available provision was small (John 6:9). To some extent, John shares the 'urban' focus of the letters and Acts.

The countryside in the teaching of Jesus

The countryside becomes most clearly visible in the teaching of Jesus. The people who inhabit the countryside and who work there emerge in the gospels as significant people. Indeed, the gospel record of Jesus' teaching has become a resource to illuminate for modern readers the social and agrarian conditions in first-century Palestine. General, non-biblical scholarship refers to the parable of the labourers in the vineyard (Matthew 20:1-16) as a telling illustration of under-employment in Palestine before the war with Rome. In a similar way the parable of the tenants (Mark 12:1-12) is used to illustrate the tension built up by Herod's policy of confiscating peasant land and of creating a number of large estates on which peasants became mere tenants. It also illuminates the other severe stresses to which peasants were subject in the lifetime of Jesus (Applebaum, 1977, pp. 367–368; Guijarro, 1997, pp. 43–46).

Guijarro in particular has pointed out the prominence of rather well-to-do people in the agrarian landscape as depicted in Jesus' parables, people such as the family of the prodigal son (Luke 15:11-31). In Jesus' references to revenue collectors gathering up the profits from their masters' tenants we see an awareness of the social upheavals of the first century, when independent peasant families were being forced by debt to become tenants of powerful elites. These elite families lived in the cities and regarded their landed estates simply as sources of income (Guijarro, 1997, pp. 48–49). The Synoptic gospels therefore contain some clear observation of what was actually happening in rural society of Jesus' day.

The social setting of Jesus himself emerges with some clarity from the gospel record. When Luke comments that the infant Jesus was laid in a manger because there was no place for him in the *kataluma* (Luke 2:7), he may have been referring to an inn. But more likely he envisaged Mary and Joseph staying in the house of an extended family member (he sees Bethlehem as Joseph's family town, Luke 2:3), in which case the *kataluma* would be the upper room of the house. The typical peasant houses of first-century Palestine were probably made of sun-dried brick, and their remains have vanished. But if they were similar to the traditional houses observed in Palestine a century or so ago, they would have had a ground floor for animal accommodation and an upper room for human habitation, with a roof of branches (Canaan, 1933). Bailey has argued for a single-storey house on two levels, the humans occupying the higher level, and mangers on the floor at the end of the higher level nearest the animals (Bailey, 1983, pp. xv–xvi). If the upper room (or the higher level) were already occupied in such a house, then the animal quarters downstairs would be the only available space for delivering the child, and the manger an obvious place to put him. Luke, with this vignette, places the family of Jesus among that large block of the population, perhaps 75%, who lived in nucleated families in such primitive housing (Guijarro, 1997, pp. 60–61).

The gospels draw attention not just to social conditions, but also to the physical aspect of the countryside. Jesus mentions the tilled land (*agros*) and its propensity to harbour colourful flowers (Matthew 6:28 *krina*). These 'flowers of the field' are usually taken to be species of *Lilium*, probably *Lilium candidum*, which occurs on rocky sites, often on cliffs, in Galilee. However, Palestine supports many showy flowers, quite a few of which grow in cultivated ground, and it is more likely that Jesus was referring to these.

The problems and opportunities of arable farming make frequent appearances in Jesus' teaching. A variety of crops can be sown, including mustard (Mark 4:30-32 and parallels) and various herbs (Matthew 23:23). Crops, once sown, are subject to a number of problems, of which poor soil would have been particularly severe in parts of Galilee (Mark 4:5-6 and parallels). Contamination by weeds was also a major difficulty, with thistles or *Eryngium* species being pernicious (Mark 4:7 and parallels), and darnel rye-grass (*Lolium temulentum*) continues to be a pest today where traditional farming methods are used in the Near East, especially in winter grain crops (Matthew 13:24-30).

Fruit production also makes an appearance in Jesus' teaching. A saying which is part of the shared Matthew and Luke tradition (the so-called 'Q' material) invites Jesus' hearers to draw their own conclusion from the fact that grapes are not found on thorn bushes or figs on thistles (Matthew 7:16, Luke 6:44). Luke has a parable about caring for a fig tree and the patience it can require (Luke 13:6-9). A particularly striking acted parable in all three Synoptics concerns Jesus' cursing of a fig tree (Mark 12:12-14, 20-25 and parallels).

As we have seen, Jesus assumes (certainly in the Synoptic tradition) that his hearers are likely to own livestock, and sheep in particular (Matthew 12:11, see also Luke 15:4). In Matthew, Jesus envisages the moral dilemma posed for Sabbath observance if a sheep falls into a well (Matthew 12:11), and his argument assumes that this was something which happened frequently enough for his hearers to have already settled in their minds what they would do about it. In Luke's similar saying (Luke 14:5), Jesus envisages objects of greater value falling into a well: a son (or a donkey, the textual witnesses are divided between *onos*, donkey, and *huios*, son) or an ox. Luke seems to have a particular interest in oxen: in Luke, Jesus uses ownership of oxen to make a point on three occasions (Luke 13:15; 14:5; 14:19). The donkey makes an appearance alongside the ox (Luke 13:15, and perhaps 14:5), probably because the two animals are bracketed together in the tenth commandment (Exodus 20:17).

It is significant that Paul takes a different view of the value of an ox. In 1 Corinthians 9:9-10 Paul refers to the saying of Deuteronomy 25:4, 'You shall not muzzle an ox when it treads out the grain'. He then asks in rhetorical fashion, 'Is it for oxen that God is concerned? Does he not speak entirely for our sake?', and the answers he expects are 'no' and 'yes' respectively. We could contrast this with a 'Q' saying in the gospels, 'Are not two sparrows sold for a penny? And not one of them will fall to the ground apart from your Father' (Matthew 10:29, Luke 12:6). While Jesus and Paul both emphasize the greater value of human over animal life (compare Matthew 10:31 with 1 Corinthians 9:9-10), they do so in very different ways: Jesus by affirming that God values sparrows (and so values humans more); Paul by affirming that God's concern is for humans (and not so much, if at all, for animals). We have already noted that Paul perceives the countryside as the blank space between one city and the next. Similarly, Paul does not deal with agrarian life, whether animals or crops, as things that are significant in themselves. Whereas for Jesus, at least in the Synoptics, the countryside is a vivid reality and while Jesus could appeal to his hearers on the basis of a shared concern for the activities and values of the farming world, for Paul agricultural activity is merely a source of metaphor, and is not a focus of concern for its own sake.

The sociological contrast between the rural setting of Jesus' ministry and the essentially city-based life of the 'first urban Christians' is now quite well-established in New Testament scholarship (for example, Theissen, 1978; Meeks, 1983). Jesus himself was one of that large block of peasants and artisans who made up the bulk of the population of first-century Palestine. The imagery and the narrative of the Synoptic gospels reflect the values and perceptions of these groups and the conditions of their lives.

The imagery used by Jesus in the Synoptic gospels and the assumptions of the Synoptic narrators contrast quite clearly with the imagery used by Paul, as well as with the assumptions of Luke as a narrator in Acts. Certainly Paul uses the imagery of agriculture (for example, planting and watering, 1 Corinthians 3:6-9), but he is clearly writing to people who buy their food in the market (1 Corinthians 10:25) rather than raising or growing it themselves. For Paul's readers, imagery of growing crops is just that, imagery, rather than the shared experience of speaker and hearer, as it was with Jesus.

This contrast in imagery and in narrative focus confirms the existence of a gap between the rural context of Jesus' ministry and the urban location of the early Christians. The countryside became invisible in the New Testament because it dropped out of the consciousness of those who became followers of Jesus after the resurrection.

What does the invisible countryside of the New Testament mean?

The invisible countryside of the New Testament leads to some significant reflections on the New Testament itself. In the case of Luke, for instance, it helps us see that he did not entirely smooth out his sources. Many scholars have come to regard Luke as essentially a theologian rather than a historian, an author who reworked his sources so thoroughly in the interests of his theological message that he is a very unreliable guide to whatever events may have lain behind the narrative he gives us. But we notice that Luke's presumably unselfconscious portrayal of the countryside remains faithful to the Synoptic tradition in his gospel, while in Acts (and particularly in his portrait of Paul's ministry from chapter 13 onwards) he shares entirely the exclusively urban focus which we also find in Paul. Luke's attitude to the countryside is a tell-tale clue to his use of sources, and it suggests that he tended to respect and reproduce their unspoken attitudes and values.

In the case of John, we have the intriguing observation that the author of the fourth gospel has a more 'urban' focus than the three Synoptics have. Certainly the countryside does not emerge in his gospel with the same clarity that we find in the first three gospels. Like Paul, John uses agrarian imagery on occasion (for example, the good shepherd in John 10, or the vine and the vinedresser in John 15:1-17). But even though he uses agrarian life as a source of imagery, John does not speak of agricultural and pastoral pursuits as a common experience, shared by speaker and hearer alike. And also like Paul, John appears to take the view that interesting things usually happen in cities. There may be a clue here toward answering the enigma of the authorship of the fourth gospel, or at least starting to specify the author's social context.

But what does the invisible countryside of the New Testament mean for us, who read and receive the New Testament as scripture today? The categories of 'urban' and 'rural' mean very different things today from their meaning in New Testament times. Our cities are not the semi-autonomous Hellenistic communities of the first-century eastern Mediterranean. Conversely, the countryside of Palestine knew nothing of our concerns with conservation and heritage, of the leisure industry, of second homes or commuting. So we cannot simply transfer what the New Testament says or assumes about city and country to our own situation.

In terms of rural theology the New Testament's treatment of the countryside shows that we cannot do without the rich fund of metaphor which agriculture provides. In the Synoptics we read of a Jesus who shares the concerns of his hearers, whether it is about a sheep which has fallen into a well or a field where the crop fails to come up to expectation. Much of the rest of the New Testament does not show this ready engagement with agrarian life. But even the 'urban' Paul freely uses the imagery of life and growth drawn from the rural context.

In one respect, for all the differences, there may be a connection between the urban/rural contrast in the twenty-first century and that of the first. Power in our society, as in that of the first century, has become focused in cities and towns. What should the Christian church do about that? The early Jesus movement of the New Testament period managed to span very different rural and urban cultures. It spoke to the interests and concerns of those different cultures. The writings now in the New Testament reflect the outlooks of both those for whom rural life was in the foreground of their consciousness and those for whom the countryside was invisible. If the Christian church today is to be true to its New Testament roots, it has to find ways of embracing the corresponding diversities, rural and urban, of our own very different society.

References

Applebaum, S. (1977). Judea as a Roman Province: The countryside as a political and economic factor. In H. Temporini and W. Haase (Eds.), *Aufstieg und Niedergang der Römischen Welt*, II:8 (pp. 355–396). Berlin: Walter de Gruyter.

Bailey, K. E. (1983). *Poet and peasant and Through peasant eyes* (combined edition). Grand Rapids, Michigan: Eerdmans.

Canaan, T. (1933). The Palestinian Arab house: Its architecture and folklore. *Journal of the Palestine Oriental Society, 13*, 1–83.

Casson, L. (1974). *Travel in the Ancient World*. London: George Allen and Unwin.

Guijarro, S. (1997). *The first urban Christians: The social world of the Apostle Paul*. New Haven, Connecticut: Yale University Press.

Theissen, G. (1978). *The first followers of Jesus*. London: SCM Press.

Chapter 4

SHEEP AND GOATS: PASTORAL IMAGERY IN THE BIBLE AND TODAY

Richard T. France*

Abstract – The Bible makes frequent use of the imagery of sheep and shepherds, both to illustrate God's care for his people and also in relation to human leaders of the nation (Old Testament) and the Church (New Testament). This article suggests some ways in which an informed awareness of the reality of a shepherd's life may enrich our understanding of such imagery. It also draws attention to some limitations of the metaphor, and warns against sentimental misconceptions of the 'pastoral' role.

Introduction

The Anglican ordination service describes the work of a priest as that of a 'servant and shepherd', who is to 'keep the Good Shepherd always before you as the pattern of your calling'. I expect other churches use similar words – after all, 'pastor' is one of the commonest terms across the denominations to describe a Christian minister.

I wonder how much that imagery means to many in our urbanized western culture. Most people know that shepherds are people who wear tea-towels on their heads at Christmas and blow their nails when icicles hang by the wall, but how many have met a real shepherd, let alone understand what the shepherd's work involves?

* The Revd Canon Dr Richard T. France is an Anglican clergyman, and a former Principal of Wycliffe Hall, Oxford. Before his retirement he was Rector of a group of seven rural parishes straddling the Shropshire/Powys border. He is an Honorary Research Fellow in the School of Theology and Religious Studies, Bangor University. *Address for correspondence:* Tyn-y-twll, Llangelynnin, Llwyngwril, Gwynedd, LL37 2QL. E-mail: dick@tynytwll.co.uk

So we country folk have an advantage. Here among the hills of Meirionnydd, one member of my ministry training group is a shepherd's wife and two others keep a few sheep, while a former member is now priest-in-charge of the same parishes where he was until recently a full-time shepherd. Such real-life links give added depth to the pastoral imagery.

In the last group of parishes I served, sheep outnumbered people by twenty to one. Sheep dominated the rhythm of life. In March one of my churches had no Sunday service, since everyone was busy lambing. We knew about the long hours out on the hills in the wind, rain and snow, the aching limbs and chapped hands. We heard about the ewes needing to be dug out of snowdrifts, and we met the cade lambs being bottle-fed in the farmhouses. We knew how good sheep are at discovering the weak points in a fence, not to mention the chaos caused by townies' dogs and gates left open. We listened all night to the chorus of bereaved ewes in the glebe field when the lambs were weaned. We waited patiently when the flocks filled the narrow lanes. Foot-and-mouth disease came just after we had left. (For a vivid portrayal of year-round shepherding in words and pictures see Keith Bowen's [1997] lovely book, *Snowdon Shepherd*.)

Shepherding, we realized then, is more than a cosy bucolic idyll. It is bloody hard work (using the first adjective both literally and emphatically). Its physical demands would cripple most desk-sitters, and the disruption of family time, especially during lambing and shearing, would not be tolerated in any decent nine-to-five job. You are responsible for hundreds or thousands of vulnerable, unpredictable and often infuriating creatures, whose dependence on your care and skill does not usually seem to be matched by a suitable sense of gratitude.

In other words, it is a very appropriate model for Christian ministry – well, sometimes!

A biblical image

Sheep and shepherding were a familiar feature in biblical culture too, from the nomadic herdsmen Abraham and Jacob to the Bethlehem shepherds watching their flocks by night. Jesus could assume that some of his Galilean audience owned sheep (Matthew 12:11; Luke 15:4), and even the urbanites of Jerusalem could hardly be oblivious to the slaughter of thousands of sheep in the temple every Passover. According to Luke, even the urban Paul (Strange, 2006) used pastoral imagery to emphasize the responsibility of the equally urban Ephesian elders (Acts 20:28-29).

Anglicans have long been used to thinking of themselves in the words of the Venite as 'the people of his pasture, the sheep of his hand' (Psalm 95:7) and in the words of the Jubilate as 'the sheep of his pasture' (Psalm 100:3). Our funeral services generally remind us of the Lord as our Shepherd who provides pasture, guidance and protection, whose rod and staff comfort even in the valley of the shadow of death. The shepherd is one of the most pervasive and most valued images for God in the Old Testament, even though its obverse, the imagery of his people as sheep, is not one of the most flattering: 'All we like sheep have gone astray ...'

But God's pastoral responsibility is shared with human agents, to whom the care of the flock is delegated. In theocratic Israel the image represents not so much religious functionaries as the political leaders of God's people. Ezekiel 34 is a diatribe against 'the shepherds of Israel', who have abused their position of responsibility by exploiting the flock for their own gain, and leaving God's sheep wandering defenceless over the hills of Israel. So God will depose the unscrupulous shepherds and will himself take charge of the flock. 'I will search for the lost and bring back the strays ... I will shepherd the flock with justice' (Ezekiel 34:16, the basis of much of Jesus' good shepherd imagery and of his 'mission statement' in Luke 19:10).

But God has still not given up on delegation. In place of the failed shepherds he will install 'one shepherd, my servant David, and he will tend them' (Ezekiel 34:23). The same imagery had been used for the historical David, who (like my former student) was called from literal to metaphorical shepherding: 'You shall shepherd my people Israel' (2 Samuel 5:2). Those words had been echoed already in the famous messianic prophecy of the ruler from Bethlehem, the new David, who 'will stand and shepherd his flock in the strength of the Lord' (Micah 5:4). Later they were to be given a new and poignant twist in the image of the shepherd rejected by his flock (Zechariah 11:4-14), pierced by the house of David (Zechariah 12:10) and smitten by the sword so that the sheep are scattered (Zechariah 13:7), a sequence of disturbing images which provided an important model for New Testament writers as they struggled to make sense of Jerusalem's rejection of her Messiah (Matthew 24:30; 26:31; 27:9-10). Thus the shepherd has become an image not only for God himself but also for his Messiah.

The good shepherd

In the light of this Old Testament imagery (and the above is only a small sample), and of the pastoral setting of his Galilean ministry, it is no surprise that Jesus portrayed himself as the Good Shepherd, an image which continued to resonate among his followers if we may judge by the art of the catacombs and by such early Christian iconography as the Good Shepherd mosaic in the tomb of Galla Placidia at Ravenna. The traditional portrayal is drawn directly from Jesus' parable of the shepherd who 'joyfully puts [the lost sheep] on his shoulders' (Luke 15:5), a parable which recurs in Matthew 18:12-13 in a form and setting which suggests a more 'pastoral' and less 'evangelistic' application than in Luke. The shepherd in these parables is not directly identified as Jesus, but that step is definitively taken in John 10:1-16, 27-29, a passage which unmistakably gives the lie to the soft sentimentality of much modern use of the shepherd image: the good shepherd lays down his life for the sheep – that is what it means to be a pastor.

A shepherd's role is to protect, to guide, to care for the health of the sheep and to ensure they are well fed. But he also takes them to market – and to the slaughterhouse. Here the imagery becomes less appealing, but there is one passage where Jesus is apparently portrayed in this more threatening role. The Son of Man will divide those who come before him at the final judgement 'as a shepherd separates the sheep from the goats' (Matthew 25:32), the first for life, the second for destruction. It is a simile of careful identification. Good and bad, saved and lost, like wheat and weeds 'grow together until the harvest' (Matthew 13:30), and it takes the practised eye of the shepherd to distinguish the two superficially similar species. Even the 'sheep' and 'goats' themselves can't see the difference (vv. 37–39, 44). Here on earth we are a mixed flock, but the shepherd-judge knows his flock better than they know themselves. That, and only that, is the point of the simile. The real shepherd does not look after his goats *in order to* destroy them, nor does he send all his goats to the slaughterhouse and keep his sheep as pets. And we do not need to explain why goats are more appropriate than sheep to represent the baddies (France, 2007, p. 962, n. 89; cf Weber, 1997); one of the two had to be chosen for the simile to work. Beware of pushing a simile beyond its role in context.

So Jesus, the Son of Man, is the true shepherd, and in his risen glory remains the 'great shepherd of the sheep' (Hebrews 13:20). That is exactly what we should expect on the basis of the Old Testament imagery of the messianic shepherd. What room does that then leave for a pastoral role for his followers? Are they not themselves simply the sheep?

'Feed my sheep'

In a sense there remains just one true shepherd, the glorified Christ. He is, for Christian believers, 'the shepherd and guardian of your souls', 'the chief shepherd' (1 Peter 2:25; 5:4). But that last expression allows for junior shepherds under the chief, and Peter seems to have found this imagery particularly appealing. (I am one of that obstinate minority who continue to believe that the apostle wrote 1 Peter, probably with the literary assistance of Silvanus, 1 Peter 5:12. See, for example, Davids, 1990, pp. 3–7; Marshall, 1991, pp. 21–24.)

He had good reason to take this imagery to heart, if we may accept the account of Peter's rehabilitation in John 21:15-17. Soon Jesus was not going to be around any more. It would fall especially to the chosen leader of his disciples, failed but now forgiven, to provide the pastoral support they will need for the indeterminate period 'until I come' (vv. 22–23). And so the threefold response to Peter's hesitant reaffirmation of loyalty rings the changes on the pastoral imagery: 'Feed my lambs … Shepherd my sheep … Feed my sheep.' The fisherman has become the shepherd.

And it is as a shepherd that Peter writes his pastoral letter to those for whom he is responsible. But he is not the only assistant shepherd, and when in 1 Peter 5:2-4 he addresses the 'elders' of the churches of Asia Minor as himself their 'fellow-elder', he depicts their role too as that of shepherds. Not that they have any proprietary rights over the flock; it is God's flock, not theirs, and they themselves remain sheep under his control. But they, like the Ephesian elders in Acts 20:28, have been appointed by the Holy Spirit to be 'overseers, to shepherd the church of God', and to protect it from the 'savage wolves' of false teaching.

The wrongs and rights of shepherding

Peter's analysis of how this pastoral role is to be fulfilled (1 Peter 5:2-3) remains significant for those of us who continue to think of our ministerial responsibility in terms of shepherding. It takes the form of three antitheses.

First, *'Not under compulsion, but willingly, for God.'* Reluctance is a familiar part of the shepherd's experience, especially in mid-winter in the early hours of the morning when the sleet is beating on the window.

Nobody does this for fun. So why do they do it? For the sake of the sheep? Yes, in the short term, but why care about the sheep anyway? Ultimately, for the owner-shepherd, for profit, and for the employee, to keep their job. But the metaphorical shepherd needs no such 'compulsion'. It is for God. The day-to-day reluctance may sometimes be very real, but it is God's work, and so, for the good pastor, the care of the sheep, with all its discomfort and frustrations, is undertaken willingly.

Second, *'Not for sordid gain, but eagerly.'* Few shepherds can aspire to affluence, but at least it's a living. And few Christian ministers, even among the decreasing percentage who are stipendiary these days, go into it for the money if they have any sense. Even in these more generous days, the rewards of ministry are not primarily in the stipend, and attempts to unionize the clergy have been remarkably poorly supported. The pay-off is not in financial profit, but in job satisfaction. 'Eagerly' may sometimes seem a slightly idealistic assessment of our approach to Christian ministry in all its variety, but most of us looking back would not have wanted to be in any other job. Perhaps here the country parson has the edge over their urban colleague: there were times when on a pastoral visit to a remote hill farm I would pull in and look out across the valley and ask myself, 'Am I really being paid to do this?'

Third, *'Not lording it over your charges, but being examples to the flock.'* Here is where the metaphor begins to unravel. The literal shepherd is not himself a sheep, and to do the job effectively he *must* 'lord it' over the sheep. He is in charge, and woe betide the flock if he forgets it. But the Christian pastor is just one of the sheep, with a special role indeed, but not from a different species. Sometimes clergy have been known to forget this, and to try 'lording it', usually with disastrous consequences. Peter's model of the good pastor is not as boss but as example to one's fellow-sheep.

But even here there may be something to be learned from the world of shepherding. Some of us will remember with pleasure Dick King-Smith's little fantasy, *The Sheep-Pig* (King-Smith, 1983), subsequently filmed as *Babe*. It is the story of a piglet brought up as part of a family of sheepdogs. Naturally when he grows up he wants to be a sheepdog too, but his porcine physique is no match for the mean athleticism of the dogs. And yet in the end he wins first prize at the trials. His secret is not physical, but psychological. He has observed that the sheepdogs despise the sheep, and take pleasure in terrorizing them. The sheep have to do what they are told in the end, but they hate the dogs, and will do anything to frustrate them. But Babe takes a different approach. He gets to know the sheep, and wins their confidence, so that in the end he has only to suggest to them where he would like them to go, and they are through the gate and into the pen before he can even catch up with them.

Sheep as shepherds?

I think Peter would have approved of the sheep-pig model of shepherding rather than that of the sheepdog. The latter used perhaps sometimes to be seen in the superior, domineering country parson of yesteryear, who existed at least in fiction, and I suspect survived in reality in some parts until quite recently. There may still be a few who would like to perpetuate that model, but fortunately few country parishes these days would let them get away with it. Even the most highly trained pastor remains in reality a sheep, a member of the flock. We forget this at our peril.

So is it a problem for shepherd imagery applied to Christian ministry that literal sheep and shepherds (and even sheep-dogs and sheep-pigs) belong to different species? The metaphor works well enough where God is the shepherd of his human flock, but when the shepherding is done by human leaders the distinction of species vanishes: the shepherds are themselves sheep.

No metaphor is perfect, and perhaps the transition is not too difficult to negotiate. But it is made even easier by a remarkable passage in John's apocalyptic vision, where the blessing of the redeemed is attributed to the care of the divine shepherd who 'will guide them to springs of the water of life'. And who is this divine shepherd? 'The *Lamb* at the centre of the throne will be their shepherd' (Revelation 7:17). Here the doctrine of the incarnation bridges the gap between the divine and human models of shepherding. The divine shepherd is himself also a lamb, one of the flock. So the legitimacy of his human assistant shepherds in sharing in this divine role depends on their responsibility to the Chief Shepherd, himself both human and divine, from whom one day they may expect to receive the shepherd's wages (1 Peter 5:4).

Shepherd imagery for the church today

Those of us who live surrounded by sheep and shepherds can more easily continue to find rich resonance in the biblical imagery of God as the shepherd of his people and of Jesus as the good shepherd who lays down his life for the sheep. For much of our modern world, however, that imagery is increasingly remote from everyday reality. Shepherd

language may still have a residual sentimental appeal, which bears little
relation to the harsh realities of life on a hill farm, but for a robust sense
of divine supervision it may sometimes be necessary to look for other,
more urban images. Some years ago Carl Burke, an American prison
chaplain, asked some of the young delinquents from the streets of New
York to recast traditional biblical images in terms drawn from their own
world (Burke, 1966). I have long ago lost my copy of the book, but I
have never forgotten the new version of Psalm 23, the shepherd psalm; it
began 'The Lord is like my probation officer ...'. The writer had probably
never seen a sheep or a shepherd, but had recognized the image as one
of caring authority. And the only person from whom that youngster had
ever experienced such care was the probation officer. A testimony to the
value of the probation service, no doubt – but also a suggestive attempt
to unpack the biblical imagery for a very different culture.

But 'pastor' language shows no sign of obsolescence in current
Christian vocabulary. For as long as it remains in use, the church will be
the better for being reminded by its rural theologians of the true reality
and cost of the shepherd life that we watch with admiration on the hills
around us.

References

Bowen, K. (1997). *Snowdon shepherd: four seasons on the hill farms of North Wales.*
    Llandysul: Gomer.
Burke, C. (1966). *God is for real, man.* London: Collins.
Davids, P. H. (1990). *The First Epistle of Peter* (New International Commentary on
    the New Testament). Grand Rapids, Michigan: Eerdmans.
France, R. T. (2007). *The Gospel of Matthew* (New International Commentary on
    the New Testament). Grand Rapids, Michigan: Eerdmans.
King-Smith, D. (1983). *The Sheep-Pig.* Harmondsworth: Penguin.
Marshall, I. H. (1991). *1 Peter* (IVP New Testament Commentary Series). Leicester:
    Inter-Varsity.
Strange, W. A. (2006). The invisible countryside of the New Testament. *Rural
    Theology, 4,* 75–84.
Weber, K. (1997). The image of sheep and goats in Matthew 25:31-46. *Catholic
    Biblical Quarterly, 59,* 657–678.

Part 2

PERSPECTIVES FROM ORDINARY THEOLOGY

Chapter 5

ORDINARY THEOLOGY FOR RURAL THEOLOGY AND RURAL MINISTRY

*Jeff Astley**

Abstract – In this article the author describes and defends the notion of a non-technical 'ordinary theology', and argues for its role as an originating source for both academic theology and official ecclesiastical theology. He relates these claims to one way of interpreting the category of 'rural theology', and identifies rural ministry as a context in which ordinary theology may be discerned most clearly and explored most successfully.

Introduction

What is rural theology? I suspect that it is too early to say, and that we shall have to wait for the publication of more books and articles that will help to exemplify and identify the subject. Most academic subjects are as a matter of fact best defined ostensibly, by pointing out the concrete manifestations of their study. This is surely as true of theology as it is of philosophy, which was once defined by G.E. Moore by pointing to the books on his shelves with the words, 'It is what all these are about.'

It does not yet appear what rural theology will be. Quite properly, it will be interpreted by some as the application of theology, itself a multi-disciplinary entity, to the area – or (happily) 'field' – of rural life and society, and their particular concerns. Some might therefore prefer to speak about a 'theology *of* the countryside' or 'theology *and* the countryside', focusing their theology on rural issues and the rural context. But such a *theology of context and concern* is likely to generate a

* The Revd Professor Jeff Astley is Director of the North of England Institute for Christian Education. *Address for correspondence*: 18 North Bailey, Durham, DH1 13RH, UK. E-mail: jeff.astley@durham.ac.uk

particular theological style, framework, pattern and procedure: in short, a *theological viewpoint* or perspective that may later be used to examine other contexts and other issues. In a similar way, feminist and other liberation theologians, and even liturgical theologians, regard themselves as having something to say about a wide range of theological topics and theological reflections. Feminist theology is not just a theology about, for or of women; nor is liturgical theology concerned only with doing theology in the context of worship, or with an explicit focus on the texts of worship. What begins with a concern for a particular context and its distinctive problems and possibilities may in this manner transform itself into a way of doing theology that demands to be recognized as possessing a much broader reference.

I am not saying that 'rural theology' has yet made or that it should make this transition. Indeed, for the purposes of this article I want to go in the other direction. For the moment I should like to treat rural theology in a fashion that may seem to some readers even more limited in its application and impact, as the sort of theology ('God-talk') that is engaged in by Christians who live and worship, and in many cases still work, in the countryside. This is rural theology understood as the theology held by rural folk. While a number of fairly obvious criticisms may be mounted against such a designation, I want to suggest that it has some merit. And, as we shall see, it is more widely relevant than at first appears. It could also serve as a first step toward developing a contextual rural theology, and a rural theological perspective, just as some other theologies might trace their origins to listening to other particular constituencies (women, black people, and so on) speaking about their ultimate concerns.

Ordinary theology?

Over recent years I have been working with the phrase 'ordinary theology' in an attempt to identify the broad type of reflective God-talk that is to be found among churchgoers and non-churchgoers who are innocent of academic theological education. This is a concept that draws on Edward Farley's claim that 'theology in its original and most authentic sense' is not a scholarly discipline or enquiry, a 'science', but is rather a fundamental dimension of every Christian's piety and vocation: what he calls 'the wisdom proper to the life of the believer'. On this interpretation, theology is not abstracted from its concrete setting, but is understood as a form of personal knowledge of God, concerned with and developed within 'the believer's ways of existing in the world before God'. Farley claims that this enduring orientation, the 'sapiential and personal knowledge' that attends salvation, is 'a part of Christian existence as such'. (See Farley, 1983, pp. xi, 31, 35–37, 156–159; 1988, p. 88.)

My concept of ordinary theology is also related to what Karl Barth called 'irregular dogmatics'. He described this as something that both precedes and continues alongside the 'regular or academic dogmatics' of the theological school (Barth, 1975, pp. 277–278). Unlike the latter, however, irregular dogmatics does not attempt to 'cover the whole ground with the same consistency'. According to Barth, it is a type of theology that is often not easily distinguishable from proclamation, and whose form is marked by the fact that it relies more on aphorism than on explicit argument. Like ordinary theology, irregular dogmatics tends to be 'strongly influenced by the person and biography of their authors'. It seeks nothing beyond a fragmentary account of faith, leaving the goal of a systematic enquiry to its academic cousin. Yet the more academic mode of theology, Barth insisted, 'has always had its origin in irregular dogmatics and could never have existed without its stimulus and co-operation'.

Following, in fear and trembling, in the footsteps of these theological heroes, I too wish to identify the reflective God-talk of the majority of churchgoers as 'theology'. More rashly, perhaps, I want to include a substantial minority (at least) of the non-churchgoing public as proper candidates for the title 'ordinary theologian'. In doing so, I am intentionally opting for a 'broad sense' of theology, as distinct from the theological enquiry that is pursued 'through a range of academic disciplines' (Ford, 1999, pp. 10, 15). That academic *subject* represents 'the most sophisticated and reflective ways of talking about God', and is therefore reserved for 'a minority of Christians, usually seen as an intellectual élite' (Macquarrie, 1967, p. 11; Sykes, 1983). But no one should deny that there are other ways of doing theology.

Although the overwhelming majority of contemporary God-talkers have not studied theology formally at all, in my view they are inevitably engaged in doing their own theology if and when they speak and think about God, or at all events when they do so with any seriousness. This is an acceptable claim if theology is essentially the attempt to speak reflectively of the divine, or more generically of what we worship. 'Ordinary theology' would then be an appropriate term for the content, pattern and processes of ordinary people's articulation of their spiritual or religious understanding.

Why 'ordinary theology'? One meaning of the word 'ordinary' is 'without exceptional experience or expert knowledge'. While I have some reservations about what we might mean by exceptional experience in this context, I am drawing on this connotation of the word (which is also captured by one sense of that other ambiguous word, 'lay'). But I have also settled on the word 'ordinary' because that is how many people describe themselves, their beliefs and believing. They say, 'I'm fairly ordinary'; 'We're ordinary folk here'; 'I don't know the right way to put this because I'm just ordinary'. Please note that I do not use the term with any pejorative overtones and neither do they, for there is nothing wrong with being ordinary. 'Ordinary' translates the Latin *ordinarius*, meaning 'regular', 'orderly', 'usual'. It labels what is 'normal' and 'of the usual kind'. But the word and its close relatives (such as 'common') are frequently employed as terms of disparagement, a word that itself originates in the Old French for marrying unequally. The language of ordinariness is then applied to what is inferior, vulgar or undistinguished. But, although we may often prefer the extraordinary, that should not blind us to the value that is to be found in things, ideas and people that are without any special status – the widespread and the everyday. Ordinary theology is in this category.

I might have chosen different language to label this common reflective faith. When politicians wish to persuade us of their origins among, or close connections with, 'ordinary people', they often use metaphorical language that is drawn from farming, gardening or Nature. So they speak of 'getting down to the grass roots', of being close to ('having their ear to') 'the ground', even of being 'down to earth'. Here too, I think, there is no sense of disparaging that which is earthy and rooted, but a welcome recognition that this is the setting and medium from which life springs, and where the truth of many a matter can be found. In the network of associations that metaphors such as these generate in our minds, earth and roots are recognized as different from the more manifest and often spectacular stems, leaves, flowers and fruits of the plant, which are organs that depend on but frequently hide their origins, anchors and 'grounding'.

In *Ordinary Theology* (Astley, 2002) I argue on two fronts for the existence and significance of a mode of reflective faith that is prior to, and serves as the basis for, the more considered, critical, technically-articulate and systematic theology that characterizes the discussions and formulations both of the academy and of official ecclesiastical contexts. Ordinary theology is original and foundational at two levels. First, it is very likely to be *each individual's* original God-talk. For that reason it is often framed in the language of conversational personal interchange, the 'rapport-language' or 'mother tongue' that forges relationships within a family and between lovers. Such language, and such a theology, normally antedates the 'report-language' or 'father tongue' that is employed by a speaker when he or she engages with a topic at arm's length, and subjects it to some form of impersonal critical appraisal. Deborah Tannen (1992) and Ursula Le Guin (1989, pp. 147–152) map this distinction onto gender differences, but Rowan Williams (2000, chapter 5) applies it more widely to a contrast between theology in personal and pastoral situations, as compared with other contexts. A related point is that theology is first done by Christians as in the posture of prayer, and tends to be expressed in the rich allusive and self-involving language of metaphor and story. It is only later, if at all, that this 'kneeling theology' is critically honed and revised 'at the desk', with the help of a sophisticated technical apparatus of concepts and under the urge to generate systematic coherence (von Balthasar, 1960, p. 224). In these ways, ordinary theology may undergird and feed into academic theology at the level of the individual. I suspect that inside many a professional theologian or ecclesiastic there slumbers an ordinary theologian that he is trying desperately to keep in.

Secondly, a similar relationship obtains at the level of the *church*, where academic and ecclesiastical theology develop from the wider church's lived experience and reflective practice. It is frequently asserted that academic/ecclesiastical theology not only arises from, but should also keep in close contact with, this more ordinary source. Like ripples spreading to the edges of a pond when a stone is thrown into the middle, these secondary forms of theology may be greatly influenced by other (critical and technical) factors, but they originate in and are continuous with the more violent and faster-moving, 'ordinary theological wavelets' at the centre of the pond – agitations that represent the first responses to religious learning, change or experience (in this analogy, to the original 'splash').

These relationships are clearly exemplified in the medium of religious language, where rich metaphors stand out in research interviews with ordinary theologians just as they do in the primary religious texts of scripture, liturgy and hymnody.

> Peculiar moments in ordinary lives, saturated by metaphor or personal symbol-making, are the stuff of religion. The sacred quality of our lives is fabricated from the metaphors we make. (Sexson, 1982, p. 3)

It is important that the secondary conceptual language of so much of Christian doctrine should appreciate its own lowlier, metaphorical origins. In Sallie McFague's words:

> Concepts are never free of the need for funding by images, the affectional and existential richness of images, and the qualification against conceptual pretensions supplied by the plurality of images. Doctrine, necessary and appropriate as it is, does not replace the metaphors that fund it. (McFague, 1983, pp. 26, 50)

Such an organic, even symbiotic, relationship should also be conceded in our debates over theological normativity. Churches and theologians are past masters at denying the influence of ordinary people, their thoughts and their values, on the more rarefied moral and doctrinal deliberations of the élite. In truth, however, most changes begin on the ground. The 'statistical norms' that describe what the majority of people (most Christians) in fact do and believe inevitably play some role in shaping the 'evaluative norms' that prescribe what they (all Christians) *should* be doing and believing. Church leaders follow the 'public opinion' of the pews more often than they realize, or at least more often than they acknowledge; and academic theologians who do not respond to some extent to influences from below (from the broader culture, as well as the broader church) will soon find themselves without an audience, even in the academy. The 'consensus of the faithful' is in reality a most potent force and, statistically speaking at least, 'ordinary theology *is* the theology of God's church' (Astley, 2002, p. 162).

Rural theology?

I want to focus now on an exploration of ordinary theology at the individual level, and to pick up once again the agricultural metaphors of roots and soil. I believe that academic theologians and church leaders need to pay more attention than they do to the roots of their own and other Christians' theology. The principle that I would appeal to here is that our theology is always a *learned* theology, and that much of its most significant elements were learned at our own ordinary theological stage. I am not claiming, of course, that we learned about the doctrine of *perichoresis* or the Irenaean theodicy as such 'at our mother's knee', or when (perhaps much later) we began to be influenced by the faith of others or to embrace a faith of our own. But I do maintain that we were formed there or thereabouts in certain values and dispositions, and that we learned in such contexts some of our more basic and non-technical theological language. These elements still have the power to mould, frame and energize our sophisticated God-talk. We may therefore claim that a complete description of our learned faith must include some reference to and some investigation of its genesis. This may be rather a messy business, as in places our theological self-exploration is likely to turn up a somewhat grubby and obscured specimen.

> It is natural, therefore, to want to sluice it down and spruce it up; removing these marks of origination so as to reveal the naked, clear and timeless cognitions that are embodied within our wind-blown, lived-in and learned beliefs, attitudes, values and dispositions. Sometimes, of course, this is exactly what we should do, not least in academic theology. But if we always operate in this way when we do theology, we shall never know the full truth about the nature of the central structures, concepts and dynamics of our own, or other people's concrete and distinctive lives of faith. The subjective meaning that a particular idea or belief has for someone depends on a range of connotations and associations, both cognitive and affective, that are peculiar to his or her life experience and past learning. This sort of learning can never be plucked out of its context and picked clean; it always carries with it some of the soil in which it was nurtured (cf. Lee, 1973, chapter 6). If we ignore the learning context of a person's Christian theology, we shall not be able adequately to understand or describe it. (Astley, 2002, p. 13)

We should, then, be more *radical*, even about our own theology. We need to avoid those superficial judgements of people's theology that are based on no more than a casual glance at the more obvious manifestations of their faith, while ignoring its deeper anchors and channels of nourishment. Although it is by my fruits that I may be known, the learning *roots* of my faith are also part of my faith flourishing. So if you want to know about my faith in any depth, you will have to take some account of them as well.

I trust that I need make no apology for employing some of these metaphors in a journal devoted to rural theology. Where may we speak of roots, if not here? Whatever the actual numbers employed in the industry, agriculture is the dominant *image* of the countryside, and the ubiquity of a less trammelled Nature is its major appeal for most of us. Many of those who are distanced from the countryside strive to re-create some of its qualities in the suburban garden or urban patio.

But the relevance of ordinary theology to rural theology is not confined to this, admittedly rather strained, metaphorical connection. I wish to argue a wider point. One possible justification for speaking of a distinguishable species of 'rural' Christian theology might be that the non-technical and non-academic ordinary theology of rural churchgoers (and non-churchgoers?) is distinctively different from that of their urban or suburban counterparts. While I am not aware of any social scientific evidence that supports this case, at the anecdotal level there are many hints that this may be so, at least in some areas of theology, and in some areas and dimensions of the countryside. Arguing *a priori*, it is surely likely that people who live, and especially those who also work, in a rural environment will view their lives and the meaning they detect in their lives rather differently from the town or city-dweller. Any deep differences of this nature in the values, attitudes and stances for living that make up their 'human faith' (Fowler, 1981) are quite likely to express themselves at some point or another in the network of explicitly religious beliefs and values that constitutes a person's ordinary theology.

Rural ministry?

Because of the differences in scale that typify the rural ministry of pastoral care and Christian communication when compared with the urban kind, and the closer links that the rural clergy are able to forge (for this and other reasons) with the everyday life of both worshippers and non-worshipping parishioners, it is also to be expected that ordinary theology will often be heard more clearly and may be examined more closely in a rural context. This suggests that rural ministry may in principle serve as the ideal testing ground for the very notion of ordinary theology, and for the requisite empirical studies that are needed in order to paint its portrait (or, rather, its variety of portraits) in sufficient detail.

Once the phenomenon of ordinary theology is taken seriously, it is non-controversial to claim that some knowledge of the ordinary theology of his or her congregation and parishioners is an essential prerequisite for the ministry of every Christian pastor, preacher or Christian educator. They need to know about the religious beliefs and values of those whom they serve and to whom they speak. They need to be familiar with their patterns and processes of believing and valuing. The church in general, and its clergy in particular, should therefore find some way, whether formal or informal, of studying ordinary theology, so that it can properly exercise its ministry of pastoral care, worship, Christian education, apologetics, preaching and evangelism, and indeed every other form of Christian conversation, leadership, concern and relationship (compare, for example, van der Ven, 1993, pp. 158, 160–161).

I believe that the first and most essential tool for this task is *theological listening*. I mean by this phrase an ability and a willingness to listen out for, and to acknowledge, the theological content that resides below the surface of the often inarticulate, hesitant and confused, but also deeply-felt reflections of those who have never been trained to express their theology any differently. In support of this stance I shall quote two philosophers of religion who have been influenced by Ludwig Wittgenstein's insistence that, in order to clarify many concepts and resolve many issues, we need to 'stick to the subjects of our everyday thinking', and to return to the 'rough ground' of actual language set within real life (Wittgenstein, 1968, pp. 106, 107). D.Z. Phillips has argued that we need to find room for 'the ugly, the banal and the vulgar for these, too, may be forms of religious belief': forms of belief in which people 'must be personal' and must speak for themselves (Phillips, 1993, pp. 248–250). Paul Holmer reminds us not only that living religion does not need the abstract, specialized concepts of academic theology, any more than the motor mechanic needs the concept of atomic weight (Holmer, 1978, p. 174); but also that 'the theologian gets no new revelation and has no special organ for knowledge'.

> He is debtor to what we, in one sense, have already – the scriptures and the lives and thoughts of the faithful ... This puts theology within the grasp of conscientious tentmakers, tinkers like Bunyan, lay people like Brother Lawrence, and maybe someone you know down the street who shames you with his or her grasp .. Theology is often done by the unlikely ... God's ways are still discovered by his friends and not in virtue of techniques and agencies of power. (Holmer, 1978, p. 21)

The respectful, listening stance toward the ordinary Christian for which I am arguing can only be adopted by those who have the ears to hear what their parishioners are saying *as theology*. Others, I fear, will be deaf to it. Too many clergy, and even more academic theologians, dismiss most ordinary theology outright as unworthy of any serious consideration. This is a great pity, not least because people very quickly know when their deepest thoughts are disregarded. I believe that a great deal of the church's alienation from ordinary people is a product of that experience. As one ordinary theologian put it to me: 'You know, religion is really for the clergy; they just let us have a lend of it.'

My guess – and it is only a guess – is that one reason why rural congregations and communities seem less prone to this form of alienation is that rural clergy have been on the whole better listeners. Perhaps they have had to be. Whatever the reason, this may be one more way in which the rural voice can teach the rest of God's church a valuable lesson about what it means to discern the body, and to exercise a Christian ministry, *wherever* it may be called to serve.

References

Astley, J. (2002). *Ordinary theology: Looking, listening and learning in theology.* Aldershot: Ashgate.

Barth, K. (1975). *Church dogmatics.* Vol. I/1. Edinburgh, T & T Clark.

Farley, E. (1983). *Theologia: The fragmentation and unity of theological education.* Philadelphia: Fortress.

Farley, E. (1988). *The fragility of knowledge: Theological education in the church and the university.* Philadelphia: Fortress.

Ford, D. F. (1999). *Theology: A very short introduction.* Oxford: Oxford University Press.

Fowler, J. W. (1981). *Stages of faith: The psychology of human development and the quest for meaning.* San Francisco: Harper & Row.

Holmer, P. L. (1978). *The grammar of faith.* San Francisco: Harper & Row.

Le Guin, U. K. (1989). *Dancing at the edge of the world: Thoughts on words, women, places.* New York: Grove.

Lee, J. M. (1973). *The flow of religious instruction: a social science approach.* Birmingham, Alabama: Religious Education Press.

McFague, S. (1983). *Metaphorical theology: Models of God in religious language.* London: SCM.

Macquarrie, J. (1967). *God-Talk: An examination of the language and logic of theology.* London: SCM.

Phillips, D. Z. (1993). *Wittgenstein and religion.* Basingstoke: Macmillan.

Sexson, L. (1982). *Ordinarily sacred.* New York: Crossroad.

Sykes, S. W. (1983). 'Theology'. In A. Richardson and J. Bowden (Eds.), *A New Dictionary of Christian Theology* (pp. 566–567). London: SCM.

Tannen, D. (1992). *You just don't understand: Women and men in conversation.* London: Virago.

van der Ven, J. (1993). *Practical Theology: an empirical approach.* Kampen, Netherlands: Kok Pharos.

von Balthasar, H. U. (1960). *Verbum Caro*, I, Einsiedeln: Johannesverlag.

Williams, R. (2000). *Lost Icons: Reflections on cultural bereavement.* Edinburgh: T & T Clark.

Wittgenstein, L. (1968). *Philosophical Investigations.* Oxford: Blackwell.

Chapter 6

THE KNEELERS ARE MOST IMPRESSIVE: REFLECTIONS ON READING A VISITORS' BOOK

*Norman Morris and Lewis Burton**

Abstract – The understanding of God and the expression of faith and belief which is articulated by ordinary people can be found in what they write in visitors' books as a response to their experience of looking around the church and its environs. In this article the record of a completed visitors' book was analysed using the analytic perspective of ordinary theology. The results show responses exhibiting spiritual reactions to the experience. They also suggest that visitors' books are perhaps not the most productive ways of seeking insights into the 'God-talk' of ordinary people, and that prayer trees or prayer boards could yield more productive results.

Introduction

According to the report *Celebrating the Rural Church: ten years on from Faith in the Countryside* (ACORA, 2000, p. 31), twenty-eight dioceses of the Church of England responded to questions regarding tourism, and some have set up appointments of Diocesan Tourism Officers to encourage rural churches to benefit from the growing number of those living in urban situations who take short holidays and days out in the countryside. This interest in encouraging rural churches to find in tourism opportunities for their own mission to visitors, as well

* The Revd Norman Morris is Rector of Wentnor with Ratlinghope, Myndtown, Norbury, More, Lydham and Snead. *Address for correspondence*: The Rectory, Wentnor, Bishop's Castle, SY9 5EE. E-mail: revnorm@btinternet.com

   The Revd Dr Lewis Burton, a retired Methodist minister, is Honorary Research Fellow in the St Mary's Centre, Wales. *Address for correspondence*: 94 Sun Street, Haworth, Keighley, BD22 8AH. E-mail: lewisburton@blueyonder.co.uk

as providing benefits of a spiritual and recuperative kind for visitors, has been strongly encouraged by the Arthur Rank Centre through the Hidden Britain Programme (2007). This is designed to promote tourism which could bring clear community benefits of different kinds to rural villages, and several Hidden Britain Centres have already been established (Country Way, 2007). The benefit of such promotion also extends to village churches in rural settings which have been persuaded to open their doors once more for the sake of their own interests and that of tourists who are attracted to the open countryside and its villages.

A result of this growing tourism is found in the comments recorded in visitors' books, reflecting on why they come, and on what the experience has meant to them. Moreover, a study by Francis and Martineau (2001, p. 49) found that just over half of the visitors to a rural church would like to find a visitors' book. These visitors' books may be a rich resource for establishing a theological understanding of what ordinary tourists think of God. What has been recorded? What clues are there in all these entries? How do visitors view the experience of 'dropping in' to a remote country church? Visitors' books thus become a source of important data regarding belief patterns.

Ordinary theology

Sometimes these entries are remarks about the physical appearance of the church or some superficial reaction to being there, but sometimes they could also be an indication of the spiritual impact the experience has made upon them. An examination of such remarks written in visitors' books can identify a broad type of reflective 'God-talk' which can be found among churchgoers and non-churchgoers alike who have never been subject to any formal theological training. This follows the principles of ordinary theology, a perspective distinctive from the disciplines of systematic or dogmatic theology, which views theology not from the Godward side, but from the understanding of individual people (Astley, 2002, 2003). God-talk arises from the processes by which ordinary people articulate their own spiritual and religious under-standing. This understanding of ordinary theology has been employed productively in three recent studies exploring different aspects of visitor responses to rural churches. In the first study, Littler and Francis (2005) used the concept of ordinary theology to explore the reactions of 4,879 visitors to the holiness perceived in rural churches. They found 68% of visitors perceived the church to be holy. Three specific issues (opportunity for private prayer, availability of information regarding the church services, and the presence of flowers in the church) were correlated with this perception of holiness.

In the second study, Keulemans and Burton (2006) addressed a number of questions to visitors to the shrine of St Melangell in the Berwyn Mountains of central Wales to ascertain what they felt about the experience. The analysis of the results shows that, for those who visit a sacred place, there are spiritual responses of different kinds which are displayed by a substantial majority of visitors.

In the third study, Brown and Burton (2007) analysed data collected from a prayer tree and a visitors' book in a village church in Cheshire. Over an eight month period in 2004 there were 58 prayer requests on the prayer tree and 419 entries in the visitors' book. Of the former all could be analysed for spiritual content, but of the latter only 8% of the entries contained a spiritual reference, 72% being an appreciation of the beauty and tranquillity of the building, 10% being gratitude for an open church, 7% being concerned with tracing ancestors, and 3% being other miscellaneous issues. The conclusion makes it clear just how personally significant the experience of visiting a rural church can be for some visitors, not only as a spiritual experience, but offering balm and solace for life's knocks, and appreciating the peace and tranquillity which a rural church can generate.

Building on these three pioneering studies, the aim of the project is to conduct a thorough analysis of the comments recorded in the visitors' book of one rural church, drawing on the perspectives of ordinary theology.

Method

The book and the church

When the visitors' book at St Mary's was full, having covered the period from October 1991 to December 2005, it became available for research purposes. The church is a small parish church which has early medieval monastic origins and lies in a valley on the Welsh borders which is full of legend and mystery. It is sited in a small, 100-strong, very scattered community of farms and cottages in south Shropshire. Little has changed over the years, though visitors have increased, especially walkers and riders. Until the 1950s there was an adjacent landed estate, the family being the benefactors of a local school which later became a Youth Hostel when a new primary school was built. A thriving public house is popular with locals and visitors. Weekly services muster between

12 and 15 people, but at Christmas, Easter, Harvest, and for baptisms, weddings and funerals, the church is packed. In recent years St Mary's has followed 'God's Acre' practice, creating 'wild' features which draw visitors who frequently refer to the attractiveness of the churchyard, as well as the church, in the visitors' book.

Analysis of the data

Although the visitors' book covers the period 1991 to 2005 it was decided to ignore 1991 entries and 2005 entries as part years. Yet another difficulty for analysis was that between April 1992, and late July 1992, the church was closed for renovation. It was officially reopened on 7 August 1992, and visitors were again admitted to the church. Because of this the period of analysis was determined as the twelve years of 1993 to 2004 inclusive. This enabled comparisons between three-year periods, 1993 to 1995, 1996 to 1998, 1999 to 2001, and 2002 to 2004. Analysis of visitor entries were made visually by the researcher and recorded as follows.

Results

Visitor numbers and numbers of comments

Table 1 displays the number of individuals who signed the visitors' book at St Mary's church over the twelve year period between January 1993 and December 2004, together with the number of comments which they made.

In interpreting the number of recorded visitors one must recognize that they are understated for a variety of reasons. First, not all those who visit a church are inclined to leave a record of their visit. Second, some who visit come as a family group and record their visit as 'the Smith Family'. Where such entries appear, families were counted in Table 1 as mother and father and two children, four visitors in total. Third, some who visit came in groups (often staying at the local Youth Hostel) and only the leader made an entry. Since it is impossible to guess the number of people in each group, group entries were counted as just one visitor.

One further difficulty in making a judgement of the comparative numbers of visitors over the twelve year period was the influence of special events. Numbers of visitors in the early years of the study had obviously been swollen by some who had come to inspect and pass judgements on the reordering of the church. Flower Festivals had also influenced visitor figures, and since their comments centred round their reaction to the displays and their gratitude to those who fashioned them, the comments of those who came to the Flower Festivals in 1996 and 2000 have been ignored. The numbers of those recording their visit in2001 were fewer in number than in any other year, presumably due to travel restrictions on local people and the disincentive for tourism caused by foot-and-mouth disease raging in the countryside during that summer. What is attempted, therefore, is to establish the pattern of 'ordinary' visitors over the twelve year period and it is the number of these 'ordinary' visitors which appear in the table.

Table 1: Numbers of recorded visitors and comments

	Visitors N	Comments N	%
1993–1995	1455	707	48
1996–1998	867	488	56
1999–2001	612	359	58
2002–2004	803	429	53
Totals	3737	1983	54

When the twelve years covered by the visitors' book are taken singly, the bumper year was 1993 with 520 entries, a number possibly swollen by the curious coming to see how the church had been altered. A more typical number for the three year period was perhaps the 465 recorded for 1994 and the 470 recorded for 1995; 2001, afflicted by foot-and-mouth disease, was a year with only 133 visitors. Taking a view over the whole twelve year period, visitors who recorded an entry in the book dwindled from around 470 in the early years to 262 in the final years of the period. Despite this decline in visitors making an entry, the proportion of comments related to numbers of visitors is fairly constant, the four triennial periods showing an average of 54%.

Analysis of visitors' comments

The principal purpose of this article was to discuss the extent to which visitors revealed something of their own Ordinary Theology through the comments written in the visitors' book. The first stage of analysis, therefore, involved locating such comment within one of the two groups: those that contained some spiritual content and those that contained no spiritual content. Comments which are included in the category of spiritual content are those which by their nature indicate that the building and the visit generated some kind of reaction which prompted them to feel some spiritual benefit. Over the twelve year period 29% of the entries revealed some spiritual content, and the proportions remained relatively consistent over the four triennial periods: 1993–1995, 33%; 1996–1998, 28%; 1999–2001, 19%; 2002–2004, 33%.

Regarding the comments without spiritual content, the largest proportion over the twelve year period (52%) focused on the church building and its contents. The architecture was admired by some, 'an architectural masterpiece', 'a gem of a church', 'a beautiful church in the middle of nowhere', 'my favourite church in the whole of Shropshire'. The stained glass windows were often remarked upon, and also the organ. The centre of attention throughout all the twelve years was the kneelers and the hassocks. The comment, 'The kneelers are most impressive', occurred throughout each triennial period. There were a number of comments about the church's good housekeeping, and about the pleasure of finding a church open, as though they expected entry to be barred to them.

Some visitors also appreciated the church in its surroundings, the graveyard and the surrounding countryside (5%). Some visitors had come for family reasons, to attend weddings or funerals or baptisms, to remember a personal anniversary, and to trace family connections (6%). Other visitors had come for nostalgic reasons, to remember pleasant experiences connected with the church in the past (8%).

Regarding the comments with spiritual content, the largest proportion over the twelve year period (83%) focused on the feeling of peace. Other comments focused on a sense of awe and wonder (6%), on God's blessing for church and people (2%), and on a wide range of other issues (9%). These themes will now be discussed in greater detail.

Feelings of peace

A very large proportion of those who made a comment which may be identified as 'spiritual' was centred on the feelings of peace and tranquillity which the experience had generated for them. Comment focused on words like 'peaceful', 'tranquil' 'restful', 'very quiet', a 'quiet little haven', 'what an oasis!', 'happy thoughts', 'secluded and peaceful', 'a sweet quiet spot'. The way of expressing such feelings in short phrases and one-word responses carries a note of surprise that they felt this way about their reaction to the church. This sense of peace and tranquillity found further description in some of the longer comments. 'Thank you for a little peace in a weary world'; 'Peace, perfect peace'; 'Peace, just what we needed'; 'Lovely, and a quiet place to think'; 'Lovely place of reflection'; 'Great to sit and contemplate'; 'Go placidly amid the noise and confusion and know that peace may be in the silence'; 'Beautiful peace, relaxing, quiet, amen'. It is only this last word in this last quoted comment that expresses some content of a traditional faith. Generally all these non-specific comments show the appreciation of a place of reflection where visitors can find an opportunity for contemplation, a sanctuary of quietness, and the provision of a place of refuge from the pressures and stresses of modern life. In this sense it shows that a substantial number of visitors realize, consciously or unconsciously, that what they have received is a spiritual experience. It is an experience which they do not find in their ordinary lives or the circumstances of their workaday world, which was generated by the spiritual ambience of the church and its surroundings. The responses are not overtly Christian in their content, but they display longings for a spiritual realization which the visitors did not find in the ordinary pattern of their lives. The visit has provided a spiritual centre which for them is normally absent (see further Astley, 2007).

Sense of awe and wonder

The realization that certain places carry with them a special aura has given rise to debate in recent times that certain places generate a spiritual consciousness in the minds of those who might visit them (Carmichael, Herbert, Reeves and Schenk, 1994). Some may associate such sacred places with the site of a saint's resting place (Keulemans and Burton, 2006), or with some significant event in church history, but this is not necessarily the case. Lane (1988) considers the sacred place as 'an ordinary place rendered extraordinary'. An ordinary place can be a sacred place when the realization comes to those who happen to be there that it is in some way special. The visitors to St Mary's were experiencing what Rudolph Otto (1923) describes as the 'numinous', that sense of mystery generated by certain surroundings which is a 'non-rational, non-sensing experience or feeling, whose primary and immediate object is outside of the self'. It would seem that this would describe the experience of some of the visitors to St Mary's who sensed the feelings of awe and wonder which the church generated.

Some 6% of those who gave a comment which could be interpreted in spiritual terms described a reaction of awe and wonder. For them the sense of peace and tranquillity developed into recognition that the church itself was different, that it was a sacred place. The ambience of the church had generated for them a spiritual experience. They were spiritually stirred by a sense of awe to an awareness of a spiritual presence. The comments were not all Christian in their connotation, but were witness to the fact that some visitors found the church to be a special place. A hymn is quoted in one comment, 'Be still for the presence of the Lord is moving in this place', but another describes the experience in a secular way, 'A church that sends shivers up your spine, a special place!' Other, shorter comments, report similar reactions, 'a real place of God'; 'the church is a beautiful and holy place'; 'no words, no comments, only God'; 'a holy and magnificent church'; 'a special place, a lovely church'.

A blessed place

The idea of blessing is particularly important in Judeo-Christian religion. God blesses and beneficently gives to the believer the gifts of grace. This feeling of being blessed was felt by 2% of visitors. They not only feel that the church is a blessed place, but feel blessed in being there, and also wish to ask God's blessing on those who worship there and make their experience possible, 'A gem of a church. God bless its ministry and its people'; 'so lovely, God bless you all'; 'I felt blessed by being here'.

Specific Christian responses

The remaining 9% of the comments classified as holding spiritual content show the visitors going beyond their own personal feelings to express a reaction which in one way or another focuses on God. In the detailed analysis these reactions were subdivided into: God's love and God's ways (2%), praise and thanksgiving (3%), expressions of hope (2%), prayer needs (1%), Christian care (> 1%), and pilgrimage (> 1%).

The experience reminds 2% of visitors of God's love and the way that God treats humanity: 'a reminder of God's peace; that God loves us and understands our mistakes and forgives us', and a response which could be Christian or not, 'a beautiful church in which to discover the true meaning of life'.

Short ascriptions and interjections of praise and thanksgiving were recorded for 2% of the visitors. Ascriptions took the form of 'A Godsend'; 'God's creation'; 'To God be the glory'; 'A house of God'. The praise form was 'Praise God'; 'Thank the Lord'; but longer thanksgivings also appeared. It is difficult to interpret some of these, since they are so short, but generated by the experience which they have received. In a Christian building, hallowed over the years by the worship of Christian people, they have obviously been moved to thoughts of God. A particular prayer of thanksgiving which will be appreciated by anyone who has ever taken an examination was, 'Thank God for good GCSE results'.

There were a number of expressions of hope, both for this present world and for eternity, although interpretation is often difficult, as those who commented in this way may only be saying that their visit was a good experience. However, if one can take the word 'heaven' to have a serious rather than a colloquial connotation, it might have some reference to hope in the hereafter. Typical responses were, 'A pleasant place, a little bit of heaven'; 'This place offers hope for the future and a better place soon'; 'a little piece of heaven, a taste of what's to come.'

A few comments included prayers, directed to God for others and not for themselves. These were prayers for clergy and church attenders, for those coming for weddings and baptism. Some were very personal: 'In love we came, in love we go and pray for Joseph's (8 months) future life.' A very poignant one was, 'My brother was involved in a tragic accident which killed a local boy. I returned to say a prayer for him, but couldn't find his grave.'

A few people thanked God for care received and linked it with the care given to the church, 'May God's peace and care abide here forever and ever'; 'A much loved church surely contains loving, caring and Christian people. An example to us all.' Finally two people had come on what they considered to be a spiritual pilgrimage, both having visited before.

Discussion

What appears from the results of the examination of the visitors' book to this local rural church is that the great proportion of comments made by visitors are prompted by the building itself. In coming to this church their focus is on the object of their visit, the church interior and its surroundings. This is the main prompt to their thinking and determines the remarks which they make.

Thus, in their secular comments they make kind remarks about the beauty of the church, the things they find there, and its setting in an attractive rural location. In their comments which have some spiritual content the church is still the focus of what they are prompted to say. It is tranquil, and quiet, a haven of peace and they find something there which is missing from their busy lives in their workaday world, some experience which is spiritual because it seems to be fulfilling an inner need which they otherwise do not experience. It may be that coming into such a church as St Mary's is not a common experience for visitors and that they realize that it is a special place, hallowed over many years by the worship of God's people. The awareness would come readily to those who are Christians and church attenders, but the proportion of those who record this as a comment suggests that awareness of sacred place stretches beyond churchgoers. The same awareness of sacred place is shown by those who feel blessed by their visit and also wish to bless those who maintain the church which has made their experience of blessing possible. Only a small proportion of visitors make spiritual comments not focused on the church, nor prompted by it. They wish to praise God, and perhaps some of their ascriptions of praise are prompted by the building, but others wish to offer their own thanksgiving for specific happenings in their lives and to offer prayer for themselves or others.

From the result of this study of comments in the visitors' book of a rural church it would seem that comments are heavily influenced by the main purpose of their visit, their interest in visiting an attractive village church in the countryside. As a source of understanding the ordinary theology expressed in visitors' remarks, it does point to a spiritual search for peace in busy lives, and an awareness of a church as a special place which creates feelings of 'the other'. It does not, however, give insight into the spiritual awareness and needs of those who might place their prayers on a prayer tree or a prayer board.

As a comparison of the productiveness of insights into the ordinary theology of visitors to a church between the data source available from visitors' books as against prayer boards, the work of Brown and Burton (2007, pp 45–52) is instructive. The categories of entries into the visitors' book confirms what we have found here in that 72% comment on the peace and tranquillity of the building, 10% expressing gratitude for finding the church open and 8% aware of it as a place of prayer. The numbers who have placed requests for prayer on a prayer board are much smaller than those who have entered comments in the visitors' book, 58 as against 419, but having the focus of personal concern rather than the church building itself, they offer much better insight into the 'God thoughts' of those who have written them.

A much more exhaustive study of the prayers which people choose to leave on a prayer board has been made by ap Siôn (2007) in her analysis of 917 prayer cards left in a chapel over a sixteen month period. The majority (893) produced intercessory and supplicatory prayer forms, and the remaining 19 included elements of thanksgiving, confession and repentance. The numbers of prayer requests enabled her to provide a thoroughgoing analysis of the nature of prayer and to provide a framework of analysis which is useful to other investigators in the field. Although her special interest is in the psychological investigation of the nature of prayer she relates her conclusion to the interest in ordinary theology.

> Many of the prayers given voice by visitors in an ancient church remain largely uninfluenced by theological reflection in the Christian tradition. Opportunities exist, therefore, for practical theologians to open the doors of more churches and to develop these buildings as inviting sanctuaries to stimulate and encourage a prayerful response. (ap Siôn, 2007, p. 224)

From the content of her study she firmly establishes the usefulness of prayer boards or prayer trees to provide insights into the theology of ordinary visitors to churches as a more productive source of detailed analysis than can be obtained from the examination of church visitors' books.

Conclusion

The examination of the visitors' book and the analysis of the comments indicate the effects which a small rural church can have as it seeks to deepen the spirituality of tourists who come to enjoy the countryside and others who might come to its premises for other reasons.

This analysis shows that those who came as visitors appreciated the church and its surroundings, and displayed their appreciation in their remarks in the visitors' books. The main object of the analysis was however to discover in their remarks something of a spiritual quality which showed more than just an aesthetic appreciation of their surroundings. This was displayed by the data in two ways. The first was the large proportion of those who made what could be categorized as a spiritual response to their experience in their appreciation of the sense of tranquillity generated by the building. It is the experience of peace generated by the ambience of the church and its surroundings which, in a world of bustle, activity and mental pressure, gives the custodians of church buildings a way in which they can promote a sense of spirituality and sanity in today's world for anyone who might visit their churches. The second is the way that visitors were moved by a sense of awe and wonder which the ambience of the church building created for them, which helped them to perceive the church as a special place, linked to a spiritual consciousness of which in the everyday world they were relatively unaware.

The few comments of a spiritual nature which were not linked to perceptions created by the ambience of the church building and its surroundings shows the paucity of the attempt to glean the 'God thoughts' of ordinary people from visitors' books alone.

A comparison of other attempts to discern the ordinary theology articulated by people at large through church sources indicates that prayer boards and prayer trees are a more fruitful source in producing this kind of investigation.

References

ACORA Publishing (2000). *Celebrating the rural church: Ten years on from Faith in the Countryside.* Stoneleigh Park: ACORA Publishing.

ap Siôn, T. (2007). Listening to prayers: An analysis of prayers left in a country church in rural England. *Archive for the Psychology of Religion, 29*, 199–226.

Astley, J. (2002). *Ordinary theology: Looking, listening and learning theology.* Aldershot: Ashgate.

Astley, J. (2003). Ordinary theology for rural theology and rural ministry. *Rural Theology, 1*, 3–12.

Astley, J. (2007). Public and personal peace in life, religion and education: an exercise in ordinary theology. In J. Astley, L. J. Francis, and M. Robbins (Eds.), *Peace or violence: The ends of religion and education?* (pp. 151–173). Cardiff: University of Wales Press.

Brown, A., & Burton, L. (2007). Learning from prayer requests to a rural church: an exercise in ordinary theology. *Rural Theology, 5*, 45–52.

Carmichael, D., Herbert, J., Reeves, B., & Schenk, A. (Eds.). (1994). *Sacred sites, sacred places.* London: Routledge.

Country Way (2007). In celebration: Hidden Britain of Cumbria. *Country Way, 44*, 8.

Francis, L. J., & Martineau, J. (2001). *Rural visitors.* Stoneleigh: ACORA Publishing.

Hidden Britain (2007). www.hidden-britain.co.uk

Keulemans, M., & Burton, L. (2006). Sacred place and pilgrimage: Modern visitors to the shrine of St Melangell. *Rural Theology, 4*, 99–110.

Lane, B. B. (1988). *Landscapes of the sacred: Geography and narrative in American spirituality.* Mahwah, New Jersey: Paulist Press.

Littler, K., & Francis, L. J. (2005). Ideas of the holy: The ordinary theology of visitors to rural churches. *Rural Theology, 3*, 49–54.

Otto, R. (1923). *The idea of the holy.* Oxford: Oxford University Press.

Chapter 7

ORDINARY PRAYER AND THE RURAL CHURCH: AN EMPIRICAL STUDY OF PRAYER CARDS

Tania ap Siôn*

Abstract – The article explores the content of ordinary people's prayers by analysing 1,067 prayer cards left in one rural church over a sixteenth-month period. The analysis is placed in the theoretical context of ordinary theology, and it uses a conceptual framework which distinguishes between three aspects of ordinary intercessory and ordinary supplicatory prayer defined as reference, intention, and objective (ap Siôn, 2007). Results of the analysis show that specific concrete issues were not included in 30% of prayer requests, but in the 70% of requests where concrete contexts were provided, 29% cited illness and 20% death. Overall, there were more examples of primary control (55%) than secondary control (45%). The results, alongside selected exemplification of categories, identify the concerns of ordinary theologians expressed in a rural ministry context and their contribution to the empirical study of ordinary theology.

Introduction

Many rural churches offer an invitation to those passing through their doors to pause, to reflect and to compose a request for prayer. The present study was established to listen to and to analyse the prayer requests left by ordinary people within one rural church. The analysis is placed within the context of ordinary theology and its practical expression through ordinary prayer.

* Dr Tania ap Siôn is Executive Director of the St Mary's Centre, Wales and Senior Research Fellow, Warwick Religions and Education Research Unit, University of Warwick. *Address for correspondence:* The St Mary's Centre, Llys Onnen, Abergwyngregyn, Llanfairfechan, Gwynedd, LL33 0LD. E-mail: t.apsion@glyndwr.ac.uk

Ordinary theology

Theology is usually regarded as an activity which lies in the domain of 'qualified' theologians within the Church or Academy. Although dialogue exists between qualified theologians and ordinary people, notably in the context of practical theology, very often that dialogue is controlled by the former. In response to this perceived imbalance, Jeff Astley (2002) introduced and defined the construct of ordinary theology, and asked whether benefits could be gained from listening to those who are technically unqualified (ordinary) people. For Astley, 'the study of ordinary theology can promote a perspective that meets the contention of Edward Farley and others that we should recover theology as a fundamental dimension of piety, an inherent part of *every* Christian's vocation' (2002, p. viii).

In terms of definition, ordinary theology is concerned with 'the theological beliefs and processes of believing that find expression in the God-talk of those believers who have received no scholarly theological education' (Astley, 2002, p. 1). This ordinary God-talk or ordinary theology is a deeply personal, 'lived' theology and may be hesitant or inarticulate because it has not been subjected to the same objective, analytical rigours required for academic theology. Ordinary theology is also concerned with understanding how the processes of believing work, which requires an appreciation of individual learning contexts and an understanding of how people learn (Astley, 2002, p. 17ff). Astley argues that learning takes place in 'experiential learning contexts' which are located outside the person (for example, the religious community) and inside the person (for example, individual life experiences), and that these two contexts for learning exist in a dialogical relationship. Therefore, in a real sense, individuals have their own theology, informed by their reflections on their individual experiences, and this theology is in a continual state of change and adaptation as individuals reflect on and incorporate new information arising from individual experiential learning contexts.

In terms of identifying the benefits of listening to and engaging in dialogue with ordinary theologians, Astley (2002, p. 145–162) provides some examples. The study of ordinary theology provides the Church with significant information about the people it serves which is essential if the Church is properly to 'exercise its ministry of pastoral care, worship, Christian education, apologetics, preaching and evangelism ...' (Astley, 2002, p. 146), which is also the perspective of practical theology. Good ordinary theology may play a useful role in the activity of doing theology; for example, it is able to test whether academic theology actually 'works' in practice, in the sense of being meaningful on the level of experience. In addition, for Astley, theology is something which should be experience based and as such academic theologians do not hold the monopoly in relation to it. By implication, this means that good ordinary theologians are able to contribute to, as well as critique, theology, and these ordinary activities will help ensure the continuing relevance of theology within an ever-changing world.

In addition to providing a theoretical model for ordinary theology, Astley also considers approaches to studying ordinary theology, where he identifies 'two areas of original research [that] are of particular importance: one is empirical and social-scientific, the other is philosophical and theological (that is, conceptual)' (2002, p. 97). With reference to the former, empirical and social-scientific studies related directly to ordinary theology are emerging, for example, the quantitative study of Littler and Francis (2005), examining ordinary ideas of holiness in a survey of 4,879 visitors to rural churches; the interview-based study of Christie (2007) who classified and exemplified the ordinary christologies of 45 Anglican churchgoers; and the qualitative study by Christie and Astley (2009) exploring ordinary soteriology.

Within a rural ministry context Astley (2003, p. 10) argues that 'rural ministry may in principle serve as the ideal testing ground for the very notion of ordinary theology, and for the requisite empirical studies that are needed in order to paint its portrait (or, rather, its variety of portraits) in sufficient detail'. In comparison with urban ministry, for reasons relating to scale among others, a closer relationship often exists between rural clergy and their church-attending and non-church-attending parishioners, which may enable their ordinary theology to be heard more clearly.

Ordinary prayer

Prayer lies at the heart of Christian practice. Studying the content of ordinary people's prayers can provide valuable insights into ordinary theologies which help to define, shape, and support their religious or spiritual lives, whether they are churched or unchurched. One approach to exploring ordinary prayer in a specific context is through the analysis of intercessory prayer requests left in churches.

A number of initial exploratory studies have been conducted which identify the main themes and characteristics of prayer requests in terms of content and frequency. For example, Schmied (2002) analysed 2,674 prayers inscribed in the prayer intention books provided by seven Roman Catholic churches in Germany. The analyses focused on four areas: the addressees of the prayers; the kinds of prayers; the reference persons and groups; and the prayer intentions. First, 72% of the prayers specified an addressee, with 27% addressed to God, 21% to Mary, and 5% to Jesus. Second, 91% of the prayers included some form of petition, while 23% expressed thanksgiving, 3% trust, 2% praise, 1% complaint, 1% love, and 2% some other concept. Third, 59% of the prayers made petition only for others, 11% for self and others, and just 15% only for self. Fourth, the prayer intentions were allocated to seven categories, with some prayers embracing more than one category. Over a quarter (28%) of the prayers referred to health or recovery of health, 21% to protection in general, 16% to religious matters (including vocations and forgiveness), 9% to specific projects (including surgical operations and long journeys), 8% to peace, 7% to faith, and 34% to other issues.

Brown and Burton (2007) analysed 61 prayer requests left in one rural church. The majority of the prayers were for people who were ill, in hospital, about to undergo operations, recovering from operations, or who had died. Only two prayers were for world situations.

ap Siôn (2007) analysed 917 prayer cards left in a rural Anglican parish church employing a framework which consisted of three main constructs: prayer reference, prayer intention and prayer objective. Results for prayer reference showed that the majority of prayer requests were for other people known personally to the prayer authors or for global issues (90%) with very few written for the prayer authors alone (4%). For prayer intention, 29% were non-specific in terms of not offering a concrete, physical context for the prayer. The next three highest categories were illness (21%), death (16%), and conflict or disaster (14%). For prayer objective, there were more examples of secondary control (57%), where prayer authors placed the outcomes of their prayers entirely in the hands of another, than primary control (43%), where prayer authors explicitly indicated the desired outcome to their prayers.

A few prayer-request studies have focused on specific areas of concern. For example, two studies have examined prayer requests left in hospital settings (Grossoehme, 1996; Hancocks and Lardner, 2007), while other studies have examined prayers for health and wellbeing (ap Siôn, 2008) and prayers reflecting the beliefs of 'ordinary theologians' about the nature and activity of God and God's concern with and impact on the everyday world (ap Siôn, 2011), both in a rural church setting.

Research agenda

The present study set out to analyse a second set of prayer requests from the same rural church as the 2007 prayer study, employing the same broad conceptual framework (ap Siôn, 2007). The analysis aims to identify and illustrate the main concerns and modes of expression of ordinary theologians and to reflect on their significance for rural ministry.

Method

Location

St Mary's church is situated in a rural location in an area of middle England highly attractive to tourists. As visitors enter the highly atmospheric space of the memorial chapel they are greeted by a notice inviting them to pause, to reflect, and to pray. They are also invited to commit their prayers to a postcard-sized prayer card and to leave these cards to be prayed by the local priest and congregation. The present study is based on the 1,067 prayer cards which were left in this chapel over a sixteen-month period.

Analysis

Of the 1,067 prayer cards analysed in the study, 1,022 were entirely concerned with intercessory and supplicatory prayer forms (96%). Of the remaining 45 prayer cards, 33 included elements of thanksgiving, five included elements of confession and repentance, and seven included elements of adoration. Within the prayer cards concerned with inter-cession and supplication, a total of 1,370 requests were made. It is these 1,370 individual requests which form the basis of the following analyses.

The conceptual framework devised by ap Siôn (2007) was employed for analysing the content of the intercessory and supplicatory prayers. The framework distinguished between three elements defined as intention, reference, and objective. The notion of *intention* is applied to distinguish among ten key areas with which the individual authors were concerned: illness, death, growth, work, relationships, conflict or disaster, sport or recreation, travel, open intention, and general. The notion of *reference* is applied to distinguish among four key foci with which the individual authors were concerned: themselves, other people who were known personally to the authors, animals which were known personally to the authors, and the world or global context. The notion of *objective* is applied to distinguish between two effects which the individual authors envisaged as a consequence of their prayers of intercession or supplication in terms of primary control and secondary control. In primary control prayer authors explicitly suggest the desired consequences of their prayers. In secondary control prayer authors place prayers and their consequences entirely in the hands of another.

Results

In relation to prayer intention, 401 (29%) requests were concerned with illness, 278 (20%) death, 242 (18%) open intention, 163 (12%) general, 91 (7%) relationships, 64 (5%) growth, 60 (4%) conflict or disaster, 42 (3%) work, 15 (1%) sport or recreation, and 14 (1%) travel. In relation to prayer reference 1,024 (75%) were requests for other people who were known to the prayer author, 222 (16%) for global concerns, 67 (5%) for the prayer authors themselves, and 57 (4%) for animals known to the prayer author. In relation to prayer objective, primary control was employed in 757 (55%) requests and secondary control was employed in 613 (45%) requests.

The following exemplification of the content of these requests explores prayer intention and prayer objective in relation to prayer reference. In the present article only selected prayer intention categories are exemplified. Examples of secondary control are denoted by an asterisk (*).

Self

Of the 1,370 individual prayer requests, 67 (5%) had the prayer authors as the key focus. Relationships featured in 32 (48%) of these requests, followed by 9 (13%) for illness, 6 (%) for open intention, 6 (9%) for work, 6 (9%) for general, 5 (9%) for growth, 1 (1%) for sport or recreation, 1 (1%) for travel, and 1 (1%) for death. Relationships, illness, and growth are exemplified. In terms of prayer objective, 54 (81%) of these prayer requests were examples of primary control and 13 (19%) were examples of implicit secondary control.

Relationships. Of the 91 prayer requests concerned with relationships, 32 (35%) had the prayer author as the key focus. Most requests referred to pre-marital or marital relationships in which the prayer authors were involved. In most cases these were indicative of primary control where the authors suggested a desired outcome such as protection, help, blessing (usually in relation to having children), love, and longevity in the relationships. For a few, possibly younger, authors the desired outcome was more concrete, referring to the hope of re-establishing specific relationships with named or unnamed individuals. The rare examples of secondary control referred to an author's marriage and thwarted love.

> [Please pray for] For our marriage.*
> [Please pray for] Me as I am so mixed up. I love him so but he loves another.*
> [Please pray for] My boyfriend NAME that we may get back together because he knows I will forgive him for all the trouble he has caused me because I love him very much.

Some requests were concerned with relationships between the authors and their families or friends, where primary control was evident in requests for re-establishing family relationships which have been broken through adoption as well as maintaining the longevity of friendships.

> [Please pray for] I also pray that one day I will have a chance to see my real mother as I am adopted although I love my mum lots.
> [Please pray for] NAME and help to keep her as my friend.

In addition, there was one prayer request set within the context of the absence of relationships, and illustrative of primary control, and one request addressed directly to an ex-partner.

> [Please pray for] Please find me a nice man.
> [Please pray for] NAME. Thanks for your memory. May you live a happy life and have a happy marriage. An old boyfriend.

Illness. Of the 401 prayer requests concerned with illness, 9 (2%) had the prayer author as the key focus. These related to physical ailments suffered by the prayer author and an operation as well as mental health in the form of depression and hypochondria. A couple of requests related to preservation of health. Primary control examples requested healing, improvement, or protection, and the one secondary control example stated the context with no indication of desirable outcome.

> [Please pray for] Me to get rid of bad pains in my lungs.
> [Please pray for] NAME Myself to come out of this depression and find peace of mind with her husband and son.
> [Please prayer for] Keep me free from cancer and heart trouble.
> [Please pray for] Me as I am a dreadful hypochondriac.*

Growth. Of the 60 prayer requests concerned with growth, 5 (8%) had the prayer author as the key focus. The types of personal growth identified by the authors included increased moral awareness and faith development. All these requests were examples of primary control apart from one.

> [Please pray for] Most of all help me to find the path I once had.
> [Please pray for] Make me a channel of your peace.
> [Please pray for] Help me to be a better person.
> [Please pray for] Me that I will try to put Christ first in my life constantly.

Other people

Of the 1,370 individual prayer requests, 1,024 (75%) had people who were known personally to the prayer author as the key focus. Illness featured in 350 (34%) of these requests, followed by 240 (23%) for death, 180 (18%) for open intention, 125 (12%) for general, 50 (5%) for relationships, 32 (3%) for growth, 29 (3%) for work, 12 (1%) for travel, 4 (1%) for sport or recreation, and 2 (1%) for conflict or disaster. Illness, death, work, and travel are exemplified. In terms of prayer objective, 557 (54%) of these prayer requests were examples of primary control and 467 (46%) were examples of implicit secondary control.

Illness. Of the 401 prayer requests concerned with illness, 350 (87%) had people known to the prayer author as the key focus. These prayer requests were mainly related to family members and friends, and employed primary control more often than secondary control. Requests referred to illnesses in general, non-specific terms or provided more detail about the nature of the problems, identifying diseases, accidents, mental health issues, operations, addiction, and pregnancy and birth, and if the conditions were terminal. Some of the requests included the families of the ill. In a number of requests additional details concerning the age, location, and personal qualities of the ill people were included. Primary control requests had desirable outcomes which included, for the ill person, improvements in health, freedom from pain, and strength, and for the ill person's family, help, strength, and ability to cope. Some requests focused on the prevention of illness and the promotion of health. Secondary control requests were characterized by their identification of context, with no desired outcomes.

> [Please pray for] NAME who is going into hospital.*
> [Please pray for] NAME who is bearing her illness so bravely.*
> [Please pray for] All members of my family that they may find health and happiness.

> [Please pray for] NAME that he may recover from schizophrenia.
> [Please pray for] My wife NAME who has been unlucky with illness –
> give her strength to carry on and enjoy life.
> [Please pray for] NAME and NAME that his suffering will soon end
> and for NAME his wife to have the strength she needs.
> [Please pray for] NAME a sweet child fighting hard against a vile
> illness. Give her strength please to be completely well.

Death. Of the 278 prayer requests concerned with death, 240 (86%) had people known to the prayer author as the key focus. These prayer requests concerned dead family and friends, and often provided dates and the time lapse since the deaths, which ranged from very recent to a few years previous or more. In many cases the prayer author's emotions relating to the dead person were noted, and, less often, the dead person's personal qualities. In some cases, the prayer author addressed the dead person directly. Some requests stated the belief that the dead person was with God, reunited with other loved ones, or in heaven. A number of requests were directed toward those who were left behind. The circumstances of the deaths were recorded mainly in very general terms, although some specific contexts were mentioned, for example, cancer.

There were more secondary control requests than primary control requests. Secondary control examples presented the context for the prayer, but suggested no desirable outcomes. Primary control requests asked for God to take care of the dead, give peace to the dead, and love or bless the dead. In some cases a request was made for a dead person to go to heaven, and one request asked for a dead friend to be brought back to life. With regard to the bereaved, a few primary control requests asked that they may be helped during that difficult time. Another aspect of primary control examples was the anticipation of future deaths of family and friends with requests for long life.

> [Please pray for] My dear mother who departed this life on August 24th
> and also for my father in law, who passed away in July. That they may
> enjoy the wonders of heaven.
> [Please pray for] NAME my mate who died a year ago and make this all
> a nightmare and bring her back so that we can all be happy again.
> [Please pray for] NAME who died a year ago. Please may she be in
> heaven and please look after her all the time and let her be by her
> friend and family all the time.
> [Please pray for] My Nan who died two months ago. She was a great
> person. I'll never forget you Nan. Thinking of you always.*
> [Please pray for] My godmother who sadly died a few years ago from
> cancer.*

One prayer request looking forward to the future asks that 'unseen friends' are present at a marriage.

> [Please pray for] NAME and NAME as they start their life together on Saturday, DATE. May all our unseen friends be with us. Especially NAME, NAME and NAME.

Work. Of the 42 prayer requests concerned with work, 29 (69%) had people known to the prayer author as the key focus. Many of these requests were related to achievement in respect of examination success, passing driving tests, or finding a job. Others focused on new beginnings in respect of starting a new school, a job interview, or retirement. In addition, work-related issues were included in some prayer requests. Most of these were examples of primary control, with desirable outcomes expressed mainly in concrete terms, for example, requests to pass exams or to gain employment, but there were a few expressed in abstract terms, for example, requests for 'peace', and 'enjoyment'. The cases of secondary control stated the context, and made no reference to a desirable outcome.

> [Please pray for] NAME so that she might pass her nursing exam.
> [Please pray for] NAME that he will settle down in his new school.
> [Please pray for] Please pray that my grand dad NAME enjoys his retirement and that my granny NAME be also able to enjoy his retirement.
> [Please pray for] NAME's dad who is on the dole. My dad who is working his fingers to the bone.*
> [Please pray for] My brother who is due to take his exams.*

Travel. Of the 14 prayer requests concerned with travel, 12 (86%) had people known to the prayer author as the key focus. Most requests concerned family or friends who were on holiday or about to emigrate, and, in some cases, the author was included in the group. Most requests were primary control focusing on safety and enjoyment. Secondary control examples stated the context with no reference to desirable outcome.

> [Please pray for] Our son NAME who will shortly depart on a long motor trip around Europe and for NAME who will leave for holidays in France.*
> [Please pray for] Please pray that all the members of our camping holiday arrive home safely.
> [Please pray for] NAME that she finds happiness in Australia.

Animals

Of the 1,370 individual prayer requests, 57 (4%) had animals which were known personally to the prayer author as the key focus. Death featured in 30 (53%) of these requests, followed by 13 (23%) open intention, 9 (16%) for illness, 4 (7%) for general, and 1 (2%) for travel. Death, open intention, and illness are exemplified. In terms of prayer objective, 37 (65%) of these prayer requests were examples of implicit secondary control and 20 (35%) were examples of primary control.

Death. Of the 278 prayer requests concerned with death, 30 (11%) had animals known to the prayer author as the key focus. Most of these requests concerned a variety of pets including cats, dogs, hamsters, and a pig which had died at specific times in the past or recently. The animals were referred to by name or species. Most requests were examples of secondary control, and these noted the pets' deaths, their place in heaven, and occasionally the circumstances and the owners' emotions in relation to the pet, with no desirable outcome. Primary control requests asked for their pets to rest in peace, to be blessed, or looked after, and included an additional focus on extant pets, that they should experience long lives.

> [Please pray for] My hamster NAME who was very ill, and died three weeks ago. I loved him very much. May you God, look after him for me, and keep him in your care. I spent many hours with him.
> [Please pray for] My bull dog. May he rest in peace.
> [Please pray for] Dog NAME who died at Christmas. She was a wonderful spaniel. God bless her.
> [Please pray for] My cat NAME who has recently been knocked over and killed.*
> [Please pray for] My dog NAME who will be gone from our lives sometime but not from our memories.*

Open intention. Of the 242 prayer requests concerned with open intention, 13 (5%) had animals known to the prayer author as the key focus. None of these prayers included a specific intention but identified a pet or pets, often by species or personal name, for which prayer was intended. Most pets were the authors' own but with occasional reference to the pets of others. In a few examples, the authors expressed their emotions in relation to the pets, which they usually identified as love. All these were examples of secondary control.

> [Please pray for] NAME my cat, and NAME my other cat.*
> [Please pray for] My dog we all love him and he is getting old.*

Illness. Of the 401 prayer requests concerned with illness, 9 (2%) had animals known to the prayer author as the key focus. The cases of primary control requested that sick pets were looked after, and, in one case, that a pet stayed healthy. The cases of secondary control stated the context without indicating a desirable outcome.

> [Please pray for] Please look after my dog who is not well.
> [Please pray for] For my dog NAME who is not well and the vet does not know what is wrong.*
> [Please pray for] NAME my hamster. He is losing the hair out of his bottom.*

World or global

Of the 1,370 individual prayer requests, 222 (16%) had a world or a global context as the key focus. Conflict or disaster featured in 58 (26%) of these requests, followed by 43 (19%) for open intention, 33 (15%) for illness, 28 (13%) for general, 27 (12%) for growth, 10 (5%) for sport and recreation, 9 (4%) for relationships, 7 (3%) for death, and 7 (3%) for work. Conflict or disaster, growth, sport or recreation, and work are exemplified. In terms of prayer objective, 126 (57%) of these prayer requests were examples of primary control and 96 (43%) were examples of implicit secondary control.

Conflict or disaster. Of the 60 prayer requests concerned with conflict or disaster, 58 (97%) had a world or global context as the key focus. In these prayer requests, both general and specific groups were selected for prayer. The general included the starving, the poor, the dying, and abused and killed animals, with no geographical or other contextualising information provided. The specific included named examples of countries, groups of people, events, and disasters. Many of these probably referred to the same contexts as the general groups. These were often related to Africa and the Middle East, with a few European examples.

There were more primary control requests than secondary control requests. Secondary control requests stated the contexts, with desired outcomes. Primary control requests included some concrete outcomes, relating to the provision of food for the starving, rain for drought, destruction of nuclear weapons, and freedom from war, for example. In addition, there were many abstract outcomes, relating to peace, love, justice, and strength.

[Please pray for] The 3rd world.*
[Please pray for] Starving people in the world.*
[Please pray for] Peace in the world and that all the starving people will get enough food and water.
[Please pray for] Peace throughout the world and the destruction of all nuclear weapons.
[Please pray for] All the animals that are experimented on, killed, shot, and run over. Help them seek a better life.
[Please pray for] World peace especially in the Middle East.

Growth. Of the 64 prayer requests concerned with growth, 27 (42%) had a world or a global context as the key focus. Many prayers were requests for conversions or 'turning to God' at two levels: in England with reference to individual churches and missions, and in the world with reference to people or categories of people in general. A few of these prayers referred to more extensive global change brought about by the power of God or the return of Jesus. In addition some prayers focused on established Christian communities or Christians in general and their faith development. Most were examples of primary control, although a few examples of secondary control were evident.

[Please pray for] For all who follow Christ as his apostles, taking up their cross daily.*
[Please pray for] the world and Jesus to come again to save us.
[Please pray for] The healing of our nation and a return to Biblical truth.
[Please pray for] All Christians that more of what they want will decrease and more of God's will increase.
[Please pray for] That the evils of our day may be overcome through the power of Almighty God.
A number of prayers included requests to develop certain qualities or attributes for application on a global level, for example, kindness, truthfulness, contentment, and moral strength. These were all examples of primary control.
[Please pray for] All the little children. May they grow up to be kind and truthful.
[Please pray for] Every thing we have. Help us not to want more.

Sport or recreation. Of the 15 prayer requests concerned with sport or recreation, 10 (67%) had a world or a global context as the key focus. All of the prayers related to named football teams or England in the world cup. Most of these were examples of primary control, requesting the success of the team, while the two secondary control prayers stated only the context.

[Please pray for] Leicester City football club.*
[Please pray for] Derby County and help them win promotion.

Work. Of the 42 prayer requests concerned with work, 7 (17%) had a world or a global context as the key focus. These included broad all-inclusive requests relating to certain categories of people such as the unemployed, nurses, and teachers. There were more examples of primary control than secondary control. Secondary control examples stated the context with no desirable outcomes identified. In primary control prayer authors requested help, strength, or a change in circumstances.

> [Please pray for] Help those who are out of work or who can't.
> [Please pray for] NAME school that they might receive a proper headmaster soon.
> [Please pray for] All those out of work.*
> [Please pray for] People and teachers who help us in hard stages in life.*
> [Please pray for] All nurses that they may find courage to continue their work despite the heavy burdens which they are forced to carry. May God bless them and watch over them, helping them to ease the dissolution of their work.

Conclusion

On the basis of the present study of prayer requests, two conclusions emerge which relate to specific results found within the analyses. First, the conceptual framework employed in the analysis of prayer requests is helpful for the identification and illustration of the concerns and beliefs of ordinary people when engaged in this form of ordinary prayer. Three features of the results are of particular note. In relation to reference, only 5% of prayers were for the prayer authors alone while 91% of prayers were for other people either known personally to the prayer author or other people in a world or global context. These results are almost identical to the previous prayer-card study (ap Siôn, 2007), and this imbalance is broadly supported by Schmied's research (2002). Again, questions arise regarding why so many people do not choose to pray for themselves. Is there a common view that Christian prayer is essentially an altruistic activity, performed for other people, and that the self is not perceived as a natural or appropriate subject of prayer?

In relation to intention, illness and death were the most popular categories, closely reflecting the results of the earlier study (ap Siôn,

2007), and also supported by other prayer-request studies (Schmied, 2002; Brown and Burton, 2007). From this it may be concluded that when an opportunity to offer a prayer is provided, the majority of people feel that illness and death are the most important (or appropriate) topics of prayer, and perhaps over which they have least control. In relation to objective, primary control was favoured over secondary control. In the previous study secondary control was favoured over primary control by around the same margins, indicating one is not favoured over the other. However, there are intention categories where primary control or secondary control is favoured in both studies. Therefore, in both studies secondary control is favoured in prayer cards relating to death, and primary control is favoured in relation to illness, growth, work, and relationships. This may indicate that in certain circumstances, prayer authors may have a greater immediate concern to ensure a desired outcome or that the desired outcome is more readily identified and easier to articulate.

With reference to the practical applications of studies involving prayer requests, a further three conclusions emerge from these data. First, analyses of prayer requests help to inform the Church and Academy about the concerns and beliefs of ordinary people. This can play a role in the dialogue that Astley envisages taking place between Church and Academy and ordinary theologians, in which both sides reap mutual benefits. Second, although the depth in which it is possible to explore the prayer authors' beliefs is limited through the short format of the prayer request, prayer requests provide an opportunity for general, large-scale studies to be conducted which can reliably identify appropriate areas for further research from the perspective of ordinary theology. This identification of appropriate areas can support the development of both quantitative and qualitative research tools which are designed to explore prayer in more controlled, systematic ways. Third, there is a need to replicate prayer request studies in other rural church settings in order to test these conclusions.

References

ap Siôn, T. (2007). Listening to prayers: An analysis of prayers left in a country church in rural England. *Archiv für Religionspsychologie, 29,* 199–226.

ap Siôn, T. (2008). Distinguishing between intention, reference and objective in an analysis of prayer requests for health and well-being: Eavesdropping from the rural vestry. *Mental Health, Religion and Culture, 11,* 53–65.

ap Siôn, T. (2011). Interpreting God's activity in the public square: Accessing the ordinary theology of personal prayer. In L. J. Francis & H-G. Ziebertz (Eds.), *The Public Significance of Religion* (pp. 315–342). Leiden: Brill.

Astley, J. (2002). *Ordinary Theology: Looking, listening and learning in theology.* Aldershot: Ashgate.

Astley, J. (2003). Ordinary theology for rural theology and rural ministry. *Rural Theology, 1*, 3–12.

Brown, A., & Burton, L. (2007). Learning from prayer requests in a rural church: An exercise in ordinary theology. *Rural Theology, 5*, 45–52.

Christie, A. (2007). Who do you say I am? Answers from the pews. *Journal of Adult Theological Education, 4*, 181–194.

Christie, A., & Astley, J. (2009). Ordinary soteriology: A qualitative study. In L. J. Francis, M. Robbins, and J. Astley (Eds.), *Empirical Theology in Texts and Tables: qualitative, quantitative and comparative perspectives* (pp. 177–196). Leiden: Brill.

Grossoehme, D. H. (1996). Prayer reveals belief: Images of God from hospital prayers. *Journal of Pastoral Care, 50* (Spring), 33–39.

Hancocks, G., & Lardner, M. (2007). I say a little prayer for you: What do hospital prayers reveal about people's perceptions of God? *Journal of Health Care Chaplaincy, 8*(1), 29–42.

Littler, K., & Francis, L. J. (2005). Ideas of the holy: The ordinary theology of visitors to rural churches. *Rural Theology, 3*, 49–54.

Schmied, G. (2002). God images in prayer intention books. *Implicit Religion, 5*, 121–126.

Part 3

THEOLOGICAL AND SOCIOLOGICAL PERSPECTIVES

Chapter 8

ENCOUNTERING NEW AGE SPIRITUALITY: OPPORTUNITIES AND CHALLENGES FOR THE RURAL CHURCH

John Drane*

Abstract – This article reviews the rise of New Age spirituality, locating its origins in widespread disillusionment with the western cultural paradigm and difficulties faced by the Church in offering relevant answers to new questions. At the same time, it argues that the Church has resources, particularly in its rural manifestations, that can begin to address the concerns of today's spiritual searchers.

Introduction

Whenever the expression 'New Age' is used in a rural community, it often conjures up images of scruffy dropouts travelling around the countryside in beaten-up buses, camping on other people's land, and playing havoc with local economies. Though that phenomenon is there, describing such people as '*New Age* travellers' can create the impression that 'New Age' concerns only a minority fringe element within society. The reality is, however, quite different, and exponents of mainstream 'New Age' spirituality are to be found in all walks of life. Moreover, they are actually raising some fundamental questions about the future of western civilization which, through the impact of globalization, might also be about the future of the world.

* The Revd Dr John Drane is a freelance researcher and theological consultant, a Fellow of St John's College, Durham and Adjunct Professor of Practical Theology at Fuller Seminary, Pasadena, California. *Address for correspondence*: Cairneve, Ellon, Aberdeenshire, AB41 7TU. E-mail: cairneve@aol.com

Origins

Before turning to the 'New Age' proper, it is important to note that it is not the same thing as those organizations that are referred to as 'New Religious Movements', or more popularly 'cults' (Barker, 1989; Saliba, 1995; Arweck, 2002). Whereas a New Religious Movement (NRM) is typically a highly structured organization, with clear boundaries and definitions of membership, the 'New Age' is a much more diffuse category demonstrating a high degree of ambivalence and with no clear boundaries and certainly no concept of membership. As a discrete category, 'New Age' may ultimately turn out to be unserviceable, though the phenomenon to which it refers is real enough (Sutcliffe and Bowman, 2000, pp. 1–13). Some prefer to speak of 'new spirituality', though there is no consensus on an appropriate alternative term, either among scholars or practitioners. The expression 'New Age' seems to have come into common currency in the mid-1980s, with the launch of the *New Age Journal* in the United States of America. But it was certainly not freshly created then, and can be traced as far back as the earliest decades of the twentieth century, if not earlier (Sutcliffe, 2003). In more recent times, however, the notion of a coming new world order that would usher in an era of transformation had been popularized through the counter-culture of the 1960s, most notably in the musical *Hair* with its song declaring 'This is the Age of Aquarius'. That musical itself was scarcely 'New Age' in the later technical sense of the word, but the lyrics of its opening scene highlight one of the strands that fed into the current fascination with new or 'alternative' spiritualities. Traditional astrological lore regards the Age of Aquarius as the final (seventh) stage in the story of human development that began 14,000 years ago with the age of Leo, proceeded through the ages of Cancer (approx. 8000–6000 BC), Gemini (approx. 6000–4000 BC), Taurus (approx. 4000–2000 BC), Aries (approx. 2000–0 BC – the 'age of the Father'), and Pisces (the fish – 'age of the Son', approx. 0–2000 AD), and is now culminating in the age of ultimate enlightenment and transformation, typified by Aquarius the water-bearer, ushering in the 'age of the Spirit'.

None of this is new, and that is indeed one of the notable characteristics of much that is encompassed by the New Age: with one or two exceptions (mostly related to science fiction), much of it is quite ancient. Though it is impossible to generalize in this area, some aspects of New Age spirituality undoubtedly bear more than a passing resemblance to ancient Gnosticism (Ellwood, 1992; Drane, 2000a, pp. 36–56). The rise

of organized forms of alternative spiritualities can be traced back at least
to the first half of the nineteenth century, and the fascination for esoteric
knowledge that dominated the early years of the formation of the United
States of America (Melton, 1992; Alexander, 1992). The north-eastern
states in particular gave birth not only to new religious movements such
as the Mormons and Christian Scientists, but also encouraged interest
in numerous arcane healing therapies, while the experiences of the Fox
sisters, Kate and Margaretta, who in 1848 allegedly connected with the
spirit world at a house in Hydesville, New York, led to a burgeoning of
interest in contacting other worlds. When Helena Blavatsky established
the Theosophical Society in New York in 1875, and subsequently brought
Swami Vivekananda to the World's Parliament of Religions (Chicago,
1893), she and her collaborators were working ground that was already
fertile and receptive to new ideas.

In Britain, the First World War became a major catalyst for the
popularization of some of the same interests (Sutcliffe, 2003, pp. 31–54).
Spiritualism in particular flourished, as bereft relatives tried to get
in touch with their departed loved ones. At the same time, the sheer
number of men killed in that war created a new awareness of the dark
side of technology and industrialization, and its philosophical base in
the Enlightenment notion of inexorable progress. Mechanization was
turning out to be a mixed blessing, with the benefits of things like
sanitation and electrification balanced by a new and terrifying capacity
for people to kill their enemies in ever more efficient, if inhumane, ways.
At roughly the same time Arthur Waite, an English aristocrat, defined
the modern Tarot as a tool for connecting with ultimate spiritual
realities (Drane, Clifford and Johnson, 2001). Nor was he alone in such
esoteric interests: he was a member of the Hermeneutical Order of the
Golden Dawn, along with other well-known cultural leaders of the day,
including the Irish poet W.B. Yeats – forerunners of an interest in all
things alternative that still persists today in aristocratic circles. It would
be easy to dismiss the emergence of such concerns among this stratum
of society by reference to Maslow's hierarchy of human needs (Maslow,
1970), by observing that when people have nothing else to worry about
they do indeed tend to turn to philosophical and religious speculation. It
is also tempting to understand it in the light of the well-documented fact
that, whenever the credibility of political institutions is threatened, they
often claim privileged access to secret information as a way to either
establish or shore up their power base. It happened at the time of the
French Revolution (when the Tarot, which had previously been a pack of

playing cards, was first reinvented as a mystical tool), and Hitler used the same appeal to mystical powers to establish his own empire in the early twentieth century (the Order of the Golden Dawn being one of several secret societies that interested him). But it would be a mistake to regard this emerging interest in mystical knowledge as a concern only of the idle rich, eager to maintain their position of wealth and power.

By the 1930s, there was considerable interest in such topics among working-class populations in Yorkshire and Lancashire, and the Mazdaznan movement was a significant social force in many northern mill towns during that period. Its founder was Dr Otoman Zar-Adusht Ha'nish, an Oxford medical graduate and eastern guru, and his meetings in cities such as Leeds and Huddersfield were attended by thousands, as he proclaimed his belief that it would be possible to bring all things into balance through a combination of breathing exercises and diet, which would lead to nerve and gland regeneration. There are still people alive today who can remember its social impact, and remain true to its teachings. At the same time, many of these same ordinary people began to be disillusioned with urban life – especially its mechanized manifestations in mills and factories – and sought spiritual regeneration in the countryside. Intentional communities were established with a 'back to the land' philosophy, not least through the agency of the influential Co-operative movement.

By the 1960s, dissatisfaction with the culture of modernity was even more widespread, and it was at this time that major players in the alternative spirituality scene began to emerge, including the Findhorn Foundation in north-east Scotland (Riddell, 1990; Sutcliffe, 2000, 2003, pp. 150–194) and the Esalen Institute in California (Alexander, 1992). The proliferation of nuclear devices was threatening world stability, and the terrible possibilities of technology without boundaries was becoming more widely recognized as evidence of the Nazi death camps began to filter out. In due course, this awareness was supplemented by the knowledge that western lifestyles were damaging the actual stuff out of which the planet is made, and the scene was set for a widespread questioning of the ideology which had brought us to this situation. In addition, as former colonies around the world claimed their independence from Britain and other western powers, it became clear that civilization as we had inherited it had been bought at a very high price, paid by people of other cultures.

Increasing numbers of people today are, if anything, even more concerned about the possibilities for disaster on a larger scale than was previously imagined. The search for some resolution, some hidden wisdom that might help to chart a new way forward for the global community, is more urgent than ever. So where can wisdom be found? A hundred years ago, British people would automatically have looked to the Church as their spiritual guardian. In times of outstanding crisis, they still do: after 9/11 there was a discernible, if short-lived, increase in attendance at church services in England, while a few years earlier the death of Princess Diana had evoked a similar reaction (Drane, 2000a, pp. 78–103). The 2001 United Kingdom census figures show that, in England, 71.7% of people regard themselves as Christian, and though that scarcely seems to translate into an active and regular commitment to Christian faith, there is still plenty of evidence of a concern for 'spirituality without religion' (Davie, 1990, 1994; Hay and Hunt, 2000; Heelas, 2002). That concern does not necessarily lead to any connection with an identifiable community, but in so far as it does, such spiritual searching appears more likely to find expression in a New Age context than through regular involvement with any sort of mainstream faith tradition, whether Christian or any other.

Changing culture

What exactly is the 'New Age'? In previous writings, I have proposed a fourfold taxonomy that may be used to define and describe the characteristic practices of this emerging spirituality, and there is no need to repeat that here (Drane, 1999, 2000a, pp. 8–35). What I want to do is to reflect on some of the important changes in western society over the past fifty years or so that have facilitated the emergence of this kind of thinking, as a way of understanding the reasons why so many people take it for granted that they will not find spiritual meaning in the Church, while apparently being prepared to believe almost anything else that might be offered to them. There are four factors in this, two of them specifically related to the Church, and the other two to cultural change. A key element is the obvious fact that the Church itself, once an important part of our culture, is today on the margins of society. There are many reasons for this, but one that is frequently articulated by spiritually serious people is that the Church – because of its close historical alignment with the state – is part of the problem, and therefore cannot be part of the solution. Christians, so the argument runs, colluded with all the negative aspects of empire building, and in some cases used their theology to justify the exploitation of both people and the natural environment. That being the case, how can Christians now claim to have any sort of answer to the human predicament – especially since they have had two thousand years to get it right, during which time things seem to have gone from bad to worse? Like many historical judgements on the Church, this one has important elements of truth as well as some falsehoods. Overall, though, more of it is true than not, and we do well to accept that the Church has baggage which it is finding very difficult to own, still less to work through and discard. It is also an institution, and institutions of all sorts are deeply distrusted nowadays, whether it be politicians, the law, bankers, accountants, or any number of others.

This is not the only challenge to the Church, however. There is such a confusing religious mix among Christians today that spiritual searchers with no previous understanding can find it all mystifying – and, therefore, irrelevant. Ordinary people outside the Church simply cannot understand why there should be so much division among Christians. The distinctives of various denominations mean little or nothing, while the matters on which churches do make pronouncements are generally regarded as introverted, if not incomprehensible. An obvious recent example would be the seemingly endless debate about matters such as homosexual clergy, which is not only meaningless to the average person, but by comparison with the enormous issues facing the world today seems extraordinarily trivial. There are many reasons why the Church ends up projecting itself as apparently being interested in trivialities that no-one else cares about, and much of the difficulty is probably not created by the issues at all, but by Church leaders who are naïve when it comes to dealing with the media. Whatever the explanation, Christians are regularly perceived as people who have no idea what they think, and who argue about matters that are only peripherally 'spiritual', if at all – and who probably have hang-ups about things that other people take for granted. Many genuinely spiritual people feel that they have enough problems of their own, without joining the church and being introduced to a whole world of arguments they never thought about before.

It is, therefore, not altogether cynical to claim that, if the Church has a problem with spiritually-sensitive people searching elsewhere for the answers to life's deep questions, it only has itself to blame. But there are two other factors that also encourage people to look more widely in their search for a spiritual dimension to life. Though still only a very small percentage of the total United Kingdom population, there is a strong presence of traditional non-Christian faiths that are now accepted as part of a multicultural society. Moreover, the adherents of other world religions are increasingly found not only in major urban centres, but in rural settings throughout the British Isles. There is a widespread recognition that, though most people would not wish actually to convert to such faiths, they cannot be altogether wrong, and there must be some wisdom to be found in each of them. Moreover, we have become increasingly aware of other forms of spirituality, particularly those associated with first-nation peoples (Harrod, 2002) as well as the old pagan ideas which dominated these islands long before the arrival of Christianity (Pearson, 2002). There is a questioning of the cultural imperialism which formerly assumed that only people like us could know the truth, and a recognition that – while we may not wish to revert to any of these other worldviews *per se* – there must be some useful wisdom to be found in such places. This interest is often borne of a sense of despair with where western ideology is taking us, and a desperation to grasp hold of anything that might offer an alternative way. This intuition is then backed up by the consumerist mentality of our culture, for if we pick-and-mix everything else to ensure we get the best deal for ourselves, then surely we ought to be able to do the same with spirituality. This explains why, at the average New Age festival, one might find a whole range of spiritual tools or disciplines on offer, ranging from angels to tarot cards, astrology, rebirthing, spirit guides, reincarnation – and much more besides.

Prophetic or pathological?

Some regard all this as an incomprehensible jumble, and therefore dismiss the New Age as, at best, meaningless, if not a sign of the terminal decline of civilization as we know it – evidence of what Neil Postman (1986) colourfully called 'amusing ourselves to death'. The view that it is the product of a self-centred individualism, spelling the end of rational discourse altogether, is shared by people as diverse as religion scholar Paul Heelas (1996), neo-fundamentalist Carl Trueman (2003), and journalist Roland Howard (2001, p. 275) who claims that 'New Age spirituality seems the ultimate religion of privatized global capitalism'. Even those opinions, however, are relatively benign when compared with many within the Christian world who regard it all as dangerously occult, and its practitioners as demon possessed (Cumbey, 1983; Groothuis, 1988; Morrison, 1994). Some caution against trying to define it at all. Denise Cush (1996, p. 196) identified the New Age as 'a cluster of related ideas, teachings and groups, not altogether coherent, most of which would identify with this title', which sounds like a counsel of despair until we learn that even those such as the Findhorn Foundation, who have in the past promoted themselves as central to the movement, 'are now a little wary of this description ... because in popular thought it has become connected with the sensation seekers ... whose interest lies less in seeking spiritual transformation than in dabbling in the occult, or in practicing classical entrepreneurship on the naïve' (Riddell, 1990, p. 64). Even those who find themselves attracted to it offer no single consistent understanding. Writers like ex-Dominican Matthew Fox see it as the essential coming-together of different spiritual traditions that will lead to the reconciliation of our fractured world (Fox, 1988). His one-time colleague, the self-styled 'Jewitch' Starhawk, however, warns against people who are 'spiritually starved in their own culture ... unwittingly [becoming] spiritual strip miners damaging other cultures in superficial attempts to uncover their mystical treasures' (Starhawk, 1989, p 214) – a perception that correlates with the position advanced by Muslim scholar Ziauddin Sardar, who regards the emergence of designer spiritualities in the West as just another twist in the knife of imperialist oppression (Sardar, 1998).

Though I have serious disagreements with some of his conclusions (Drane, 2000b), I am personally more inclined to stand alongside Matthew Fox in regarding the New Age as a purposeful spiritual path, rather than to side with its cynical detractors. If pressed to give definition to the New Age, I would suggest it is a personal search for spiritual tools to overcome our hurts, to realize our hopes, and to make the world a better place. Within that frame of reference, one can identify a unifying theme that runs through all the apparently disparate and disconnected spiritual disciplines and practices that are employed. That unifying theme is the search for a way of empowerment that will help us to live effectively in the everyday world by awakening our spirituality. In other words, the key questions to which New Age spiritual practices purport to offer some answers are the classic, age-old questions of human identity and purpose: who am I, where did I come from, what does my life mean, and how can I make a useful contribution to the life of this world? Far from being a self-centred narcissistic movement, it is in fact a response to the failure of modernist culture to deliver on its promises, and represents a genuine search for a new worldview that will chart a safer course for the future of the planet and all its people. These questions are now so pressing, and other possible responses so unclear, that the New Age has in effect become the dominant spiritual outlook in our culture. Of course, there will be some people who are exploiting others by selling them artifacts or programmes they do not need, and Carol Riddell is right to draw attention to this possibility. But my consistent experience of New Age people over the past fifteen years or so is that there is no more exploitation here than one could find in many churches, and many sincere individuals who are concerned to leave the world a better place than they found it.

Making connections

The world of nature – and therefore the rural world – is one of the consistently recurring features in many aspects of New Age spirituality. The tour documented in Roland Howard's book *Shopping for God* features more rural locations than urban ones (Howard, 2001), while a visit to the Mind, Body, and Spirit shelves of any high street bookstore will confirm the impression that New Agers generally think it is easier to be spiritually connected in the countryside than it is in the city. Part of this can no doubt be attributed to the more general romanticizing of rural life by those who feel themselves alienated from urban civilization, and who hanker for the peaceful country lifestyle they imagine their forebears enjoyed. But there is among many New Age communities a genuine concern for rural issues, whether the environment itself or the need to sustain a more holistic lifestyle. At places like Findhorn, this translates into adventurous eco-village projects, offering sustainable housing of a sort that could enhance the rural environment anywhere, including an impressive sewage disposal facility that is operated entirely by natural means (plants and insects). More often, it might manifest itself in teenagers from the city going to a field at the summer solstice to dance and perform nature-based rituals. They might well be inspired primarily by television programmes such as *Buffy the Vampire Slayer* or *Sabrina the Teenage Witch*, but they are also reflecting a theme that is well represented in the Bible, which also portrays the countryside as a place to meet with God and the city as a place that is likely to be more hostile to true spirituality. It is no coincidence that those aspects of the Christian tradition that spiritually searching people find most appealing today – and there are many – are those which highlight this contrast between urban and rural living. In New Age circles, the medieval mystics are widely admired as people of great spiritual integrity, at the same time as urbanized Christians are distrusted. Francis of Assisi is much more warmly admired than John Calvin could ever hope to be, while the Celtic missionaries from even earlier centuries are valued as spiritual role models over against Constantine and Roman Christianity. Grace Jantzen (1998) proposes that behind this preference is an intuitive move away from an over-emphasis on the imagery of death in favour of a more holistic understanding of the imagery of birth when talking of spiritual connections, since death imagery focuses on the past, apportioning blame and meeting out judgement, whereas birth imagery points to the future, offering new opportunities for growth and change. This certainly makes sense when we realize that neo-paganism is one of the fastest-growing areas in popular spirituality today, with its concern to live in harmony with the environment rather than seeing nature as a battleground (York, 1995; Harvey and Hardman, 1995; Harvey, 1997).

It strikes me that in this context, the rural way of being Church has something distinctive and valuable to contribute to the spiritual search of our culture. In their book *Jesus and the Gods of the New Age*, Australians Ross Clifford and Philip Johnson (2001, pp. 40–55) offer an impressive theological analysis of the common ground between Christians and pagans, which would certainly justify further reflection by those who regularly meet such people. But there might also be more straightforward contributions that the experience of the average rural congregation can offer.

Rural Christians have always had a more open understanding of what is now called 'implicit religion' (Bailey, 1998). There has always been an openness to 'popular' or 'folk' traditions, and correspondingly less interest in what might be called an 'official' book-centred religion, which places more emphasis on beliefs and carefully argued propositions. In this frame of reference personal experience is highly valued, and narrative theology is a natural way of living and believing, as the Gospel story is intertwined with personal stories and the work of God so as to become part of the fabric of a community and its life. Not only does this connect closely with Jesus' style of teaching and ministry, but it also models a form of spiritual exploration that many New Agers are looking for, where one's personal insights and experience can validate the metanarrative of salvation, rather than the metanarrative being a given which requires personal experience to be conformed to it. Examples of this from the past can be found in customs such as traditional well-dressing in Derbyshire or Whitsunday marches in Lancashire, both of which have close parallels with a 'pagan' worldview, but which have been happily blessed and identified with the Christian tradition.

Given the rising interest in such matters among today's pagans, perhaps churches that are involved in such activities ought to consider whether they cannot now become more intentional in regarding such traditions as evangelistic opportunities in a way that was neither necessary nor relevant in the recent past. This would require careful reflection, and a recognition of the innate spirituality of the natural world, rather than the imposition of an external doctrinally-determined agenda, but there are resources that could inform and inspire along these lines (Clifford and Johnson, 2001). Creative thinking will identify many other similar possibilities. There may be a difference between English and Scottish churches in this respect, as the Presbyterian tradition undoubtedly tends to be more dualistic, and dominated by doctrines and ideas, sermons and theological abstractions to a much greater extent than the Anglican tradition, where the natural rhythms of life and its mystical and symbolic dimensions are more happily celebrated. But the sense of community should be common to both, and is perhaps the one thing that New Agers are looking for above all else. Indeed, it may not be going too far to suggest that the features of the Christian Church that are most problematic to today's spiritual searchers are actually features of the urban church – in which case rural Christian spirituality might have more to offer to the future of the world than any of us yet appreciates.

References

Alexander, K. (1992). Roots of the New Age. In J. R. Lewis and J. G. Melton. *Perspectives on the New Age* (pp. 30–47). Albany, New York: State University of New York.

Arweck, E. (2002). New religious movements. In L. Woodhead, P. Fletcher, H. Kawanami and D. Smith (Eds.), *Religions in the Modern World* (pp. 264–288). London: Routledge.

Bailey, E. (1998). *Implicit religion: An introduction.* London: Middlesex University Press.

Barker, E. (1989). *New religious movements.* London: HMSO.

Clifford, R., & Johnson, P. (2001). *Jesus and the Gods of the New Age.* Oxford: Lion.

Cumbey, C. (1983). *The hidden dangers of the rainbow.* Lafayette, Lousiana: Huntington House.

Cush, D. (1996). British Buddhism and the New Age. *Journal of Contemporary Religion, 11,* 195–208.

Davie, G. (1990). Believing without belonging: Is this the future of religion in Britain? *Social Compass, 37,* 455–469.

Davie, G. (1994). *Religion in Britain since 1945.* Oxford: Blackwell.

Drane, J. (1999). *What is the New Age still saying to the Church?* London: HarperCollins.

Drane, J. (2000a). *Cultural change and biblical faith.* Carlisle: Paternoster Press.

Drane, J. (2000b). Matthew Fox. In T.A. Hart (Ed.), *The dictionary of historical theology* (pp. 218–220). Carlisle: Paternoster Press.

Drane, J., Clifford, R., & Johnson, P. (2001). *Beyond prediction: The tarot and your spirituality*. Oxford: Lion.

Ellwood, R. (1992). How new is the new age? In J. R. Lewis & J. G. Melton, *Perspectives on the New Age* (pp. 59–67). Albany, New York: State University of New York.

Fox, M. (1988). *The coming of the Cosmic Christ*. San Francisco, California: HarperCollins.

Groothuis, D. (1988). *Confronting the New Age*. Downers Grove, Illinois: InterVarsity Press.

Harrod, H. L. (2002). Native American religions. In L. Woodhead, P. Fletcher, H. Kawanami, & D. Smith (Eds.), *Religions in the modern world* (pp. 231–248). London: Routledge.

Harvey, G., & Hardman, C. (1995). *Paganism today*. London: Thorsons.

Harvey, G. (1997). *Listening people, speaking earth: Contemporary paganism*. London: Hurst.

Hay, D., & Hunt, K. (2000). *Understanding the spirituality of people who don't go to church*. Nottingham: University of Nottingham School of Education.

Heelas, P. (1996). *The New Age movement*. Oxford: Blackwell Publishers.

Heelas, P. (2002). The spiritual revolution: From 'religion' to 'spirituality'. In L. Woodhead, P. Fletcher, H. Kawanami, & D. Smith (Eds.), *Religions in the modern world* (pp. 357–377). London: Routledge.

Howard, R. (2001). *Shopping for God*. London: HarperCollins.

Jantzen, G. (1998). Necrophilia and natality: What does it mean to be religious? *Scottish Journal of Religious Studies, 19*, 101–121.

Maslow, A. (1970). *Motivation and personality*. New York: Harper and Row.

Melton, J. G. (1992). New thought and the New Age. In J. R. Lewis, & J. G. Melton (Eds.), *Perspectives on the New Age* (pp. 15–29). Albany, New York: State University of New York.

Morrison, A. (1994). *The Serpent and the Cross*. Birmingham: K. and M. Books.

Pearson, J. (2002). *Belief beyond boundaries: Wicca, Celtic spirituality and the New Age*. Aldershot: Ashgate Publishing and Open University.

Postman, N. (1986). *Amusing ourselves to death*. New York: Penguin.

Riddell, C. (1990). *The Findhorn Community*. Findhorn: Findhorn Press.

Saliba, J. A. (1995). *Understanding new religious movements*. Grand Rapids, Michigan: Eerdmans.

Sardar, Z. (1998). *Postmodernism and the other*. London: Pluto Press.

Starhawk (1989). *The spiral dance*. San Francisco, California: Harper and Row.

Sutcliffe, S., & Bowman, M. (2000). *Beyond New Age*. Edinburgh: Edinburgh University Press.

Sutcliffe, S. J. (2000). A colony of seekers: Findhorn in the 1990s. *Journal of Contemporary Religion, 15*, 215–232.

Sutcliffe, S. J. (2003). *Children of the New Age*. London: Routledge.

Trueman, C. (2003). Boring ourselves to life. *Themelios, 28*(3), 1–4.

York, M. (1995). *The emerging network: a sociology of the New Age and neo-pagan movements*. Lanham, Maryland: Rowman and Littlefield.

Chapter 9

GOD IN CREATION: A REFLECTION ON JÜRGEN MOLTMANN'S THEOLOGY

William K. Kay*

Abstract – Jürgen Moltmann's fine book God in Creation makes a contribution to one type of rural theology. Although the book is concerned with the totality of the relationship between God and the created order, it is, nevertheless and consequently, a stimulus to reflection on a theology of the environment and a theology of the rural church. The book itself was delivered in 1984–85 in the Gifford lectures (which tend to deal with science and religion) and this article places it both within the biography of Moltmann himself and in relation to his intellectual oeuvre.

Introduction

In a consideration of the concerns of rural theology, there has historically been an emphasis on the care of the created order although, latterly, climate change has become a predominant theme. Both these concerns, despite their enormous importance, are driven by essentially pragmatic factors. It is helpful from time to time, however, to step back from pragmatism to wider and larger perspectives, and it is this that Moltmann's theology enables us to do. But first, it is necessary to make a distinction between four theological enterprises. There is a long tradition of *natural theology* going back in Christian history at least as far as St Paul and the first chapter of the Epistle to the Romans and, in Jewish history, to the Psalms and the declaration by the heavens of the

*   The Revd Professor William K. Kay is Professor of Theology at Glyndŵr University, Wales. *Address for correspondence*: 7 Croft Way, Everton, near Doncaster, DN10 5DL. E-mail: w.kay@glyndwr.ac.uk

glory of God (Psalm 19.1). Natural theology was given a succinct shape and central place in the writings of Thomas Aquinas where the cosmological argument provides one of the proofs for the existence of God (McDermott, 1989, pp. 12–13). William Paley (1802) elaborated the argument; he contended that the design, intricacy, harmony and variety of the world all point to a rich and beneficent creator.

To this must be added a *theology of the environment*. This is 'green theology', the theology developed out of the Christian tradition that delineates the relationship between the natural environment and humankind showing how the environment ought to be protected, treated, valued, and conceived of in the light of the ravaging exploitation wrought by the greedy quest for economic growth, whether in the West or in the post-communist East (McGrath, 2002). That this theology may include a form of pantheism (God is the totality of the world) or panentheism (God is in and beyond the world) is not central to its primary thrust, which is the protection of our natural heritage.

The *ecclesiology of churches in rural environments* is concerned with the particular shape the church takes within a rural setting, whether this emerges from the low population density of the countryside or from the slower rate of social change within rural settings (Church of England, 2004). Here, in the quiet of the village, the church cannot operate as a cellular structure like that advocated in Korea or South America (Bunton, 2002; Green, 2002) nor can it regularly muster the celebratory gatherings beloved of Restorationist groups (Walker, 1998). Instead, a pattern fitted to a different rhythm of life must be constructed.

And then there is an attempt to discern the *entire relationship between God and nature* stretched over historical time, but also extending into eternity. This endeavour was made by one of the great Protestant theologians of the latter part of the twentieth century, Jürgen Moltmann, whose Gifford Lectures of 1984–85 attempted to summarize the complex and mind-stretching concepts related to the creation of the world in time and space by a Trinitarian God in eternity, outside time and space, who makes human beings in the divine image (Moltmann, 1985).

These distinctions give rise to the structure of this article. An abbreviated account of Moltmann's magisterial text will be presented and this will then be interrogated from the perspectives of natural theology, environmental theology and ecclesiology as a way of further clarifying the distinctions and exploring the implications of Moltmann's work. First, however, it is necessary to give a sketch of Moltmann's life and theological development so as to illuminate the personal context from which the Gifford Lectures sprang.

The prisoner who finds hope

Born in Hamburg, Germany, in 1926, Moltmann was brought up in a secular home that valued the poets and philosophers of German idealism. He read Lessing, Goethe and Nietzsche and, when he was drafted into the German army in 1944, he took with him as reading material Goethe's poems and *Faust* as well as Nietzsche's *Zarathustra*. He fought for six months before surrendering to British troops in Belgium in 1945. In the next three years he was confined to prisoner of war camps, first in Belgium and then in Scotland and England. He observed how many of his fellow prisoners relapsed into depression as they abandoned hope, and many died for a lack of any purpose for which to live.

While in Belgium, an American military chaplain gave him a copy of the New Testament and Psalms and he began to read the text behind barbed wire. Although his initial reason for reading the Bible was one of intellectual boredom, he soon found that the words of scripture spoke to his own experience and nourished him even though his apprehension of the presence of God was elusive. Subsequently he studied theology at an educational camp run by the YMCA and supervized by the British Army before returning to Göttingen in Germany in 1948 when he began his theological studies in earnest. His teachers had been influenced by Karl Barth and he imbibed theological dialectics at this stage before moving beyond Barth in his desire to address the historical realities of the post-war world.

Moltmann's early trilogy included *The Crucified God* (1976), *The Church in the Power of the Spirit* (1977), and *Theology of Hope* (1983). These three books represent three aspects of the theological programme by which Moltmann reinstated eschatology as the source of human hope. Yet Christian eschatology also functions to make theology relevant to the modern world – and this in contradiction of Schweitzer (1933, 1935, 1937 and 1968) and Bultmann (1980/1983) who had stripped eschatology out of Christianity as a feature of the church's thought alien to the modern mind. On the contrary, hope is vital to the programme of the church and to the contribution that Christianity can make to solve the crises facing the human race.

In *The Crucified God* Moltmann developed his doctrine of God in three ways. First, when the Son dies on the cross, the whole of God suffers the desolation that separates Father from Son, and so Trinitarian language must emphasize the inter-subjective relationship between the divine Persons. Second, since God clearly suffers pain during the process of crucifixion, the doctrine of divine impassibility – that God is incapable of knowing suffering – must be rejected, because God can truly be affected by creation. This said, Moltmann is careful to indicate that God is not open to every kind of suffering but only suffering that is undertaken freely in love. Love is a fully-fledged two-way interaction between Creator and creation and not a kind of nominal or sampling process whereby God feels an occasional twinge for selected human beings. Third, Moltmann rejects the traditional distinction between what God essentially and eternally is and what God is as a consequence of interaction with the world. Consequently the doctrine of the Trinity is to be understood as a narrative not only of the changing relationships between the divine Persons, and they do change, but also of the simultaneous relationship those Persons share with the universe itself.

Moltmann understands the church as a messianic community in-dwelt by the Holy Spirit. He fractures the more rigid and exclusive connection in Barth between the Holy Spirit and revelation by emphasising the work of the Holy Spirit in relation to life, the eternal life granted by God, but also life preserved and renewed daily. He also gives a place for religious experience as a correlate of the revelation built into the Word of God, and such a conception of the Spirit underlines the continuity between God's life and the life of creation and draws together creation and salvation.

All this, in terms of theological method and emphasis, while retaining elements of the dialectic inherited from Barth, is much more orientated toward a theological task that seeks to *change* the world in readiness for the coming of the eschatological kingdom. Moreover, Moltmann is unsatisfied with theology as merely a theory of practice or praxis and, instead, wishes to make theology more doxological, that is, to bring human beings into a relationship of praise and worship with God. In addition, because of the open nature within the Trinity and between the Trinity and creation, there is a deliberate rejection of tidy theological systems and a desire to create a structural openness which, nevertheless, in its faithfulness to Jesus Christ permits critical dialogue with other forms of discourse.

God in Creation

Moltmann begins his book with a recognition that, whereas in the 1930s the struggle was between the Confessing Church (which resisted Hitler) and the remainder of Protestant theology (which justified Hitler's rise to power by reference to the will of God at work in history), there is now a vast ecological crisis that threatens the created order itself. 'Today the theological adversary is the nihilism practised in our dealings with nature' (Moltmann, 1985, p. xi). And, as a way of emphasising his concerns, the creation is understood not only as the place where the Holy Spirit is at work, but ecological in the sense that ecology is a doctrine of the *oikos* or house, that is, it is a doctrine that implies that the creation is a place where the Creator, through the Spirit, dwells.

According to the Christian interpretation, creation is a Trinitarian process whereby the Father creates through the Son in the Holy Spirit (John 1:1-2). We are told in Psalm 104 'you send forth your breath, they are created'. And, according to the Nicene Creed, the Holy Spirit is the giver of life who is poured out into creation. Indeed, Paul's sermon to the Athenians declares, 'in him we live and move and have our being' (Acts 17:28). As a consequence, God the Spirit is immanent in creation but not related to it like the world soul of Stoic philosophy because, while God acts into and penetrates the world, God is not merged with it. Yet, while we see the presence of the divine Spirit in creation, we must differentiate this theologically from the redeeming and reconciling work of the Spirit. Beyond this, the relationship between God and the world is only with difficulty analysed in terms of causality since 'creating the world is something different from causing it' (Moltmann, 1985, p. 14). This is because God is present in the world as well as being Creator of it, with the result that we need not set God against creation but rather see the creation as starting from an immanent tension in God himself.

Of the ecological crisis facing us, it is enough to say that the modern sciences developed in a political and social context that, following Descartes, understood science as intended to make human beings masters and possessors of the natural order: the wildness and dangers of fallen creation were there to be subdued, not guarded. One of the most telling criticisms of the 'dominion' theology, however, is that the biblical narrative itself clearly instructs human beings to cultivate and protect their world (Genesis 2:15).

These considerations must be brought against the Marxist doctrine describing alienation between human beings and nature, an alienation only abolished at the expense of nature itself since, in Marxist thought, nature is largely a treasure house to be plundered in the quest for consumer goods. For Marx what matters is that the workers overthrow their capitalist overlords, not that the world itself is redeemed. Against this doctrine, the biblical vision is of a liberated nature enabled by and based upon Christ's glorious atonement (Romans 8:26). 'The messianic era does not merely bring an *outpouring* of the gifts of the Spirit on men and women. It also *awakens* the Spirit itself in the whole enslaved creation' (original emphasis, Moltmann, 1985, p. 69). Human beings may now be freed by Christ through the operation of the Spirit from the bondage of sin and lifted to a new panoramic understanding of the sufferings 'of the present time' by relativizing them in the light of an impending cosmic celebration.

Moltmann then turns to the creation itself which, while it is a demonstration of divine power, is also an act of self-communication springing from divine freedom. It is a creation from nothing, *ex nihilo*, rather than the rearrangement of pre-existing matter and it has no analogy in any human activity. It is a creation from nothing, not from God; a creation out of absolute nothingness, which, nevertheless, must be made in the space that, as it were, God 'vacates' in order to give it room for existence. This is because God's omnipresence does not pre-suppose the omnipresence of space (Moltmann, 1985, p. 155). Or, reflecting a dispute between Newton and Leibnitz, we can conceive of space without conceiving of objects within it: in Newton's terms we can conceive of absolute space, that is, the eternal dwelling space of God and of the relative space of the created world, and we do not have to assume that the space of the world impinges on God's space for, if we did, we should have to grant that matter is eternal. According to Moltmann the solution between these two kinds of space is to be found within Jewish Cabbalistic thinking that presumes that the infinite God whose light originally occupied the whole universe withdrew his light and concentrated it on his own substance, thereby creating the space where the universe is. Thus the created world does not exist in the absolute space of the divine Being but rather 'exists in the space God yielded up for it through his creative resolve' (Moltmann, 1985, p. 156).

Similar complications arise in respect of time since, if we asked *when* God created the world, we have no answer since time itself is contingent upon the existence of the world. If we attempt to say that time exists prior to the creation of the world in relation to the eternity of God's existence, we have no answer to the question that is comprehensible in terms of our own experience of time. For how can our consciousness of time be equated with the eternal consciousness of God?

Following Augustine, we must see time as part of creation so that God did not create the world in time but with time, and time is only created time. There is no eternal time, no clock by which eternity is measured, but rather the entire spread of the duration of historical time is equally present before the divine mind in one continuous act of omniscience. Even so, there are questions to be asked about the relationship between time and eternity, especially if time and eternity are defined over and against each other. They are in danger of cancelling each other out; eternity may incorrectly be seen as the infinite extension of time and time may incorrectly be seen as something to which the eternal God is subject. So, according to Moltmann, the answer to the dilemma is that God resolved to withdraw his eternity into himself in order to make time for his creation.

How are we to understand the duality of heaven and earth? Here we have to face the fact that if heaven and earth are not distinguished qualitatively then 'what results is the concept of homogeneous and self-contained universe' (Moltmann, 1985, p. 181) that cannot be open to God. Consequently 'heaven' represents the 'beyond' of the world, the possibility of transcendence and the sphere of God's creative potentialities toward the world.

In a chapter on evolution and creation that is all of a piece with the foregoing theological discussion, we are led to comprehend the evolutionary cosmos as an irreversible system opened to the future that is to be understood as an interplay between God's transcendence in relation to the world and his immanence in that world (Moltmann, 1985, p. 206). Human beings, while made in the image of God, are called to bear the image of Christ and their final destiny is to rejoice in the kingdom of divine glory. Even though human beings are simultaneously in God's likeness and sinners, this is not as paradoxical as it might seem: the intellectual and spiritual nature of human beings corresponds to the nature of God, and is God's image in the whole of our existence including the bodily nature and the sexual differentiation between masculine and feminine, a differentiation that presumes the existence of community; our sinfulness is finally ended through our conformity to the image in Christ.

So far as the structure of human beings is concerned, Moltmann considers both the Platonic soul and the more mechanistic model of Descartes. He understands the human likeness to God in the context of interrelations within the Trinity. He therefore views the relationship between soul and body, conscious and unconscious, as one of mutual interdependence and differentiated unity.

The final and concluding flourish of Moltmann's book, and one that gives it individuality and a satisfying resolution, concerns his exposition of the Sabbath as the 'feast of creation'. The whole work of creation was performed *for* the Sabbath. It is the completion and consummation of the creative process because on the seventh day God *finished* his work (Genesis 2:2). 'His works expressed God's will, but the Sabbath manifests his Being' (Moltmann, 1985, p. 280). So, while the mighty creation demonstrates God in his outward power, the Sabbath demonstrates the inwardness of the eternal God and directly points to the One who rests in glory. In this respect the Sabbath stands as a symbol of the end of all things and the climax of the ages.

Reflection

Any reflection on Moltmann's theology must take account of hope. It is fundamental to his own understanding of God in the dark days after 1945 and it is an underdeveloped theme within theology as a whole and in competing secular ideologies. *God in Creation* is a book that could not have been written without hope even if there are intrinsic complications in the relationship between hope and time. For hope must be orientated toward the future, whereas a God outside time does not need hope. Thus hope is related to our humanness and our ability, from within the horizons of time, to perceive a future that results from the perspective of eternity.

The theological method adopted by Moltmann is partially iterative in that he re-visits the debates of the past and reinterprets them or utilizes aspects of them to establish his own position. He enriches the Christian tradition without negating it and widens the traditional conception of theology that, perhaps too easily within the patristic period, adopted the categories and concepts of Greek philosophy, especially those which presumed that timeless perfection must be static since any failure of stasis would imply a failure of perfection. In other words, Greek philosophy, and hence the doctrine of divine impassibility, could not perceive of a change from perfection to perfection but only a change from perfection to imperfection.

The coinherence of the members of the Trinity provides an important model for relationships between God and creation and the church and creation. The notion of mutual indwelling in love points toward a cooperative relationship between human beings and God and between human beings and their natural environment.

Natural theology

The apologetic purposes of natural theology find little place in Moltmann's account. He makes no attempt to establish the existence of God by inference from the natural world. Instead, the natural world is to be understood by reference to the creative resolve of God and the interpersonal relations within the Godhead. It is God who brings meaning to the space and time of the natural world and whose existence illuminates both the origins of the material realm and its final state.

Theology of environment

An understanding of the crisis facing the environment is derived from Moltmann's theology. He goes far further than specifying a Christian attitude toward the environment or providing a justification for environmentally friendly behaviour. His concern is to show the created order (including human beings) is to be subsumed within the vast purposes of God. In other words, this is not a book about your garden or your coastal walk but about the universe itself against the backdrop of eternity. Your garden and your coastal walk as well as all the plants and animals they contain are important because of the value placed upon them by God. But it would be a mistake to sentimentalize them or nature itself by reference to pictures of primal innocence. Nor would it be wise to radicalize nature by attributing consciousness to it. On the contrary, the natural world is to be understood as waiting to manifest the messianic kingdom by which God will show forth divine glory. In this sense nature and nature's destiny are to be understood through Christ, and not apart from him.

Ecclesiology

There is nothing in Moltmann about the kind of church that ought to exist within a sparsely populated rural area. However it should be said that *God in Creation* is part of a series of 5 volumes of Moltmann's theology (see bibliography for R. Bauckham 1987, 1995, 1997). There is no reference here to liturgy, to church buildings, to the ministerial life or to evangelism. Nor is there any advice about the best way that the church community can be built from the natural community of the village. Yet, for those who look for them, there are straws in the wind.

Human beings are designed to function in community reflecting the social relations of the Trinity; human beings are designed to bear the image of Christ in their concern for the poor and disadvantaged; human beings are to interpret their existence in the light of God's existence and purposes rather than through the transient pressures of political agendas or earthly cares. Moreover the existence of the Holy Spirit in the world and as giving life to human beings indicates Christian worshippers should not only pour out praise to God for their 'creation, preservation and all the blessings of this life' but also that they should in some fashion convey the life of God. Thus the church is not to be fixed in time and stamped with one historical format but is to be part of the created order, sharing its development and variety, eagerly looking forward to the eventual liberation of the universe in the messianic kingdom. These are not reflections to encourage small-mindedness. Rather they encourage the church to partake of the great sweep of the Divine will.

The final biblical picture of the Church is of the Garden City at the end of the *Book of Revelation*. Here, where God's presence is immediate, the river of life flows out to nurture the trees for the healing of the nations. It is this combination of city and garden, of buildings and trees, that brings together both the original unspoiled greenery of creation with the organized and civic life of human beings that is the apogee of the vision. Now human beings may live harmoniously with each other and with their God. This synthesis places the multitudes of the redeemed within a purified environment, whether earth or heaven is not clear, perpetually lit by the light of the glory of the Lamb.

References

Bauckham, R. (1987). *Moltmann: messianic theology in the making.* London: Marshall Pickering.

Bauckham, R. (1995). *The Theology of Jürgen Moltmann.* Edinburgh: T & T Clark.

Bauckham, R. (1997). Jürgen Moltmann. In D. F. Ford (Ed.), *The modern theologians.* Oxford: Blackwell.

Bultmann, R. (1980/1983). *New Testament theology* (Volumes 1 and 2). London: SCM Press.

Bunton, P. (2002). *Cell groups and house churches.* Ephrata, Pennsylvania: House to House Publications.

Church of England (2004). *Mission-shaped church.* London: Church House Publishing.

Green, M. (Ed.). (2002). Church without Walls: a global examination of cell church. Carlisle: Paternoster.

McDermott, T. (Ed.). (1989). *Summa Theologiae: A concise translation.* London: Methuen.

McGrath, A. E. (2002). *The Re-Enchantment of Nature.* London, Hodder and Stoughton.

Moltmann, J. (1976). *The Crucified God.* London: SCM Press.

Moltmann, J. (1977). *The Church in the power of the Spirit.* London: SCM Press.

Moltmann, J. (1983). *Theology of hope.* London: SCM Press.

Moltmann, J. (1985). *God in creation: An ecological doctrine of creation.* London: SCM.

Paley, W. (1802). *Natural theology; or evidences for the existence and attributes of the deity, Collected from the Appearances of Nature.* Publisher unknown.

Schweitzer, A. (1933, 1935, 1937). *My life and thought.* London: George Allen and Unwin Ltd.

Schweitzer, A. (1968). *The Kingdom of God and primitive Christianity.* New York: Seabury Press.

Walker, A. (1998). *Restoring the Kingdom* (fourth edition). Guildford: Eagle.

Chapter 10

BELONGING TO RURAL CHURCH AND SOCIETY: THEOLOGICAL AND SOCIOLOGICAL PERSPECTIVES

David S. Walker*

Abstract – Recent writing has focused on the 'network' dimension of belonging, with the inference that geographical belonging is of more limited importance. This article examines the continuing significance of the latter concept with reference to the rural English community and parish church. Key categories of individuals with a claim to belong in the English countryside are identified and the notion of belonging as a theological concept is expanded. A fourfold model of belonging to activities, people, events and places is developed and used to investigate how the ministry of the parish church relates to those who would define themselves as belonging with it.

Introduction

Much has been written in recent years to put forward the theory that in British society belonging is now less to do with neighbourhood or geography than with communities of interest. *Mission-Shaped Church* (Archbishops' Council, 2004, p. 4) states, 'In a network society the importance of place is secondary to the importance of "flows".' There is some truth in the increased importance of non-geographical belonging, and the need for churches among others to be attentive to the challenges and opportunities presented, but this should not be allowed to cloud the fact that for many people their belonging with, or alienation from, specific geographical communities plays a vital role in their lives;

* The Right Revd David S. Walker is Bishop of Dudley within the Diocese of Worcester. *Address for correspondence:* Bishop's House, Bishops Walk, Cradley Heath, B64 7RH. E-mail: bishopsofficedudley@cofe-worcester.org.uk

perhaps no more so than in the countryside, where the connection with place may remain at its strongest.

This article follows the definitions of Francis and Robbins (2004), over against Davie (1994), in taking Christian belonging as 'self-defined religious affiliation' rather than collapsing it into either doctrinal affirmation or participation in specified activities. Even in looking at the wider concept of rural living, the distinction between participation in activities and general notions of identity remains extremely useful. Using the language of 'social capital' (Putnam, 2000), belonging to a specific group is closely aligned with bonding capital, while notions of belonging that allow diverse groups to belong with the same institution or place is conducive to the creation of bridging capital.

Diverse ways of belonging in rural communities

There is a huge diversity of interests in rural Britain. Not everybody wants to belong in the same way or to the same extent. Different expressions of belonging exist in some tension and conflict. Not all are present in all communities. To understand this better, the present article offers a series of types or categories. These are intended to be illustrative rather than exclusive or comprehensive. Few people fit entirely and solely into one type. Moreover, they include not only those living within the rural setting but others who still belong there but have either chosen to leave or been forced out.

Commuters. These may or may not be long time residents. Their work takes them out of the community frequently, usually to urban centres. Particularly if they are longstanding residents they may feel that they belong to the place where they live. Time and energy spent both working and travelling limit their ability to participate in rural activities. For some, workplace relationships are more significant than neighbourhood ones, and belonging is felt more strongly to organizations based around work rather than around home. Others seek ways to enhance their belonging to the local community, as long as the time and effort is affordable.

Privacy seekers. Some people move to the countryside to get away from the noise and intrusions of urban life. Many remain deeply connected to urban society, not least through holding down substantial profes-sional roles. Their social lives and any church membership are likely to be outside the rural community. Others have a high sense of belonging associated with the property where they live, and express that through objections to planning applications which impact upon it.

Trophy owners. Rural homes are often purchased as a symbol of success. For some who do so their primary belonging is with their achievements. While many are looking for privacy, others see the rural lifestyle, as well as the rural location, as part of the prize. Some wish to carve out a status within the local community. They are likely to be articulate and accustomed to leadership and thrive in structures that imitate those of the business or commercial world. They often seek to take prominent roles in activities with which they engage. Some resent the arrival into the community of others who are perceived as less worthy of the prize.

Established residents. Those who have lived in a locality the longest are the most likely to have an innate sense of belonging to their rural community that does not require high levels of active participation to sustain. In principle many are happy for others to run things, but some react negatively if local institutions are taken in new directions. They are likely to have specific family ties within the community including relatives buried in the churchyard.

Travellers and gypsies. These are among the most marginalized in many rural communities. Historically the rural economy has depended on them for both seasonal agricultural work and general manual labour. Today they compete with urban labourers and migrant workers. Their distinctive lifestyle and sense of belonging to their own community is frequently perceived as threatening and intrusive by other rural dwellers. They are likely to have a strong sense of belonging with the places around which they travel, including rural church buildings. They often experience problems in accessing basic services such as education and healthcare. They are unlikely to be welcome participants in many rural activities, except those arranged by their own community.

Lifestyle shifters. Some urban dwellers who experience an attachment to the countryside make a definite choice to move there in order to be part of rural life. They have a great deal invested (often literally) in the success of the move. Many are seeking a sense of peace, to re-engage with the type of community they remember from many years previously, to tend a garden, or to be part of a smaller, more manageable community. Some are putting into effect a belonging they have long felt with a specific location or the countryside in general. As well as 'pull' factors there are also 'push' elements such as the desire to escape from a rushed urban existence, the fear of crime or the ethnic and cultural diversity of many towns and cities. Moving out from high price areas in London and the South East of England releases capital to fund a less busy existence or a higher standard of living. They are less likely than others to wish to maintain strong patterns of belonging with their former neighbour-hoods and networks. Some look to participation in local institutions as the way of forging a new sense of belonging.

Absent friends. Former residents and the descendants of such are among those who have a sense of belonging with a rural community in which they are not living. Many still have family living there as well as graves in the churchyard. The place provides a sense of home to an experience of living in exile. Because the attachment is rooted in history, they may well have much of their sense of belonging invested in things remaining as they formerly were. They are far more likely to contribute to an appeal to restore the parish church than to support efforts to re-order its internal furnishings and decor. They will expect the church to be available for their rites of passage. Distance makes it unlikely they will be active participants in many activities.

Full-time dwellers. There are still many who spend the substantial bulk of their waking hours within the rural community. Some are members of the same household as individuals in one of the earlier categories, for example the non-working or home-working partner of a commuter. Home-workers are increasing in number through the opportunities presented by information and communications technologies. Others are retired residents, the relatively few who go out to work within the community, and children. They are likely to have less disposable income than others and to be more dependent on facilities in the community itself. Some have time and energy to put into local institutions. Many less mobile, often older, residents suffer from isolation.

The missing vulnerable. Whereas fifty years ago the typical life story of a British citizen was one of stability and steady progression (through adulthood, marriage, family and career and toward greater financial security) the present picture is much more one of cycles, with significant downturns such as the need to make a complete change of career, the breakdown of a close personal relationship, or a prolonged period of dependency through illness. The almost total collapse of rural social housing has removed what small provision previously existed to sustain individuals and households in their village through such a crisis. Divorcing couples, young adults reaching independence and older persons requiring sheltered or supported accommodation (for example) are forced into the towns at their moment of greatest need. In doing so they are cut off from the places where they feel that they belong, and from the people and institutions to which they would naturally turn for support and with which they participate.

Arriving vulnerable. As a counterpoint to the previous group there are those who arrive in the countryside at a moment of vulnerability. For example, older adults or those with increasing care needs who relocate near to where family members are living, but have no other natural links or connections in the locality. There is evidence of single parents or divorcing partners moving to rural areas where house prices are lower. Many look for support through belonging in the community.

Tourists and visitors. From the mass trespasses of the 1930s onwards, urban Britons have been staking their own direct claim of belonging with regard to the countryside (Walker, 2004, p. 82). Visitors come to what they see as 'their' countryside. They take possession of it by walking unhindered over its land, by recording it photographically and by entering its premises. Their belonging is enhanced by adequate (preferably free) car parks, waymarked and well-maintained footpaths, prepared attractions, public lavatories, gift shops and refreshment facilities. Visitor books attest the significant role that the parish church often plays in enhancing their experience. For some who live in those areas that attract significant numbers of visitors the experience is one of invasion, especially where local facilities emphasize the belonging of tourists over residents (for example shops stocking gifts rather than basic commodities).

The British public. The emergence of the Countryside Alliance at the end of the 1990s was a response to what some saw as interference by the national political apparatus into the rural way of life. Powerful feelings emerged on both sides in a battle over whether the countryside belongs to all of society or more exclusively to those who live in it. More recently the European Union has replaced production subsidies by the Single Farm Payment Scheme, which will increasingly require farmers to deliver environmental enhancement to priorities set by central government. This may in time prove to be one of the most profound assertions that the countryside belongs to the whole nation.

These examples of rural 'belongers' demonstrate the potential for conflicts between different categories. When a planning application is made to replace an old house in large grounds by several smaller domestic properties, it is welcome to those wishing to move into the community and to others looking for new friends or potential helpers in local causes, but not welcome to those who fear that it is an intrusion into their privacy, a diminution of their trophy, or an act of vandalism to a piece of local heritage. Beyond the areas of conflict there are developments that encourage belonging among some groups that are at worst neutral or irrelevant to most others. Only the most partisan privacy seeker objects to improved public transport. Schemes to support higher employment levels or to encourage the development of small rural businesses are not usually divisive. In addition, some institutions and activities in rural Britain continue to receive widespread support across most of the groups mentioned, and little objection from others. Village halls offer a venue for a wide range of events and activities. The rural school retains widespread support. A high percentage of the population expresses concern at proposals to declare the church redundant.

This characterization of the range of stakeholders in the rural community demonstrates that belonging is a complex phenomenon. Some find accessible activities and institutions through which to express and effect their belonging. Others with an equally deep sense of belonging are either unable to engage with frequent participation in activities, or are not naturally inclined to express their belonging in such a way. To engage more deeply with how belonging is effected it is necessary to develop a theological model.

Belonging: a theological concept

From a Christian perspective the prime 'belonging' relationship is with God. The Old Testament notion of the 'People of God' is the best developed corporate understanding of what it is to belong. Indeed, without a developed sense of an afterlife, it is the present belonging with God rather than the promise of a future destiny that lies to the fore. This belonging is expressed in many ways, from a series of covenants to the poetic and erotic language of the Song of Songs. God belongs with specific persons, such as Abraham, Isaac and Jacob. Both the individual and corporate aspects are developed in the New Testament. The Farewell Discourses of John 13-17 with their message of a mutual indwelling in love between God and the disciples are perhaps the most powerful expression of this belonging, but the concept is ubiquitous. This concept of belonging fits more naturally with the definitions of Francis and Robbins (2004) rather than with those popularized by Davie (1994) which are centred on participation in activities. Key to all these biblical examples is the idea that belonging is not unidirectional but mutual. 'We are your people and you are our God.'

From this divine belonging a fourfold natural belonging arises: belonging with people, activities, events and places. Again mutuality is an abiding factor. To speak of 'belongings' is not simply to describe objects in ownership but to acknowledge two-way ties.

Belonging with people. The Children of Israel belong, in the Old Testament, not only with God but with each other. The Jewish Law seeks to manage this belonging, and the prophets repeatedly call the people to repentance for failing to maintain the standards of justice that such belonging requires. The Pastoral Epistles of the New Testament pick up the secular model of a 'household', built around a network of interpersonal relationships, and adopt it to construct the emerging notion of a church, with bishops, presbyters and deacons who both lead the community and model the Christian life for others. Several major denominations still define themselves as being those in communion with a particular senior bishop.

Belonging with activities. Activity, as it is understood today, is much less to the fore in the Bible. The Old Testament has its daily temple rituals performed by priests, but there is little that speaks of demands on individual Israelites for frequent and regular participation. By the time of Jesus the synagogue is a significant locus for activity, and the early disciples quickly pick up the pattern of weekly observance that remains familiar today. Paul's various lists of spiritual gifts attest to a range of individuals regularly applying their skills to further the life of the church.

Belonging with events. The notion of expressing religious belonging through events is evident in the various covenant makings of ancient Israel as well as in the rites for circumcision, purification of women, and cleansing of lepers. Baptism lies to the fore as the main event-based expression of religious affiliation in the Early Church. The notion of affirming religious identity at a variety of rites of passage builds on this over successive centuries.

Belonging with places. The importance of the land in ancient Israel is explored in detail by Brueggemann (2002). The author identifies that the Old Testament:

> was not all about deeds, but was concerned with *place*, specific real estate that was invested with powerful promises (p. xi).

Brueggemann also describes the:

> dialectic in Israel's fortunes between landlessness (wilderness, exile) and landedness, the latter either as possession of the land, as antici-pation of the land or as grief about loss of the land (p. xi).

The notion of Jerusalem as a place of especial significance pervades the Jewish scriptures. Above all other land there is a special relationship with the particular place where someone lives. The Jubilee laws of Leviticus 25 cover the purchase and sale of domestic properties, distin-guishing carefully between homes in walled towns and those in villages or open countryside. Whilst place features less centrally in the New Testament the Early Church soon begins to hallow particular locations such as the sites of martyrdoms. Meanwhile the eschatological vision of the heavenly Jerusalem in the Revelation of John draws Christians to identify themselves with a future place.

Belonging and the rural church

There are some who see 'self-defined Christian affiliation' as at best a potential for being drawn into a 'proper' faith, and others who consider it as a hindrance to or vaccination against evangelism. Against this Thomas (2003, p. 7) distinguishes between 'participant' and 'associate' membership and warns the church against a policy of working solely to maintain the former while ignoring the latter. He remarks on how people choose to identify with 'brands and ideas' rather than 'groups and meetings' and notes that successful organizations are often those that 'enable us to support them without requiring our participation in the organizations themselves'.

The stance of this article is that belonging as a theological concept is sufficiently powerful to demand the church pays full attention to it, both responding appropriately to its manifestations and promoting it at various levels of its work. By doing so the belonging of far more than the 7–8% of the population who reportedly attend a church on Sunday (Brierley, 2001) can be described. The importance of this can be seen from the 2001 National Census returns showing over 70% of the UK population claiming to be Christian and the British Social Attitudes Survey of 2000 (De Graff and Need, 2000) showing 52% professing to believe in God.

In this section rural church belonging is analysed under the four categories of activities, people, events and places, developed above.

Belonging with activities

Activities are those things that take place on a regular and frequent basis, and where individuals are expected to engage not just on a specific occasion but with the series. For example, Sunday services, youth groups, home fellowships, Mothers' Union, toddler groups, and Parochial Church Council meetings are examples of church-run activities. By contrast, Christmas services, baptisms, funerals, garden fetes and concerts are categorized here as events.

Taking part in activities requires a significant investment of time and energy. It is not unusual in a rural community to find the same individuals maintaining a variety of them. It is often those who like activities who run the events, maintain the buildings and act as the significant individuals in the community. Some activity-led people grumble that others do not join in as much as they should, or deprecate the genuineness of a belonging that is not activity based.

Among the categories that have been identified, full-timers are likely activists. Along with them are some lifestyle shifters, established residents and the arriving vulnerable. Some commuters are inclined to activity if it can be planned to fit in with their time constraints. If trophy owners are involved they are probably more interested in running activities than participating. Those who come to visit, travellers passing through, individuals forced to live away and privacy seekers are the least likely to take part, either through lack of opportunity or lack of desire. There are also many in the more obvious catchment groups for whom activity is not their mode of belonging.

Activities on the whole are not hugely contested. Those who do not wish to involve themselves do not take part. An exception is Sunday worship, where one person's preferred style and timing may conflict with the preferences of another person.

Belonging with people

Within the rural community the church has its lay and ordained ministers and officers. These are individuals who are associated with the church in the minds of others. What they do is, to a greater or lesser extent, seen as the church doing it. Some hold formal office, as clergy, churchwardens, readers, or members of a local ministry team. Others are simply recognized for what they do: visiting, flower arranging, organizing events.

The same groups that are most likely to produce activists are also most likely to include those who belong to the rural church or other rural institutions. However, because relationships of this nature are often built up over a considerable period of time there is a skewing of those who belong in this way toward longer-term residents.

Belonging with people offers a route for those who, for reasons of time or distance, are not taking part in regular activities. For many missing vulnerable and absent friends the most significant way of sustaining belonging is through key people visiting them in their places of exile, or inviting them to visit in turn. Where visiting is not possible, regular letters, parish magazines or telephone conversations can have a vital part to play. For some commuters it is more practicable to retain relationships with significant individuals than to fit in with the relatively less flexible diary of a regular activity. Those passing through or seeking privacy are unlikely to have or to generate belonging in this way.

Conflict in this area of belonging arises through personality clashes and through competition between individuals for recognition, authority and status. One example is of tension between newer arrivals with enthusiasm to run things, and those who have traditionally been focal for belonging in the community, where the latter express gratitude for the new energy of incomers but feel marginalized by them.

Belonging with events

Most rural churches undertake a range of events that engender belonging. The occasional offices are crucial. They express a belonging with the church and with God at key moments in the lives of the individuals directly concerned. They place the church at the centre of how a network of friends, relatives and neighbours expresses its belonging together. Major festivals such as Christmas and Harvest allow a belonging with the Christian story to be expressed and enacted. Concerts, fetes, garden parties and other social events offer a belonging together in the community, with the church acknowledged as having an explicit part in that belonging.

Some communities engender a significant amount of belonging through secular events that are not part of an organization with wider aims. The well dressings of rural Derbyshire and the open garden weekends of Worcestershire are examples. Often the church, or its core membership, plays a central role in arranging and promoting such events. They illustrate that there can be two levels of belonging going on at the same time. There is a basic level of belonging with rural life offered to those who visit the events. At the same time, there is a deeper sense of belonging engendered in many of those who plan and deliver such occasions.

Because these events are essentially 'one-off' activities, they allow a different and wider range of people to be involved. They are not the main aspect of belonging for those who are activists, some of whom disparage event-based belonging. However, they offer the main way of belonging to longer-term residents who are not otherwise active.

Public events such as fetes allow individuals to express support without making an ongoing commitment. They attract absent friends and vulnerable missing. Tourists and visitors are often drawn to them. One of the trickiest issues may be identifying appropriate means of communication so that those who would want to come know that the event is happening. Churches are traditionally poor at maintaining contact with those who live outside of the parish unless they are regular worshippers.

Occasional offices are legally public but are seen by most as essentially private affairs, directed toward the invited guests of those concerned. Each of these rites brings with it areas of contention. The practice of pressing for baptisms to be held during a regular Sunday main service is a good example of the activist seeking to enforce their own understanding on event-belongers. The current residence requirements within the marriage preliminaries threaten the belonging of travellers, absent friends and the missing vulnerable. Clergy who use their discretion not to offer Archbishop's Licences, or who restrict the availability of marriage services in the case where a participant is divorced are also denying belonging, as are those who refuse the funerals of non-residents. Where the rites are made generally available they provide belonging for members of every group mentioned in our earlier list. Even the privacy seeker may be drawn to hold a family occasion in the church.

Belonging with places

In many rural communities the church and churchyard are the most significant spaces in terms of contributing to belonging. Rural churches are almost invariably the oldest, or among the oldest, buildings in the area. One of their functions is to stand as a symbol of permanence amidst a society of change. That permanence looks backwards in providing a sense of belonging to the heritage of the community, and makes the church the natural location for memorials to significant persons, institutions or events. It also looks forwards, for example expressing in stone and wood the permanence that a couple are seeking when they make their marriage vows.

The church is often the visual symbol of the identity of the village, and as such features on any community website, or memorabilia. Parish churches are also seen by many outside the Christian faith as being 'spiritual space'. They use the church as somewhere holy to come and be quiet while they undertake their own spiritual journey, which does not recognize a need for liturgies, doctrine or ministers. The churchyard affirms the belonging both of those who lie beneath its surface and of the community who remember them. Indeed the expectation that it will be there in future to receive one's own remains offers belonging to the living.

Belonging with the place matters to just about all of our categories. It is often the most important tie for those who are not resident. It is also the point where the wider belonging by the public in general is asserted; a belonging chiefly focused on the preservation of heritage. The faculty jurisdiction system recognizes a range of individuals whose belonging with the church must be taken into account, giving them rights of petition and objection. Diocesan Advisory Committees involve the amenity societies representing a range of specific interests. English Heritage has the dual roles of both offering critical comment on proposals and providing core funding for restoration work. This may conflict with the desires of the present congregation to make the building congenial for present uses, and to economize on construction costs.

There is a link between belonging with place and belonging with events in that place. Events are for many the primary way through which belonging to place is expressed. The church building which has hosted generations of a family's rites of passage is hallowed by that history and also by the promise of its future availability. However, it is important not to collapse places back into events. Schemes for the internal re-ordering of churches, to make both activities and events more comfortable, and more resonant with current worship styles, often fall foul of this. Once a place has become sacred then any alteration to it runs the risk of being seen as sacrilege. A good demonstration that it is the building rather than the event which carries this status can be seen in the much more positive attitude that those who belong through place or event are seen to have with regard to modern liturgies, wedding marches and funeral music than to the re-ordering of buildings.

Place belonging in the churchyard can be contentious when space is short and restrictive criteria are introduced. But by far the most frequent cause of conflict is over monuments. Having the gravestone one wants, within the churchyard one wants, and being able to plant, tend, edge or otherwise mark out the grave space plays a central role in many a grieving family's assertion of belonging with their deceased. However, a totally unregulated graveyard, subject both to the whims of individuals and competitive demonstrations of mourning, detracts from the belonging of the wider community, including the heritage interests.

Conclusion

This article sets out to demonstrate that geographical belonging still matters. There are powerful forces in the formation of church policy that assert that modern society has lost its roots of belonging and that networks giving identity are more significant. This leads some to suggest that the parochial system, giving each a place of belonging according to residence, has now become superfluous; that the provisions for ministry, including church, parsonage and minister, should be relocated or assigned to new tasks relating to the fluid and unpredictable networks.

Currently the Government is showing fresh interest in the potential contribution of faith groups to local regeneration and other positive aspects of community life. It would be important for the rural Church to maintain its place in rural life at the time when more might be expected of it, rather than allowing a view from the urban experience to sacrifice its place in rural life.

It would be important to conduct further research to examine some of these assertions before dispensing with valuable and possibly irreplaceable assets. A number of counter claims have been set out in this article that also need examining. Issues that merit further enquiry include the value that rural residents, whether commuter or indigenous, place on the local church and the worship and prayer for which it provides; the significance of the burial ground to local people; the contribution of local faith groups to community vibrancy; the possibilities that come with the development of local ministry; the potential for local faith groups to make a full contribution to the inclusivity of the rural society.

References

Archbishops' Council (2004). *Mission-shaped church*. London: Church House Publishing.

Brierley, P. W. (2001). *UK Christian Handbook, Religious Trends No 3, 2002/2003*. London: Christian Research.

Brueggemann, W. (2002). *The land: Place as gift, promise and challenge in biblical faith* (second edition). Minneapolis, Minnesota: Fortress Press.

Davie, G. (1994). *Religion in Britain since 1945: Believing without belonging*. Oxford: Blackwell.

De Graff, N. D., & Need, A. (2000). Losing faith: Is Britain alone? In R. Jowell, J. Curtice, A. Park, K. Thomson, L. Jarvis, C. Bromley, & N. Stratfords (Eds.), *British social attitudes: The seventeenth report* (pp. 119–136). London: Sage.

Francis, L. J., & Robbins, M. (2004). Belonging without believing: A study in the social significance of Anglican identity and implicit religion among 13–15 year old males. *Implicit Religion*, 7, 37–54.

Putnam, R. D. (2000). *Bowling alone: The collapse and revival of American community*. New York: Touchstone.

Thomas, R. (2003). *Counting people in: Changing the way we think about membership and the Church*. London: SPCK.

Walker, D. S. (2004). Private property and public good. In J. Martineau, L. J. Francis, & P. Francis (Eds.), *Changing rural life: A Christian response to key rural issues* (pp. 79–98). Norwich: Canterbury Press.

Part 4

HISTORICAL PERSPECTIVES

Chapter 11

BLACKSHAWHEAD: A LOCAL CASE HISTORY IN RURAL CHURCH CATEGORIZATION

Lewis Burton*

Abstract — A number of studies have sought to categorize churches according to their location in situations which can be said to be rural or urban, or some mix of each of these two types of settlement patterns. Such categorization has uncertainties, and the attempts to refine systems sometimes give rise to debate about the criteria to be used, and to contradictions between the resulting scales suggested by different studies. This article seeks to question existing criteria and systems of categorization by using a local church's experience as a case history, and also to point up other issues related to small church experience in an isolated situation. It also seeks to draw attention to the value of the study of the local church for more general issues in rural theology.

What is rural?

A recent publication, *Sowing the Seed* by the Churches' Regional Commission for Yorkshire and the Humber (2003), describes its area of rural concern as 'not only the vast rural tracts of North Yorkshire, the Dales and the North York Moors, but also the Wolds of the East Riding; west of Halifax to Todmorden, and north toward Keighley; south and east of Huddersfield' and so on. In the text which follows, however, it describes Christian initiatives for neighbourhood communities only in the well cultivated and fertile parts of the region and has nothing to say about the rolling vast areas of moorland where nothing grows except

* The Revd Dr Lewis Burton, a retired Methodist minister, is Honorary Research Fellow in the St Mary's Centre, Wales. *Address for correspondence*: 94 Sun Street, Haworth, Keighley, BD22 8AH. E-mail: lewisburton@blueyonder.co.uk

rough grass and heather, and which is populated only by sheep and the occasional isolated farm.

The description quoted is the opening of an introductory section entitled, 'Setting the scene: what is rural' and it goes on to say, 'The typical village scene has at its centre a church, and this is of course the case, since the development of churches went alongside the development of rural settlements, towns and villages' (Churches' Regional Commission, 2003, p 11).The image is that mythical countryside of many an urban dweller's dream, and the whole weight of what follows in the publication is of activity in the lush valley pastures and the rolling green hills of North and East Yorkshire and its villages. It neglects the vast unpopulated acreage of moorland and rough pasture which separates the broad acres of Yorkshire from the countryside of Lancashire.

Definitions of rurality

Such considerations put up the question, 'What is rural?' yet again. It is a question which has been well exercised in recent years and various definitions and categorizations have been suggested to cover the case.

The Rural Church Project was an investigation of rural situations in five Anglican Dioceses covering large areas of countryside which provided evidence used in the production of *Faith in the Countryside* (Archbishop's Commission on Rural Areas, 1990). This report provided recommendations for the future work of the Church of England in rural situations.

The findings of the project are summarized in *Church and Religion in Rural England* by Davies, Watkins and Winter (1991). In the course of their introductory chapters they ask the question, 'What is rural' (1991, p. 57) and review some of the ways in which a church can be categorized as 'rural.' Following Wibberley (1972) they ask if the difference between rural and urban areas is a distinction of land use. This has something to commend it, but the difficulty is that raised by marginal cases. A more comprehensive measurement of rurality is needed and this was attempted by Cloke and Edwards (1986) based on the 1981 Census. This has the assumption that the sparser a population and the greater distance from the urban centre, the more 'rural' a district will be. From ten variables, four categories were recognized: extreme rural, intermediate rural, non-rural and extreme non-rural. Quoting Hoggart (1988) and Pahl (1968, p. 293) they admit that the scale must be used with caution, as it cannot be used in comparisons of smaller areas or as a way of explaining geographical variation in economic conditions. After the examination of these other categorizations they derive an alternative index based upon clergy assessments: a five-fold scale of totally rural, partly rural, small country town, part urban or non rural, and urban.

The difficulties of defining what is rural are also discussed by Anthony Russell (1986, p. 3) in *The Country Parish*. Four types of countryside are defined, each of them envisaged as concentric rings around urban conurbations: the urban shadow countryside, the accessible countryside, the less accessible countryside, and the marginal remote countryside.

A brief review of some of the suggestions for the categorization of any individual church as urban or rural on some kind of continuum or by some significant criteria indicates that the exercise is problematical. Local situations and topography vary tremendously between one area of the country and another and the situation of one church and another.

To return to the concerns of the introduction, can a village church in the rolling green countryside of East Yorkshire be placed in the same category of rurality as a church of similar denomination and membership in a village of the same population size in the Pennine hills? If not, then how can a church in Pennine hill country be categorized, rural or urban, or is it in a category quite separate and on its own? An attempt to do this and also to chart some development over the years of the twentieth century has been made in a case study of Blackshawhead, a small Pennine community with a Methodist chapel at its heart.

Blackshawhead

Participant observation over a period of six years, while the writer had pastoral charge of this village community, is the main technique used for this case history. It is supplemented by in-depth face to face interviews with two people, one male and one female, one who had attended the church all of seventy years and one who had moved into the village some twenty-five years ago. The church was the smallest of four churches in the pastoral group of the minister, the main church being a large church in the local valley town. All four churches were in the Methodist circuit which served the upper reaches of the Calder Valley in West Yorkshire.

Blackshawhead chapel lies within the civil parish of Blackshaw at map reference SD 959276 (Ordnance Survey, 1977). The population of the civil parish is 845 (1991 Census). The Church of England has up to recent times divided Blackshaw between the parishes of Heptonstall and Hebden Bridge. Heptonstall parish covers a number of square miles of moorland without any significant population. The parish of St James', Mytholm, covers the area of Hebden Bridge, the town in the valley bottom. The confusion of the parish boundaries and the distance of Blackshawhead from Heptonstall have given significance to the Methodist chapel which stands at the centre of the village. Recent decisions of the Diocese of Wakefield have created a united benefice of the two parishes. This centres Anglican work in the town and gives the incumbent little chance to minister to outlying villages and scattered farms on the moorland fringe.

Blackshawhead lies at an altitude of 1,100 feet on the terrace of level ground between the valley bottom of the Calder and the high moorland. The descent from the village to the valley is incredibly steep, falling 500 feet over a distance of a mile and a quarter. The high moorland rises to a spot height of 1,405 feet. These terraces of cultivable land between the steep valley sides and the high moor on the north side of the valley are typical of the landscape. The terrain is treeless and bleak with occasional outcrops of millstone grit showing through thin earth.

It is over these terraces between the steep slopes of the valley side and the higher moorland that transport of goods was possible before the river valley became passable with the construction of a turnpike road in the late eighteenth century (Jennings, 1994, p. 99). The old pack horse road was called 'The Long Causeway' and ascended from the old bridge at Hebden Bridge very steeply to Heptonstall and then across moorland to Blackshaw and then to Burnley. A spur of this road circled the high cliffs on which Heptonstall stands and came up the westerly slopes, appropriately called 'The Steeps', and joined the Long Causeway at Blackshawhead. It is in the junction of these two roads that Blackshawhead chapel is located and the village, hardly bigger than a hamlet, gathers around it. The former paved way is now a C class road connecting Hebden Bridge to Burnley.

Farming has always been the local industry, principally in a number of small holdings which have provided a living for a family unit not much above subsistence level. The soil is poor and at the altitude of Blackshaw it is not possible to grow any crop for the market. It is possible, however to graze cattle and so some store cattle and some dairying take place. Potatoes and kale were grown in farm gardens for pig feed and winter feed for cattle. The main interest is in sheep and many of the small-holdings have grazing rights on the moor.

Manufacturing industry has been located in the main towns of the upper Calder Valley. Two of these towns are about three miles from

Blackshawhead. Hebden Bridge has been a centre for the manufacture of corduroy cloth and the making up of this cloth into trousers. Todmorden has been a historic centre for the cotton trade. Both towns have now lost their industry and Hebden Bridge particularly is a centre for tourism in the central Pennine area.

With the difficulties of terrain the village has always been rather inaccessible and at one time a post office which was also a general trader and a branch of Hebden Bridge Cooperative Society, and three public houses supplied local social and economic needs without resort to the town.

Transport by an hourly bus service is provided to and from Hebden Bridge and this has been in place since the 1920s. A car-owning generation has made a great difference and opened up Pennine villages in modern times to the wider world.

Chapel life

After the First World War chapel life at Blackshawhead was much as it had been since the chapel was built in the 1870s. It was supported by people drawn from the surrounding farms and from farm workers' cottages which clustered around the road junction and the ribbon development on the old road which led down to the Steeps. On Sundays it had a service very much in the old Methodist tradition at 2.30 in the afternoon which allowed farmers to do the morning milking and return home for the similar task in the evening. Although in the care of a minister based in Todmorden or Hebden Bridge (it has changed circuit from time to time), the services were mostly staffed by local preachers who travelled from a distance.

The chapel was not only the provider of spiritual values to the village, but was also the main centre where the people of the village could gather for their social activities and their communal endeavour. These social activities clustering around the worshipping community and providing communal entertainment, both on Saturday evenings and on evenings throughout the week, were typical of what was happening at the time in both urban and rural chapels.

The civil parish of Blackshaw at that time was very much a rural community and the chapel represented the only religious centre and the only 'respectable' social centre for the farming community and the cottagers in and around the village. Smallholdings tended to be mostly in the hands of families, with the father and older sons working the cattle and the stock, mother doing the traditional tasks around the house, but grown up daughters tending to supplement the family income by finding employment in Hebden Bridge, where female labour in the local mills or sewing shops was always in demand. In large families, and sometimes in stringent economic conditions, some of the men sought work in the town and farmed part-time.

The Second World War seems to have been a watershed, both for chapel life and life in the village generally. It was a time when for social and economic reasons the village became more dependent on the local town. Activity in the chapel dwindled, although services were maintained. Congregations were smaller and by the mid 1950s there were only perhaps fifteen people gathered for Sunday afternoon service. The families who had held power in the chapel for many years had now gone and leadership had passed to others. In the chapel's social life there was great decline; the sparkle was no longer there.

By the late 1970s the church building was in difficulty. It is a small chapel with a balcony, and a corridor separates the chapel from two rooms on the ground floor and the schoolroom above. At the balcony level there is access from the chapel to the schoolroom. The building stands high, and without any shelter it falls an easy victim to the rain-soaked westerly winds which sweep across the open landscape. A new roof was needed. The congregation had dwindled to seven, meeting in one of the rooms. Closure became a real possibility as resources to do any repair work did not exist.

Rescue came first in the form of a very formidable lady who had been associated with the chapel in the past. Her determination that closure should not happen provided a breathing space to rally those who had associations with the chapel who were of the same mind. She was joined by another very capable lady who had spent her childhood not far from the village centre. She had developed a social concern that the village should not be without a rallying point for the community. By that time both the post office and the shop and one of the public houses had closed and within a few years the other two were destined to go. News of the problem came to the parish council and they encouraged the chapel people not to close a building which was in fact the only place for public meetings in Blackshaw.

Social change came to their assistance. With the development of easy communication by car, people no longer needed to live near where they worked. Country cottages became attractive dwellings, even in isolated places like Blackshawhead, and conversion grants were available to make them into acceptable dwelling houses despite old inconveniences. An architect, a lapsed Methodist, and his wife and family moved into a cottage in the ribbon development on the lower road. Not a regular attender at any church at that time, but as one who attended occasionally, the plight of the village chapel appealed to his good nature to help in any way he could. Through his professional skills and his contacts, and the hard work of those keen to see the chapel whole, contractors were organised, old friends of the chapel were rallied, money was raised, and the roof was repaired.

As happens in many a completed building scheme, the effort put into the project resulted in some regeneration of church life. Those who had been at the centre of the building project had their spiritual interest quickened and stayed on as the new leadership of the church. Chapel life also benefited from the widespread tendency of professional people at that time to move out into country areas and commute to their work. This movement was encouraged by the construction of some middle class houses, where old property had been pulled down, adjacent to the chapel at the intersection of the two roads in the centre of the village. A number of families moved into the village, both into some of the new houses and also into older properties. They were mostly young parents with small children and a number threw in their lot with the chapel's congregation.

Perhaps they were also attracted because they found a ready welcome. Those who were leaders in repairing the roof still attended and were open to new ideas and worship styles, but they themselves were in-comers. There was a group of people in the congregation who remembered the past and were long-time members, so the transition from the worship of a traditional Methodist chapel with the emphasis on the sermon and the singing of Wesley and Watts did not happen without pain. The newcomers had already experienced in previous churches the new charismatic style of worship with choruses and songs and open prayer and more congregational participation than the traditionalists were used to. The person whose skills as an architect had facilitated the repair of the roof became the acknowledged leader of the chapel and was trusted by the locals, the old residents, and was open to new ideas, motivated at the same time to push the chapel into new ways of worship and service to the village. The process, however, was not without its dangers. A few of the locals ceased their association with church, some ceased to come every Sunday to worship but still maintained some connection. The decline in numbers, however, was made up by the newcomers to the village and also some others attracted by the new worship styles. As happens in a village, what was going on in the chapel became common parlance and was no doubt exaggerated somewhat, and the congregation gained the reputation of being 'religious freakies' which threatened the good work which they were trying to do for neighbourhood needs. There were indeed some in the new congregation who wanted to push the chapel more into a charismatic, conservative evangelical position, and perhaps to the credit of the whole congregation a spirit of toleration enabled them to hold together for a number of years. However the strains created by differing religious convictions finally took their toll and two families left for worship with a charismatic group some distance away.

One other major shift in policy which the newcomers eventually influenced was a change in service time. Afternoon services are too intrusive on time available for family activities and a decision, brewing for some time, was finally taken to move the service to Sunday morning. The change was an indication both that the rhythm of tasks in a farming community no longer mattered and that the newcomers had gained the upper hand in church council decisions. By the time of this change, in the early 1990s, the character of land use in Blackshaw civil parish was changing. The local farmhouses and barns were being converted to dwellings whose owners were professional people from the town. Farming was still carried on but the smallholdings of some 33 acres of the past were no longer typical and aggregation of land had happened to make larger farm units.

The changes and controversies which newcomers into the district made in the chapel worked themselves out only over a number of years, but by the middle of the 1990s the chapel was able to set itself up to be a neighbourhood centre, able to work out its religious calling not only in the spiritual life of local people but also for service to the whole community. The set pieces of the chapel's year, such as the Anniversary, Harvest and the Christmas christingle and carol services once again draw a full congregation, and also the great occasions in the Christian calendar are well attended. A Kid's Club is run for a week in the summer and there is a Girls' Club and a Boys' Club meeting in alternate weeks. The church throws its weight into the annual village fete organized by the parish council. The council itself meets on chapel premises and there is much support from the secular authority into what the chapel is trying to do for the local community. There is a mutual desire to foster a true sense of community into a straggling village which has no natural centre except the chapel. When one of those interviewed, the lay leader of the chapel, was asked how much time the chapel building was used for spiritual or secular use, he was taken aback at the nature of the question, but after some thought he said, 'About fifty fifty.'

Blackshawhead chapel: a rural church?

What does this case history say to us, not only about the categorization of Blackshawhead chapel as a rural church, but how safe such categorizations are? In this particular case what can also be observed is a definite shift in the rural/urban nature of this particular church over time.

Thirty or forty years ago Blackshaw civil parish was certainly a rural community. Land use was still in small units and the village still had some of the necessary services to make life possible within the village rather than to travel a distance to seek such services elsewhere. The two interviewees, when asked whether Blackshawhead was a rural community responded directly that it was. One of them had lived in the village all her life, the other was a newcomer. The newcomer then had second thoughts and attempted to define what was 'rural'. He instanced population density and said that by this definition his village was rural. He then went to other possibilities and instanced land use. If there are more houses than fields, he said, then it is suburban or urban; if more fields than houses, then it is rural, and this latter was certainly the case for Blackshawhead. Interestingly he returned to the subject at the end of the interview showing uncertainty about his previous definitions. The conversation of the interview had prompted him to think again and to retract some of them. His opinion was that any rural-urban divide in the categorization of any church was a simplification of reality. There had to be a wide variety of churches which eluded precise classification. Reflecting again on the composition of his church he noted the presence of a majority of middle class professional people in the present congregation and that well over half of both men and women worked in an urban setting, some commuting to Leeds or to Manchester. In some respects he felt that Blackshawhead was more urban than some urban churches. On being prompted he felt that for many church people their place of occupation created an urban mind-set which they brought to some aspects of the church's life. On the other hand, he was sure that Blackshawhead was not just a dormitory village as the enthusiasm which such people put into the church and creating social capital and community in the village was evidence of a commitment to the neighbourhood where they lived.

Where does Blackshawhead fall in the categories of rural church suggested by others? The criteria of land use applied by Wibberley (1972) would seem to make it rural, as also density of population suggested by Cloke and Edwards (1986). The latter, however, using the notion of distance from urban centres, might place it in their category of 'intermediate rural'. Among the fivefold categorization of Davies, Watkins and Winter (1991) it would seem to be 'partly rural'. The basic assumption of Russell (1986) of using as a basis of categorization concentric circles based on a large urban unit is undermined by the nature of the terrain in the South Pennines where urban development is determined by the river valley. 'Urban shadow' is too urban for Blackshaw and somehow neither 'accessible countryside' nor 'less accessible countryside' seems to fit.

There are many studies of the practice and ethos of rural churches which attempt to distinguish the church in a rural situation from that in an urban one, but it is obvious that precise classification of a church in one category or the other eludes us. Yet there is still the gut feeling that the rural church is different. How can sociologists of religion proceed to study the rural church and its difference from that in an urban setting, if definition and categorization is so elusive? The only answer is to use whatever method of categorization seems to be the most reasonable. Then out of further empirical study it might be truly determined that the 'rural church is different' without the qualifications which seem currently to apply.

Conclusion

Individual case histories show the difficulties of categorizing rural as against urban churches. Perhaps a more fruitful way might be to designate types of rural settlement by population size together with location. Thus a designation of Blackshawhead chapel could be 'Pennine hill village' and offer some comparison of type with many other villages in the Pennine hills or in similar terrain elsewhere.

A major conclusion from this case study is how quickly the nature of categorization of rural and perhaps also urban settlements can change in response to social and economic change in any particular case. This makes comparison of village communities difficult and also comparison of the same village community over time.

The spiritual and the social impact of newcomers into village church situations is considerable. The way that adjustments to dislocation and accommodation resulting from different religious positions and social values in such situations have been resolved would repay further detailed study.

Small village churches in a rural situation benefit greatly from the energy and vision and experience of newcomers when the existing congregation is open and tolerant enough to accept their contribution. For many churches such inward mobility is crucial for their continuing life. On the other hand, such newcomers, apart from those newly retired, tend also be outwardly mobile in due course. The small village church then becomes vulnerable. Some attention needs to be given to patterns of mobility for the sake of such small churches.

This case study shows that the presence of a committed and able lay person who is both a natural and accepted leader can make a great difference to the life of a small village church and to its service in the neighbourhood community. In Methodist circuits or in Anglican united benefices where ministerial and clergy attention is minimized there is evidence here that suitably chosen and trained lay people who feel called to such a voluntary or part-time ministry would be of great benefit to a village church and its community.

References

Archbishops' Commission on Rural Areas. (1990). *Faith in the countryside.* Worthing: Churchman.

Churches Regional Commission. (2003). *Sowing the seed.* Leeds: The Churches' Regional Commission for Yorkshire and the Humber.

Cloke, P., & Edwards, G. (1986). Rurality in England and Wales. *Regional Studies, 20,* 289–306.

Davies, D., Watkins, C., & Winter, M. (1991). *Church and religion in rural England.* Edinburgh: T and T Clark.

Hoggart, K. (1988). Not a definition of a rural area. *AREA, 20,* 35–40.

Jennings, B. (Ed.). (1994). *Pennine Valley.* Skipton: Smith Settle.

Pahl, R. E. (1968). The rural urban continuum. In R. E. Pahl (Ed.), *Readings in urban sociology* (pp. 205–263). London: Pergamon.

Russell, A. (1986). *The country parish.* London, SPCK.

Wibberley, G. P. (1972). Conflicts in the countryside. *Town and Country Planning, 40,* 259–265.

Chapter 12

IS THE RURAL CHURCH DIFFERENT? THE SPECIAL CASE OF CONFIRMATION

David W. Lankshear*

Abstract – The nationally published statistics of confirmation candidates in the Church of England between 1950 and 1999 are explored for three groups of dioceses. These groups are the most rural, the most urban and a group that lies around the centre of the continuum between rural and urban. The decline in the number of candidates after the 1960s is traced. The figures are also compared with the population of the dioceses, the members of the electoral roll and the numbers of Easter day communicants. The gender balance with confirmation candidates is also explored for this period. Attention is drawn to the differences between the urban and rural patterns of presentation of candidates for confirmation and the changes in these during the fifty year period being considered. A number of explanations for the differences noted are advanced and it is suggested that these possible explanations are best tested through research at diocesan level. Attention is also drawn to the weaknesses inherent in the rural/urban model when it is used as a descriptor of the Church of England.

Introduction

In her article 'Is the rural Church different', Roberts (2003) presented a careful assessment of the potential of the statistics published by the Church of England for enabling informed debate about the differences between different parts of the church. Roberts focused particularly on

* Dr David W. Lankshear is Research Fellow in the Warwick Religions and Education Research Unit. *Address for correspondence:* 22 Shrub End Road, Colchester, Essex, CO2 7XD. E-mail: dandclankscol@hotmail.com

two dioceses as representative of the rural and urban church, Hereford and Birmingham respectively. The intention of this article is to build on the insights that Roberts presented by using a more detailed focus on the issue of confirmation across a broader spectrum of dioceses and a larger time frame.

In their article 'The rural church is different', Francis and Lankshear (1997) drew four conclusions from studying the Church of England's practice in the presentation of confirmation candidates. These conclusions were: that rural churches present more candidates than urban churches as a proportion of the population; that rural churches present a higher proportion of male candidates than urban churches; that rural churches present a higher proportion of teenager and pre-teenager candidates than urban churches; and that the presentation of young candidates for confirmation by rural churches is associated with church growth.

Francis and Lankshear (1997) used questionnaire survey techniques to obtain their data and were thus able to obtain the numbers, ages, and gender of confirmation candidates and to identify specific parishes as being rural, urban, or suburban. It cannot be assumed that taking figures aggregated to diocesan level will show similar patterns. Indeed, because no information is published consistently at the national level about the age of confirmation candidates, it is not possible to explore issues related to the age of candidates at the national level. It is important in what follows to avoid making the assumption that confirmation candidates are all teenagers or that the decline in the number of confirmation candidates is associated with a decline in the church's ministry with any particular age group.

Building on the earlier work of Francis and Lankshear (1997) this study uses the information published nationally by the Church of England over a fifty year period to seek to establish whether the rates of decline in the numbers of confirmation candidates within the Church of England are the same as the rates of decline of measures of church membership in general. Using the national data it should also be possible to identify differences between the urban and rural dioceses in the rate of decline of these measures. Given that the last decade of this period was designated within the Churches as a decade of evangelism, it might be particularly important to identify any growth in numbers of confirmation candidates in this decade, or at least a slowing down in the decline.

Method

Roberts (2003) has drawn attention to the problems associated with the analysis of the national data, published by the Church of England. Lankshear (1992) drew attention to the occasional variations away from the overall trend of figures, in the published figures on confirmation candidates from individual dioceses as published in the national statistics. In order to overcome some of these difficulties with the data and to identify overall trends, the published figures for confirmations for all dioceses in the Church of England for the period between 1950 and 1999 were collated from published Church of England resources. It proved possible, using a variety of published sources, to find these figures for every year in this period. Data were also collated for diocesan population, electoral roll, and Easter day communicants, over the same period, although these data are not complete, because they are not published for every year in this period.

The dioceses were then placed on a continuum from most rural to most urban using the factors to identify rurality first used by Francis (1985) and further developed by Lankshear (2001). The dioceses were then split into five groups according to their position on this continuum. The most rural group, referred to in this study as 'rural', consisted of Hereford, Norwich, Lincoln, Carlisle, St Edmundsbury and Ipswich, Salisbury, Gloucester and Truro. The most urban group, referred to in this study as 'urban', consisted of Wakefield, Rochester, Sheffield, Liverpool, Manchester, Southwark, Birmingham, Chelmsford and London. The group in the centre of the continuum, referred to in this study as the 'mixed' group consisted of Chichester, Leicester, Canterbury, Derby, Ripon, Coventry, Newcastle and Lichfield.

Results

The total population, electoral roll membership, Easter day communicants, male, female and total confirmation candidates for each of these groups of dioceses and for all the dioceses were aggregated and divided by the number of dioceses in the relevant group to produce a composite 'rural', 'mixed', 'urban' and average or 'mean' diocese; this latter 'diocese' being representative of the Church of England as a whole. These composite figures were employed to eliminate individual local fluctuations in particular years and therefore focus on overall trends.

The data were further aggregated to provide a mean population, electoral roll and Easter day communicants for each decade of the period. For male, female and all confirmation candidates the figures were aggregated for five and ten year periods during the fifty year period. This was possible because of the complete data available for these variables.

In order to compare the rates of change the mean figures for each decade were converted into a percentage of the mean figures for the first decade (the 1950s).

Confirmation candidates

The number of confirmation candidates presented in the Church of England rose during the 1950s and early 1960s and then fell away sharply in the late 1960s and early 1970s. Thereafter the decline has been slower, but at a steady rate. For every 100 candidates presented in the 1950s only 30 candidates were presented during the 1990s. Detailed analysis of these figures is presented in table 1 (see appendix).

As will be clear from table 1 initially the level of decrease was higher in the 'urban' diocese, and the rate of decline was steeper during the 1960s and 1970s. In the 1980s and 1990s the rate of decline was steeper in the 'rural' diocese so that by the late 1990s the figures for the 'urban' and 'rural' dioceses were almost identical. Generally the 'rural' diocese followed the same pattern as the 'mean' diocese that is the Church of England as a whole, except for the early 1960s.

A preliminary consideration of the confirmation figures produced using this methodology is of limited use because of the different sizes of the dioceses. For this reason comparisons were undertaken with the population, electoral roll and Easter day communicant figures.

Population

Over this period the population of the 'urban' diocese was broadly similar in each decade. In the 1990s the mean figure for population in the 'urban' diocese was 98% of the mean population of the diocese in the 1950s. By contrast the population in the 'rural' diocese had risen steadily throughout the period and during the 1990s the mean figure for population was 134% of the mean population for the 1950s. Details of the population figures for the rural, mixed, urban and mean dioceses and the rates of change are shown in table 2.

This must not be interpreted to imply that those living in urban dioceses had remained in these dioceses during this period, or that there had been a 34% flow of incomers into the 'rural' dioceses. The overall movement of population, including the results of immigration and emigration at national level, has resulted in a net 'no growth' situation in the 'urban' diocese and a net 34% growth in the population of the 'rural' diocese. It must also be clear that it is likely that during this period the proportion of the population that adhered to faiths other than Christianity would be higher in the 'urban' dioceses than in the 'rural' dioceses. Until the results of the 2001 census are mapped on to the diocesan boundaries there is no way of testing this assumption.

It is apparent that when the numbers of confirmation candidates are expressed in terms of the number per thousand of the population the rate of decline in the 'rural' diocese is higher than the rate of decline in the 'mean' diocese, that is the Church of England as a whole, which in turn is higher than the rate of decline in the 'urban' diocese. This difference is apparent in the 1960s and 1970s and is at its greatest in the 1980s. Table 3 shows the numbers of candidates per 1,000 of the population and the rate of decline in this figure.

The raw numbers in table 3 support the statements that the 'rural' church is presenting more candidates (per thousand of population) than the urban church. The more rapid rate of decline observed in the 'rural' diocese across this period also supports the concern expressed by Roberts (2003) that, although the rural church is still stronger than the urban church, when population is taken into account those differences may be disappearing.

Electoral roll

Roberts (2003) has drawn attention to the issues that arise in using electoral roll membership figures. These largely arise from the changes introduced during this period to the age at which people can first be admitted to the roll and the introduction of a total revision of the rolls every six years beginning in 1972. The first of these two changes should tend to increase the numbers on the rolls. The second created a significant decrease in the overall numbers on the roll.

Table 4 shows the number of members of the electoral roll in the 'rural', 'mixed', 'urban' and 'mean' dioceses for the period. From this table it is apparent that the membership of electoral rolls fell more steeply in the 'urban' diocese than in the 'rural' or 'mixed' diocese. The rolls in the 'rural' diocese fell less than the 'mixed' diocese or than the rolls in the Church of England as a whole (represented by the 'mean' diocese).

Before those in rural dioceses take too much comfort from these figures it is important to draw attention to the impact of the overall changes in the population of the different types of dioceses on these figures. When the membership of the electoral roll is expressed in terms of numbers per thousand of population a different pattern emerges. Table 5 shows that throughout the period a consistently higher proportion of the population of the 'rural' diocese was on the electoral roll than in the 'mixed', 'urban' or 'mean' dioceses and that the proportion of the population in the 'urban' diocese that was on the electoral roll was consistently less than in other dioceses. What the table also shows is that the rate of decline in the proportion of the population that is on the electoral roll was very similar across the different dioceses.

The Church of England Year Books consistently present warnings about using Electoral roll membership as a measure of the membership of the Church of England (see Roberts, 2003). However it seems to be a reasonable assumption that those who are being confirmed might be expected to join the electoral roll of their church as soon as they are of an age to do so. If they are already in their late teens or older this could be immediately; if they are being confirmed before they are old enough to be on the roll then it must be assumed that the continuing Christian nurture that they received after their conformation will have as one of its aims becoming full committed adult members of the church who participate in its organization and governance. For these reasons it is important to compare the numbers of confirmation candidates with the numbers of electoral roll members. From a comparison of tables 1 and 4 it will be apparent that the numbers of confirmation candidates have been falling more rapidly than the numbers of members of the electoral roll since the 1960s. This has happened despite the changes in the rules concerning electoral rolls which produced a sharp fall in their numbers through the 1970s. Table 6 shows the number of confirmation candidates presented per thousand members of the electoral roll.

From this table it is apparent that the rate of decline has been greatest in the 'rural' diocese and least in the 'urban' diocese. This is to be expected given that it has already been noted that numbers of members of the electoral rolls was falling more sharply in urban dioceses during this period. In the 1950s the Church of England was confirming sufficient candidates to renew its electoral roll membership every eighteen years if all those who were confirmed joined the electoral roll. In the 'rural' diocese it would have taken twenty-one years to renew the Electoral roll and in the 'urban' diocese it would have taken seventeen. By the 1990s the time taken to renew the electoral rolls to their 1990s levels, which were much lower than their 1950s levels would have been thirty-seven years in the 'rural' diocese, twenty-five years in the 'urban' diocese and thirty years in the church as a whole.

Easter day communicants

Historically in the Church of England one of the results of being confirmed was admission to communion. The rubric in the *Book of Common Prayer* suggests that everyone who is confirmed should receive communion at least three times a year, one of which should be at Easter. The count of Easter day communicants is the only published data available throughout the period which could be used as a measure of the extent to which confirmation candidates are renewing the numbers who are making their communion on this day. Table 7 shows the number of people who make their communion on Easter day in the 'rural', 'mixed', 'urban' and 'mean' dioceses for the period. The immediate matter to note in this table is that the numbers of Easter day communicants is falling much more slowly than the numbers of Electoral roll members or the numbers of confirmation candidates. In absolute terms the number of Easter day communicants has fallen more slowly in the 'rural' diocese than in the 'mixed', 'urban' or 'mean' dioceses, with the 'urban' diocese showing the sharpest fall.

When population is taken into account, however, this article has already demonstrated that a different picture can emerge. Table 8 shows the number of Easter day communicants per thousand of population. These data demonstrate that although the 'rural' diocese has a consistently higher proportion of Easter day communicants in its population than the other dioceses, the rate of decline in this figure is the same in the 1990s as the rate of decline in the 'urban' diocese. Both the 'rural' and 'urban' diocese show a slower rate of decline than the 'mixed' diocese in the 1970s, 1980s and 1990s and a slower rate of decline than the Church of England as a whole in the 1980s and 1990s. It was results like these that led Lankshear in his 2001 study to question whether a model of the Church of England based on the rural/urban continuum was adequate to understand and account for all the differences that could be observed.

Easter day is the only occasion in the year when everyone who is confirmed is expected to make their communion. The proportion of confirmation candidates to Easter day communicants therefore represents one of the potential measures of the extent to which the Church of England is able to renew itself. Table 9 shows the number of confirmation candidates per thousand Easter day communicants. From table 9 it will be clear that the proportion of candidates to Easter day communicants is lowest in the 'rural' diocese and highest in the 'urban' diocese. The rate of decline of this proportion is also highest in the 'rural' diocese. During the 1950s the 'rural' diocese and the 'mixed' diocese were confirming sufficient numbers to renew their Easter day communicants every 13 years. In the 'urban' diocese the renewal was taking place in 12 years. By the 1990s this figure, even allowing for the lower number making their Easter day communion, had dropped significantly. In the 'rural' diocese at the rate of confirmation then taking place it would take 33 years to renew the Easter day communicants. In the 'mixed' and the 'mean' dioceses this figure was 27 years and in the 'urban' diocese 22 years.

Gender balance

The limitations of the figures collected at national level make it difficult to understand what is happening to confirmation within the Church of England beyond what has already been presented, with one exception. The confirmation figures have been presented consistently divided into male and female candidates. Therefore, it is possible to trace changes in the gender balance amongst the overall numbers of candidates. Table 10 shows the proportion of female confirmation candidates presented in the 'rural', 'mixed', 'urban' and 'mean' dioceses for each of the decades.

One factor emerges very clearly from this table. The proportion of confirmation candidates who were female in the 'rural' diocese in the 1950s was much lower than in the rest of the Church of England, although it was still biased toward female candidates (55:45). By the 1990s this difference between the 'rural' diocese and the rest of the Church of England had evened out, despite a slight growth in the proportion of female candidates generally. None of these composite dioceses now had less than 60% female candidates.

Discussion and conclusion

One of the problems of discussing confirmation trends based on national statistical evidence is that it is not possible to include consideration of the age of confirmation candidates, as there is no consistent publication of candidates' ages.

Three significant issues emerge from the data that has been presented in this article. The first of these concerns the numbers of confirmation candidates being presented by parishes in the Church of England. These numbers have been falling since the late 1960s. There are some who will argue that this is a good thing as it represents a move away from 'social confirmation' toward confirmation of those who are 'committed believers' or who are being closely nurtured in their faith by their family or the local church community.

The rate of decline of the numbers of confirmation candidates is higher than the rate of decline of electoral roll membership and of Easter day communicants. This should be of concern to those who are committed to the continuing development of the Church of England, for it is difficult to see how such development can be sustained if the church is not bringing significant numbers into full adult membership of the church.

The second issue concerns the rate of decline in the number of confirmation candidates in both rural and urban areas. Although the rural church has a higher starting point the rate of decline is similar in rural and in urban areas, before the effects of change in the numbers of residents in the area are taken into account. Given that by the end of the period two factors within society might tend toward an opposite assumption this is difficult to explain. The first factor concerns the withdrawal, in some rural areas at least, of Christian denominations other than Anglican which could be seen as having the effect of leaving the Anglican Church in a monopoly situation. The second factor concerns the growth in more urban areas of a significant proportion of the population who adhere to faiths other than Christianity. The first factor is likely to raise the number of Christians seeking full membership of the Anglican Church in rural areas. The second factor is likely to reduce the overall numbers of Christians living in urban areas, where the population has been shown to be falling slightly. Therefore both these factors should tend to make it less likely that numbers of confirmation candidates would decline in rural areas than in urban areas. In fact this is not the case as when population is taken into account, the rate of decline in rural areas is higher than that in urban areas.

The rates of decline of electoral roll membership and Easter day communicants are similar in different parts of the church only after population is taken into account. This is more easily understood in the context of theories which propose that the role of the church within society is becoming more marginal or that there is an increasing pattern of 'believing but not belonging' (Davie, 1994).

A number of explanations for the more rapid decline of confirmation candidates in rural areas could be advanced. The first of these focuses on the changing age profile in rural communities and proposes that a growing proportion of more mature people in rural areas means that it is less likely that many of them will be seeking confirmation. A second explanation suggests that the rural church may be failing to engage the 'new' population of rural areas and may be too closely associated with traditional rural issues and way of life. This explanation suggests that as a result the 'incomers' may not be identifying with the rural church. A third explanation takes the disassociation of young people from village life in general and the village church in particular caused by the location of their secondary schools outside the home area as a reason why young people may not be coming forward for confirmation in rural areas. A fourth explanation, drawing on the work of Francis and Lankshear (1992), suggests that the cause of decline is associated with the challenges facing rural clergy who serve a number of villages, but who live in only one of them.

These explanations, and others that might be advanced, need further exploration. Such exploration is beyond the scope of this study and would need to employ research techniques beyond the secondary analysis of published data. In order to inform the debate, affirm or refute the theories and speculation, work has to be undertaken using material which is only available at parochial or diocesan level.

The third issue focuses on the gender of the candidates. The proportion of female confirmation candidates has risen slightly over the period and now stands at over sixty per cent in all the different groups of dioceses. The rate at which this proportion has risen is most marked in the 'rural' diocese where at the start of the period the proportion of female candidates was only just over fifty-five per cent.

This review of the available data over a significant period of time has demonstrated that differences remain between the rural and the urban churches although the gap between the rural and the urban church is narrowing. What has also been demonstrated, almost incidentally, is that the contrasts between the urban and the rural church do not provide the whole picture. The group of dioceses used in this study to provide the composite 'mixed' diocese do not always fall neatly between the 'urban' and the 'rural'. They do, however, reflect closely the Church of England as a whole, represented in this study by the 'mean' diocese. In future it may be important for the Church of England to use a more sophisticated model than a continuum between the 'rural' and the 'urban' church, when seeking to use statistical methods to inform the debate about policy and practice. It will also be important that further research into the trends identified and the reasons for them is conducted either at the diocesan or parochial level, because of the limits to the information which is made available at the national level.

Acknowledgement

The statistics have been drawn from *Church of England Year Books* and their *Statistical Supplements* (1953–2002 inclusive).

References

Davie, G. (1994). *Religion in Britain since 1945*. London: Blackwell.

Francis, L. J. (1985). *Rural Anglicanism*. London: Collins.

Francis, L. J., & Lankshear, D. W. (1992). The rural rectory: The impact of a resident priest on local church life. *Journal of Rural Studies, 8*, 97–103.

Francis, L. J., & Lankshear, D. W. (1997). The rural church is different: The case of Anglican confirmation. *Journal of Empirical Theology, 10*(1), 5–19.

Lankshear, D. W. (1992). The episcopal moment, a study of confirmation in the Church of England, unpublished MPhil dissertation, University of Wales, Lampeter.

Lankshear, D. W. (2001). One Church or three? Using statistics as a tool for mission, unpublished PhD dissertation, University of Wales, Lampeter.

Roberts, C. (2003). Is the rural church different? A comparison of historical membership statistics between an urban and a rural diocese in the Church of England, *Rural Theology, 1*, 25–39.

Appendix

Table 1: Confirmation candidates

	Rural N	%	Mixed N	%	Urban N	%	Mean N	%
1950s	2,647	100	3,694	100	5,214	100	3,699	100
1960s	2,519	95	3,531	96	4,814	93	3,566	96
1970s	1,686	64	2,352	64	2,957	57	2,321	63
1980s	1,298	49	1,736	47	2,268	43	1,806	49
1990s	788	30	1,035	28	1,458	28	1,096	30

Note: Throughout the tables the symbol % above a column means that the column shows the N for that period as a percentage of the N for the 1950s

Table 2: Population

	Rural N	%	Mixed N	%	Urban N	%	Mean N	%
1950s	463,854	100	916,598	100	1,897,126	100	971,191	100
1960s	491,320	106	984,158	107	1,926,822	102	1,023,890	105
1970s	545,888	118	1,050,096	115	1,860,809	98	1,069,667	110
1980s	581,436	125	1,049,093	114	1,821,011	96	1,084,608	112
1990s	621,150	134	1,057,538	115	1,863,311	98	1,126,815	116

Table 3: Confirmation candidates per thousand population

	Rural N	%	Mixed N	%	Urban N	%	Mean N	%
1950s	5.71	100	4.03	100	2.75	100	3.81	100
1960s	5.13	90	3.59	89	2.51	91	3.48	91
1970s	3.09	54	2.24	56	1.59	58	2.17	57
1980s	2.23	39	1.65	41	1.25	45	1.67	44
1990s	1.27	22	0.98	24	0.78	28	0.97	25

Table 4: Electoral rolls

	Rural N	%	Mixed N	%	Urban N	%	Mean N	%
1950s	55,553	100	65,983	100	91,163	100	67,484	100
1960s	51,825	93	62,827	95	83,743	92	63,493	94
1970s	40,962	74	47,976	73	55,173	61	47,287	70
1980s	34,826	63	37,106	56	42,588	47	38,482	57
1990s	29,230	53	30,610	46	37,082	41	32,455	48

Table 5: Electoral rolls per thousand of the population

	Rural N	%	Mixed N	%	Urban N	%	Mean N	%
1950s	120	100	72	100	48	100	69	100
1960s	105	88	64	89	43	90	62	90
1970s	75	63	46	64	30	63	44	64
1980s	60	50	35	49	23	48	35	51
1990s	47	39	29	40	20	42	29	42

Table 6: Confirmation candidates per thousand members of electoral roll

	Rural N	%	Mixed N	%	Urban N	%	Mean N	%
1950s	47.65	100	55.98	100	57.19	100	54.81	100
1960s	48.61	102	56.20	100	57.81	101	56.16	102
1970s	41.16	86	49.02	88	53.59	94	49.08	90
1980s	37.27	78	46.78	84	53.25	93	46.93	86
1990s	26.96	57	33.81	60	39.32	69	33.77	62

Table 7: Easter day communicants

	Rural N	%	Mixed N	%	Urban N	%	Mean N	%
1950s	35,372	100	48,080	100	62,186	100	47,175	100
1960s	35,584	101	47,239	98	57,864	93	46,150	98
1970s	30,263	86	35,922	75	40,780	66	35,708	76
1980s	30,658	87	34,467	72	39,267	63	35,025	74
1990s	26,346	74	27,844	58	32,698	53	29,252	62

Table 8: Easter day communicants per thousand population

	Rural N	%	Mixed N	%	Urban N	%	Mean N	%
1950s	76	100	52	100	33	100	49	100
1960s	72	75	48	92	30	91	45	92
1970s	55	72	34	65	22	67	33	67
1980s	53	70	33	63	22	67	32	65
1990s	42	55	26	50	18	55	26	53

Table 9: Confirmation candidates per thousand Easter day communicants

	Rural N	%	Mixed N	%	Urban N	%	Mean N	%
1950s	74.83	100	76.83	100	83.85	100	78.41	100
1960s	70.79	95	74.75	97	83.66	100	77.27	999
1970s	55.71	74	65.48	85	72.51	86	65.00	83
1980s	42.34	57	50.37	66	57.76	69	51.56	66
1990s	29.91	40	37.17	48	44.59	53	37.47	48

Table 10: Proportion of confirmation candidates who were female

	Rural N	%	Mixed N	%	Urban N	%	Mean N	%
1950s	55.05	100	59.13	100	61.06	100	58.61	100
1960s	56.70	103	59.91	101	61.45	101	59.23	101
1970s	60.19	109	61.02	103	62.32	102	60.86	104
1980s	61.55	118	61.86	105	63.47	104	61.24	104
1990s	61.70	112	60.86	103	63.37	104	61.50	105

Chapter 13

RURAL ANGLICANISM: ONE FACE OR MANY?

Carol Roberts*

Abstract – Over the last twenty years the use of statistical analysis to inform church studies has developed apace. Increasing numbers of empirical studies are concerned with the 'rural church'. A key problem with regard to these studies is the definition of 'rural church'. A variety of approaches has been taken in respect of studying 'Rural Anglicanism': the single diocese approach, the five-diocese approach, and the 'average diocese' approach. This article takes data for seven rural dioceses and examines changes between the late 1950s and early 1960s and the year 2000, in relation to indicators of church vitality. These indicators relate to churches, clergy, laity, membership, and seasonal practice. Differences between the dioceses are noted, and questions for further research are raised. The data suggest that 'Rural Anglicanism', as reflected in rural dioceses, is complex. As autonomous administrative units, the dioceses may have considerable say in their destinies through diocesan policies. It is argued that to think in terms of the many faces of 'Rural Anglicanism' rather than one 'Rural Anglicanism' may be more appropriate.

Introduction

Good statistics properly used should be able to provide a sharp tool for analysing the strengths and weaknesses of an organization and for predicting future trends. Exponents of the branch of practical theology known as empirical theology have argued that the tools of statistical analysis are properly able to draw attention to matters of concern in areas such as ministry and mission, and exercise a proper prophetic function. (van der Ven, 1993, 1998)

* The Revd Dr Carol Roberts is Assistant Curate in the Parish of Bangor. *Address for correspondence:* Tu Hwnt i'r Afon, 55 Braichmelyn, Bethesda, Gwynedd, LL57 3RD. E-mail: davecas@tesco.net

In his book *Rural Anglicanism*, Francis (1985) set out to employ the tools of statistical analysis to draw a picture of strength and weakness in rural Anglicanism. In the following two decades a number of studies have added to this tradition. For example, statistical analysis has been used to examine the church school system in one rural diocese (Francis, 1986), the impact of baptism policy on church growth in rural, urban, and suburban parishes (Francis, Jones, and Lankshear, 1996), the impact of a resident priest on the life of the local rural church (Francis and Lankshear, 1992a), the liturgical work of rural clergy (Francis and Lankshear, 1992b), the practice of confirmation (Francis and Lankshear, 1997; Lankshear, 2004), and clergy stress (Francis and Rutledge, 2000).

Statistical analysis also underpins the five volume *Parish Workbook* series focusing on the rural church. Each volume presents statistics, offers a reflection, activities, and suggested talking points, in order that Parochial Church Councils and church groups think seriously about the way their church functions, and what they as a church might do to develop in the fields of worship (*Rural Praise*, Francis and Martineau, 1996), ministry (*Rural Ministry*, Francis, Littler, and Martineau, 2000) working with young people (*Rural Youth*, Francis and Martineau, 2001a), welcoming visitors (*Rural Visitors*, Francis and Martineau, 2001b), and mission (*Rural Mission*, Francis and Martineau, 2002).

A key problem in assessing these studies concerns the definition of 'Rural Anglicanism'. In his original study, *Rural Anglicanism*, Francis (1985) argued that it was sensible to study one rural diocese as an example. He challenged others to test his findings by replication studies.

In the decades that have followed, studies have taken various approaches. The single diocese approach continued to be used by Francis when he undertook his survey of the church school system (Francis, 1986). Roberts (2003) again used a single diocese approach by analysing one rural diocese and one urban diocese for comparative purposes. Davies, Pack, Seymour, Short, Watkins, and Winter (1990a, 1990b, 1990c, 1990d) analysed five dioceses in the Rural Church Project. By aggregating data for the eight 'most rural' dioceses, using the factors to identify rurality first developed by Francis (1985), Lankshear (2004) created an 'average rural diocese', in order to examine differences between rural Anglicanism and urban Anglicanism in respect of confirmation and membership.

However, what if the Church of England is not like that? Each diocese has a great deal of autonomy; suppose diocesan policy actually influences outcome? The aim of the present study, therefore, is to compare and contrast a limited number of rural dioceses; seven rural dioceses are examined in relation to ten indicators of church vitality, in order to test how reasonable it is to speak in terms of 'Rural Anglicanism'. The seven rural dioceses are Carlisle, Exeter, Lincoln, Norwich, Salisbury, St Edmundsbury and Ipswich, and Truro. The ten indicators are churches within the parochial structure, full-time stipendiary parochial clergy, ratios of full-time stipendiary parochial clergy to populations, non-stipendiary and ordained local ministers, licensed readers, electoral rolls, baptism candidates, confirmation candidates, Easter day communicants, and Christmas eve and Christmas day communicants.

Method

Materials published in the *Statistical Supplements to the Church of England Yearbooks*, their successor publications *Church Statistics* and *Statistics of Licensed Ministers*, and three *ad hoc* publications *Some Facts and Figures about the Church of England* are analysed in order to establish the changes that have taken place in the seven dioceses from the late 1950s and early 1960s to the year 2000. Details of all publications used as sources are provided in appendix 2.

The average figures for the late 1950s and early 1960s were established for most categories of data against which the figures for the year 2000 could be compared in both absolute and percentage terms. Tables were generated to illustrate changes over time. The one category of data treated differently concerns the numbers of churches, where the figures for one year (1960) are employed as the basis for comparison. The tables are presented in appendix 1, where full details of the years used to calculate the average figures are provided for each category of data. In each case where the data in the final column of the table is a percentage figure, the position at the year 2000 is expressed as a percentage of the average, or in the case of churches, as a percentage of the 1960 figures.

Results

Churches

One consequence of a reduction in financial resources can be the downsizing of an organization, in terms of both personnel and infra-structure. Have rural dioceses experienced downsizing in respect of numbers of parochial churches? How similar are the experiences of different rural dioceses?

All seven of the rural dioceses in this study saw a reduction in numbers of churches between 1960 and 2000 (table 1) with the losses in both absolute and percentage terms varying considerably between dioceses.

Taking the dioceses which fared best and worst in terms of percentage loss is a useful indicator of variance. The diocese of Exeter saw its number of churches reduce by 4% (or 25 churches); in the diocese of Salisbury the figure was 10% (63 churches); in the diocese of Lincoln it was 13% (or 93 churches). In terms of pastoral reorganization the data suggest that quite different policies have been adopted with regard to church closures.

Clergy

All seven of the rural dioceses experienced losses in terms of full-time stipendiary parochial clergy (table 2). It is clear, however, that the losses varied considerably in both absolute and percentage terms. Again taking the dioceses which fared best and worst in terms of percentage loss demonstrates the variation between rural dioceses. In the diocese of Truro full-time stipendiary parochial clergy numbers were 70% of the mean at the year 2000 (a loss of 53 clergy). In contrast both the diocese of St Edmundsbury and Ipswich (with a loss of 111 clergy) and the diocese of Norwich (with a loss of 148 clergy) had full-time stipendiary parochial clergy numbers of 56% of the mean at the year 2000.

In terms of ratios of full-time stipendiary parochial clergy to population, the variations visible in the late 1950s and early 1960s were also present in the year 2000, with the dioceses of Lincoln and Carlisle clearly illustrating this. In the late 1950s and early 1960s the diocese of Lincoln had a ratio of one full-time stipendiary parochial cleric per 2,284 people, and the diocese of Carlisle had a ratio of one full-time stipendiary parochial cleric per 2,038 people. In the year 2000 the diocese of Lincoln had a ratio of one full-time stipendiary parochial cleric per 4,639 people, and the diocese of Carlisle had a ratio of one full-time stipendiary parochial cleric per 3,443 people (table 3).

The data suggest that the various clergy deployment formulae have impacted on all seven dioceses. The intention of the formulae was for each diocese in the Church of England to have an equitable share of ordained Anglican clergy. The formulae included all diocesan clergy, not just parochial clergy, although parochial clergy comprise by far the greater proportion of the workforce. It is thus valid to consider changes to full-time stipendiary parochial ministry in this context. In 2000 part-time stipendiary clergy were also included. Of the seven dioceses analysed in this study, five had clergy numbers which were under share in 2000, and two had clergy numbers which were over share. The variance ranged from two over share for the dioceses of Carlisle and Truro, to 15 under share for the diocese of Lincoln.

Non-stipendiary ministry has developed since its inception in the early 1970s. Given the pressures created by reducing full-time stipendiary clergy numbers in the seven rural dioceses, to what extent has the non-stipendiary ministry developed? Have the seven rural dioceses shared a common experience, or have some dioceses been more inclined than others to take this form of ministry forward?

The data demonstrate that non-stipendiary ministry and ordained local ministry appear to have been embraced to varying degrees (table 4). The diocese of Salisbury fared best, with 60 non-stipendiary ministers and 23 ordained local ministers in 2000. The diocese of Carlisle fared worst with 27 non-stipendiary ministers and six ordained local ministers in 2000. The diocese of Lincoln was at the centre of the range with 30 non-stipendiary ministers and 21 ordained local ministers in 2000.

The diocese of Lincoln had the lowest full-time stipendiary cleric to population ratio in 2000 (1:4639). The dioceses of Salisbury (1:4071) and Carlisle (1:3443) had the highest full-time stipendiary cleric to population ratios in 2000. From the late 1950s and early 1960s to the year 2000 full-time stipendiary parochial clergy numbers reduced by 34% (111 clergy) in the diocese of Salisbury. Over the same period, full-time stipendiary parochial clergy numbers reduced by 37% (120 clergy) in the diocese of Lincoln, and by 39% (88 clergy) in the diocese of Carlisle.

Salisbury, which had experienced a 34% reduction in numbers of full-time stipendiary parochial clergy, had the highest number of non-stipendiary and ordained local ministers of the seven dioceses. Carlisle had the lowest number of stipendiary and ordained local ministers and yet had a 5% greater loss in numbers of full-time stipendiary parochial clergy.

The data indicate that these ministries have not grown to meet the gaps resulting from a decline in numbers of stipendiary clergy and suggest that diocesan policies may be encouraging non-stipendiary ministry and ordained local ministry in ways so as to mitigate against them being perceived as ministries to meet 'the gaps produced by the decline in the stipendiary ministry' (Francis, 1985).

The reasons for the variation in numbers of non-stipendiary and ordained local ministers may be simply that fewer candidates are coming forward in some dioceses. Different diocesan policies may also encourage non-stipendiary ministry and ordained local ministry to greater or lesser degrees.

Licensed readers

In view of the reduction in numbers of full-time stipendiary parochial clergy, and the development of non-stipendiary and ordained local ministry, what happened to licensed reader ministry over the period? To what extent has this form of lay ministry been embraced, to compensate for the decline in stipendiary ordained ministry? Have rural dioceses all embraced the ministry of licensed readers with equal fervour?

In terms of both percentage change and absolute change from the late 1950s and early 1960s to 2000, the seven dioceses show considerable variations in licensed reader ministry (table 5). In the diocese of Norwich, which fared best, numbers of licensed readers were 252% of the mean (an increase of 159 licensed readers). The diocese of Exeter fared worst, and was the only one of the seven dioceses to experience a reduction in numbers of licensed readers, at 83% of the mean (a loss of 32 licensed readers). The other five dioceses fell into a range of 110% to 134% of the mean at the year 2000, reflecting increases of between 13 and 47 licensed readers. The data suggest that different dioceses take different approaches to the promotion of licensed reader ministry.

Electoral rolls

While there is no one single definition of church membership in relation to the Church of England, electoral rolls are one proxy for church membership, and as such warrant consideration in any assessment of longitudinal change. The requirement to produce new electoral rolls every six years was introduced in 1972. Those years when new rolls are produced can often see a marked reduction in numbers, with a gradual increase in numbers in subsequent years, until the next new rolls are produced, when numbers drop again. During the period under review, new rolls were last compiled in 1996, which means that the figures for 2000 are likely to provide a somewhat more optimistic view than would be found on a year when new rolls were compiled.

The seven rural dioceses all experienced losses in numbers on electoral rolls (table 6) from the late 1950s and early 1960s to the year 2000. The diocese of Salisbury experienced the lowest percentage loss, at 64% of the mean (a loss of 27,386). The diocese of Exeter experienced the highest percentage loss, at 39% of the mean in 2000 (a loss of 54,914). These losses should be seen within the context of changes in population levels; not one of the seven dioceses saw a reduction in population levels when the 1961 census figures are compared with the 2001 census figures.

Baptism candidates

Baptism can also be taken as a proxy for church membership. There have been changes to the way infant baptism figures are reported during the period under review in this study. Prior to 1978 there was no formal definition of 'infant'; from 1978 infants were defined as under one year of age for the purposes of statistical reporting on the annual returns. In order to compare like with like, this review will be restricted to total baptism candidate numbers.

All seven dioceses experienced decline in numbers of baptism candidates between the late 1950s and early 1960s and 2000. The data demonstrate considerable variation between the dioceses in both absolute and percentage terms (table 7). The diocese of Truro saw the least decline in terms of percentage losses. Total numbers of baptism candidates in 2000 were 60% of the mean, reflecting a reduction in numbers of candidates baptized of 40% or 1,138 candidates. The diocese of Norwich saw the highest percentage decline, with numbers of baptism candidates of 42% of the mean in the year 2000. This reflects a decrease of 58%, or 3,550 baptism candidates.

Confirmation candidates

Another proxy for church membership is confirmation. The picture in respect of numbers of confirmation candidates is bleaker than for baptism candidates, with all seven dioceses experiencing losses in excess of 75% (table 8) when data for the late 1950s and early 1960s are compared with data for 2000.

The diocese of Salisbury fared best in percentage terms, with confirmation candidate numbers at 24% of the mean, reflecting a reduction of 76% or 3,191 confirmation candidates. The diocese of St Edmundsbury and Ipswich fared worst with confirmation candidate numbers at 15% of the mean, reflecting a reduction of 85% or 2,318 candidates.

Easter day communicants

Numbers of Easter day communicants have declined between the late 1950s and early 1960s and 2000. The degree of decline differs in the seven rural dioceses (table 9).

In 2000, in the diocese of Truro, Easter day communicant numbers were 81% of the mean, reflecting a reduction in numbers of 19% or 4,983 communicants. The diocese of Norwich had Easter day communicants at 64% of the mean, reflecting a loss of 36% or 14,422 communicants. The diocese of Carlisle appears to have fared worst, at 48% of the mean, reflecting a loss of 52% or 21,963 communicants. In other words, in the diocese of Carlisle, numbers of Easter day communicants had more than halved over the forty year period.

Christmas communicants

Christmas eve and Christmas day communicant numbers have not declined as greatly in percentage terms in comparison with Easter day communicant numbers. The variation between dioceses is clearly evident (table 10).

In 2000 the diocese of Truro had Christmas eve and Christmas day communicant numbers at 106% of the mean, reflecting an increase of 6% or 1,176 candidates. In contrast, Christmas eve and Christmas day communicant numbers in 2000 in the diocese of Lincoln were 65% of the mean, reflecting a loss of 35% or 14,359 communicants.

In the late 1950s and early 1960s all seven dioceses had more communicants on Easter day than on Christmas eve and Christmas day. By 2000 the picture had changed with six of the seven dioceses (the exception being Carlisle) having more communicants on Christmas eve and Christmas day than on Easter day.

The data for 1998, considered for comparison purposes, confirm that patterns are changing, with all seven dioceses having more communicants on Christmas eve and Christmas day than on Easter day. Of course Easter communion can be taken in Easter week; unfortunately the Church of England has ceased to publish figures of Easter week communicants. Such information would inform studies concerned with changing patterns of worship, and particularly as to whether Christmas is becoming a more popular festival than Easter at which to take communion. In addition, it would then be possible to examine differences between rural dioceses in this regard.

Conclusion

Patterns of ministry have changed in the last half of the twentieth century; church closures and reducing clergy numbers have meant that, both among the clergy and laity, some individuals will have found themselves having to travel greater distances to attend church. In some country churches services may be held only fortnightly or monthly. The examination of the data for seven rural dioceses has clearly demonstrated that different policies are pursued with respect to church closures. What has been put in place to help those whose church has closed but who have no transport? Are different dioceses more or less supportive in these situations? Further research at the level of the diocese is needed to address these issues, and may help explain the differences between the experiences of rural dioceses.

To what extent have changes in patterns of ministry been examined in relation to church attendance and mission? To what extent have dioceses which pursue a policy of closing churches tested the impact of such closures on mission and ministry? How do church closures impact on levels of church attendance, numbers of communicants, and on numbers of baptism and confirmation candidates? In the answers to such questions may lie some of the differences in the experiences of rural dioceses over the last forty years. Further statistical analysis of the nationally published data can help with such questions.

Losses in numbers of full-time stipendiary parochial clergy have been experienced in all seven dioceses examined. To what extent has the reduction in numbers of full-time stipendiary parochial clergy impacted on church attendance, numbers of communicants, numbers of baptism and numbers of confirmation candidates? Again, further statistical analysis of the nationally published data can help with such questions.

Electoral roll numbers have reduced in all seven dioceses. If this trend continues dioceses may find that rural parishes are faced with problems of governance. To what extent does the move away from this type of commitment impact on the ability of the church to manage its own affairs effectively?

Do rural churches struggle to fill key posts such as warden, treasurer, Parochial Church Council secretary? If pressures to fill such posts exist in rural parishes, to what extent, if any, have they impacted on pastoral reorganization in terms of the unification of parishes? What effect does it have on people's sense of belonging? The answers to such questions will certainly be needed if the parochial system is to be sustained long term. Further research at the level of the individual diocese, and at parish level, is required in order to ascertain the extent to which such problems exist.

Numbers of baptism candidates have reduced in all seven dioceses, with variation evident in their experiences. What factors lie behind the differences? To what extent does this impact on confirmation candidate numbers and on numbers on electoral rolls?

The data also demonstrate differences between the dioceses with regard to confirmation candidate numbers. Are some rural dioceses more effective in supporting the faith development and commitment of those baptized at Anglican fonts? Do some dioceses put more emphasis on nurture courses than other dioceses? Is it the case that within certain dioceses there has been a move away from 'social confirmation' toward the confirmation of those who are 'committed believers'? How have the profiles of each of the seven rural dioceses changed in terms of numbers of young people? As suggested by Lankshear (2004) such questions need addressing by further research. This would require further research at the level of the individual diocese and at parish level.

Further research using the nationally published data, providing information by dioceses, permits questions on the impact of reducing confirmation candidate numbers on electoral roll numbers, Easter day communicant numbers, and Christmas eve and Christmas day communicant numbers to be further explored.

Easter day communicant numbers have decreased in all seven dioceses examined. One reason suggested for this decrease is the availability of and ease with which many can now take foreign holidays. This may be the case to some degree, but surely cannot account for the considerable differences in the experiences of the seven dioceses over the last forty years. What factors lie behind the differences between the dioceses? Have church closures played a part? To what extent have reducing clergy numbers played a part? Such areas require further research, and the nationally published data are a resource for such future research.

In spite of the pressures created by reducing clergy numbers, it has been possible to achieve growth in Christmas eve and Christmas day communicant numbers in one diocese (Truro). Other dioceses, for example Lincoln and Carlisle have had quite different experiences. What factors lie behind this? To what extent do reducing clergy numbers and church closures impact on this? Again the nationally published data can help in addressing such questions.

The data on these seven rural dioceses support Lankshear's (2004) view that research needs to be conducted at the level of the individual diocese, and also at parochial level, in order to gain a fuller understanding of what has been happening in the Church of England in the second half of the twentieth century. The seven rural dioceses examined in this study have not shared common experiences in relation to the indicators reviewed. Whereas the story has generally been one of decline, the dioceses show marked differences in the extent of that decline. Evidently they do not perform in a consistent way.

The nationally published data examined here suggest that we do not have one 'Rural Anglicanism', and thus do not support the view propounded by Francis (1985) that it is sensible to study one diocese as an example. The data support the view that 'Rural Anglicanism' has many faces. As autonomous administrative units rural dioceses certainly warrant further investigation. Research at diocesan level is required, and this may well be the key to unlocking reasons for differences in experiences between rural dioceses. Such research, combining statistical analyses of the nationally published data with additional information from dioceses, could provide valuable insights on the many faces of rural Anglicanism as exemplified by rural dioceses.

Acknowledgements

I am grateful to the Mulberry Trust for providing funding for this research.

References

Davies, D., Pack, S., Seymour, S., Short, C., Watkins, C., & Winter, M. (1990a). *Staff and buildings: Rural church project*, volume one. Cirencester: Centre for Rural Studies, Royal Agricultural College.

Davies, D., Pack, S., Seymour, S., Short, C., Watkins, C., & Winter, M. (1990b). *The Clergy life: Rural church project*, volume two. Cirencester: Centre for Rural Studies, Royal Agricultural College.

Davies, D., Pack, S., Seymour, S., Short, C., Watkins, C., & Winter, M. (1990c). *Parish life and rural religion: Rural church project*, volume three. Cirencester: Centre for Rural Studies, Royal Agricultural College.

Davies, D., Pack, S., Seymour, S., Short, C., Watkins, C., & Winter, M. (1990d). *The views of rural parishioners: Rural church project*, volume four. Cirencester: Centre for Rural Studies, Royal Agricultural College.

Francis, L. J. (1985). *Rural Anglicanism: A future for young Christians?* London: Collins.

Francis, L. J. (1986). *Partnership in rural education?* London: Collins.

Francis, L. J., Jones, S. H., & Lankshear, D. W. (1996). Baptism policy and church growth in Church of England rural, urban and suburban parishes. *Modern Believing, 37*(3), 11–24.

Francis, L. J., & Lankshear, D. W. (1992a). The rural rectory: The impact of a resident priest on local Church life. *Journal of Rural Studies, 8,* 97–103.

Francis, L. J., & Lankshear, D. W. (1992b). The rural factor: A comparative survey of village churches and the liturgical work of rural clergy. *Modern Churchman, 34,* 1–9.

Francis, L.J., & Lankshear, D. W. (1997). The rural church is different. *Journal of Empirical Theology, 10*(1), 5–20.

Francis, L. J., Littler, K., & Martineau, J. (2000). *Rural ministry.* Stoneleigh: ACORA Publishing.

Francis, L. J., & Martineau, J. (1996). *Rural praise.* Stoneleigh: ACORA Publishing.

Francis, L. J., & Martineau, J. (2001a). *Rural youth.* Stoneleigh: ACORA Publishing.

Francis, L. J., & Martineau, J. (2001b). *Rural visitors.* Stoneleigh: ACORA Publishing.

Francis, L. J., & Martineau, J. (2002). *Rural Mission.* Stoneleigh: ACORA Publishing.

Francis, L. J., & Rutledge, C. J. F. (2000). Are rural clergy in the Church of England under greater stress? *Research in the Social Scientific Study of Religion, 11,* 173–191.

Lankshear, D. W. (2004). Is the rural church different? The special case of Anglican confirmation. *Rural Theology, 2,* 105–117.

Roberts, C. (2003). Is the rural church different? A comparison of historical membership statistics between an urban and a rural diocese in the Church of England. *Rural Theology, 1,* 25–39.

van der Ven, J. A. (1993). *Practical Theology: An empirical approach.* Kampen: Kok Pharos.

van der Ven, J. A. (1998). *Education for reflective ministry.* Louvain: Peeters.

Appendix 1

Table 1: Number of churches

Diocese	1960	2000	Change	%
Exeter	646	621	-25	96
Truro	332	313	-19	94
St Edmundsbury and Ipswich	511	478	-33	94
Carlisle	378	350	-28	93
Norwich	700	646	-54	92
Salisbury	643	580	-63	90
Lincoln	741	648	-93	87

Table 2: Full-time stipendiary parochial clergy

Diocese	Mean	2000	Change	%
Truro	175	122	-53	70
Salisbury	322	211	-111	66
Lincoln	325	205	-120	63
Carlisle	228	140	-88	61
Exeter	416	237	-179	57
St Edmundsbury and Ipswich	251	140	-111	56
Norwich	333	185	-148	56

Mean = average of the published figures for 1959, 1960, 1961, and 1962

Table 3: Full-time stipendiary parochial clergy: population ratios

Diocese	Mean	2000
Lincoln	1:2284	1:4639
Exeter	1:1972	1:4532
Norwich	1:1721	1:4422
St Edmundsbury and Ipswich	1:1657	1:4243
Truro	1:1963	1:4115
Salisbury	1:1839	1:4071
Carlisle	1:2038	1:3443

Mean = populations at 1961 census divided by average of the published figures for stipendiary parochial clergy for 1959, 1960, 1961, and 1962

Table 4: Non-stipendiary and ordained local ministers in 2000

Diocese	NSMs	OLMs	Total
Salisbury	60	23	83
St Edmundsbury and Ipswich	29	46	75
Norwich	26	29	55
Lincoln	30	21	51
Exeter	47	0	47
Truro	25	10	35
Carlisle	27	6	33

Table 5: Total licensed readers

Diocese	Mean	2000	Change	%
Norwich	104	263	+159	252
St Edmundsbury and Ipswich	138	185	+47	134
Carlisle	106	142	+36	134
Lincoln	132	170	+38	129
Truro	102	115	+13	113
Salisbury	173	190	+17	110
Exeter	186	154	-32	83

Mean = average of the published figures for 1956, 1958, 1962, and 1963

Table 6: Numbers on electoral rolls

Diocese	Mean	2000	Change	%
Salisbury	76086	48700	-27386	64
Truro	31834	18000	-13834	57
St Edmundsbury and Ipswich	51318	26900	-24418	52
Lincoln	69066	31600	-37466	46
Norwich	59501	26700	-32801	45
Carlisle	58716	25300	-33416	43
Exeter	89614	34700	-54914	39

Mean = average of the published figures for 1956, 1957, 1958, 1959, 1960, and 1962

Table 7: Total baptism candidates

Diocese	Mean	2000	Change	%
Truro	2878	1740	-1138	60
Salisbury	6215	3680	-2535	59
Lincoln	9107	5000	-4107	55
St Edmundsbury and Ipswich	4262	2010	-2252	47
Carlisle	5563	2620	-2943	47
Exeter	7965	3730	-4235	47
Norwich	6150	2600	-3550	42

Mean = average of the published figures for 1956, 1958, 1960 and 1962

Table 8: Total confirmation candidates

Diocese	Mean	2000	Change	%
Salisbury	4215	1024	-3191	24
Lincoln	3389	696	-2693	21
Norwich	2411	491	-1920	20
Exeter	4756	912	-3844	19
Truro	1525	269	-1256	18
Carlisle	3711	611	-3100	16
St Edmundsbury and Ipswich	2732	414	-2318	15

Mean = average of the published figures for 1956, 1958, 1960 and 1962

Table 9: Easter day communicants

Diocese	Mean	2000	Change	%
Truro	25583	20600	-4983	81
Salisbury	51183	40100	-11083	78
St Edmundsbury and Ipswich	32530	22800	-9730	70
Norwich	40022	25600	-14422	64
Exeter	70111	39700	-30411	57
Lincoln	43004	22600	-20404	53
Carlisle	42463	20500	-21963	48

Mean = average of the published figures for 1956, 1958, 1960 and 1962

Table 10: Christmas eve and Christmas day communicants

Diocese	Mean	2000	Change	%
Truro	21024	22200	+1176	106
Salisbury	46989	46800	-189	100
St Edmundsbury and Ipswich	27692	25700	-1992	93
Norwich	34223	28100	-6123	82
Exeter	60804	45200	-15604	74
Lincoln	31089	22500	-8589	72
Carlisle	41559	27200	-14359	65

Mean = average of the published figures for 1956, 1958, 1960 and 1962

Appendix 2

Church of England. (1959). *Facts and Figures about the Church of England 1959.* London: Church Information Office.

Church of England. (1961). *Official Yearbook of the Church of England 1961.* London: The Church Assembly and SPCK.

Church of England. (1962). *Facts and figures about the Church of England 1962.* London: Church Information Office.

Church of England. (1962). *Official Yearbook of the Church of England 1962.* London. London: The Church Assembly and SPCK.

Church of England. (1965). *Facts and figures about the Church of England Number 3.* London: Church Information Office.

Church of England. (1965). *The Church of England Yearbook 1965.* London: The Church Assembly and SPCK.

Church of England. (2003). *Church of England Yearbook 2004.* London: Church House Publishing.

Church of England: The Archbishops' Council. (2000). *Church Statistics: Parochial membership and finance statistics for January to December 1998.* London: Church House Publishing.

Church of England: The Archbishops' Council (2002). *Church Statistics: Parochial membership, attendance and finance statistics for January to December 2000.* London: Church House Publishing.

Church of England: The Archbishops' Council. (2003). *Church Statistics: Parochial membership, attendance and finance statistics for the Church of England, January to December 2001.* London: Church House Publishing.

Chapter 14

PASTORAL FRAGMENTS: DISCOVERED REMNANTS OF A RURAL PAST

Trevor Kerry*

Abstract – The article records the discovery of pages from an unpublished manuscript of an autobiography by Jean Blathwayt, daughter of the rector of Melbury Osmund, Dorset, the Revd Francis Blathwayt, who held the living from 1916 until 1929. The intention of the article is to extract elements from this fragment that throw light on life in the rural rectory during the 1920s, and to examine these against the broad social and religious context of the period. Jean's work is also located in the context of what is known from other sources about the family of the Revd Francis Blathwayt. An attempt is made to assess the value of the manuscript from an historical perspective, to link its concerns with a theory of the rural church and to explore briefly its insights into rural theology.

Introduction

In 2004 I set about a task I had promised to do some thirty years previously: I researched and recorded the life of a parson-naturalist, the Revd Francis Linley Blathwayt (Kerry, 2005). As a result of publishing this biography I corresponded, and in some cases met, with current members of Blathwayt's family. As a result of these meetings and further consultations of Blathwayt's diaries (twenty-two volumes held by the Dorset County Museum) I was able to augment my picture of the man (Kerry, 2006a, 2006b, 2006c). Family members were unreservedly generous and allowed me to use private papers to flesh

* Professor Trevor Kerry is Professor Emeritus in the University of Lincoln. *Address for correspondence:* TKConsultancy, 15 Lady Bower Close, North Hykeham, Lincoln, LN6 8EX. E-mail: tk.consultancy@ntlworld.com

out my picture of him still further. Among these was a hand-written manuscript by one of Francis's daughters, Jean Blathwayt (1918–1999). This manuscript comprised two fragments of an account of her life and that of her family in the parish of Melbury Osmund, Dorset, where Francis was rector from 1916 to 1929. The present article examines some aspects of these fragments, attempts to place them in the socio-religious context of the time, and considers the view they reflect of rural ministry of the period.

Family context

To understand Jean Blathwayt it is important to understand the milieu which nurtured her. Her father, Francis, was the child of a civil servant in the Raj, sent home at age three to an English education when his mother died. He was of the aristocratic lineage that owned Dyrham Park, Gloucestershire, but he was not in line to succeed to its ownership. In keeping with the temper of the times he attended Malvern College, then Oxford University, and trained at Lincoln theological college for the ministry, being made deacon in 1900. He served two curacies in urban Lincoln, but in 1909 moved six miles west to the hamlet of Doddington as rector. Married to Marjorie (née Dennys) in 1910, also a fugitive from the Raj, they produced several children not all of whom survived. In late 1916 the family was translated to Melbury Osmund in Dorset, another tiny rural community. This was followed in 1929 by a final move, to the little village of Dyrham adjacent to the ancestral home, to a rectorship that endured until Francis died, aged 78, in 1953. Thus, Francis Blathwayt spent the whole of the period 1909–1953 as rector of three extremely rural parishes in turn, dividing his time between pastoral duties and, as recorded in *Of Roseates and Rectories* (Kerry, 2005), in making an outstanding contribution to bird-watching and bird-recording in Lincolnshire, Dorset and Somerset.

Both the Blathwayt daughters, Jean and her older sister Barbara (1914–2006), were unmarried and lived at home until their father's death. There is no evidence that either inherited their father's passion for birding; but they seem to have assisted their mother with parish activities such as running the Girl Guide companies. It has been possible to piece together a few clues (Dyrham Historical Society, personal communication) about everyday life in the Dyrham rectory from people still living who remember 'the rector', and one must assume that life in Melbury was similar. Miss Jean and Miss Barbara were liked and respected (Poole, personal communication). A visitors' book covering all three rectories is extant (Kerry, 2006d), though many visitors are family members, their dogs, and a handful of well-known bird-watchers; clergy from the Lincoln days also continued to visit and correspond.

Francis Blathwayt seems to have carried out the duties of rector assiduously, and was concerned with practical social issues such as obtaining employment for local youths. He undertook all the usual services of the church; only two examples of sermons from the period exist, both in minimal note form on postcards, and neither capable of full reconstruction. The only text of a Blathwayt sermon that remains in full is from 1907, marking All Saints' Day, and dealing with issues of science, religion and the after-life. In tracing Francis's life I have been contacted by a number of individuals who remember him (for example, Barr, personal communication); all of them wax warm in their liking for the man who 'always replied and helped me greatly'. That he came out of that distinctive line of parson-naturalists so redolent of Victorian England (he was born in 1875) is undoubted (Armstrong, 2000).

He seems to have been a man devoid of ambition for preferment. Morgan (1969) in his study of bishops in the Church of England between 1868 and 1968 identifies four pre-requisites for appointment to that office: landed gentry connections, attendance at a public school and at Oxbridge, and training at one of four major theological colleges (Cuddesdon, Ridley, Westcott and Wells). Francis fulfilled the first three but he remained resolutely a country parson, even though he rubbed shoulders with the aristocracy (Kerry, 2007).

In *Of Roseates and Rectories* (Kerry, 2005) I speculate about this and his chosen rural life. It is speculation, not fact, but Francis Blathwayt fulfils the criteria laid out by Francis, Smith and Robbins (2004) as one of those clergy who, by dint of introversion, is well suited to a 'deep rural parish'. He certainly seems to fit the pattern that 'introvert clergy may be better equipped to nurture and sustain a smaller number of relationships in greater depth than to spread their pastoral skills over a number of rural parishes' (Francis, Smith and Robbins, 2004, p. 131). (By contrast, Francis's son, Linley Dennys Blathwayt, became team rector of Melbury for a time, moved around the British Isles substantially, was a rural dean and ended his career as a canon of Salisbury cathedral). Jean's life in the rectory at Melbury (the period covered by her manuscript) and later at Dyrham was, then, a quiet, predictable, social but sedate affair.

Socio-religious context

Obelkevich's (1993) socio-historical essay, *Religion*, resonates with much that is known of the life of the rector and his family. Thus Francis was one of that breed of 'conscientious men' who were 'not so much religious specialists as gentlemen who happened to be ordained'; he had 'not studied theology' at university (Obelkevich, 1993, p. 313). Early pictures show him in a 'Roman' style cassock, his curacies were in 'high' churches, and he was close to the hounded Bishop King of Lincoln, forced to court for his allegedly Romish practices (Chadwick, 1968). Yet we know he later, in incumbencies, pursued more middle-of-the-road approaches to churchmanship (see below). His female family members took their place in pastoral activities: Marjorie is recorded as teaching singing to the local children at Doddington (school log) and Barbara and Jean joined their mother in other social work as they got older, according to Jean's manuscript. In *Of Roseates and Rectories* (Kerry, 2005), it is recorded that Francis did not engage in the higher criticism of the Bible then becoming fashionable.

Blathwayt's (1907) only extant sermon, referred to earlier, forms the sole evidence of his views on the Darwinian debate, in which he managed to hold science and religion in the same frame, at a time when pressure was for an exclusive stance on one side or the other. As a methodical scientist one might have expected an overt Darwinism to emerge in his thinking; but this is not the case, at least at that date. The sermon argues that science illuminates one aspect of the nature of Godhead, notably the desire for orderliness and invention in Creation. But, he goes on, the morality of God, and aspects such as compassion, certainly do not find illustration in the natural world, one has only to consider 'Nature red in tooth and claw' to realize that. Nature's God of electrical energy and physical laws is counter-balanced by the revelation in Jesus of the compassion and salvation wrought by God and in the moral strivings of humankind.

From the last phase of his life emerge two small pieces of paper on which sermon notes are written, but so concisely (merely a few headings) as to make it impossible to piece the gist of them together. One may have been an Easter sermon, on the theme of Philippians 3:10, 'the power of his resurrection'. The other, a little fuller, is on the person of King David whom he describes as 'a man after God's own heart yet not a good man, which gives us hope'. A printed flyer advertising services in the parish church at Doddington, found in the pages of Blathwayt's bird diaries, encourages the rural population in the observance of Rogation Sunday, 'a day of prayer to God for the fruits of the earth' and because 'it is right that in this country parish all who can should come to God's House ... and ask his blessing on the growing crops' (Kerry, 2005, p. 172).

Jean's manuscript concerns the period from about 1923 to 1929, perhaps before the advent of secularization as a force for lowering attendance, though there is a hint that this process had begun at the time of writing (around 1948, see below):

> People came to the church then more than they do nowadays in most villages.

Brown's meta-analysis (2001, pp. 149–156) of the relationship between social class and church attendance warns that few hard-and-fast conclusions can be drawn, but social class certainly had an effect on what happened in church, according to Jean:

> There was a certain amount of class segregation as regards seating; the farmers took precedence over the cottagers, and the gentry over the farmers, with slightly more superior individuals in between.

Another 'context' for the faith of the Revd Blathwayt, and presumably of his family, is an absence rather than a presence: the complete absence of anything that might have intimated an empathy with the kind of debate being conducted about the relationship between individual/ Christian morality and wider social morality. Neither extant public documents nor private family letters reveal any engagement with those issues – despite the fact that Francis lost a brother in the 1914–1918 war and that, at the very time Jean was recording, urban Britain at least was 'limping through the depression years' (Morgan, 1984, p. 542). As with his Darwinian science, Francis was able to hold critical issues at arms' length from his religious beliefs, and there is no evidence to suggest his immediate family was any more engaged. Their approach was non-judgemental, with faith less a zealous conviction and more a duty of birth and social standing. It was left to Francis's uncle, aunt and cousin (Lieutenant Colonel Linley Blathwayt, wife Elizabeth and daughter Mary) to involve themselves in one of the socio-political wrangles of the age: women's franchise (Pugh, 2001).

By the time Jean's manuscript became ink on the page there was a feeling just being realized in the life of the Church of England that, at the period of which she wrote, Anglicanism and Englishness belonged so closely the one to the other that unravelling them was difficult. This is powerfully conveyed in a caption in the Victoria and Albert Museum recorded by Lowerson (1992, p. 159) to the effect that the significance of the rural church 'transcended religion' and became emblematic of wider sentiments such as continuity and national pride.

Craig (2005) tested 2,658 rural church-goers and concluded that they were characterized by 'a more conservative approach to issues of faith and belief'; though this picture could be ambiguous in rural locations with high populations of in-comers. A more negative view was offered by the report *Renewing Faith in the Countryside* which stated that 'for members of the Church of England the idealized rural parish with its vicar epitomizes so much of the powerful paradigm with which we wrestle' (Board of Mission, 2001, paragraph 14; www.leicester.anglican. org/bsr/rural/renew_faith.htm). But the former was exactly Jean's church and precisely her Anglicanism.

Jean Blathwayt's manuscript

Jean's manuscript came to light among a collection of family papers; it consisted of an octavo school exercise book from which pages had been torn. On the remaining pages there were chapters five and six of what purported to be an autobiography. It was not clear whether chapter 6, which ends rather abruptly, had been finished. The narrative was apparently abandoned at this point. The chapters tell the story of life at the rectory at Melbury Osmund, Dorset (1916–1929), the first extant chapter being about the rectory garden and gardener, the second about parish life. There are alterations to the text but these seem not so much editorial as 'running' amendments contemporary with the first draft. As Jean was born in 1918 and appears as a self-assured child in the narrative, one must assume the starting point of the narrative cannot be until about 1922–1923. Records of events affecting the later life of the gardener and of his family, place the time of writing some years after the end of World War Two, perhaps about 1948. No-one in the Blathwayt family believed that the work had been published and no trace of such a book has been found through internet searches of author or theme. However, that Jean was an aspiring author is known; and from about 1956 she pursued a career as a children's story writer who, by the 1980s, had more than ten titles to her name. One might hypothesize that this was a first or early attempt at writing for an intended adult audience, but one she found was not conducive to her particular talents.

The manuscript has value as a piece of socio-religious history. It is retrospective, but is clearly an account of events experienced by the

writer – what we might now call 'living history'. The style is natural-
istic and personal, the immediacy suggesting a factual rather than a
carefully groomed and edited account (factual, that is, from the writer's
perspective). The manuscript rings true to what is known of similar
contexts from other sources. It commends itself, therefore, as a snapshot
of rural religious life as it was during those years. It is written in a naïve
but guileless mode which engages the reader, and with a degree of
nostalgia that suggests that the motive for writing may have been an
awareness of social change.

In what follows, therefore, ten themes are extracted from Jean
Blathwayt's manuscript. Each is analysed to see what light it can throw
on religion in this rural community at a specific moment in time.

Sundays and church attendance

The rectory family had to take a lead in church-going, inevitably. Jean's
manuscript records that her mother did not like an ostentatious front
pew, and used to sit more modestly in the middle of the congregation.
Life in the rectory would have been relatively comfortable, with a nanny,
a gardener (see below), and probably more than one domestic helper
(this was certainly so in the Dyrham rectory from 1929). Nevertheless,
as Jean's manuscript records:

> Going to church was part of Sunday. There was no question of choice.
> And it was always Sunday clothes too. I remember the feeling of my
> best dress – made by mother or nanny – clean white socks and highly
> polished shoes, and our hats – always hats. How we loved those hats,
> especially the straw ones with wreaths of artificial buttercups and
> daisies round them. The boys wore grey jackets and shorts when old
> enough, and I vaguely remember in the earlier days little suits of pale
> blue linen. I guess the grown-ups were proud of us, and we enjoyed the
> special feeling too. Sunday was Sunday, quite different from a weekday
> for the whole community. We fetched the milk ourselves on Sundays
> from a farm away across the fields ....

This allegiance to the church – we have noted above that the
manuscript records diminished but still significant attendance in the
countryside – may have been a part of what Harris (1993) calls an
'organic resistance to change' after the upheaval of the 1914–1918 war,
but if so then it is probably a rural rather than an urban response, for
the upper-class intellectuals and socialites were hardly likely to espouse
Morgan's (1984, p. 539) Sunday of this period, 'a day of tranquillity and

gloom'. Nevertheless, it is interesting that one Yorkshire countrywoman of the time (quoted by Kightly, 1984, p. 187) regarded attendance at church (as opposed to chapel) as for the 'lardy-dardies'.

Churchmanship

Francis Blathwayt was not averse to changing practice in the churches of which he was incumbent; in *Of Roseates and Rectories* (Kerry, 2005), there is a record of how he refused to give the squire any assurances that he would not change established norms when he took over his first independent living at Doddington. That he did so in Melbury, and in which directions, is recorded by Jean's manuscript:

> My father's predecessor was 'high church', perhaps a little unusual in a village of less than three hundred inhabitants, but he gently brought it down to 'middle of the road', more comfortable for everyone, and the sacristan he inherited had to learn new tricks. But I don't imagine anybody minded much. My father was always tactful and kind, and one of his great attributes was peace-making.

Whether 'anybody minded' must be open to some conjecture! This was the era of somewhat heated debate about the introduction of the 1928 *Book of Common Prayer*, after all. What Jean's paragraph makes nothing of is the fact that Francis Blathwayt himself probably started his ministry as a 'high' churchman: his curacies were in churches noted even today for that tendency and he was well disposed toward Bishop King of Lincoln (see above). But in the three rural parishes that occupied his subsequent long ministry he did not pursue this emphasis, espousing instead an inclusive stance that resonates to some degree with Walker's (2006) notion of 'belonging as a theological concept'.

Socialization into religion

Littler and Francis (2005) surveyed 4,879 visitors to rural churches of whom 68%, when invited to assess the holiness of the church they were visiting, reported that they perceived the church in question to be holy. This positive perception was correlated with three features in the church: opportunity for private prayer, availability of information about services, and the presence of flowers. This modern finding may surprise, but it also opens a debate about exactly how and by what means the sense of 'numinous', and of resultant allegiance, is conditioned. Jean's manuscript has its own slant on the matter:

I remember church as a peaceful, tuneful place. There I learned time-honoured words from the *Book of Common Prayer*, the favourite psalms, the popular hymns, and today there are certain tunes and chants which still may overwhelm me with nostalgia.

The church organ

One might argue, therefore, that the organ, or at least the hymnody which it generated, was part of that cluster of phenomena that helped to 'fix' people in a religious mould. That has been the experience of many (even D.H. Lawrence according to Obelkevich, 1993, p. 345). Such an attachment does not require either deep faith or well-organized rationality; indeed, to borrow a nice phrase only slightly out of context, 'aesthetic satisfactions may silence intellectual uncertainties' (Scharf, 1970, p. 167). But Jean's story of the organist and her assistant was probably included for no deeper reason than the gentle humour of the situation:

> The organ was played by the keeper's wife – she had a long journey to make every Sunday from the keeper's cottage way up in the park – and my mother had a green curtain put up between her and the congregation to give her the privacy she desired. The organ blower was a simple and likeable hobbledehoy, called Cyril, who earned a few pence each Sunday by keeping the organ full of air. Cyril would sing loud and tunelessly, and set the boys at the back into fits! And occasionally he would forget to pump at all, so that the organ would die just for a second or two, only to be galvanized into action in the next.

Music, especially band music, was a feature of non-conformity, but organ music and choral singing were deeply entrenched in the Anglican tradition, spilling out from the home into the public arena. Brown (2001, p. 137) quotes a certain Thomas Upton, an enthusiastic chorister from this time, as saying 'I used to enjoy that thoroughly; I don't think it made me particularly religious, but it took me to church'.

Social concern

The female members of the Blathwayt household at Melbury were engaged in good works, as was deemed appropriate for the rector's family, and were so, assiduously, throughout their lives. The manuscript records it thus:

> My mother did wonders for [the village] children, [her] mission growing with the years in the shape of rallies, camps, marching and singing competitions all over the country, as well as the basic training

and fun at home. To get anywhere it was either Mr Legg's bus (I have memories of Guides travelling on the roof!) or walking or cycling to the next village to catch the train. Under my mother's teaching they reached very high standards indeed, and on one occasion won every cup there was to win.

This picture of philanthropy is one which had guided the Victorian era, but it was a throw-back to that age. Things were moving on, accelerated by recent war, and the countryside was, in some ways, in the last throes of infancy. A new era was dawning, had already dawned by the time Jean's manuscript was written, an era which Sir Roy Strong describes in apocalyptic terms (Strong, 2000, p. 605):

> A revolution in human consciousness ... affected both social behaviour and attitude ... the era was cast as one in which all human values had to be re-thought and traditional morality of the kind rooted in Christianity was to be jettisoned .... We enter a century dedicated to Babel and fragmentation.

This was impetus enough for Jean to write her manuscript in order to capture the moment valued but past.

Social status: cottager and lady

In the 1920s in rural England the ascription of social status had not progressed much beyond the words of the now sanitized hymn: 'the rich man in his castle, the poor man at his gate'. Two extracts from Jean's manuscript show contrasting emotions. In the first, the privileged children of the rectory long to run free like the village youngsters. In the second, even the rector's wife is torn off a strip for poor child-care!

> This wall [that is, of the churchyard], with a bank up against it, was our vantage point for watching the village children playing in the wide street outside. I longed to join them, but this was not done, and they only came inside when the various age-groups met for Guides and Brownies and Wolf Cubs. How I loved the Brownie meetings, and I made many good friends among these little girls. Our uniform made us absolutely equal, and for a whole hour every week we were sisters.
>
> Lady Lilian, a local nobility [*sic*], gave demonstrations ... of First Aid and Home Nursing, two of her great interests, and once I was inveigled into acting as 'the casualty'. I had to be undressed in bed and given a blanket bath, and I hated every minute of it. Afterwards, Lady Lilian complained to my mother that I wore too many clothes, and she was probably right.

Uniformed organizations

Lady Lilian exerted a powerful influence, perhaps because she was one of the few local worthies who actually out-ranked the rector's family. She was the wife of the Earl of Ilchester, who was in turn the patron of the Melbury living which comprised both the parish church of Melbury Osmund and also the little church of St Mary's, Melbury Sampford, attached to Melbury House.

> Lady Lilian was also a keen Girl Guide and ... a District Commissioner of that area. The Brownies would trail across the fields to her lovely home to be tested for various badges, carrying their efforts with them which could even include a rice pudding. On one occasion we met the inevitable bull, and my mother was especially worried as one of the children was wearing a red coat. This was hastily taken off, and stowed underneath me in the push-chair (even before I was old enough I was paraded along with them) but we still felt vulnerable and took a safe though longer way home through the woods. Brownie Revels were held in this good lady's garden ....

School

School was much as village schools of the period are imagined to be, with harsh discipline at times and a sense of social responsibility contiguous with that of the church. Jean implies that she attended the village school, though later she was probably sent away to school as her older sister was.

> The village school was lively and full, the only education for every child up to the age of fourteen. There was the head teacher, the infant teacher, and a monitor. The head teacher was very strict and used the cane for special offences, but she loved the children and discipline was excellent. The needlework she taught to the older girls was a wonder to behold .... We children greatly respected this lady, and sometimes went to tea with her and her old father who she lived with.

But there was for Jean a shadow over this world of education, for the infant teacher was not so well loved by her. This lady was also the Sunday school teacher and made Jean feel inferior because she was not the most able reader of the biblical texts, as the manuscript records. Her social position did not protect this child of the rectory, nor lessen her vulnerability.

War

Though, as recorded by Kerry (2005), the Blathwayts provided some distinguished soldiers even in the second World War, the horror and intensity of war seems to have passed by Jean. As at the time of writing she was a woman of about thirty years of age this seems odd. One can only speculate whether it was the remoteness of the rectory, or the remoteness of the writer from the world's realities, that seemed to block out this experience. It is introduced only as a means to tell a couple of tales about the gardener, Mr Lyon, a key figure in her childhood memories. One of these tales is reproduced here:

> By nature Mr Lyon was inclined to a nervous disposition, a trait which was passed down to one of his sons. This lad, being misplaced in the gunners during the second World War, was reputed to have fallen over every time the big guns went off. Quite rightly, he was demobbed, and went to work as general *factotem* in a boys' prep school where everyone loved him. Mr Lyon himself survived the first World War, serving with the Lincolns.

Relations with retainers and the locus of authority

So finally, we come to a major figure in the upkeep of the rectory, and in the up-bringing and even the education of the Blathwayt children, Mr Lyon, the gardener.

> If nanny was guardian of our nursery then Mr Lyon was certainly the keeper of our garden hours. He had been head gardener at the Hall in a little Lincolnshire village where my parents first set up home together, working up to that exalted position from gardener's boy. But when they moved to Dorset he very soon followed with his family, to become the rectory gardener, and stay with us until he retired.

There are plenty of accounts about servant life at this period, its hardships and the complicated socially stratified relationships between the servants themselves (Benson, 1998, p 24). I have been able to discover none with such explicit accounts of the relationship between children and any domestic employee other than the nanny herself. The senior gardener was, according to Kightly (1984, p. 161) relatively well paid compared with agricultural labourers, though this may have been more true in larger households and estates than for a rectory gardener. But Mr Lyon looms large in these fragments of manuscript.

> To my parents he was Tom. To us children, who held all adults in respect, he was always Mr Lyon. But that respect was much more than

deferential esteem. Mr Lyon was an integral part of our growing up, the joiner-in of marvellous games, the encourager of our every effort, and we loved him dearly. When we were turned loose in the garden our very first call was, nearly always, 'Mr Lyon, where are you?'

This respect between master and servant was becoming more the norm by the 1920s (Horn, 2002, p. 142), but servants and their employers, even their children, did not mix socially, as in the story of the maid who was sacked for leading an employer's child to see her own house while she was taking him for a walk (Horn, 2002, p. 147). So Mr Lyon's relationship with the children, and theirs with him, was distinctive.

> The kindness and friendship of Mr Lyon greatly enhanced the joy of our garden freedom. He was so enthusiastic about our little discoveries and achievements, and he was always willing to look and listen. To run over the flower beds or vegetable patches was obviously frowned upon, 'keep off the garden' was the way he put it, and if we unintentionally disobeyed him in the heat of some game we would quite rightly be reprimanded. But I only remember him being really angry once.

The relationship endured, at least to a degree, for Jean records visiting him, at his daughter's home in Lincolnshire long after he had retired, and his joy at the meeting.

Summary

In reading current literature about religion in the countryside one is left with a sense that everything has changed and nothing has changed. The Arthur Rank Centre's (2006) report surveys the role of parishioners in today's crises, foot-and-mouth disease, funding the rural church and so on, in the language and milieu of a government White Paper. More user-friendly is the document *Seeds in Holy Ground* (Hopkinson, 2005). Thus, after the presentation of the bones of the problem (9,639 places of worship, 19.5% of the population as rural dwellers) there are practical involvements exemplified by the Rural Strategy Group of General Synod. The Church of England's National Rural Officer is optimistic:

> My hope is that rural churches will read *Seeds in Holy Ground*, and that they'll enjoy forming a small group to study it ... and out of working through it they'll decide to do something new for mission in their community – something that will make a difference to that community and to themselves.

Here, and in Gaze (2006), are the coffee mornings, the breakfast clubs and the schemes to take over local post offices, the farmers' markets and suggestions to use school buildings after hours to organize café-style events to reach out to rural communities: community service and support not much different in kind, only in context, from the world of Jean Blathwayt's manuscript.

Jean's manuscript has, we have seen, an immediacy, a realism, a self-effacing honesty about life in Melbury St Osmund parish in the 1920s. What makes it important in an historical context is its very spontaneity, unselfconsciousness and parochialism and, as Mink (1978, p. 148) points out, the significance of past occurrences is best understood as they are placed in 'the ensemble of interrelationships' that can be grasped through the narrative form. Stylistically, the manuscript is autobiographical, but it is strangely out of kilter with the tenor of both religious and secular literature of the time. According to Brown (2001) the literature by and of women of the era was more typically either of an overtly evangelical and missionary nature, or was developing a secular brashness based on women's new-found employment opportunities. Here, there are threads of continuity with our own times, and there are discontinuities brought about by advances in travel, technology, social change and employment patterns.

Jean's world as she presents it is a romantic world, in the true sense of the word. Yet the years covered by her narrative saw a shift of workers away from the land – land being returned to grazing – while jobs in urban environments were also diminishing. More and more people were buying houses in the country or at least in the rural fringe, but they were middle class buyers with no roots in the soil. The Communist Party of Great Britain was set up in 1920, and the General Strike occurred in 1926. Nevertheless, full democracy was finally achieved in England by 1928, even if Wall Street crashed the following year. This was the moment when T.S. Eliot (1968) was writing of the churches the overtly critical lines in *The Hippopotamus*.

> I saw the 'potamus take wing
> Ascending from the damp savannas,
> And quiring angels round him sing
> The praise of God, in loud hosannas ....
>
> He shall be washed as white as snow,
> By all the martyr'd virgins kist,
> While the True Church remains below
> Wrapt in the old miasmal mist.

Strong (2000, p. 607) says of the period that these were decades 'of industrial turmoil and class confrontation on such a scale that it is surprising that revolution did not actually take place'. Yet Jean's 'nostalgic' view of the world was not hers alone; the authors of Arthur Mee's (1936, p. 8) *King's England* books about our heritage and landscape, were patting themselves on the back that they had 'made up their minds to put down nothing bad ... but to be recording angels'.

As has been shown, even in the Church's current deliberations the old dichotomies still exist, these tensions between present reality and romantic past. Jean's work remains, perhaps for this reason, a window into history through which one can gaze with empathy and with a sharpened appreciation of life in another era. Through this window it is possible to discern a theory of the rural church if not a rural theology. The latter suggests a rational and structured view about the relationship between God and the rural community. Jean's manuscript is shot through with images of the first: of pastoral people and pastoral activities. In this she echoes the New Testament concerns, well documented over the years in writers from Johns (1887) to Strange (2006), with wildlife, crops, animals and the daily round of life in the countryside. Her work is predicated on a social gospel too, with the society being that of a rural community. It would be for readers of the whole of Jean's text to decide for themselves whether this theory of the rural church is one strongly rooted in faith: the question here would be whether her silence means faith is taken for granted or simply ignored.

Astley (2002) would have us accept that 'ordinary theology' is discernible in the talk of ordinary people about their religion, and Jean does this in her manuscript. Certainly there is in the manuscript a theology of *caritas* and a theology of *communitas*, and these are significant concepts. There is also on Jean's part an acceptance of the sacraments as part of the Christian life, and of worship as both duty and pleasure. Also present is an Old Testament sense of God as the source of Creation, and of the value of the natural world, a position doubtless shared within the Blathwayt family. There can be little doubt that the Revd Blathwayt himself, with his keen interest in ornithology, was one of the forerunners of what Armstrong (Astley, 2002, p. 180) labels ecotheology; the movement that demands the stewardship of the natural world and its conservation as a duty laid down at Creation, although modern thought questions the simplicity of that view (for example, Russell, 2004).

Overall, then, in the decades that have passed since Jean Blathwayt wrote, it cannot be said that much has altered in the nature of these debates, even though the contexts may have changed.

References

Armstrong, R. (2000). *The English parson-naturalist.* Leominster: Gracewing.

Arthur Rank Centre. (2006). Faith in rural communities: Contributions of social capital to community vibrancy. Accessed 21 November 2006: www. arthurrank-centre.org.uk.

Astley, J. (2002). *Ordinary theology: Looking, listening and learning in theology.* Aldershot: Ashgate.

Barr, L. J. T. (2006). Personal communication, 15 May.

Benson, J. (1998). *The working class in Britain 1850–1939* (third edition). Harlow: Longman.

Blathwayt, F. L. (1907). *I and my Father are one: A sermon preached by the Revd F. L. Blathwayt.* Lincoln: printed with his permission by the vicar and a few friends, 9 November.

Board of Mission. (2001). *Renewing faith in the countryside* (GS1418). London: General Synod.

Brown, C. G. (2001). *The death of Christian Britain.* London: Routledge.

Chadwick, O. (1968). *Edward King Bishop of Lincoln 1885–1910* (second series, number 4). Lincoln: Lincoln Minster Pamphlets.

Craig, C. (2005). Psychological type preference of rural churchgoers. *Rural Theology* 3(2), 123–131.

Doddington School Log. Accessed in the Lincolnshire Archive Office.

Dyrham History Society. (2005). Personal communication, 22 October.

Eliot, T. S. (1968). *Collected poems 1909–1935.* London: Faber and Faber.

Francis, L. J., Smith, G., & Robbins, M. (2004). Do introverted clergy prefer rural ministry? *Rural Theology, 2,* 127–134.

Gaze, S. (2006). *Mission-shaped and rural: Growing churches in the countryside.* London: Church House Publishing.

Harris, J. (1993). Society and the state in twentieth-century Britain. In F. M. L. Thompson (Ed.), *The Cambridge social history of Britain 1750–1950: Social agencies and institutions* (volume 3) (pp. 63–118). Cambridge: Cambridge University Press.

Hopkinson, J. (2005). *Seeds in Holy Ground: A workbook for churches.* Stoneleigh Park: Acora Publishing.

Horn, P. (2002). *Life below stairs in the twentieth century.* Gloucester: Sutton Publishers.

Johns, C. (1887). *Bird life of the Bible.* London: Longmans Green.

Kerry, T. (2005). *Of Roseates and Rectories.* Lincoln: PintailTKC.

Kerry, T. (2006a). Blathwayt's birds: The contribution of a Lincolnshire parson-naturalist. *Lapwings, 121,* 12–13.

Kerry, T. (2006b). A day's birding in Kent: In 1924. *Kent Life,* November.

Kerry, T. (2006c). Re-assessing a former president: The Revd Francis Linley Blathwayt. *The Lincolnshire Naturalist: transactions of the Lincolnshire Naturalists' Union for 2005*, 148–152.

Kerry, T. (2006d). *Unpublished Inventory of Blathwayt Papers.* Lincoln: TKConsultancy.

Kerry, T. (2007). Birding with Blathwayt in Somerset. *Exmoor Country Magazine, 40*, 30–32.

Kightly, C. (1984). *Country voices: Life and lore in farm and village.* London: Thames and Hudson.

Littler, K., & Francis, L. J. (2005). Ideas of the holy: The ordinary theology of visitors to rural churches. *Rural Theology, 3*, 49–54.

Lowerson, J. (1992). The mystical geography of the English. In B. Short (Ed.), *The English rural community: Image and analysis* (pp. 152–174). Cambridge: Cambridge University Press.

Mee, A. (1936). *Enchanted land.* London: Hodder and Stoughton.

Mink, L. (1978). Narrative form as a cognitive construct. In R. Canary and H. Zozicki (Eds.), *Literary form and historical understanding* (pp. 129–149). Wisconsin: University of Wisconsin.

Morgan, D. (1969). The social and educational background of Anglican bishops. *British Journal of Sociology, 20*, 295–310.

Morgan, K. O. (Ed.). (1984). *The Oxford illustrated history of Britain.* Oxford: Oxford University Press.

Obelkevich, J. (1993). Religion. In F. M. L. Thompson (Ed.), *The Cambridge social history of Britain 1750–1950: Social agencies and institutions* (volume 3) (pp. 311–356). Cambridge: Cambridge University Press.

Poole, C. (2005). Personal communication, 22 June.

Pugh, M. (2001). *The Pankhursts.* London: Penguin.

Russell, A. (2004). The priesthood of creation: The Hulsean Sermon 2004. *Rural Theology, 2*, 119–125.

Scharf, B. (1970). *The sociological study of religion.* London: Hutchinson University Library.

Strange, W. (2006). The invisible countryside of the New Testament. *Rural Theology, 4*, 75–84.

Strong, R. (2000). *The Spirit of Britain.* London: Pimlico.

Walker, D. (2006). Belonging to rural church and society: Theological and sociological perspectives. *Rural Theology, 4*, 85–97.

Part 5

LISTENING TO VISITORS

Chapter 15

I WAS GLAD: LISTENING TO VISITORS TO COUNTRY CHURCHES

Keith Littler, Leslie J. Francis and Jeremy Martineau[*]

Abstract – A major national visitors' survey asked visitors and tourists to rural churches to rate on a five-point scale how much they liked to find certain features when they visit churches. Of the 12,757 individuals who completed the rating scales, 765 took the additional effort to add further personal comment. The qualitative data arising from these personal comments have not previously been evaluated. The present analysis of these data provides a valuable guide to visitors' views about the provisions churches should make for visitors and tourists.

Introduction

Writing in the introduction to the Church in Wales report, *Rural Wales Consultative Document*, Robin Morrison (2003) recognizes the need to reconstruct the future of our rural communities. He goes on to ask questions about the role, to this end, of all relevant agencies, including that of local churches. 'How will the churches have to change', he asks, 'in order to engage in new ways?' The report concludes with wide-ranging

[*] The Revd Dr Keith Littler is Research Fellow at St Mary's Centre, Wales. *Address for correspondence:* Myrtle Hill Cottage, Broadway, Laugharne, Carmarthenshire, SA33 4NS. E-mail: ktlittler@btinternet.com

The Revd Canon Professor Leslie J. Francis is Professor of Religions and Education at the Warwick Religions and Education Research Unit. *Address for correspondence:* Warwick Religions and Education Research Unit, Institute of Education, The University of Warwick, Coventry, CV4 7AL.
E-mail: leslie.francis@warwick.ac.uk

The Revd Canon Jeremy Martineau OBE is Director of the Centre for Studies in Rural Ministry. *Address for correspondence:* 11 New Hill Villas, Goodwick, Pembrokeshire, SA64 0DT. E-mail: jeremy.m@talktalk.net ideas and proposals among which are key recommendations concerning local churches. Included among these recommendations is the statement that churches should open their doors and let the world rediscover their true role. The report goes on to insist that many local churches need a massive image make-over, and that clergy need to be more people friendly, welcoming, proactive, open, and involved.

This notion of churches needing an image make-over is taken up by others. Indeed, given a backcloth of controversial trends in what some see as challenges to the orthodoxy of the Anglican Church, coupled with financial difficulties and falling attendance, it is perhaps not surprising to find that there is a trend among theological writers to see major changes in the way the Anglican Church should present itself. Ward (2003) urges a move away from the traditional idea of the local church as a gathering of people meeting in one place and to become a more dynamic series of relationships. Thwaites (2003) similarly advises that it is time for the churches to move beyond their present focus on the congregation and place greater emphasis on integration into the community. Hybels (2003) presents a notion of the local church as being so important that he describes it as the hope of the world and calls for a more creative and courageous leadership.

These works are interesting and innovative, and seek new ways for churches. They leave open, however, the question of what people actually expect or want to find in a local church in the twenty-first century. Hobson (2003) gives some insight into this issue by reporting visits to several churches in his locality, to see which would best suit his needs. He was, therefore, attending services rather than visiting empty buildings, but was clearly much influenced by general appearances and first impressions. He concludes that he was unimpressed by the extremes which he witnessed, and he gave up the search. His critical concern is responded to by Dennen (2003) who ventures to advise about what the twenty-first century religious consumer wants, likes and needs from their church: worship of a decent quality, significant relationships and hospitality. Whether, however, Dennen's criteria are equally true for every worshipper who is shopping around or casually visiting a church as a tourist or visitor, is another matter. Hobson (2003) was seeking somewhere to worship. Many churches find that more people come to church as visitors rather than as worshippers and the importance of responding to the needs of the casual visitor or tourist is being increasingly recognized. Rosemary Watts, church tourism officer for the Lincoln diocese, clearly agrees and is credited with the comment that tourism is, 'absolutely embodied in what the church is about. It is not a tack-on' (Adams, 2003). Durstan (2003) reminds us that 'visiting churches and cathedrals is now a significant tourist pastime'.

Visitors' views

Tourism is, then, clearly important, as also is the first impression a church gives to the casual visitor, and churches have a part to play in encouraging and supporting the tourist industry. If, however, churches are really to play a part in encouraging and supporting tourism, then there is substantial room for change in the image portrayed by the church. Furthermore, in order to produce a change in the image portrayed by the church, the church must listen to what visitors and tourists are saying.

Francis and Martineau (2001) have produced a research report on visitors' reactions to the rural church, designed specifically to help rural churches reflect on their work among visitors and tourists, both in the church and in the wider community. In addition to the twenty-two issues discussed in detail, the authors stress the importance of churches being open and welcoming. They refer to earlier research (Countryside Commission, 1995) which found that over 40% of the rural churches are unlocked during the day time and that some are unlocked all the time because the keys are long since lost. The report by the Countryside Commission (1995) claimed that many have a key-holder notice which, in many places, is a system so full of hazards that it is practically worthless. Key-holders worry about whether they should hand keys over to a stranger or whether they should go with a visitor to the church, the key-holders themselves often feeling vulnerable. Francis and Martineau's (2001) statistics are drawn from a national visitors' survey, which was a response to a recognition of the growing importance of tourism and the opportunity that is provided for churches to renew the reputation for which they were in earlier centuries renowned: hospitality to visitors and pilgrims.

Method

A national visitors' survey asked visitors and tourists to rural churches to rate on a five point scale how much they like to find certain features when they visit churches. The features ranged from 'somewhere quiet to pray' to 'information about things to do in the area'. Churches in membership of the National Church Tourism Group (now Church Tourism Association) were invited to take part in the survey. Survey forms, a poster advertising the presence of survey forms and a box into which completed forms were to be put were sent to the 163 churches that responded. There was no assumption that these churches would have anyone on duty to promote the survey, although some did so. The survey is therefore of visitors who chose to complete a form and is not a survey of all visitors to these churches. The survey took place during the months of June, July and August 1999.

The questionnaire included a space for further comment, thereby allowing the opportunity for both quantitative and qualitative data to be collected. Of the 12,757 questionnaires completed and returned, 765 respondents took the additional trouble of making further comments. The quantitative data has been analysed and the resulting discussion is presented elsewhere (Francis and Martineau, 2001). What has not been discussed, however, are the respondents' further comments. A qualitative analysis of these comments is presented below.

Results and discussion

It was to be expected that not every respondent would make a further personal comment. In practice the number who did so was quite small. Of the 765 respondents who did make a further comment, a number made generalized comments such as 'nice church', or 'interesting', or 'thank you'. These have been excluded from the analysis. A small number of respondents commented in a very personal and non-relevant way. These have also been excluded. In some cases the questionnaire was completed after attendance at a service in church, but very few comments were made about the liturgy or worship. These comments are also excluded. This left a total of 518 comments, the majority of which it was possible to categorize under seven headings. These headings and the proportion of the total comments under each heading are as follows: History of the church and the locality (34%); Peaceful atmosphere, opportunity for prayer and spiritually uplifting (30%); Praise for the church being open (11%); Critical of facilities and lack of welcome (11%); Comments on the condition of the church and the churchyard (9%); Praise for the availability of a gift shop (3%); Family research (1%). Each of these seven categories will be discussed in turn.

History of the church and the locality

A third of all visitors and tourists who passed comment (34%), made reference to the history of the church and its artefacts or to the history of the locality. It would seem that for many visitors the building and its historic contents were seen more as a museum than a place of worship. There is no doubt that the architecture, stained glass windows, murals, etc., are seen as an important part of the national heritage, separate and distinct from the prime purpose of the church as a place of worship. Indeed, such terms as 'a good church' and 'very interesting' clearly equated in the minds of many tourists with 'good architecture' and 'interesting artefacts' and the building was viewed as somewhere to visit because its features were deemed to be of national importance. It was not possible to separate comments on the history of the church from comments on the history of the locality, since visitors and tourists generally referred to the church and the locality in a single context. Haworth Church, for example, was obviously a focal point of attraction to visitors because of its association with the village of Haworth and the former inhabitants of the vicarage.

Peaceful atmosphere

Given the likelihood of overstatement in the previous category, it is especially noteworthy that 30% of those visitors and tourists who included a further comment on the questionnaire, recorded their appreciation of a peaceful atmosphere, opportunity for prayer and feelings of being spiritually uplifted. It was clear from the further comments made by many people that they placed importance on being able to withdraw, albeit briefly, from the world and find a place of peace and tranquility. Some of those visitors and tourists who commented in this way had attended a service in the church and this may have influenced them in finding peace and prayerfulness in the church. Most, however, had not attended a service, and were referring very specifically to a sense of peace in the general atmosphere of the church building. This was often expressed by the visitor wishing to say 'thank you' for this opportunity to escape from the pressures of the world. For some visitors it was an opportunity for prayerful silence, while for other visitors it was an experience of tranquility and calm, which they found spiritually uplifting and fortifying.

Praise for the church being open

More than one in ten of all visitors and tourists whose further comments were recorded on the questionnaire, made direct reference to the fact that they found the church open and how much they applauded this.

In all cases these comments were either a simple statement of gratitude that they had been able to gain access to the church or a sentence or two of praise for those responsible, coupled with criticism that many other churches they had visited elsewhere were found to be closed.

Critical of facilities and lack of welcome

While it is noteworthy that 11% of visitors and tourists who commented expressed gratitude and praise for the church being open, it does not follow that all who gained access necessarily discovered the church's true role and neither were they necessarily pleased with what they found. Conditioned, perhaps, by increasingly high expectations of service and comfort in public places, 11% of those visitors and tourists who commented were disappointed by the churches' lack of provisions. Some were critical of the lack of toilets, others criticized the absence of a restaurant, inadequate heating, lack of guide books, absence of back-ground music, or inadequate signposting, while many regretted the non-availability of a person to welcome them at the door and to show them round. While many of these expressions are unrealistic, when more than a tenth of tourists' and visitors' personal comments are critical of the facilities that churches offer, then churches must be prepared to consider whether their facilities really are adequate in the twenty-first century.

Comments on the condition of the church and churchyard

Nearly one in ten of the comments (9%) related to the condition of the church and churchyard and most of these comments were either complimentary or at least understanding of the problems involved in maintaining old buildings. Although a small number of people commented critically, the greater majority were praiseworthy of the condition of the church and of the upkeep of the churchyard. Those who did not give outright praise nevertheless understood the difficulties of maintaining an ancient building and expressed empathy with those who strove to raise money to carry out repairs and renovations. A common expression designed to show that the work of those caring for the church had been noted was the phrase, 'the church appears to be loved'.

Praise for the availability of a gift shop

Although the figure is quite small at 3%, it is perhaps a little surprising that so many tourists and visitors to churches made comment on the lack of availability of a gift shop. This may, of course, simply reflect a common inclination of tourists to acquire a souvenir of their visit, but it may also indicate a desire to take away and retain, and perhaps share with others, something of a desirable experience.

Family research

Very few visitors (1%) made mention of family research being an aspect of their visit. This may reflect the increased availability of alternative methods for carrying out family research or simply that most tourists and visitors who commented on the questionnaire in this survey were visiting churches with no particular historic connection to their ancestry. Either way, as important as churches may have been for family research in the past, comments made by visitors and tourists in this survey suggest that this was a key factor for but very few people.

Conclusion

Any analysis of a section of a questionnaire left open for further comment will be subjective. Even so, the number of comments showing interest in the history of the church and its immediate locality (34%), and the number of comments on the peaceful atmosphere, opportunity for prayer and sense of being spiritually uplifted (30%) suggest that genuine visitor preferences are being expressed. If this is so, then churches do well to listen to what visitors are saying. While criticism of churches' lack of facilities may seem unrealistic, such criticism is made by too many visitors and tourists to be ignored. Tourism is important and churches have a part to play in welcoming tourists and visitors, as well as those who migrate from one parish to another and need to shop around for a church to attend. Our church buildings are national treasures and it is right that we respond to visitors' interest in them. It is also right that we listen to what visitors say to the churches and it seems that what they say most clearly and repeatedly is that they wish to find the church open and to be able to avail themselves of a few minutes for quiet peaceful meditation, when they can come close to God or simply escape from a busy world. Bernard Gribbin (2003) reminds us that church buildings are an extravagant act of devotion, bringing to mind Mary Magdalene and the precious ointment. They can be described as reflections of God's superabundance in creation, or even of the complexity, beauty and order of God's nature. They are a means of lifting our spirits into God's presence. First, however, the visitor and tourist must step inside and whatever it is that they are seeking, unless the church is open and welcoming, they will not find it and will stay away.

References

Adams, S. (2003). Get on the tourist map. *Church Times, 7327,* 8 August, p. 16.

Countryside Commission. (1995). *Sustainable rural tourism: Opportunities for local action.* Cheltenham: Countryside Agency.

Dennen, L. (2003). Comment on Hobson makes his choice. *Church Times, 7315,* 16 May, p. 19.

Durston, D. (2003). Thoughts that lie too deep for tears. *Church Times, 7327,* 8 August, p. 16.

Francis, L. J., & Martineau, J. (2001). *Rural visitors: A parish workbook for welcoming visitors in the country church.* Stoneleigh Park: Acora Publishing.

Gribbin, B. (2003). Don't duck the religious bit. *Church Times, 7327,* 8 August, p. 14.

Hobson, T. (2003). Hobson makes his choice. *Church Times, 7315,* 16 May, p. 18.

Hybels, B. (2003). *Courageous leadership.* Grand Rapids, Michigan: Zonderman.

Morrison, R. (2003). *Introduction: Looking to the future – rural communities, economic and social change.* A report by the Department for Church and Society. Cardiff: Church in Wales.

Thwaites, J. (Ed.). (2003). *The church beyond the congregation: The strategic role of the church in the postmodern era.* Carlisle: Paternoster Press.

Ward, P. (2003). *Liquid church.* Carlisle: Paternoster Press.

Chapter 16

SACRED PLACE AND PILGRIMAGE: MODERN VISITORS TO THE SHRINE OF ST MELANGELL

*Michael Keulemans and Lewis Burton**

Abstract — The two concepts of sacred place and pilgrimage are explored in relation to the shrine of St Melangell at Pennant Melangell in Mid Wales. An empirical study was mounted during the first three months of 2004 when visitors to the shrine were presented with a questionnaire to ascertain their reactions to sacred place and pilgrimage stimulated by their visit. Analyses of resulting data show that many visitors today are aware of sacred place and can be described as being on pilgrimage. Data also show possibilities for energizing small local rural churches which at the present time might be in danger of redundancy.

Introduction

Jones (2002) identifies nine functioning centres of modern pilgrimage in Wales of which four are particularly popular. The principal one is that of David, the nation's patron saint, located in the West Wales cathedral town that bears his name. Winifred's shrine at Holywell on the Dee Estuary in North Wales, has the longest history of continuous pilgrimage and enjoys increasing popularity today. In a more remote location off the Lleyn Peninsula is Bardsey Island, the shrine of Cadfan, the fifth century Breton saint. The fourth is the shrine of Melangell, set in a valley deep within the Berwyn mountains of Mid Wales.

* The Revd Dr Michael Keulemans served as chaplain of Liverpool Nautical Sixth Form. *Address for correspondence*: The Poplars, Porth y Waen, Oswestry, SY10 8LR. E-mail: roseandmike@tiscali.co.uk

The Revd Dr Lewis Burton, a retired Methodist minister, is Honorary Research Fellow in the St Mary's Centre, Wales. *Address for correspondence*: 94 Sun Street, Haworth, Keighley, BD22 8AH. E-mail: lewisburton@blueyonder.co.uk

All four shrines are dedicated to saints with their own history and mythology. The associations of the locality with the saint, together with the holiness and aura attached to the saint's life, have created a sacred place, a particular geographical locus where the saint can be remembered and venerated and where the pilgrim may still find personal benefit today through the atmosphere and spiritual influences encountered in that place. Allchin (1991, p. 91) says of the sacred place that it marks 'the meeting of time and eternity in the life and utterance of a particular human being [and] creates the fabric of human history'. Carmichael, Herbert, Reeves and Schenke (1994, p. 3) say of a sacred place that 'it carries with it a whole set of rules and behaviour in relation to it, and implies a set of beliefs to do with the non-empirical world', while Lane (1988) considers the sacred place 'an ordinary place rendered extraordinary'.

St Melangell's shrine

The shrine of St Melangell at Pennant Melangell fits very well into these descriptions and its sense of holiness is undoubtedly enhanced by its remoteness and inaccessibility. The church is sited near the head of a deep glacial valley, nestling beneath the open moorland tops of the Berwyn mountains, which rise to nearly 2,000 feet. Just beyond the churchyard wall the rapidly flowing Nant Ewyn comes down to join the Tanat not long after it has plunged from the mountain summit in a mighty waterfall. Opposite the church are the towering crags of the Gwely Melangell, while just up the Ewyn is a sacred well long reputed to possess healing properties. The churchyard itself is positioned on a classically well-drained site, precisely where the flat valley bottom begins to rise. Modern excavations by Britnell (1994) have uncovered evidence of Bronze Age burial pyres and a twelfth century construction of a stone church and shrine immediately above them (Radford and Hemp, 1959; Heaton and Britnell, 1994).

The legend which originally brought pilgrims to the site is displayed in the frieze of Pennant's remarkable fifteenth-century rood screen and in a brief *Life of Melangell* (Cunliffe, 1992), which, in its present form, probably also dates from the late-fifteenth century. The original text of this *Historia Divae Monacellae* is no longer extant, but five manuscripts and one early printed transcript provide evidence of its original content (Price, 1994). The basis of the story revolves around the Prince of Powys hunting on horseback in the valley with his dogs and chasing a hare into a bramble bush, behind which was a holy virgin engaged in prayer. The prince, impressed by the woman's sanctity and *sang-froid*, gifted the valley to her and her holy companions as 'a perpetual sanctuary, asylum or most sure refuge of the wretched' (Price, 1994, p. 40).

Records of pilgrimage to the shrine in the Middle Ages are sketchy, which is hardly surprising considering its tiny scale and its remote and inaccessible location, but Chapman (1994) quotes the will of Sir Morgan Herbert of 1526, buried at Ribbesford near Kidderminster, which determines that his servant should go on pilgrimage on his behalf to six Welsh shrines, one of which was to be Melangell's. The shrine must have attracted a good number of pilgrims as it amassed the not insubstantial votive offerings of £2.16s.8d in 1535. The saint's legend was elaborated over the years and cherished by the locals, since in such a barren place pilgrims must have been a help to the local economy; but records do not indicate visitor numbers.

By the 1980s the church of Pennant Melangell had slipped into disrepair and was in danger of demolition. In the meantime, the Revd Paul Davies, incumbent of Meifod, not far away, faced a personal crisis when his wife Evelyn was diagnosed with cancer. After recovering from major surgery she discovered that other people facing the same crisis came to see her and her husband for emotional and practical help. Paul decided to purchase a cottage alongside the churchyard in 1986 and in due course the Bishop of St Asaph licensed him to look after the church on a voluntary basis. Under his leadership the church was totally repaired, the shrine reassembled and the cottage adapted to create a Cancer Help Centre. In 1994 Paul himself succumbed to cancer, but Evelyn pressed on regardless, developing the healing, counselling and pilgrimage ministry of both the church and the centre. In 2000 Evelyn left Pennant Melangell. After a lull in the counselling work, Linda Mary Edwards arrived in 2003. Here she has expanded the scope of her personal ministry in line with her own qualifications and mental health experience.

Questions about pilgrimage

Pilgrimage might seem a rather outmoded concept to many today, but there is no doubting its growing popularity. The number of people who crowd to Lourdes and other notable Roman Catholic shrines, or those from different traditions who go to Walsingham, Iona, Lindisfarne, or even Epworth may be counted as modern pilgrims. Can we also count as pilgrims those who visit the cathedrals of England and gaze upon the tomb of some saint while on their holiday? How deep is their religious interest, their quest for blessing, or their search for something of spiritual worth? Or are these visitors merely curious tourists, seeking an interesting diversion to fill leisure time? The shrine of St Melangell at Pennant provides a test site where some of these questions can be answered. It is a sacred place dedicated to a Celtic saint and in recent years there has been a huge resurgence of interest in Celtic Christianity both from the institutional Church and from new thinkers inside and outside its boundaries (Bradley, 1999, 2003). In this changed environment, the shrine of St Melangell has found a new purpose and function in alternative medicine.

This study seeks to explore the motivations of modern pilgrims to the shrine at Pennant Melangell in an effort to offer some enlightenment to the Church at large on how to receive visitors, not only to the shrines of saints, or to great cathedrals, but also to other much humbler churches scattered around the remoter countryside of Britain.

Method

The period in which research data were collected commenced on New Year's Day, 2004 and ended on Easter Monday, 2004. The researcher was present on the site one whole day at the beginning of this period and one whole day at the end, when he asked interviewees to complete a questionnaire which he presented to them in person. During those two days he was available to answer questions about the research and to record additional comments. During the intervening months, a stack of questionnaires and stamped addressed envelopes were left prominently displayed in the church porch under a large notice explaining the project, with the request that completed questionnaires should be returned to the researcher's home address. Although data were collected in the depths of winter, there was an advantage in that the number of visitors was much lighter and more dispersed than would have been the case in the summer months, thus allowing people time to participate in far less pressured circumstances.

There were sixteen questions. The first five sought personal information: sex, age, distance travelled from home to Pennant, employment status and occupation. Question six asked for the frequency of the respondent's attendance at church. The next three questions sought details regarding the visit: was it planned or spontaneous, had they visited previously, and using a Likert scale to assess reactions to six possible reasons, how did they assess the strength of the motivations which prompted them to make the visit? The next two questions aimed to elicit responses to their experiences from the visit. The first of these asked, from a list of eleven possibilities, what they had been moved to do while they were in the church. Then, using a Likert scale to ascertain the strength of their reaction to twelve different responses, they were asked to rate the spiritual impact which the visit had made upon them. Two questions followed, again using a Likert scale, to assess whether the visit had made a positive or negative effect on their attitude toward the Christian faith and the institutional Church. Finally, there was a question asking whether respondents knew of Ann Griffiths, a notable young mystic and hymn-writer who lived and died in the late-eighteenth century in a village only a few miles from Pennant. As she presented a reasonable modern counterpart to St Melangell, it was thought worthwhile asking a second question: would respondents visit her grave or had they already done so? A final, open-ended question offered plenty of blank space for other observations or comments.

Results

The total number of responses collected during the fifteen-week period was 107, although some did not complete all sections. Of the total respondents, 43% were male and 57% were female; 7% were under fifteen, 2% were aged between sixteen and twenty-five, 10% were in their twenties and thirties, 49% were in their forties and fifties, 26% were in their sixties and 6% were 70 or over; 72% of visitors had travelled over 30 miles to be there, with 17% travelling less than 10 miles and 11% between 10 and 30 miles. Only 47 of the 107 visitors were willing to divulge their home town or district, but of these 36% came from within Wales, 29% from Central England, 11% from North West England, 1 each from London and Scotland and 3 from overseas. Among those from England and Wales it was clear that accessibility by main road played a major part.

Regarding employment status, 41% were in full-time work, 14% in part-time work, 31% were retired, 7% described themselves as housewives or carers, and 7% did not respond to this question; 57% were from the professional classes, 26% described themselves as semi-professional, 10% described themselves as skilled or semi-skilled manual workers, and 7% did not respond to this question. Visitors to Pennant, therefore, did not reflect the social composition of the general population, but were more typical of those today who have the money and leisure time to indulge in tourist activity. This hints at the fact that Pennant and its shrine have some special attraction which draws visitors to them rather than to other more accessible and more popular tourist venues.

In the second group of questions, 42% were weekly churchgoers and another 20% attended once a month. Only 17% were non-churchgoers, but another 20% put themselves in the once a year category, women appearing in greater proportion here. The majority, 70%, had planned to come to Pennant and were therefore not casual visitors, 41% were on their second to fifth visit and 19% had visited six or more times, 40% were on their first visit. Of those who had travelled the furthest, more than 30 miles, one third were on the second to fifth visit and 13% in the six plus visit category. This confirms a tendency for repeat visits, as might be expected of people who were especially attracted to the saint, her shrine or its location, though a few regulars stated that they came to visit family graves in the churchyard. Some of these deceased relatives had themselves been regular visitors from afar and requested burial in the churchyard, thereby confirming a tendency toward modern pilgrimage and an appreciation of the site as a sacred place, and incidentally continuing a pattern of pilgrim burials at Pennant known to have started during the Middle Ages.

When respondents were asked why they had come to Pennant, 78% expressed a spiritual motive, with women scoring marginally higher than men; 65% expressed an historical interest, and 64% an archaeological interest, while architectural interest came last with 30%. When these proportions were scored against church attendance, it became clear that for churchgoers the spiritual motivation was overwhelming, while for non-churchgoers, though the spiritual motive was by no means absent, the country setting and the historical interest were of more importance.

Of the spiritual activities which might engage people while they were within the church building, silent prayer gained a 78% response, lighting a candle 60% and meditation 57%, with smaller proportions praying at the shrine, praying generally, making a written prayer request or purchasing a prayer card. The focus upon prayer is major and noteworthy. Over half (54%) explored Melangell's story and 51% purchased a souvenir. In terms of spiritual impact, 76% claimed they were helped toward a sense of peace; 72% felt that they wanted to pray; 69% were prompted to think about God; and 57% were prompted to think about the meaning of life, the same proportion professing a sense of Melangell's presence, but slightly more feeling some undefined spiritual presence. Interestingly, 16% felt that God had spoken to them.

Overall, 56% of the respondents reported a quickening of their interest in the Christian faith and 45% in the Church, but proportions among non-churchgoers were less, at 34% and 32% respectively. Considering this from a negative viewpoint, only 8% of churchgoers reported that they were more dubious about their faith and about the institutional Church, whereas the proportions of non-churchgoers who responded negatively rose to 15% and 24% respectively. Further analysis of the data revealed that 85% of churchgoers had spiritual motives for their visit, but so did 51% of the non-churchgoers. Of the most overtly 'Christian' activities reported by respondents while they were in the church, churchgoers scored 62% against the non-churchgoers' 38%. Taken together, these statistics are impressive evidence of spiritual potential among non-churchgoers as well as among regular worshippers.

As for knowledge of Ann Griffiths, the local mystic and hymn-writer, 78% had never heard of her and of those who had, all were Welsh. Nonetheless, half the sample said that they had already visited her grave or would now do so. This response clearly demonstrated the potential for encouraging visits to other locations connected with equally worthy but lesser known Christian personalities.

Those who completed their questionnaires by interview in the car park and those who returned them by post had ample opportunity to make their own extended comments to the open-ended question. Indeed, 62 out of the sample of 107 (59%) did so, some at considerable length. Their comments were necessarily diffuse and thus difficult to report: 26 remarked upon the peace of the place; 2 women, who rarely attended church back home, felt that Pennant had become their 'own' parish church; a young male manual worker considered it 'out of this world' that such a well-stocked church book and souvenir shop could be left unattended in this day and age.

Both churchgoers and non-churchgoers reported finding solace, help and a measure of healing from physical and emotional problems. One particularly interesting comment indicated that the respondent felt that the site was a spiritual rather than a Christian place, this being echoed by another who expressed the view that this was indeed a sacred place, but one that had been in existence as such long before Christianity arrived.

Discussion

Historic pilgrimage

The theological significance of place has become increasingly recognized by scholars such as Inge (2003). This sense of place has been significant since the Old Testament. Where God appears to the people, that place is marked for ever as the scene where the divine and the human have made contact. The fugitive Jacob has a vision of angels as he sleeps (Genesis 28). When he awakes, he says, 'How awesome is this place. This place is none other than the house of God and this is the gate of heaven.' He sets up a memorial stone and gives the place its new name of Bethel. Later, on his way to meet his brother Esau, Jacob finds himself wrestling unawares with God (Genesis 32). His response is to name that place Peniel as a memorial of this experience. Sacred places were also prominent in the religion of peoples with whom the Israelites came into contact during their desert wanderings and Moses issues instructions to destroy such places (Deuteronomy 12). On the entry into Canaan and throughout a long period of Jewish history, the sacred places and groves connected with the fertility religion of the inhabitants of the land were denounced by prophet and priest alike.

The archaeological evidence shows that the beginnings of Pennant Melangell as a sacred place are somewhere in the late Bronze Age. Pennant could be said to exhibit a religious culture which Moses and the prophets of Israel despised, for it was a religion centred upon mountains, springs, rivers, trees and other striking natural phenomena. The sacred place at Pennant lies in precisely such a location and its setting still attracts those who seek out such places of awe-inspiring natural scenery. One third of the non-churchgoers among the respondents gave as their motive 'the beautiful country setting' of the site.

In the New Testament the mention of sacred places is rare, but in the early Christian centuries those associated with the life, death and resurrection of Jesus came to be regularly visited by pilgrims. There is strong archaeological evidence that the burial places of the earliest saints also turned into holy places of pilgrimage (Ward-Perkins and Toynbee, 1956; Edwards, 2002).

The Celtic Church, to which Melangell belonged, saw no clash of theology between the fully developed Christian idea of the immanent God, who can turn every place into hallowed ground, and the holy site, linked specifically to the last resting place of some outstanding Christian believer. Neither did the Christian Celts see any reasons to found new holy places to replace those hallowed by time-honoured use. They respected the old sites and instead colonized them for Christ. Although the archaeological record is not clear that the site of Melangell was used continuously from the Bronze Age to the present day it may be that the Christian Celts perceived that they were colonizing a sacred site for Christ, perhaps a site of continued and long-standing significance. Whether the Celtic Christians were aware or not that this location was the focus of pagan antecedents is debatable. However, we may assume that in this location at least, the transition to a Christian sacred site was a total rather than a partial one. This was still reflected today in the survey by the fact that among regular churchgoers an overwhelming 85% had a spiritual motive for coming to Pennant. While this dropped to 51% among non-churchgoers, it must be acknowledged that for both sets of visitors the nature of the place was recognized as sacred.

Pilgrimage today

There is a stark contrast between the pilgrims of the Middle Ages and the pilgrims of today. In earlier times deep penitence was expected from those who went on pilgrimage since their motive was primarily to be shriven of their sins by the mortification of the flesh and the hardships which they were willing to endure (John and Rees, 2002). At Pennant and other Welsh shrines they were visiting places where the Celtic saints had themselves lived lives of devout and conscientious asceticism. Chaucer, however, not only illustrates the mechanics of pilgrimage in his own time, but also demonstrates that the journey itself could have different values for its various participants. At Pennant it is at times difficult to assess whether the value of the journey is in the excursion itself or in the satisfaction or spiritual uplift resulting from the visit to the shrine of the saint. From the data in this study it seems that motivations are mixed, but it is clear that physical surroundings are still paramount in the recognition of a sacred place. The complete rural peace of Pennant, commented upon by so many respondents, is a function of the grandeur, the remoteness and the unspoilt beauty of its setting, which is undoubtedly of great value to many who have to endure the daily grind of urbanism, with the frenetic pace of its way of life.

It is clear, however, that although spiritual motives still fire visitors to travel to Pennant, they are very different from those of the mediaeval pilgrim. In an increasingly secular and materialistic society many visitors arrive without any sort of clear-cut faith, yet with a sincere intention of seeking an alternative to what they perceive as the barren and unsatisfying philosophies of the age. At the shrine they find the space and the opportunity for a variety of spiritual responses. The survey has proved the value to most churchgoing and non-churchgoing visitors alike of silent prayer, lighting a candle, meditation and several other activities, which allow for as much or as little anonymity as they want. At Pennant they are finding they can get away from the noise and confusion of modern life to what Archbishop Rowan Williams (2001) has called 'a spiritual hearth'. Pilgrims to Pennant are part of the increasing pilgrimage traffic which has been noted by observers and which points to a seeming urgency among modern Christians and others to rediscover the historical importance and significance of pilgrimage (Jones, 2002).

Conclusion

Both the Church in Wales (Board of Mission Rural Commission, 1992) and the Church of England (Archbishops' Commission on Rural Areas, 1990) have examined the role of the Church in the countryside and there have been a number of suggestions as to how functioning country churches can find creative ways of using their resources to welcome visitors (Francis and Martineau, 2001, 2002). The research carried out for this study at Pennant Melangell demonstrates that there is also an alternative and equally worthwhile future for the tiny disused church building lost in the hills or hidden in the marshes. If this is so at Pennant, then it could point the way to a revived role for other country churches in similar situations. With the pressures of urban life being as severe as they are, such places could provide 'away days' of peaceful, relaxing teaching and learning opportunities for church communities visiting from the big cities, while at the same time encouraging a wide clientele of urbanites to begin the search for their spiritual roots and to contemplate the Christian tradition.

The survey shows that people are fascinated by the story of Melangell, despite the fact that it is little more than a wafer-thin and relatively lacklustre narrative. It could be that other rural churches might capitalize on their own stories of worthy people who have led notable Christian lives. Latent possibilities for such opportunities would need to be thoroughly researched and developed. Visitors to Pennant were interested in travelling to the grave of Ann Griffiths at nearby Llanfihangel-yng-Nghwynfa, but had they gone there they would have found a sadly neglected church, a disappointing Victorian granite pyramid marking her grave and literally nothing on show to remind them of this gifted Welsh poetess.

A fruitful suggestion might be that each of the major conurbations of Britain needs four or five 'Pennants' in remote rural areas, but within manageable travelling distance. The essentials are a small and cosy church building of sufficient antiquity and interest, a good scenic setting, access by only the tiniest of minor lanes and footpaths, and a personality somewhere in the church's history who is properly revered (though not necessarily widely) for faith, holiness and good deeds.

As at Pennant, there could be a parallel development of a specific ministry to particular groups, somehow linked to the history of the church or to the life of the personality who is being remembered within it. There are valuable areas to be exploited here, such as counselling and help for bereavement, stress, relationship breakdown, single parenting, eating disorders or addiction. Stibbe (1995) has watched contemporary culture and found that first world societies like our own are becoming anaesthetized and numb through addictive behaviour, which he defines as 'something we are all doing, every day, to drive off the boredom, to mask the pain and to take a holiday from reality'.

If this sort of Christian counselling initiative were to be tried at Ann Griffiths's Llanfihangel, the obvious link would be to single parenthood, but there might be an equal case for focusing upon mothers who have given birth to stillborn children. There may be heavy initial outlay in restoring this sort of historic church and providing ancillary services, but heritage funding is available and there are good prospects for such schemes to become self-financing as they establish a niche for themselves and become better known and utilized.

All this would obviously entail the employment of suitably trained staff, but there would also be ample opportunity to enlist the enthusiasm of local volunteers, who generally come to the fore whenever a country church is threatened with closure. The provision of ministry to develop these specialist possibilities, as well as to host the urban visitors, could also provide a viable future for tiny local congregations, who would continue to have their Sunday services with their resident minister at minimal cost to central ecclesiastical coffers. Francis and Lankshear (1992) have demonstrated the value of a resident ministry to the rural parish.

The results of this survey show that there is an unfulfilled demand for things spiritual across a broad swathe of the population in today's world, but that it needs to be met imaginatively, sensitively and appropriately in those locations supremely suited by nature and history for this purpose. This has been achieved at the shrine church of Pennant Melangell. What has been done there could act as a precedent, catalyst and model for remote rural churches in many other parts of the country.

References

Allchin, A. M. (1991). *Praise above all: Discovering the Welsh tradition.* Cardiff: University of Wales Press.

Archbishops' Commission on Rural Areas. (1990). *Faith in the countryside.* Stoneleigh Park: Acora Publishing.

Board of Mission Rural Commission. (1992). *The Church in the Welsh countryside: A programme for action by the Church in Wales.* Penarth: Church in Wales Publications.

Bradley, I. (1999). *Celtic Christianity: Making myths and chasing dreams.* Edinburgh: Edinburgh University Press.

Bradley, I. (2003). *The Celtic way.* London: Darton, Longman and Todd.

Britnell, W. J. (1994). Excavation and recording at Saint Melangell's shrine. Pennant Melangell. *Montgomery Collections, 82,* 147–165.

Carmichael, D., Herbert, J., Reeves, B., & Schenke, A. (Eds.). (1994). *Sacred sites, sacred place.* London: Routledge.

Chapman, M. L. (1994). Transcript of the will of Morgan Herbert, Kt., dated 19 July 1526. *Montgomeryshire Collections, 82,* 126.

Cunliffe, B. (1992). *The Celtic world.* London: Constable.

Edwards, N. (2002). Celtic saints and early medieval archaeology. In A. Thacker and R. Sharpe (Eds.), *Local saints and local churches in the early medieval west* (pp. 267–290). Oxford: Oxford University Press.

Francis, L. J., & Lankshear, D. W. (1992). The rural rectory: The impact of a resident priest on local church life. *Journal of Rural Studies, 8,* 97–103.

Francis, L. J., & Martineau, J. (2001). *Rural visitors: A parish workbook for welcoming visitors in the country church.* Stoneleigh Park: Acora Publishing.

Francis, L. J., & Martineau, J. (2002). *Rural mission: A parish workbook for developing the mission of the rural church.* Stoneleigh Park: Acora Publishing.

Heaton, R. B., & Britnell, W. J. (1994). A structural history of Pennant Melangell church. *Montgomery Collections, 82,* 103–126.

Inge, J. (2003). *A Christian theology of place.* Aldershot: Ashgate.

John, T., & Rees, N. (2002). *Pilgrimage: a Welsh perspective.* Llandysul: Gomer Press.

Jones, A. (2002). *Every pilgrim's guide to Celtic Britain and Ireland.* Norwich: Canterbury Press.

Lane, B. C. (1988). *Landscapes of the sacred: Geography and narrative in American spirituality.* Mahwah, New Jersey: Paulist Press.

Price, H. (1994). A new edition of the Historia Divae Monacellae. *Montgomeryshire Collections, 82,* 23–40.

Radford, C. A. R., & Hemp, W. J. (1959). Pennant Melangell: The church and the shrine. *Archaeologia Cambrensis, 108,* 81–113.

Stibbe, M. (1995). *O brave new church: Rescuing addictive culture.* London: Darton, Longman and Todd.

Ward-Perkins, J. B., & Toynbee, J. (1956). *The Shrine of St Peter and the Vatican excavations.* London: Longmans.

Williams, R. (2001). The Church in Wales and the future of Wales. *Transactions of the Honourable Society of Cymrodorion* (pp. 151–160). London: Cymrodorion Society.

Chapter 17

VISITOR EXPERIENCES OF ST DAVIDS CATHEDRAL: THE TWO WORLDS OF PILGRIMS AND SECULAR TOURISTS

*Emyr Williams, Leslie J. Francis, Mandy Robbins and Jennie Annis**

Abstract – The remote and rural St Davids Cathedral in West Wales receives a steady flow of visitors throughout the year. In order to develop its ministry in this field, a sample of 514 visitors completed a detailed questionnaire designed to explore their experiences of the cathedral, together with a measure of their personal church attendance. The data demonstrated clear differences between the experiences of pilgrims (defined as visitors who attend church services weekly) and the experiences of secular tourists (defined as visitors who never attend church services). The implications of these findings are discussed for cathedral ministry more generally.

* Dr Emyr Williams is a Lecturer in Psychology at Glyndŵr University. *Address for correspondence:* Division of Psychology, Institute for Health, Medical Science and Society, Glyndŵr University, Plas Coch Campus, Mold Road, Wrexham, LL11 2AW. E-mail: emyr.williams@glyndwr.ac.uk

The Revd Canon Professor Leslie J. Francis is Professor of Religions and Education at the Warwick Religions and Education Research Unit. *Address for correspondence*: Warwick Religions and Education Research Unit, Institute of Education, The University of Warwick, Coventry, CV4 7AL.
E-mail: leslie.francis@warwick.ac.uk

Dr Mandy Robbins is Senior Lecturer in Psychology at Glyndŵr University. *Address for correspondence:* Division of Psychology, Institute for Health, Medical Science and Society, Glyndŵr University, Plas Coch Campus, Mold Road, Wrexham, LL11 2AW. E-mail: mandy.robbins@glyndwr.ac.uk

The Revd Dr Jennie Annis is associated with the St Mary's Centre, Wales. *Address for correspondence*: Glanafon, Trecwn, Haverfordwest, SA62 5XT.
E-mail: jennie.annis@btinternet.com

Introduction

Some argue that cathedrals have been sources of tourism since their establishment (Lewis, 1996). Both the importance of tourism for cathedrals, and the importance of cathedrals for tourism, have been highlighted by *Heritage and Renewal,* the report of the Archbishops' Commission on Cathedrals (1994, p. 135):

> Tourism is of great significance to cathedrals – in terms of their mission of teaching, evangelism and welcome, and as an important source of income. Cathedrals also play a major part in the nation's tourism.

Comparatively little is known, however, about who visits cathedrals, why they visit, and what they make of the visitor experience. Answers to such questions are particularly pertinent to illuminating why places of religious interest, especially cathedrals, are so central to tourism in what some commentators currently regard as the post-Christian context of contemporary Britain (Brown, 2001).

One of the first to explore such questions about cathedral visitors with some scientific rigour was *English Cathedrals and Tourism*, a report produced for the English Tourist Board (1979). A questionnaire was sent to 45 cathedrals and greater churches in England, of which 39 were subsequently visited. This postal questionnaire was then supplemented by two surveys specifically concerned with visitor numbers and expectations within cathedrals. The first survey obtained the number of visitors in a fortnight to 26 cathedrals. The second survey, conducted by Public Attitude Surveys Ltd, comprised interviews with a representative sample of 3,812 visitors to 11 cathedrals to profile the characteristics of these visitors and their interest in the cathedral. This report heralded a new era for cathedral life: now visitors were becoming the focus of attention for cathedral staff (voluntary and paid). The report included practical suggestions that would help both the cathedral staff and the local tourist board. The suggestions included providing tours, improving shops, giving better publicity for services, and enhancing facilities such as car parks, lavatories and restaurants. Recommendations were also proposed for managing visitors to help prevent damage to the cathedral.

The report *English Cathedrals and Tourism* (1979) struck a balance between the need to improve visitor facilities in cathedrals and the need to ensure that cathedrals remained first and foremost places of worship. For example, the disruption of worship is reported as being one of the main problems generated by visitors exploring the cathedral at will (p. 66), although the report argued that the undesirability of such disruption should be considered alongside the desirability of opportunities for mission and ministry among people who may not normally be associated with the Church.

Gasson and Winter (1994) conducted a study among 814 visitors to four English cathedrals: Coventry, Ely, Lichfield and Wells. The information was gathered by interviews conducted by members of 'Cathedral camps', a system whereby young people participate in a week of work concerned with cathedral life. Each interview took ten minutes and included a series of dichotomous yes/no questions. Of the sample, 79% were British and 21% were overseas visitors. Of these overseas visitors 46% were from European countries and 25% were from the United States of America. The majority of overseas (40%) and British (35%) visitors were aged between 26 and 45. A quarter (25%) of all visitors were from lower professional or technical employment. Over two fifths (41%) claimed affiliation to the Church of England, though the majority (36%) did not attend Sunday services. Nearly two thirds (65%) of the visitors claimed that they were visiting the cathedral for architectural experiences. In terms of the spiritual quest among visitors, only 23% claimed that they were there as pilgrims. Of this group of pilgrims, 79% experienced 'peace and quiet', 72% experienced the architectural side of the cathedral and 76% experienced the historic side of the cathedral. Only 52% of the pilgrims stated that their experience could be defined as emotional. This survey informed some of the conclusions drawn by the Archbishops' Commission on Cathedrals (1994).

Jackson and Hudman (1995) conducted a survey among visitors to five English cathedrals during August 1993. Of the 483 respondents (55% female and 45% male) 68% were in the area on holiday, 18% were visiting family and friends, 10% were on business, and less than 4% were visiting for religious reasons. In terms of their motivation for visiting the cathedral, 23% stated a religious reason, 25% stated an interest in the historical aspects of the cathedral, 17% stated an interest in the architecture, 9% visited out of curiosity, and 25% had 'other' reasons for visiting. The respondents were also asked to comment on what they believed to be the *most* impressive feature of the cathedral: 71% named the architecture, 12% named the size, 12% named the religious feeling within the cathedral, and 5% identified something else. When asked what feelings they associated with the cathedral, 32% of the visitors stated that they felt the cathedral was a religious symbol for the country, 19% stated that they had a spiritual feeling, 17% stated that they had a feeling of architectural awe, and 14% stated they felt that the cathedral was a personal religious symbol, and 17% ticked the 'other' category. Jackson and Hudman (1995) also found that age functioned as an important predictor of a person's motivation to visit a cathedral. While a religious motivation for visiting the cathedral was important to just 13% of the younger respondents (those who were aged 'nearest 20'), the proportion rose to 20% among those aged between 30 and 50, and to 49% among those 'nearest 60' (p. 43).

Voase (2007) conducted a qualitative study, instigated by the Dean and Chapter, among visitors to Lincoln Cathedral, through a focus group involving nine people who had visited both Lincoln Cathedral and other cathedrals within the last twelve months. His research drew three main conclusions. First, Voase noted that most visits to the cathedral were not the primary purpose for visiting the city, which was usually shopping or sight-seeing. Although members of the focus group did not intentionally come to the city for the cathedral, they admitted that the cathedral was part of the attraction in coming to the city. However, they also made it clear that they would not enter the cathedral if an admission charge was made, but would be willing to give a donation at the end of the visit. Second, Voase discovered that the visitor experience was primarily a response to the atmosphere generated by the cathedral. Members of the focus group mentioned the desire to look around the cathedral at their own pace with the possibility of stopping to reflect in silence and to be solitary. They were critical, however, of what Voase termed 'conscience-pricking' and were not willing to be exposed to evangelization within the cathedral if an admittance fee had been charged. Third, Voase discovered that many members of the focus group left cathedrals feeling empty. The focus group noted how they longed to experience some of the 'human connectedness' of the cathedral, rather than just experiencing the cathedral as a piece of history.

While these studies have been conducted among relatively small samples of cathedral visitors, the potential within such research conducted on a larger scale has been well demonstrated by the study among 12,679 visitors to rural churches reported by Francis and Martineau (2001) and developed further by Littler, Francis and Martineau (2004). One of the major strengths of this survey, given the sample size, concerns the systematic analyses of how expectations and experiences associated with visiting rural churches vary between different groups of visitors. Francis and Martineau (2001) begin by profiling the differences between men and women. For example, women were more likely than men to respond to the spiritual dimensions of rural churches: 45% of women appreciated somewhere to write prayer requests, compared with 36% of men; 46% of women appreciated lighting candles, compared with 36% of men. Women were also more appreciative than men of finding fresh flowers in the church (72% compared with 57%). Second, Francis and Martineau (2001) turn attention to the differences between age groups. For example, younger people under the age of forty were more likely to appreciate sensory aids to enhance the spiritual atmosphere of their visit: 24% of those in their twenties and thirties appreciated the smell of incense, compared with 14% of those aged sixty or over; 47% of those in their twenties and thirties appreciated candles to light, compared with 28% of those aged sixty or over. For those aged sixty or over a welcome and a guidebook took on greater significance: 42% of those aged sixty or over appreciated someone to welcome them during their visit, compared with 27% of those in their twenties and thirties; 60% of those aged sixty or over appreciated being able to buy a guidebook, compared with 48% of those in their twenties and thirties.

The most important and interesting factor reported by Francis and Martineau (2001), however, concerned the different views of regular churchgoers and of individuals who had no current contact with the church. Significant differences occurred in the responses of these two groups across a wide range of issues explored in the survey. For example, regular churchgoers showed much greater interest in the explicitly religious aspects of rural churches: 57% of weekly churchgoers were interested in news of church services, compared with 24% of those who attended infre-quently; 80% of weekly churchgoers were interested in finding somewhere quiet to pray, compared with 55% of those who attended church infre-quently. On the other hand, similar proportions of both groups appreciated hearing music when they visited rural churches (between 39% and 41%) or finding candles to light (between 39% and 44%).

Against this background, the aim of the present study is to investigate how individual differences in religiosity, as measured by church attendance, are related to the experiences of the cathedral visitor. Do frequent churchgoers have different expectations and experiences of visiting cathedrals compared with tourists who are not church attenders? If so, there may be important implications for the ways in which cathedrals welcome and cater for these two constituencies. In order to sharpen the research questions, the analysis will look at four main domains of the visitor experience. The first domain concerns the 'overall impression' generated by the cathedral. This will ask visitors to describe their overall impression of the cathedral and the atmosphere created by it. Second, the 'spiritual and religious' domain will be investigated. This domain will assess how visitors are connecting with the transcendent within the cathedral and ask what role they believe prayer has for their visit. Third, the 'aesthetic and historic' domain will be explored. This domain will investigate how visitors connect with the historic, intellectual and cultural aspects of the cathedral, and seek their opinions on charging to enter the cathedral. Finally, the domain of 'commercialization' will be explored. This will ask visitors to assess the availability, use and effectiveness of the cathedral shop and website.

Method

Sample

A sample of 514 visitors to St Davids Cathedral in West Wales completed the questionnaire. Of the total sample, 44% were male, and 56% were female; 10% were under the age of twenty, 12% in their twenties, 12% in their thirties, 11% in their forties, 22% in their fifties, 20% in their sixties, and 13% were aged over seventy. Three fifths (58%) of the sample came from England and over a third were from Wales (34%). Overseas visitors accounted for less than a tenth (8%) of the sample. In terms of religious affiliation, 77% of the sample said they were Christian, 21% said they did not belong to any religious group, and the remaining 2% comprised a few Buddhists, Hindus, Jews, Muslims and Sikhs. The largest denominational affiliation was to Anglicanism with 62% of the sample describing themselves as such.

Instrument

Alongside questions concerned with age and sex, the questionnaire included items concerned with personal church attendance and with experience of visiting the cathedral.

Church attendance was measured on a five point scale: 'never', 'annually', 'monthly', 'fortnightly' and 'weekly'.

Experience of visiting the cathedral was assessed by four sets of seven items concerned with the four domains of 'overall impression', 'spiritual and religious', 'aesthetic and historic' and 'commercialization'. Each item was assessed on a five-point Likert scale ranging from 'agree strongly', through 'agree', 'not certain' and 'disagree', to 'disagree strongly'.

Data analysis

The data were analysed by the SPSS statistical package, employing the frequencies and cross-tabulation routines. Statistical significance testing was conducted by the chi square statistic based on dichotomizing the responses. In the case of the items assessed on the five-point scale of attitudinal intensity, comparison was made between the people who checked 'agree' or 'agree strongly' and those who checked 'not certain', 'disagree' or 'disagree strongly'.

Responses to the question concerning public religious practice were employed to define three conceptually distinct and empirically defined subgroups within the database: those who never attended a place of worship, those who attended a place of worship from time to time but less often than weekly (styled occasional attenders), and those who attended a place of worship on a weekly basis. According to this definition within the present sample, 17% were defined as never practising, 49% were defined as practicing occasionally, and 34% were defined as practising on a weekly basis. The weekly churchgoers are those currently immersed within Christian culture, belief and practice. When visiting a cathedral they may well bring with them the worldview of pilgrims for whom the cathedral is a sacred space continuous with their local church but on a grander and more significant scale. The individuals who never attend church are those currently living at a greater distance from Christian culture, belief and practice. When visiting a cathedral they may well bring with them the worldview of secular tourists for whom the cathedral is unconnected with a current religious belief system. Such a comparison allows us to assess how the cathedral connects with two conceptually and empirically distinct constituencies.

Results and discussion

Table 1 presents the main findings from the study, comparing the responses of the three groups to four conceptually defined areas: overall perception, spiritual and religious domain, aesthetic and historic domain, and commercialization. The chi-square test examines the statistical significance of differences between the three groups. Differences which failed to reach the five percent probability level are classified as non-significant (NS).

Table 1: Comparisons between public worship attendance

	N %	O %	W %	χ^2	$p <$
Overall impression					
I found the cathedral uplifting	77	84	95	15.71	.001
I found the cathedral inviting	88	96	97	8.33	.05
I found the cathedral clean	97	99	99	2.66	NS
I found the cathedral warm	87	83	89	2.97	NS
I found the cathedral surprising	46	49	45	0.75	NS
Cathedral staff were welcoming	82	91	94	7.99	.05
Cathedral staff were well informed	51	66	75	11.05	.01
Spiritual and religious					
I felt a sense of God's presence from my visit	18	50	77	62.97	.001
Cathedral staff should lead public prayers	19	32	42	10.66	.01
I found the cathedral spiritually alive	35	61	73	28.30	.001
I found the cathedral awe-inspiring	68	79	87	11.78	.01
I felt a sense of the spiritual from my visit	31	57	72	30.78	.001
I felt a sense of peace from my visit	50	81	88	40.12	.001
My visit was an emotional experience	21	46	56	22.31	.001
Aesthetic and historic					
I found the information leaflets useful	42	63	66	11.91	.01
I would be prepared to pay admission charge	50	55	46	2.09	NS
I made a donation	73	76	84	3.98	NS
Visitors should know running cost of the cathedral	79	86	92	4.97	NS
I felt an appreciation of history from visit	87	94	94	4.07	NS
I felt an appreciation of the architecture	96	94	94	0.17	NS
I felt a sense of Welsh culture	54	61	60	1.16	NS
Commercialization					
I visited the cathedral shop	49	61	73	10.59	.01
Good range of products available in shop	41	60	74	20.78	.001
Product prices are reasonable in shop	34	53	73	28.59	.001
I made a purchase in the cathedral shop	31	29	55	19.66	.001
Have accessed the website	15	15	30	11.04	.01
Information on website helpful	18	20	37	9.61	.01
Information on web clear and informative	20	24	40	8.62	.05

N = Never, O = Occasionally, W = Weekly

Overall impression

The data revealed that the cathedral studied tends to be appreciated more by those who attended church on a weekly basis. In terms of finding the cathedral uplifting the proportions differed significantly depending on how often visitors attended church: while 95% of those who attended church weekly found the cathedral uplifting, the proportions fell to 84% among those who occasionally attended church, and to 77% among those who never attended church. Similarly, while 97% of those who attended church weekly found the cathedral to be inviting, the proportions dropped slightly to 96% among those who occasionally attended church, and further to 88% among those who never attended church. The data also demonstrate how perceptions of the cathedral staff differed among churchgoers and non-churchgoers: while 94% of those who attended church weekly found the cathedral staff welcoming, the proportions dropped to 91% among those who occasionally attended church, and further still to 82% among those who never attended church. The three groups also differed significantly in terms of seeing the cathedral staff as well informed: while 75% of those who attended church weekly believed the staff were well informed, the proportions fell to 66% among those who occasionally attended church, and to 51% among those who never attended church.

Despite these significant differences between the three groups, there were other areas in which the responses of the groups were not significantly different. A large percentage of each group felt that the cathedral was clean (between 97 and 99%) and warm (between 83 and 89%). Nearly half of each group felt that that cathedral was surprising (between 45 and 49%).

Spiritual and religious

Within the spiritual and religious domain, the differences between the three groups were even more pronounced than within the overall impression domain. Low proportions (18%) of those who never attended church felt that they had a sense of God's presence during their visit, but this proportion rose to half (50%) of those who attended church occasionally, and even further to 77% of those who attended church weekly. Low proportions of those who never attended church believed that cathedral staff should lead public prayers (19%), but the proportions rose to 32% among those who attended church occasionally, and to 42% among those who attended church weekly.

Ideas concerning the spirituality felt within the cathedral were not as greatly divided as those concerning the presence of God. While over a third (35%) of those who never attended church found the cathedral spiritually alive, the proportions rose to 61% among those who attended church occasionally, and further to 73% among those who attended church weekly. While just under a third (31%) of those who never attended church came away from their visit with a sense of the spiritual, the proportions rose to 57% among those who attended church occasionally, and further to 72% among those who attended church weekly.

Significant differences also emerged between the three groups when describing their experiences of visiting the cathedral: while over half (56%) of those who attended church weekly described their visit as an emotional experience, the proportions dropped to 46% among those who occasionally attended church, and to 21% among those who never attended church. Significant differences also emerged between the three groups in terms of feeling some sense of peace from their visit: while 88% of those who attended church weekly described feeling a sense of peace, the proportions dropped to 81% among those who occasionally attended church, and to 50% among those who never attended church. Finally, while 87% of those who attended church weekly were more likely to describe the cathedral as awe-inspiring, this proportion dropped to 79% among those who occasionally attended church, and to 68% among those who never attended church.

Aesthetic and historic

Within the aesthetic and historic domain there are not many significant differences between the three groups. Only assessment of the usefulness of an information leaflet distinguished between the three groups: while 42% of those who never attended church found the information leaflet useful, the proportions rose to 63% among those who occasionally attended church, and to 66% among those who attended church weekly.

In the rest of the section the three groups did not differ significantly. Around half of each group stated that they would be prepared to pay an admission charge: 46% of those who attended church weekly, 50% of those who never attended church, and 55% of those who attended church occasionally. A high proportion of each group stated they had made a donation: 73% of those who never attended church, 76% of those who occasionally attended church, and 84% of those who attended church weekly. The proportion of people who believed that visitors should know about the running costs of the cathedral were also comparable in all three groups: while 79% of those who never attended church believed visitors should be aware of the running costs, the proportions rose (but not significantly) to 86% among those who occasionally attended church, and to 92% among those who attended church weekly. Similar proportions also felt an appreciation for history (87% among those who never attended church, 94% among those who occasionally attended church, and 94% among those who attended church weekly) and an appreciation for the architecture (96% among those who never attended church, 94% among those who occasionally attended church, and 94% among those who attended church weekly). Finally, the proportions of those who stated that they felt a sense of Welsh culture are consistent across the three groups: while 54% of those who never attended church gained a sense of Welsh culture, the proportions rose (but not significantly) to 61% among those who occasionally attended church, and to 60% among those who attended church weekly.

Commercialization

Within the domain of commercialization of the cathedral there are many areas in which the three groups differ significantly. Levels of response to the cathedral shop are significantly different among the three groups. While 49% of those who never attended church visited the cathedral shop, the proportions rose to 61% among those who occasionally attended church, and to 73% among those who attended church weekly. Differences can also be seen in opinions concerning the range of products available in the shop: while 41% of those who never attended church thought the range of products was good, the proportions rose to 60% among those who occasionally attended church, and further still to 74% among those who attended church weekly. Differences also emerge in relation to views on the price of the products in the shop: while 34% of those who never attended church thought the prices were reasonable, the proportions rose to 53% among those who occasionally attended church, and further to 73% among those who attended church weekly. Finally, in terms of actually making a purchase, the groups differ significantly: while 29% of those who attended church occasionally made a purchase in the cathedral shop, the proportions rose to 31% among those who never attended church, and further to 55% among those who attended church weekly.

In terms of using the cathedral website, clear differences emerge between the three groups: the data demonstrated that 30% among those who attended church weekly had accessed the site, in comparison with 15% among those who occasionally and never attended church. In terms of the helpfulness of the information on the website, while 18% of those who never attended church said they found it helpful, the proportions rose to 20% among those who occasionally attended church, and to 37% among those who attended church weekly. Finally, differences emerge when the visitors were asked if they found the information on the website clear and informative: while 20% of those who never attended church thought that the information on the website was clear and informative, the proportions rose to 24% among those who occasionally attended church, and to 40% among those who attended church weekly.

Conclusion

This study has built on a small but important research tradition concerned with listening to, describing and analysing the expectations and experiences of visitors to the cathedrals of England and Wales as exampled by the English Tourist Board (1979), Gasson and Winter (1994), Jackson and Hudman (1995) and Voase (2007). By using a self-completion questionnaire survey among 514 visitors, the present study has offered two useful refinements of the conceptualization of the research agenda. The first refinement concerns developing a conceptual map of the aspects of visitor experience. The present study distinguished between four areas: the overall impression generated by the cathedral, the spiritual and religious aspects of the cathedral, the aesthetic and historic aspects of the cathedral, and the commercialization taking place in connection with the cathedral. Future studies should be encouraged to develop this task of conceptualization further by developing a more refined map of visitor experience. The second refinement concerns distinguishing between different categories of cathedral visitors and modelling data analysis on the separate categories. The present study distinguished between three categories of visitors according to levels of church attendance: weekly attenders, occasional attenders, and non-attenders. Future studies should be encouraged to develop a more skilfully nuanced model of the religiosity and spirituality of cathedral visitors. Three main conclusions emerge from the data generated by the present study.

The first conclusion concerns the responses of the visitors who are regular churchgoers. These are the visitors who have been shaped and formed by the Christian tradition, who feel at home not only in their own parish churches but in the great cathedrals as well. In many senses these are the visitors most likely to stand in the ancient tradition of pilgrims; and it is to these visitors that the cathedral speaks most clearly. The majority of these pilgrims walked away satisfied and refreshed by their visit, having found the cathedral inviting (97%) and uplifting (95%). The majority of these pilgrims responded to the cathedral as a source of spiritual sustenance, having found in the place a sense of peace (88%), an awe-inspiring experience (87%), and a sense of God's presence (77%). It is among these pilgrims that the cathedral shop did its business, with nearly three quarters visiting the shop (73%), appreciating the range of products (74%) and judging the products to be reasonably priced (73%). Over half of these pilgrims (55%) had made a purchase in the cathedral shop. Overall, the cathedral seems to have positioned itself well for a valued ministry among today's generation of pilgrims.

The second conclusion concerns the responses of those visitors who never attend church services on a Sunday. These are the visitors who currently stand outside the Christian tradition, who may not feel at home in their parish church and who also seem not to feel fully at home in the cathedral. In many senses, these are the visitors who are now replacing the pilgrims of an earlier age as more secular tourists; and it is to these visitors that the cathedral speaks with less clarity and certainty. However, the cathedral is far from silent in its call to these secular tourists. Although only 18% of the secular tourists felt a sense of God's presence from their visit, 35% found the cathedral to be spiritually alive, 50% felt a sense of peace from their visit, and 68% found the cathedral awe-inspiring. Over three quarters of the secular tourists found the cathedral uplifting (77%) and inviting (88%). The majority of the secular tourists felt an appreciation of history from their visit (87%) and felt an appreciation of the architecture (96%). Thus, many aspects of the visit were able to stir the soul. The cathedral shop, however, is much less well positioned to do business among these non-churchgoing secular tourists than among the churchgoing pilgrims. Just half of the secular tourists (49%) visited the cathedral shop, compared with three quarters of the pilgrims (73%). Just two fifths of the secular tourists (41%) considered the cathedral shop to carry a good range of products, compared with three quarters of the pilgrims (74%). Under one third of the secular tourists (31%) made a purchase in the cathedral shop, compared with more than half of the pilgrims (55%).

These findings suggest that the cathedral shop (either intentionally or unintentionally) is positioning its trade more toward the pilgrim than toward the secular tourist. On one account, this is a reasonable strategy. Where else are pilgrims likely to be able to purchase books (like the Bible), artefacts (like crucifixes) and recorded music (like sacred organ recitals) within the secular city? On another account, however, such a strategy misses the great challenge held out by the Archbishops' Commission on Cathedrals (1994) of engaging in their mission of teaching, evangelizing and welcome among secular tourists. More problematic still is the implication of the finding that the positioning of the cathedral shop is symptomatic of the positioning of the whole cathedral which seems to understand the secular tourist so much less adequately than it understands the pilgrim. It may well be the case in today's secular society that cathedrals possess a unique opportunity to draw back the veil between the secular worldview and the worldview of transcendence, and to build bridges between contemporary spiritualities, implicit religious quests, and explicit religious traditions. If this is the case, then the present data suggest that future research needs to listen much more carefully to views of the secular tourists visiting cathedrals in order to be better informed regarding ways in which cathedrals may respond more effectively to the challenge to extend their ministry among this key constituency.

References

Archbishops' Commission on Cathedrals. (1994). *Heritage and renewal.* London: Church House Publishing.

Brown, C. G. (2001). *The death of Christian Britain.* London: Routledge.

English Tourist Board. (1979). *English cathedrals and tourism: Problems and opportunities.* London: English Tourist Board.

Francis, L. J., & Martineau, J. (2001). *Rural visitors: A parish workbook for welcoming visitors to the country church.* Stoneleigh Park: ACORA.

Gasson, R., & Winter, M. (1994). *A survey of visitors to four English cathedrals.* Cheltenham: The Church Study Unit.

Jackson, R. H., & Hudman, L. (1995). Pilgrimage tourism and English cathedrals: The role of religion in travel. *The Tourist Review, 50,* 40–48.

Lewis, R. (1996). Cathedrals and tourism. In I. M. MacKenzie (Ed.), *Cathedrals now* (pp. 25–41). Norwich: Canterbury Press.

Littler, K., Francis, L. J., & Martineau, J. (2004). I was glad: Listening to visitors to country churches. *Rural Theology, 2,* 53–60.

Voase, R. (2007). Visiting a cathedral: The consumer psychology of a 'rich experience'. *International Journal of Heritage Studies, 13,* 41–55.

Part 6

LISTENING TO THE COMMUNITY

Chapter 18

SOCIAL CAPITAL GENERATED BY TWO RURAL CHURCHES: THE ROLE OF INDIVIDUAL BELIEVERS

*Keith Ineson and Lewis Burton**

Abstract — Extended interviews were conducted in 2003 with eight people who had affiliation with two churches within a large village. The interviews were analysed to assess whether these individuals were contributing to the social capital of their own church-related community (bonding social capital), and whether they were contributing to the social capital of the wider community (bridging social capital). The data demonstrated a positive answer on both accounts.

Introduction

Social capital has been developed in recent years as an analytical tool which explores the nature of social cohesiveness and the value which can be added or subtracted from social life by the contribution arising from social activity and social networks in a given population. It has been broadly defined as based on 'connections among individuals – social networks and the reciprocity and trustworthiness that arose from them' (Hall, 1999, p. 417). An alternative definition is given by Robert Putnam as 'features of social organization, such as networks, norms, and trust that facilitate coordination and cooperation for mutual benefit' (Putnam, 2000, p. 18). L.J. Hanifan, a pioneer of the concept, illustrates

* Canon Keith Ineson is Agricultural Chaplain for Churches Together in Cheshire, and Coordinator for Cheshire Farm Crisis Network. *Address for correspondence*: Worsley House, Minshull Vernon, Cheshire, CW10 0LT.
E-mail: keith@ineson.freeserve.co.uk

The Revd Dr Lewis Burton, a retired Methodist minister, is Honorary Research Fellow in the St Mary's Centre, Wales. *Address for correspondence*: 94 Sun Street, Haworth, Keighley, BD22 8AH. E-mail: lewisburton@blueyonder.co.uk

how it applies to individuals defining social capital as 'those tangible substances [that] count for most of the daily lives of people: namely, goodwill, fellowship, sympathy and social intercourse' (Hanifan, 1916, p. 130).

These definitions, though couched in very general terms, show that human life-chances and general welfare are affected by the quality of social interaction within social institutions, but also relate to the quality of input which individuals subscribe to the ongoing life of their local community. One could say, then, that the Christian Church as a social institution has had its influence on social capital in the past, perhaps both in positive and negative ways (Putnam, 2000, pp. 65–79), and that individuals who make up the constituency of local churches, can also be influential in increasing the social capital of their local neighbourhood community.

Robert Putman, in *Bowling Alone*, extends the basic concept by defining two kinds of social capital formation, that of bonding, and that of bridging (Putnam, 2000, p. 22). This distinction is especially relevant when investigating the activity of individual church people who create social capital. People especially active in the local church and who devote a good deal of energy in the leadership of the church and its activities build up the social cohesiveness and the wellbeing, the social capital, of the local church group. They create a bonding relationship. At the same time, some also spend their energies and time, not only in the church, but in various activities in the church's surrounding neighbourhood, spending themselves for the benefit of other people, thus contributing to the social capital of their neighbourhood community, the bridging effect.

The distinction between these two types of social capital in a church context also gives rise to questions regarding the Church's mission in the general community. Within Christian thought there are the two traditions of how Christians engage with the world, which are seen in denominational thinking and policy: the world-embracing attitude and the world-negating attitude (Wilson, 1966).

The two questions which then emerge are these. In what way do individual church members contribute to the social capital of the neighbourhood community in which they live? Do different denominations demonstrate through the action of their members different measures of bonding social capital and bridging social capital which seem to match the expected denominational stance regarding the mission of the church? The present study is an attempt to answer these questions.

Method

In order to establish a result that was both verifiable and repeatable elsewhere, a choice had to be made of a neighbourhood community which was large enough to give significant social networks in which the social interaction of individuals could be observed, but not overlarge, in which individual contributions to the common life would be submerged by a host of other factors. Such considerations suggested a neighbourhood community of a typical country village. Proper names have been replaced throughout this report in order to preserve the anonymity of both the village and the interviewees involved.

The place

For such reasons it was determined that Oxenly was suitable for such a study. Oxenly is a large rural community with a population of just under 10,000. Since parts of Oxenly have been designated a Conservation Area it has managed to keep its character, and some restrictive policies have prevented the erection of new buildings. However, the nature and extent of local commerce has changed considerably over the recent past. All goods and services are available locally, although many residents travel to outlying supermarkets and retail parks to do their shopping. Limited employment is given to the villagers by local retail and financial concerns situated in the High Street and there are two small employment areas accommodating offices and light industrial premises, but the majority of those in employment commute, often over long distances, to work in neighbouring conurbations. The attractive setting of Oxenly and a range of speciality shops and services bring in visitors. There are a number of leisure facilities and voluntary services with activities in Oxenly. The locality is also fortunate in having its own independent cottage hospital.

The churches

Oxenly has four churches: Anglican, joint Baptist/Methodist, Pentecostal and Roman Catholic. To obtain a clear contrast within the limits of a small study it was decided to sample from the lay leaders of the joint Methodist/Baptist church and the Roman Catholic Church. There has been a Baptist church in Oxenly since 1830 and a Methodist church since the early expansion of the Methodist movement. In the 1950s, when both churches were experiencing difficulties, a violent storm removed the roof from the Methodist church and the Baptists offered the Methodists the hospitality of their building for worship. This temporary arrangement continued for several months until the Methodists decided that they did not intend to repair their building. Since joint usage of the Baptist building was proceeding smoothly it was decided that Methodists should be given some security of tenure with the signing of a sharing agreement under the provisions of the Sharing of Church Buildings Act of 1969. In 1986 this simple sharing of a building was extended when it was officially recognized as a full Local Ecumenical Project, as the arrangement was called at that time. Since that time the church has thrived both numerically and spiritually. The general pattern of worship in the church is a preaching service held every Sunday morning at 10.30am.

In the late 1930s there was no Roman Catholic Church locally. The Salvatorian Fathers came from a village about ten miles away to say mass in the upstairs room of a local shop. During the war a local café, used by servicemen from a local camp as a recreational centre, provided a mass centre serviced by the Forces Chaplain. After the war the site was developed, coming into full use as a church in the late 1960s. The present parish embraces not only Oxenly, but also another church in a nearby village. Oxenly has two masses on a Sunday and three during the week. There is little social activity based at the church through the week although there are many Roman Catholic families in the area, resulting in large congregations for Sunday masses. The church has, however, a very active St Vincent de Paul Society with members who visit housebound and needy and do practical work to support local people in difficulty.

The sample

Four Baptist/Methodists and four Roman Catholics were chosen to provide representatives from the two local churches in order to examine the way in which typical churchgoers contributed to both bonding and bridging social capital.

Interviews

The investigation was carried out by face-to-face interviews at a convenient time and place determined by prior consent with the interviewee. As a prompt to ensure that the same ground was covered in all eight interviews, an interview schedule was used. Responses were recorded on tape, and transcribed later. Each response took the form of a brief life history, followed by an account of the activity of the interviewee both inside the church and outside the church in the neighbourhood community.

Results

The Baptist/Methodists

John Billings is 66 years of age and has lived in or around Oxenly all his life. He is a semi-retired joiner still working part-time for the local high school where he is well respected. He is a leader in the church and very active in organizing the smooth running of arrangements for worship and the transportation of people to church. He is the general handyman for the upkeep of the church property.

His activity stretches beyond the church in that he arranges the collection of waste paper in a skip on the church car park, not only for church people, but for the whole neighbourhood, and coordinates church and community charities and events. He visits patients in the cottage hospital and sees this as part of his Christian service. 'I prefer going to the hospital and getting them laughing to being part of a prayer meeting. It's just the way I work out my Christian service.'

Quite apart from any church activity he has a long history of involvement in public life. He has served twenty-five years, longer than anyone else, as a member of the parish council, and has been its chairman twice. He has a strong concern for providing low-cost housing for local people, and because of lack of other transport facilities is working with others to open the railway station with a view to providing a coordinated transport service. He is also the chairperson of the local Community Centre Trust, a position he has held for thirty years, which lets rooms to local businesses and to local leisure interest groups.

John obviously finds great satisfaction from the service which he gives both to the church and to the local neighbourhood community. The appreciation of local people is seen in that they nominated him to attend a royal Garden Party at Buckingham Palace.

Jean Fellows is 71 years of age and is a retired schoolteacher. Originally living in Derbyshire she moved to Oxenly after widowhood, when she married again. For a while she attended the parish church, but then decided with her husband to join the Baptist/Methodists.

Within the church she is a leader and shares in the services as a reader. She organizes coffee after the Sunday service, acts as treasurer of a women's weekly meeting, and helps with the mums-and-toddlers group. She also devotes much time to keeping the church garden tidy and colourful. In the activity which combines both church and community interests she organizes the annual Women's World Day of Prayer service. She has been a member of the Parish Council since 1991 and has a special interest in affordable housing and village footpaths. She serves on the Cheshire Community Council and has served recently as a judge on the Community Pride Scheme.

She sees her service as part of her faith. She contributes to the general good because she enjoys it and when asked if she would do the work if she were not a Christian she replied, 'I cannot separate the two.'

Norah Henry is 81 years of age and has been retired for 21 years. She is a native of Northern Ireland, but has lived in Oxenly for over 50 years. Her last employment was as a warden of the local sheltered housing complex. She has been very active in the church, but in recent years age has taken its toll. She has been a leader, taught in Sunday school, served as church secretary, helped with the Sacrament of Holy Communion and also has taken a lead in the church's week day activities.

She became involved in local neighbourhood service as an adjunct to her job as old people's warden. Her involvement in this way put her in an advantageous position for other community involvement. She was in the past secretary of the Scouts' committee, the local Women's Institute, and the Autumn Club (a club for retirees).

Jane Williams is 57 years of age and is a part-time library assistant in Oxenly. She was originally a Baptist, but later was confirmed in Oxenly parish church and worshipped there with her husband on an occasional basis. Later they both became members of the Baptist/Methodist church where her husband became a leader. She is the church organist and has led the choir in the past. She is an assistant to the church treasurer and has been involved in fund raising for Christian Aid and also with the annual Christmas card sale. She also helps with the Saturday coffee morning.

Her main activity outside the church has been through her membership of Inner Wheel, open mainly to the wives of the Rotary Club members. She has offered support in all the charitable work sponsored by her husband's club and also has been an effective participant in the charitable work sponsored by the Inner Wheel.

The Roman Catholics

Mary Lewis is managing director of a freight haulage company, started by her husband some time ago. He now has minimal involvement due to illness. She is 58 years of age and lives outside Oxenly in a nearby village. The company is located in a neighbouring town.

She is a cradle Roman Catholic, although with a history of involvement in an Anglican church when they lived elsewhere. She attends the Roman

Catholic Church in Oxenly at least once a week with other involvements at times of the great Christian festivals.

Opportunities for some Roman Catholics in the day-to-day running of church life are not as numerous as those from the Free Churches owing to different perceptions of the role of the laity. Distinct opportunities for service in the community are presented, however, in some of the organizations which the Roman Catholic Church sponsors. Mary is heavily involved in the local St Vincent de Paul Society which does work to help people in need. As Mary describes it, 'Where there is need, we help irrespective of whether they are members of the church or not.' She was a co-founder of the St Vincent de Paul Society in Oxenly a few years ago, and is vice president of the local organization. A useful contact with local people who need help in emotional, physical or financial distress is through her daughter who works in the local hospice. She prefers to relate to people on a one-to-one basis and has provided care and support over the years for a number of local families. Within the neighbourhood of Oxenly she has also held the post of a governor of the local school and the local college, has helped with luncheon clubs, meals on wheels and entertainment groups. She is a director of the Chamber of Commerce and a member of the local Economic Prosperity Group. She has had membership of similar bodies in the region in the past and has been asked to work for the Area Growth Strategy Group. 'Why do I do it all?', she says. 'It is hard to analyse why I do it. I want to be more than a Christian who just goes to mass. I get a lot of pleasure from it and I know there is a terrific need in the community.' She was awarded an MBE in the Honours list of 2001.

Ted Simpson is in his seventies and is a retired industrial chemist. He is a cradle Roman Catholic and is very active in the Oxenly church, both in his attendance at church and also in sponsoring and administering some initiatives regarding church finances. He is also a Eucharistic Minister assisting the priest in church duties. In recent times he has been a moving force in bringing the churches of Oxenly together. He says that he feels it is important to be involved in church life, seeing it as his duty, as well as obviously enjoying the involvement.

In the neighbourhood community he has been involved with others in the local Allotment Association, both in its running and also in defending the allotments against being sold off for other purposes. Since the owners of the land were the local British Legion he joined the local association which led subsequently to membership of its committee on which he held a key position. The allotment holders' confidence in him is seen in that over the years he has been their secretary, treasurer and president. His activity outside the church has also stretched to an involvement with the local Probus Club and with hands-on service with Age Concern. In recent years he has organized, in the local Baptist/ Methodist church, the annual sale of charity Christmas cards which has resulted in considerable sums of money being raised.

Margaret Simpson is Ted's wife, also in her seventies, and is a retired pharmacist. They have four children, one of whom is severely handicapped and needs Margaret's care. She has, however, been a constant support to her husband and without this she says that he would not have been able to do all the things that he has. Despite all the calls on her time and energy, she has been very active herself. In church she has been a regular attender at mass and other services and is an official church reader. She has also initiated, and is responsible for the running of, a ladies' group.

In the neighbourhood community she has worked in practical ways with Age Concern in the care and visitation of the elderly and has helped Ted in the annual Christmas card sale. She sees all this as the outworking of her Christian faith. 'I've always been a practical person. I'm not one who spends a lot of time on my knees.' She feels that her motives have been influenced by the fact that she has a handicapped child and there was a tradition of service to the community in her family. 'We've always had a history of helping', she says.

Louise Stanton is 54 years of age and works as a nurse at the cottage hospital on the night shift. She was trained in Dublin, for she is native to Ireland, and in Glasgow. She attends church once on a Sunday and perhaps twice during the week. She is on the rota for looking after the altar linen and has helped with catechism classes and coordinates the local collections for missionary work.

Her main area of work outside the church is again through the local activities of Age Concern where she undertakes the weekly visitation of the housebound, some of whom she has been visiting for a number of years. At the hospital she is engaged in public relations and in raising money. She is also a member and a past treasurer of the Oxenly Branch of the National Women's Register. She also takes an active part in money raising activities for Christian Aid. She says that she never consciously thinks of her work in the community as being done as the result of her faith, but after giving it some thought felt that this was her way of putting her faith into action.

Discussion

Motivation

The first question to address is that of motivation. These eight people have clearly a significant contribution to the social capital, not only of their church, but also to the neighbourhood community in which they live, but why? One could say that the motivation comes from the pleasure and self-satisfaction which they gain from the social exchange with other people that such activity demands. They may also feel that their own sense of self-worth is improved by helping those who are less favourably placed than they are. One of the interviewees is a member of the Inner Wheel organization, her husband a member of Rotary, and there are many rotarians who are not churchgoers, but still engage in all the good works which the Rotary movement promotes. What makes the eight interviewees of this study different from all those other individuals who are not churchgoers or Christians but who are involved in the creation of social capital? The answer to this question must lie in the value system of the eight individuals concerned, which may spring from their Christianity and their church allegiance.

It is from what they say at the end of their interviews that their motivations become plain. A straightforward response from one of them was, 'Why do I do it? It's hard to analyse why I do it! I want to be more than a Christian who just goes to mass. I get a lot of pleasure from it and I know there is a terrific need in the community.' There are a number of motivations within that admission. Similar sentiments are observed in the responses of the others.

Denominational differences

In considering the question of motivation, that provided by their Christianity is clearly seen, but value systems relating to biblical inter-pretation and theological stance differ between Christian denomina-tions. The sample for this study comes from two different Christian traditions, Roman Catholic and English non-conformist, and it is possible that the value systems of one favour world-embracing attitudes more than the other, making for differing results in the creation of bridging social capital. The spiritual focus of Roman Catholicism is centred in the mass, the people of God gathered at the altar, celebrating the sacrifice of Christ. Both the Methodist and the Baptist traditions derive their theology from the insights of the Reformation and focus their worship on the people of God gathered to hear the word of God

(Avis, 2004, p. 92). This difference in the understanding of the nature of the church leads to different understandings of the mission of the church, and the nature of evangelism. The imperative for mission for the Roman Catholics has been to increase an awareness and an understanding of the spirituality associated with the mass, and the other sacraments of the Church. It is this focus on the sufferings of Christ in the mass which leads to their concern for the world expressed in social action. For Methodists and most Baptists the imperative of mission has been to take the word of God out of the church setting and engage with unbelievers in bringing them to conversion. The spiritual value system of Roman Catholics would lead one to suppose that at Oxley they would be church centred. For the Methodist and Baptist traditions, as they are represented at Oxley, one would suppose that besides worship, Bible values would lead them also to engage with the world in outreach, both to convert unbelievers (Matthew 28:19), and to serve its needs (Luke 10:25-37). Were then the people in the Roman Catholic Church at Oxley less involved in outreach to the world, and therefore in the creation of bridging social capital, than the Methodist/Baptists?

The Roman Catholics were more church centred than the Methodist/ Baptists. With the two masses on a Sunday and the three during the week the whole church community was centred on what was going on in the church. Out of the sample of four, three were very active in both supporting the sacramental life of their church and assisting the priest, both in the mass and in church organization. All the sample were frequent attenders at mass. They were more regular attenders at worship than the Methodist/Baptist sample and were more caught up in the structures of their church. One main activity for outreach to the local church's neighbourhood in ministering to people's needs was through the St Vincent De Paul Society, an organization within church structures, common in the church at large and sponsored and staffed locally. There was, however, much engagement with local needs through individual action.

The Methodist/Baptist sample were also all caught up in the organizational activity of their church, both in provision for worship, and in some of its weekday activities, but the hold of the church organization itself was much weaker than that of the Roman Catholic sample, and their activities, which were numerous and varied, were outside the boundaries of church activity and can be assessed as making a strong contribution to the building of neighbourhood bridging capital.

On the other hand one must acknowledge that bridging capital was created by the activities of the St Vincent de Paul Society, even though this was a church sponsored and church staffed organization. In addition to whatever involvement some of the Roman Catholic sample had in the work of the St Vincent de Paul Society, all of them were engaged as individuals in activities which served the neighbourhood community and which were outside the jurisdiction and the influence of their local church and its priest.

Some differences which sprang from the different value systems and theology of their parent denominations were observed in this study. This, however, must be a tentative judgement, and needs further research. It is clear that in the responses concerning motivation, Christians from both denominations see outreach and service to others as part of Christian activity, and also as a way of personal fulfilment and satisfaction. It is a personal choice made whatever the overarching value system of their parent denomination happens to be.

Aging Christians

If it is possible to assume in the light of current surveys of church attendance (Brierley, 2000, 2001) that the eight people who were identified are typical of their two churches, then it must be noted that older people make a distinct contribution to both bonding social capital within their own churches and bridging social capital within their neigh-bourhood communities. Of the eight subjects of these case histories the youngest was 54 and the oldest was 81.

The simplest explanation for this age profile is that service in the church and in the community offers opportunities in which retired people can find fulfilment, and that, with retirement, time for such purposes is readily available. The obverse of this is that younger people do not have the same time or energy to devote themselves either to the organization of the church, or to good causes outside its structures. They are busy working and earning a living and they need to devote time to their families, and leisure. For younger churchgoers it may be the only time that they can give to their Christian obligation is worship on a Sunday.

This may be a part truth, but one suspects that greater forces are at work which influence the age profile of church attenders. Modern quantitative research surveys show that young adults and people in their middle years do not feature in the same proportions as once was the case and that the older age groups predominate (Brierley, 1991, 2000, 2001). Thus, if there is to be a contribution to social capital of any kind from church people, it would seem to be that it must come from the older, more numerous age group.

Transmission of religious values

Modern surveys suggest that the situation regarding church affiliation is that not only are the numbers of young and middle aged people in local churches smaller in number than was the case in the mid-twentieth century, but that the same trend is evident among all age groups. There has been a general falling away of numbers associating themselves with the institutional church. In the past forty years theories of secularization have been thought to lie behind this cultural change (Wilson, 1966), but observations that people are investing in other kinds of spirituality have brought such theories into question (Davie, 2003, p. 30). The mainstream denominations and the institutional church generally, it is argued, are no longer the main expressions of spirituality, but individual spirituality is in modern times expressed in many other ways (Richards, 2003, p. 87). If we are to understand that social capital is being created by local church people within the institutional church framework then how does this augur for the creation of social capital in the future? Such diminution of possibilities would seem to indicate a decrease in social capital in community activities (Putnam, 2000, pp. 65–79).

What becomes important in this situation, then, is the transmission of Christian values from one generation to the next, the socialization of the younger people in local churches. The challenge of the transmission of Christian values from one generation to another is not only a problem for the local church, but also in the present religious and social climate a problem for the whole of the institutional church (Percy, 2003, pp. 106–122).

Conclusion

In the light of eight case histories from people in the Baptist/Methodist and the Roman Catholic churches in the large village of this study it can be clearly seen that a contribution was being made to social capital. The eight interviewees were active in their church's social networks and in the creation of social interaction and cohesion in their own community, thus creating bonding social capital. They were also successful in creating bridging social capital in the village by their participation in a number of different voluntary and statutory community agencies.

The motivations which led them into this activity were created by their own perception of Christian values. It was something that they felt they had to do because of their commitment to Christianity.

There were indications that differences in the value system of the two churches made some difference to the way that bridging social capital was created, and its amount, but this needs further investigation.

One factor common to all of them was that they were elderly Christians, which raises questions about the participation of younger Christians in the creation of social capital and also the possible decline of the Church's contribution to social capital formation with the decline in numerical size of the institutional church in recent years and the diversification of spiritual beliefs and religious attitudes with economic and cultural change.

The decline in numbers of those church people active in social change, especially among mature Christians, raises questions regarding the church's mission, and the transmission of religious values in the institutional church across the generations.

References

Avis, P. (2004). Rethinking ecumenical theology. In P. Avis (Ed.), *Paths to unity: Explorations in ecumenical method* (pp. 91–106). London: Church Publishing House.

Brierley, P. (1991). *Christian England*. London: Marc Europe.

Brierley, P. (2000). *The tide is running out: Results of the English church attendance survey 1998*. London: Christian Research.

Brierley, P. (Ed.). (2001). *UK Christian handbook, religious trends No. 3: 2002/2003*. London: Christian Research.

Davie, G. (2003). Seeing salvation: The use of text as data in the sociology of religion. In P. Avis (Ed.), *Public faith? The state of religious belief and practice in Britain* (pp. 28–44). London: SPCK.

Hall, P. A. (1999). Social capital in Britain. *The British Journal of Political Science, 29*, 417–461.

Hanifan, L. J. (1916). The rural school community centre. *Annals of the American Academy of Political and Social Science, 67*, 130–138.

Percy, M. (2003). Mind the gap: Generational change and its implications for mission. In P. Avis (Ed.), *Public faith? The state of religious belief and practice in Britain* (pp. 106–122). London: SPCK.

Putnam, R. D. (2000). *Bowling alone: The collapse and revival of American community*. New York: Simon and Schuster.

Richards, A. (2003). Interpreting contemporary spirituality. In P. Avis (Ed.), *Public faith? The state of religious belief and practice in Britain* (pp. 78–91). London: SPCK.

Wilson, B. R. (1966). *Religion in secular society*: London: Watts and Co.

Chapter 19

LOCAL FESTIVALS IN TWO PENNINE VILLAGES: THE REACTIONS OF THE LOCAL METHODIST CHURCH CONGREGATIONS

*Sue Pegg and Lewis Burton**

Abstract – National and local festivals, carnivals and processions are a feature of social life and the way in which the human race has celebrated in its leisure moments. This article examines the reaction of two local Pennine village churches to a festival in each of their communities. It highlights certain features of the relationship between village festivals and the life of the local church.

Introduction

Festivals, carnivals and the gathering of people for local celebrations are part of social life. People come together in large groups to follow some interest, or to mark some local or national achievement, and have done so since early times. It is through such occasions that the stresses of ordinary life can be put aside, and enjoyment found in social pursuits with others. The Bible witnesses to the fact that religion has often been the initiator of such celebrations. Examples can be found throughout the Old Testament of how Israel came together on great days to celebrate both national and religious events. The story of how David brought the Ark of the Covenant to Jerusalem, told in 1 Chronicles 15, is one example

* The Revd Sue Pegg is Methodist minister in the Market Weighton section of the Pocklington and Market Weighton Methodist Circuit. *Address for correspondence*: Beverley Road, Market Weighton, YO43 3JN.
  E-mail: revsuepegg@tiscali.co.uk
    The Revd Dr Lewis Burton, a retired Methodist minister, is Honorary Research Fellow in the St Mary's Centre, Wales. *Address for correspondence*: 94 Sun Street, Haworth, Keighley, BD22 8AH. E-mail: lewisburton@blueyonder.co.uk

of how such happenings were integral to the religious and political life of the people of Israel. The ritual significance of such events is apparent. Psalm 24 is another example, where the repetitive question and answer in the text suggests that it is a part of a liturgy associated with some great political or religious event in the life of the people of Israel. One can imagine the procession approaching the closed city gates and the ritual question and answer as the gates are opened and the procession moves into the city for the climax of the event.

In the New Testament one observer has associated the Palm Sunday procession of Jesus with a carnival. In this image it becomes a glorious colourful procession, something both of beauty and the grotesque, with the children waving, and people dancing and singing and laughing and tumbling in the streets (Durbar, 2004).

In modern times carnival and religion find themselves together in the Mardi Gras of Catholic countries on Shrove Tuesday as a way of celebrating the last of the good times as the strictures of Lent and the preparation for Easter take over daily life. The word carnival itself has this Christian connection as it is derived from the Latin *carnem levare*, 'the putting away of flesh', as the fasting of Lent begins. In more modern times such celebrations have been secularized in the colourful processions such as the Notting Hill carnival and those other similar high days by which immigrant populations have lightened up staid English ways.

Carnivals were not always strangers to England, however, and local communities, here and there throughout the land, have organized their own festivals at different times of the year, sometimes for religious purposes, sometimes to raise money for good causes, and sometimes just for the pleasure and the excuse of letting the hair down and taking a break from the more serious purpose of making a living (Walvin, 1978; Walton & Walvin, 1983). By and large, however, it is the secular element which has taken over the local festivals and carnivals which were once partly the prerogative of the church and the church stands by to watch, sometimes critically, sometimes with neutral views, but not often in an organizational or initiatory capacity. Should the church be involved in such local festivals? How much should it be involved, especially when the festival is centred round an interest with little or no religious context, or when that interest seems adverse to the Christian message? Can it use the local festivals sponsored and organized by secular bodies to its own advantage? An attempt to answer such questions by determining the reactions of people attending a Methodist church in each of two

Pennine villages in 2004 was made, using questionnaires framed to elicit attitudes and possibilities.

The Jazz Festival

The Jazz Festival was first celebrated in the village of Marsden in 1991. The first venue was in the Mechanics Hall, a large community hall in the centre of the village, which had just been re-furbished at the time. The Artistic Director of the Mikron Theatre Group, which is based at the Institute, was anxious to attract a range of different events to the venue and a music festival was the one idea which was considered. After discussion it was felt that a jazz festival would be the best option. A number of people who were active in the jazz scene locally were contacted and the first Marsden Jazz Festival was the result. The festival which took place in 2004 was the thirteenth, and jazz concerts took place in a variety of venues around the village, mainly in public houses and clubs over a period of Friday, Saturday and Sunday in October. On the Saturday afternoon a jazz procession moved down the village street, followed by performances in various venues, and on the Sunday morning a jazz service was held in Marsden United Church (Methodist/URC). The festival is funded in a number of ways: by ticket receipts, by a number of donations from local sponsors, and by a number of small grants from various bodies. The organization of the event is by volunteers, the majority of whom live in Marsden.

The Moonraker Festival

The Moonraker Festival is an annual event in the village of Slaithwaite (pronounced locally as Slowit, the 'ow' voiced as in cow). It was created and organized jointly by the Satellites, a local arts organization, and the Slaithwaite Community Association in 1985. Originally the festival is based on a local legend. The story is that sometime in the nineteenth century a batch of smuggled brandy was hidden in the canal at Slaithwaite. One cloudless night the villagers were caught by excise men as they attempted to fish out the contraband from the canal. The quick thinking villagers attempted to avoid capture by pretending that they were 'trying to rake out the moon' which rather inexplicably had got itself into the water. The excise men then thought them to be fools or mad or drunk, and moved on, leaving the villagers to recover, not a reflected moon but their brandy.

In later years the event grew in size as the Slaithwaite Moonraker Festival Organizing Group was formed. This management group is locally based and the actual preparations include many local volunteers. The core feature of the event is a parade of people with lanterns, an idea brought from Ulverston by some members of the founding Satellite group. This provides a spectacular scene during the dark evenings of February. The half-term holiday means that many schoolchildren can be involved, not only in the event, but also in the making of the lanterns. In 2005 almost six hundred lanterns were made and carried, which is an indication of the popularity of the event. After the procession around the village participants finally congregate at the canal, ranging along the canal bank, where the climax of the festival is a ceremonial raking out of a 'moon'.

There was no involvement of the churches in the festival before 2000, when the local Anglicans decided to make an angel lantern and join the procession. The Methodists began to participate in 2003. In 2004 the Methodists held a Sunday morning service on Moonraker weekend, and a joint Service of Light involving Methodists and Anglicans was held on the evening of the procession.

Method

The villages

Marsden and Slaithwaite are both situated in the upper Colne Valley which runs in a south westerly direction from Huddersfield into high Pennine country (Ordnance Survey, 1970). The villages are in a deep valley and the hills either side climb sharply to the high moor. Both villages have been the centre of the woollen textile industry, but now the mills are closed and job opportunities have to be sought elsewhere. Recent developments have helped both villages. Marsden is at the top of the valley and has recently developed a tourist trade with the refurbishment of the Huddersfield narrow canal. Marsden tunnel end marks the eastern entry of a three mile tunnel where in the canal's working days barges were 'legged' through into Lancashire. Slaithwaite, two and a quarter miles down the valley toward Huddersfield, has not benefited from tourism and is somewhat smaller in population size. The M62 motorway has taken much of the passing road traffic and both villages are much quieter. Nevertheless, both have become commuter villages, as train services to Manchester, Huddersfield and Leeds provide rapid transit to jobs elsewhere. This, coupled with the fact that house prices have been somewhat cheaper than elsewhere, has attracted new people to both places. This demographic change has altered the social mix of the local populations and brought new skills and understandings for supporting community activities and new strength to village organizations.

The questionnaires and samples

Although the main questionnaire used for both village churches was essentially the same, slight differences between the two were necessary. After a preamble to explain the point of the survey reactions were tested from both churches to festivals which were church organized. The questions asked were in four sections. The first section was the same for both churches and related to events which were organized by the church, gauging reactions to the services both for the great Christian festivals and also to those which marked local church celebrations and events, such as the Sunday School Anniversary. How easy was it to invite others to such occasions, and whether attendance brought forth some spiritual reaction were subjects of enquiry. The second section was directed to those festivals which were village organized. For Marsden they related to the Jazz Festival and for Slaithwaite to Moonraker. Most of the questions in this section were the same for both villages. A third section of the questionnaire explored reactions to the kind of music which members of each congregation favoured in church worship, Marsden having an extra question regarding the reaction to the playing of jazz in a church service. Sections two and three employed a series of short items designed for assessment on a five-point Likert scale (agree strongly, agree, not certain, disagree and disagree strongly). In the last section general information was gathered relating to the respondents' sex, age, frequency and duration of attendance at church, together with any involvement in the organizing of the festivals. This main questionnaire was distributed to the members of the congregations of both churches shortly after the festivals took place.

In a preliminary study concerned with the composition of the congregation at the Jazz Festival service at Marsden, a short questionnaire was circulated after the service to gather information about the geographical origin of members of the congregation.

Results

The Jazz Festival

The response to this preliminary short questionnaire circulated to the 160 people who had attended the Jazz Festival service resulted in 100 responses. From this it appeared that of those attending and responding, 27% lived in Marsden, 36% in the surrounding area, and 37% were visiting especially for the occasion and lived outside the area. Of the 27% who lived in Marsden, 14% attended the United Church regularly, 9% attended for both village and church festivals, and 4% attended only for the jazz service. Of the 36% who lived in the surrounding area, 7% attended the United Church regularly, 14% worshipped in the area in which they lived, 11% worshipped occasionally at church festivals, and 4% attended only for the jazz service. Of the 37% who lived outside the area, 11% worshipped regularly in the place where they lived, 1% were of another faith, 23% worshipped occasionally for church festivals, and 2% attended only for the jazz festival.

Francis and Martineau (2001, p. 28), in their examination of church visitors, state that the number of visitors to a church from the surrounding area was 50% compared with the 37% at Marsden, but for those who travelled from outside the area proportions were comparable, 41% as compared with 37% at Marsden, which suggests that the Jazz Festival does provide a place of worship for jazz enthusiasts who come from some distance away as compared with occasional worshippers at the church. The proportions generally show that the Jazz Festival service does cater for the kind of visitor from some distance away but does not necessarily attract Christian jazz enthusiasts from the immediate surrounding area who may choose to worship in their own local church that morning. On analysis it seems that the fact that the service was especially connected to the jazz festival, and had a significant jazz content, did not have a significant effect on the numbers who regularly attended ordinary services.

The main, more detailed questionnaire, prepared for both Marsden and Slaithwaite was given to regular worshippers at Marsden at an ordinary service two weeks after the Jazz Festival. This was completed by 40 people, 25% male and 75% female. Over three quarters of these (83%) were over 41 years old, with most of them (68%) being over 60 years. Only 8% were under 30 years. Of the 40 respondents, 63% came to church on a weekly basis, 18% monthly and 10% occasionally. Just over a third (38%) had been attending church for over twenty years, and 47%

had attended for less than ten years; 15% were comparative newcomers. A similar age structure is reflected in Francis and Martineau's (2001) research which showed that 31% of church visitors are aged 60 years or over, and that twice as many women visit churches as men, and that this closely matches the proportions of women and men who attend church services.

In the analysis of the items in sections two and three, the two categories 'agree' and 'agree strongly' were combined to form the positive response and the two categories 'disagree' and 'disagree strongly' were combined to form the negative response. All the respondents gave a positive response to the first prompt regarding the celebration of Christian festivals such as Christmas, Easter and Harvest in church. Those who found these celebrations spiritually uplifting represented 85% whereas 15% were unsure. The lack of enthusiasm on the part of some may be explained by the fact that the respondents had a high proportion of the elderly, especially elderly females living alone, who found the great festivals of the church a lonely time, particularly when services on such occasions tended to be focused on families. For local celebrations, such as the Sunday School Anniversary, rather than the great festivals of the Christian year, those who found them to be spiritually uplifting represented 90% of respondents. The difference between the spiritual response to the great Christian festivals and the local church festivals might be that the elderly turn out more for these local occasions. What draws them to the local festival is the strong nostalgic component, a tendency manifest in the whole of West Yorkshire Methodism, and it is this nostalgia which gives a particular appreciation for the local festivals and the feeling of benefit received from them. If this is so, the point above about elderly attendance at the great festivals is reinforced.

Festival services appear to be times when many church members feel that they can invite others along to worship. Family members were targeted by 70% of respondents while only 60% thought that they would invite friends and neighbours. This latter percentage was hardly different from that of 59% who felt that they could invite people to an ordinary service. It was felt, however, that the special occasion did provide some incentive to regular churchgoers to invite family and friends to church. Only 42% of those who had responded to the invitation to join in worship at festival times had received positive feedback regarding spiritual response, and only 22% for those who were attending an ordinary service.

Of those people who responded, 98% thought that events such as the Jazz Festival make a valuable contribution to village life, and 90% also thought that it made a valuable contribution to church life. It does seem, though, that some think that church and village life should remain separated. However, 95% felt that it was of value for the Jazz Festival to come to church and 83% felt that they could invite family, friends and neighbours to the festival service. Of those who had done so 45% had received feedback that the service had been spiritually helpful. Every respondent agreed that the church should be involved in festivals irrespective of whether they made a valuable contribution to the life of the church, and all agreed that the festivals were good for the village compared with the 95% who also thought them to be good for the church. The latter percentage suggests that there are a few, perhaps those who experience loneliness, who are afraid of being in large crowds, and some who find large numbers in church difficult. For these it would appear that the festival service does not meet their personal needs.

Organists and other church musicians can also be wary of jazz musicians who displace them. Traditional church music was supported by 28% of respondents, but 60% were sure that music in church should not be limited to organ or piano. This sits oddly with the 92% who liked to hear a variety of musical instruments in church, probably weighted by the fact that the church sponsored a young people's music group. Brass bands are a feature of this part of West Yorkshire, every village either having one, or at one time had one, and 68% enjoyed the prospect of them playing in the church. The prospect of jazz music as a regular feature of church music met with approval from 78%, a somewhat larger proportion than those who appreciated brass bands, which perhaps indicates that local tastes may be changing, perhaps as a result of changes in the local demography.

The Jazz Festival on the whole seems to cater for those whom John Drane in his book *The McDonaldization of the Church* (Drane, 2000, p. 65) calls party-goers. He explains that by becoming almost different personalities at week-ends people find inner strength to cope with the rigid structures in which they find themselves enmeshed during the week. He points out that unless Christians engage with these underlying concerns they will have nothing to say to people. Drane concludes that an effective spirituality which can engage play as worship and see God's kingdom as a party would cater for such people. The Jazz Festival in Marsden seems to do just this which could perhaps explain its popularity. John Clarke (1995) demonstrated the importance of targeting non-Christians, enquirers and seekers in the development of the Willow Creek Community in Chicago. Church growth can occur when worshippers invite friends who are on their personal fringe. He abjures worship content which puts pressure on worshippers to voice what they may not mean and suggests that this be replaced by the use of creative arts. The services at the Jazz Festival and the Moonraker Festival are lively and use creative arts in worship.

The Moonraker Festival

The questionnaire for the Moonraker Festival was distributed to worshippers at Slaithwaite Methodist Church after a Sunday morning service. There were 40 responses, 6 males (15%) and 34 females (85%). Ages ranged from twenty to over seventy; 5% were in their twenties, 3% were in their thirties, 5% were in their forties, 10% were in their fifties, 37% were in their sixties, and 40% were over seventy.

When asked about celebrations, 95% said that they always enjoyed the great festivals of the church year and 90% said that they found them spiritually fulfilling. When asked about the special celebrations such as the anniversaries of the local church 93% enjoyed them and 80% found them spiritually fulfilling. However, fewer were convinced that the Moonraker Festival should be celebrated in church, 60% thinking that it was of value that the church joined in the village event; and only 55% feeling that they could invite their family to a Moonraker service. These proportions indicate some suspicion of a Moonraker Festival service as a 'proper' service, but an anecdotal story can be told concerning a couple who requested the baptism of their baby at a Moonraker Festival service as they thought the service sounded 'fun'. This incident chimes with Michael Fanstone's research (Fanstone, 1993, p. 66), when he suggests, using interviews carried out with church leavers, that a substantial proportion thought that church services were dull and boring. It would seem that a large minority of respondents at Slaithwaite preferred traditional worship content, rather than things out of the ordinary. Despite their reservations 76% of respondents felt that the church should be involved in some way with the Moonraker Festival and 71% felt that they were good for church life. Only 8% saw them as being detrimental.

In the matter of church music at Slaithwaite opinions were rather contradictory: 85% of respondents liked to hear a variety of musical instruments played in church, but 38% said they preferred only organ or piano for music in church services. Despite the local tradition of brass bands, only 35% felt that their music was acceptable for a service in church. As those who approved represented only 5% of the sample there were obviously a good number in the congregation who, for one reason or another, were neutral on the issue.

Discussion

One of the assumptions made in this discussion is that both the churches have similar attitudes which colour their reaction to the festivals which take place in the two villages. They both share in the Methodist tradition, although Marsden is a Local Ecumenical Partnership (LEP) with the United Reformed Church. Both churches have been, and currently are being, served by a minister from the Huddersfield Pennine Methodist Circuit. The age profile and regularity of attendance of the two congregations are very similar, with Marsden having over two thirds of those who responded in the over 60 age group compared with Slathwaite's three quarters. Slaithwaite, however, has a wider spread and slightly more in younger age groups than Marsden.

If one makes this assumption, which seems reasonable, each church's reaction to its village festival can be assessed in a comparative way. One question to be asked is, 'Is the content and action of the festival an acceptable activity for a village Christian congregation?' Certainly both churches support their own festivals, both those which are major events of the Christian year and those attached to celebratory occasions in their own history, but do they view the secular festivals of the village with the same acceptance? Among the respondents at Marsden there was a very positive acceptance of the Jazz Festival, both as a village event and in the way that it made a valuable contribution to church life. The enthusiasm was only very slightly below that given to church festival events but both types of festival received a very positive endorsement. Perhaps it was hardly surprising that this should be so when at the jazz Sunday service there was a bumper congregation, the 160 attenders far outnumbering the 40 to 50 for ordinary services. The data provided by these 160 attenders demonstrated that 43 of them would have come to a service in this church on an ordinary occasion. This is an indication of the support which regular attenders gave to the jazz service. Another endorsement which respondents from the Marsden church were willing to give to the Jazz Festival is also seen in their views of the type of music which is suitable for the local church. Organ and piano only were thought to be suitable instruments for services at Slaithwaite by over two thirds of respondents, whereas at Marsden only one quarter subscribed to this view, over 90% liking a variety of instruments for use in church. Similar differences of opinion existed in the two churches, with 78% in Marsden regarding jazz music to be appropriate for a church service, compared with 15% in Slaithwaite. This greater openness to musical innovation at Marsden than at Slaithwaite confirms the positive attitude at Marsden for the Jazz Festival service.

Respondents from the congregation at Slaithwaite were much more reticent in welcoming the prospect of a service in church connected to the Moonraker Festival. There 60% of people thought that such a service would be of value and 50% would be prepared to invite their family to it. This contrasted with the value they saw in celebrating the festivals of the church year and their own local church festivals. Their approval for this latter type of festival was much the same as at Marsden and was very positive. There could be a number of reasons for this. A conservative attitude is shown in their response to music in church, as we have already seen, and this may be an indication of a conservative attitude which touched other aspects of church life. Another factor is that the Jazz Festival at Marsden had been established longer, and the churches there have a history of involvement stretching over a number of years. The church at Slaithwaite has no such experience and the churches of the village have only recently made tentative steps to be involved with the village organization. Perhaps the main reason is that the nature of the two festivals makes a difference. The churches of Huddersfield and the Colne valley have always had a musical tradition and one might therefore suppose that an extension of this to jazz is not a very large step, whilst Moonraker, although a village legend, has nothing of religion to commend it and can be viewed in a certain way as being at best rather foolish and at worst having something of the pagan about it. In the light of this one can understand that the people of the church could be a little more reticent in taking the Moonraker Festival to their hearts. However, despite this greater reticence at Slaithwaite, for one reason or another, there were over two thirds of respondents from the church who thought that such village events were good for church life.

What is apparent at Marsden is that the church there was aware of what was happening around it in the village and recognized this as a situation which provided opportunities at various levels. It provided occasions where the church's participation in village events could indicate clearly to the local community its interest in village community affairs and its willingness to participate, thus encouraging positive perceptions on the part of non-churchgoing villagers. Its sponsorship of the jazz service brought people into church who followed the jazz interest and engaged with them in Christian worship. It thus provided a unique evangelistic opportunity. Slaithwaite church had not developed the potential that the Moonraker Festival offered, but there were those among the respondents who realized that opportunities were there to be grasped. What was important in both places, and to some extent had been achieved, was that church people understood that they must have an important ongoing relationship with the village community, and for the sake of its own mission have an attitude of openness to the opportunities that the village provides. This would be more than a mission opportunity for it would also create social cohesion which would be of benefit to all. On the theological level Martineau (1999) has suggested that community is central to the Christian faith, and is at the heart of God in the sense that it is this sort of relationship which is proclaimed by the existence of the Trinity. It is imperative that the church relates to the secular community if it is to be truly faithful to Trinitarian doctrine. The Church's task is not simply to form an association of like-minded people but to call the whole world into the kingdom. Christians both at Marsden and Slaithwaite are feeling their way to this end in making the most of relationships with the secular communities of their villages.

Conclusion

Five main themes emerge from this study of two Pennine villages which may have wider implications for rural ministry. First, local secular festivals provide evangelistic opportunities for local churches. Second, traditional attitudes and practices can prevent churches making the most of such evangelistic opportunities. Third, some discernment is required as not all secular festivals are equally compatible with Christian values and expectations. Fourth, with open and welcoming attitudes built between the church and the village community at festival time, benefits for both church and village can ensue. Fifth, festivals enable the church to be perceived as an integral part of village life, rather than something apart, if the opportunities created by festivals are securely grasped.

References

Clarke, J. (1995). *Evangelism that really works*. London: SPCK.
Drane, J. (2000). *The McDonaldization of the church*. London: Darton, Longman and Todd.

Durber, S. (2004). *Carnival.* Retrieved from www.website.lineone.net/~susandurber/sermon36.html, accessed 1 March 2006.

Fanstone, M. J. (1993). *The sheep that got away.* Tunbridge Wells: Monarch Publications.

Francis, L. J., & Martineau, J. (2001). *Rural visitors.* Stoneleigh Park: Acora Publishing.

Martineau, J. (1999). *Bridging the gap.* Stoneleigh Park: Acora Publishing.

Ordnance Survey. (1970). 1:25000 Marsden Sheet SE 01.

Walton, J., & Walvin, J. (Eds.). (1983). *Leisure in Britain 1780–1939.* Manchester: Manchester University Press.

Walvin, J. (1978), *Leisure and Society 1830–1950.* London: Longman.

Chapter 20

EXTENDED COMMUNION: A SECOND BEST OPTION FOR RURAL ANGLICANISM?

*Stella Mills**

Abstract – Extended communion has been used as a solution for the increasing shortage of ordained ministers; it is not, however, without critics who identify theological problems with its usage. In particular, the three concepts of the Divine Presence, of celebration, and of the communion of the faithful raise questions for congregations utilizing extended communion. Furthermore, the use of lay ministers in the service of extended communion can lead to isolation of the parish priest as well as high-lighting issues about lay presidency. This article discusses these themes in the context of an evaluation of an extended communion scheme in a parish of the Church of England. While there is some evidence for the isolation of the rector, congregational perceptions make no distinction between extended and holy communion services. In the case of home (extended) communions, however, the absence of worship space plays an important part – something about which the literature is silent.

Introduction

With the shortage of clergy in the Church of England, problems have arisen as to how to accommodate the Sunday services of holy communion which require an ordained priest to preside. A number of suggestions have been put forward including non-stipendiary ministers (NSMs) and ordained local ministers (OLMs) as well as local non-stipendiary

* Professor Stella Mills is Professor of Multimedia Technology at Staffordshire University, and Methodist Local Preacher in the Dove Valley Circuit. *Address for correspondence*: Faculty of Computing, Engineering and Technology, Staffordshire University, Beaconside, Stafford, ST18 0AD. E-mail: s.f.mills@staffs.ac.uk

ministers (LNSMs) (Smethurst, 1986, p. 19). In addition, it is now commonplace for lay people to distribute the blessed elements during a service of holy communion. More radical calls have also been made for lay presidency which can be seen as threatening ordination theology. Another alternative (Russell, 1993, p. 172) is that of extended communion where the elements are blessed through priestly presidency in the usual way within a service of holy communion but after the eucharistic prayer of thanksgiving, two lay ministers leave to take these elements to another service in another building. Tovey (2001, p. 12) noted that the term *holy communion* is used when a priest is present to celebrate and the term *extended communion* is used when the communion is distributed during an act of worship which is led by a lay minister. Thus the term *extended holy communion* is not used.

However, there are some theological concerns with extended communion and this article explores some of these within the practical context of a case study in the North of England. First, though, we turn to the theological problems associated with extended communion.

Themes of theological concern

The literature concerning extended communion identifies a number of key themes. Theologically, there is the issue of celebration which is coupled to the concept of presence and the congregational link with the communion of the faithful. Then there are more practical issues associated with lay presidency and lay leadership and the corresponding isolation of the parish priest which the use of laity can bring. Within a short article it is impossible to explore all these themes in any detail but the main points identified by the literature concerning each will now be discussed.

Celebration and divine presence

The divine presence rests on the promise of Jesus to be with his disciples for evermore (Matthew 28:20b) but the New Testament is quiet about the details of holy communion (that is, Lord's Supper) liturgy, including the prayer of invocation. Article 28 of the *39 Articles of Religion* does not speak directly of the divine presence at holy communion but the modern *Methodist Catechism* (Methodist Church, 2000, p 26) states that 'In the Lord's Supper Jesus Christ is present with his worshipping people and gives himself to them as their Lord and Saviour.' Neither the *39 Articles* nor the *Methodist Catechism* identifies the exact nature of this presence at holy communion but they agree that it is spiritual. For Roman Catholics, the presence is realized through transubstantiation, mirroring the 'fully empowered proclamation of the Easter mystery' (Ratzinger in Dulles, 2002, p. 163) while for Orthodox Christians, the 'bread and wine, having been offered as an oblation and set apart for sacrifice, have now the sacred characters of an *ikon*' (Underhill, 1937, pp. 153–154). For Smithson (1998, p. 8), it is a transfiguring through Christ's grace that for the priest extends well beyond holy communion into the whole priestly life. This transfiguring is celebrated at holy communion and differentiates celebration from extended forms of holy communion.

The community of the faithful (present and departed)

All worship joins the Christian with the communion of saints but certain parts of the liturgy emphasize this more than others. Thus, the Methodist Church uses the link of holy communion to the Messianic Banquet/Feast, founded on Isaiah, 25:6-8 (Schweitzer, 1936, pp. 377–378, footnote 1, p. 377). The means of this link is faith (*Book of Common Prayer, Article 28*). However, in more recent years, emphasis has been placed on the worshipping community itself as a social experience (Underhill, 1937, p. 159), recalling the early Christian celebrations of holy communion, which were focused on the (human) unity of the gathering (Roloff, 2002, p. 138).

Within the New Testament, detailed accounts of the liturgy and procedures used during holy communion (or more exactly, in New Testament terminology, The Lord's Supper) are scanty (Newbigin, 1996, p. 368) but Paul gives direction to the Corinthian church (1 Corinthians 11:23-26) which emphasizes that holy communion is not only at the heart of the worshipping community but also that the community owns the celebration and the action becomes 'an aggregate communal responsibility' (Roloff, 2002, p. 129). It is thus through the celebration of holy communion that the worshipping community is joined to the community of the faithful departed.

The celebrant – ordained or lay?

For the Church of England, an ordained priest must act as the celebrant at holy communion (Littler, Francis, & Martineau, 2000, pp. 42–43) since ordination yields an authorizing of certain activities including presiding at holy communion. However, Newbigin (1996, pp. 369–370) goes further and argues that ordination confirms the ordinand's relationship not only with the whole body of the baptized but also with God. Thus, the priest is the 'integration and coordination of all the charisms in a way that serves the unity of the Church' (Dulles, 2002, p. 157), where ordination becomes a sacred action with the priest emanating holiness and separation from 'secular distractions' (Dulles, 2002, p. 159).

On the other hand, many (lay) church office holders have the dual relationship of God in Christ and duty to the community without being ordained. Indeed, Reader (1987, p. 185) suggests that ordination 'is a symbol required by man [*sic*], not a status granted by God' and claims it creates divisions between clergy and laity which still inhibit the ministry of the whole church (Reader, 1987, p. 187). This view is echoed by Williams (2004, p. 31, p. 45 in particular) who argued for a much more people-focused church rather than one dominated by the priest's role.

Given that New Testament celebrations of holy communion were in house churches, it is likely that the head of the family would have presided at the celebration and would also have been responsible for the associated preparation of the meal and the collection for the poor. Clearly, this creates a tension today between those who call for a return to biblically-based practices, where the community is the centre of its own determining, subject to biblical constraints, such as can be seen in the many growing house churches today and the practices of the established churches. For the Anglican Church and its celebration of holy communion, this becomes essentially a question of who should be allowed to preside. New Testament theology strongly suggests that it is the leader of the Christian community who should preside (Roloff, 2002, p. 137 and Smithson, 1998, p. 6). However, it is Christ who invites and presides at the meal and, for the established denominations, Christ's presidency is represented by the priest or minister (World Council of Churches, 1982, M14).

Isolation of the parish priest

As extended communion is given to congregations by lay ministers, this can lead to an isolation of the parish priest in that this person is no longer seen to be the congregation's leader in an administrative and/or spiritual sense. However, the absence of the priest can lead to a flowering of lay leadership where readers and other church officials can develop their own *charisms* for the greater good of the worshipping community. This can, though, lead to tensions between different worshipping groups as well as between priest and lay ministers.

These themes were explored in a case study using mainly qualitative methods and it is to this we now turn.

Method

Parish profile

The Anglican parish of Overtown (names have been disguised to keep anonymity) is situated in the north of England and is centred on a market town. Besides the historical large parish church of St Columba, there are three smaller, satellite churches all of which have lay leaders. One rural church, St John's is some three miles from Overtown, while both of the other churches are situated on the outskirts of the town. St James' meets in a non-conformist chapel and has extended communion fortnightly, while St Jude's was founded just over 100 years ago on an industrial estate. Both St John's and St Jude's only occasionally have extended communion.

Procedure

Because of the conceptual nature of the evaluation of an extended communion scheme, a mainly qualitative approach was used. In-depth semi-structured interviews were undertaken with all the key stake-holders while focus groups were used with the three smaller churches. Because of practical restraints, a partly quantitative questionnaire was used with the main parish church.

Three visits were made to the parish of Overtown, the first of which was used to obtain information about the stakeholders' views on the communion, the presence and other theological aspects. On this first visit, semi-structured interviews were held with the rector, the pastoral visitors' co-ordinator who is also a reader, the home communions co-ordinator (who has oversight of St James') and a reader who has pastoral oversight of St Jude's. All interviews were audio-tape recorded and further telephone and e-mail correspondence filled in details that were found to have been inadvertently omitted from the formal interviews.

The second visit gathered data from those who receive communion by extension at home. There are about six such people in the parish but due to age and infirmity, only four of these were able to take part in semi-structured interviews, and two of these were husband and wife. Thus, three homes were visited and the home communions co-ordinator was present throughout the interviews, consequently easing ethical consid-erations. In addition, two focus groups were held with the congregations of St James' (14 present) and St John's (10 present) as well as a semi-structured interview with the reader who has pastoral charge for St John's. Although the focus groups were rather large, the people all knew each other and good discussion prevailed especially at St James'. Again, all the interviews and focus groups were audio-recorded.

The third visit was made to St Jude's in order to obtain data from a focus group. Six members of the congregation attended in addition to the reader who has oversight of the church. The discussion was audio-recorded.

In addition to these visits to the parish and at the request of the rector, extended communion at an evening service at St Columba's was evaluated. This was necessary as the rector had to be away at short notice and the service was taken by a reader. The rector was particularly interested in this evaluation as the congregation were young people and the worship rather more informal than at the other services which had been visited. Unfortunately, the researcher could not be present in person due to other commitments and so this evaluation utilized a short questionnaire which combined questions from the prompts used in the focus groups and the questions used in the home visits.

In all cases, participants were allowed to leave at any time and all participation was voluntary. Indeed, in all cases, the arrangements were made by the local leaders concerned.

Results

Focus groups

As is usual with focus groups, the discussions revealed much data beyond the questions asked. At St James', the congregation saw themselves more as a fellowship with the intimacy of an 'extended family' where sharing with each other was easy and all had a feeling of belonging. For elderly folk living alone, this was important as was the distance from home to the place of worship, given that they wanted to keep their independence by walking. They all recognized the rector as their leader and would have liked more contact with him but they recognized the commitments he had and they would not 'bother him' unless there was something 'really important'. By far the most important point made was the worship space, sitting in a circle rather than in pews, and the plain décor allowing focus on the liturgy more directly. They agreed that the parish church worship was 'so impersonal' by comparison. They preferred this worship space even though the worship often lacked music and a formal sermon, although a meditation was used frequently.

Both St James' and St John's congregations agreed that participating in extended communion felt no different from holy communion, although St John's had infrequent extended communion services. However, St John's looked to the reader as their leader and would approach her for pastoral care needs, although in the case of a funeral, they 'would have to go to the rector'. St John's seemed rather wary of involving the rector since it transpired a previous rector had tried to close the church with the result that people had started attending from a wide area. The reader is attempting to build bridges with St Columba's and already St John's is being supported by pastoral visitors from the parish church. St John's had no difficulties with confidentiality or professional issues in lay pastoral care but the congregation agreed that trust depended on personalities rather than ordination or position.

Like St John's, St Jude's had no problems of confidentiality with lay pastoral care and they also saw the reader with pastoral oversight as the leader of the worshipping community. Again, along with St John's and St James', they doubted whether the general populace would know the rector, from whom the congregation felt isolated except on the two or three occasions in each year when they worshipped at St Columba's. No one felt there to be any differences between holy communion or extended communion, although the latter only occurred infrequently.

All three satellite congregations were more concerned with being closed through lack of numbers than any theological or practical issues with extended communion.

Interviews

Four people, all attached to St Columba's church, were interviewed as recipients of extended communion at home and they all very much appreciated being able to receive. They all made the comment that without this service, they would have little contact with the church, apart from pastoral visits. None of the interviewees had problems with the lay administration of extended communion, although one admitted to having concerns at first. However, when she discovered that 'the lay people … [did] it properly', these concerns were removed and she now is completely happy receiving extended communion. Only one of the interviewees had received holy communion from an ordained priest at home and this person reported feeling no difference in the two services, either theologically or practically. Both were conducted with reverence and enabled her to worship. Three of the four participants felt extended communion linked them to St Columba's, while three definitely felt isolated from the rector; the fourth was unsure. None of the participants had any doubts about lay ministers keeping confidentialities or not being as 'professional' as clergy, because the lay ministers acted properly and with decorum. In short, there was no differentiation between lay ministers and clergy.

Perhaps the most surprising point made by all four participants was that they all preferred communion in church, not because of any theological associations with the communion and its liturgy, but because of the worship space in terms of surroundings and atmosphere. Thus, extended communion 'is not the same as going to church', even though the ministers are 'very friendly and nice' and 'it makes us feel that we still belong to the Church'. The advantages of extended communion were seen as reaching out to 'people who cannot reach church' and the service was seen as helpful. Indeed, one participant remarked that he was 'pleased as it is' and he would 'miss it' if it were stopped. There were no discriminatory comments from any participant.

Questionnaires

Of the 25 people attending the evening service, only 11 question-naires were returned. The age range of these participants stretched from teenage years to 60 years with an even spread of distribution. All except one participant, aged between 46 and 50 years, agreed that there was no difference between communion services at which the rector presided and those at which extended communion was given. Similarly, it was only this same respondent who would have problems with lay presidency, although one other felt that the president should be 'anointed' as being authorized by God to preside but need not be ordained; the other nine respondents stated that they would not have problems. Unfortunately, the single respondent against lay presidency did not answer the qualitative question about the reasons for having problems or as to how the communion from the rector felt different from that of extended communion.

Discussion

The data gathered have revealed a number of themes relating to those which the literature also showed as being of importance in extended communion and pastoral care. Interestingly, two areas for discussion, worship space and closure of a church, emerged from the fieldwork as important by-products and these, together with the other themes, will now be considered in turn.

Celebration and presence

The stakeholders in the extended communion scheme who were involved with its administration were all aware of the theological problems of consecration and the presence and it is significant that the only reference to communion being administered 'properly', by priestly consecration, was from one of the lay ministers. None of the lay participants, either within the housebound group or the satellite communities, felt any difference in taking extended communion or holy communion (Tovey, 2001, p. 12), and most verbally confirmed that both distributions felt the same. In addition, only one questionnaire respondent had problems with extended communion but did not elaborate on these. Theologically, this raises practical issues about the necessity of celebration as far as holy communion is concerned and the real significance for the congregation participating in the prayers of consecration and thanksgiving as part of the communion of the faithful (World Council of Churches, 1982, chapter 2). With the liturgy of both services being similar (but different in those two aspects), the worshipping communities still felt they had been to services of holy communion, even though strictly they had not. Amongst the congregations there was no admittance of extended communion being 'second best' and the special presence of Christ in the communion was felt (Hurtado, 1999).

Lay presidency

For the stakeholders involved in the scheme's administration, the question of lay presidency and the associated question of the meaning of ordination in the context of priestly presidency raised a variety of answers. Those lay members who were of Evangelical tradition, rather than Catholic, admitted some reservations about the need of priestly consecration of the elements, especially in the light of the 'priesthood of all believers' (1 Peter 2:9). Only one lay minister was adamant that the priest was necessary to consecrate and she admitted being of Catholic disposition. On the other hand, as a result of this evaluation, one of the readers confessed to having serious doubts as to whether ordained presidents were needed. Thus, tradition is important here and involves the perception of the priestly role within the worshipping community.

Given that many, though not all, of St Columba's worshippers are Evangelical, this may reflect the small number of worshippers with reservations about lay presidency. It may also reflect the growing trend of worshippers to question (or ignore?) the underlying theology of the liturgy (Wilson, 2004). Certainly the 26% of rural congregations found by Littler, Francis and Martineau (2000, p. 50) to be in favour of lay presidency is far surpassed in Overtown.

It remains, however, against Anglican Canon Law for a lay person to preside (Tovey, 2001, p. 22) although Davies (2004, p. 11) argued that for Evangelicals the word carries equal weight with holy communion and that participation by the people is more important than the ordination of the celebrant. For Anglo-Catholics the consecration itself is seen as most important, thus again indicating that the churchmanship is the crucial point.

Isolation of the priest

While the extended communion scheme is working well within the satellite churches of Overtown, there was a feeling of isolation from the rector (Archbishops' Commission, 1990, p. 187) with St James' wanting to see the rector a little more (perhaps by presiding three times a year). However, it is well known throughout the parish that the rector wants to close this church. The congregation hopes that by coming to the worship, the rector may relent and allow such a friendly and supportive group to continue.

St John's, however, was much more isolated and looked to the lay leader (a reader) for immediate leadership in all forms except where a priest was essential. The isolation here was seen as positive in that the congregation felt less threatened by an absent priest than if she or he were more active, because the worry of this community is that of closure. They welcomed holy communion from retired clergy who were seen as less threatening than the rector since their remit was celebrating holy communion at the invitation of the lay leader. Here, then, are two different situations in terms of isolation of the priest – St James' felt the isolation in terms of that discussed in the literature (for example, Archbishops' Commission, 1990, p. 187) while St John's is seen as isolation helping to heal previous wounds.

The congregation of St John's trusted the lay leader who was sensitive enough to build the necessary bridges slowly and gently. For example, linking St John's back to the pastoral care rota and the prayer chain, both being based at St Columba's, has proved to be an acceptable start in the rehabilitation process. At St John's, then, the isolation of the priest had little to do with extended communion, which, in any case, only happens rarely, but had much more to do with history and personalities.

Those who received extended communion at home certainly felt isolated from both the priest and their respective church. This group was very appreciative of the extended communion as without it they would have felt even less part of the communion of the faithful (World Council of Churches, 1982, chapter 2); such nurturing is an important part of pastoral care (Vickers, 2003, p. 13). Indeed, there is already evidence in Overtown that some readers are being asked to take funerals as a sign of this valued ministry (Gledhill, 2003, p. 183). This is good as it illustrates clearly that leadership in the church today has to be teamwork (Gledhill, 2003, p. 6).

Lay leadership

The extended communion scheme involved a number of lay, licensed ministers who were active in taking the communion to the worshippers both in the satellite churches and to those at home. Clearly, the lay involvement in the scheme was essential for its flourishing but it also meant that many more lay people were involved in an important part of church life than would be the case if there were no such scheme. This work has involved both retired and fully employed people and allowed gifts to flower which otherwise may have been neglected. The lay workers were rehearsed in the theological difficulties of extended communion and exhibited a mature faith which can only be an advantage to the wider church. In addition, they have been trained (Gledhill, 2003, p. 88), which may revitalize the whole community (Clinebell, 1984, p. 396), possibly making it grow (Gledhill, 2003, p. 180), while also making a 'constructive and unique contribution' (Clinebell, 1984, p. 397) to the worshipping community.

Worship space

Where extended communion was felt to be different from 'church' was in the surrounding worship space. All the housebound made the point that the worship space was important for celebration, much more than the ordination, or otherwise, of the ministers. Of course, we need to remember that extended communion has been consecrated by an ordained minister but the participants missed the atmosphere and décor of 'church', something that can be a prime aid or hindrance (Bogle, 2004, p 41). This was a surprising result as the literature is quiet about extended communion being seen as 'second best' because of the lack of a formal and traditional worship space. Perhaps it is the eternal values and truth of God's kingdom which sacred buildings can represent (Russell, 1993, p 174) which is important here. Linked to this, was the assertion by St James' congregation that the ability to sit in a circle for worship, together with the plain décor of a non-conformist worship space lacking icons and rich symbolism, enabled the community to concentrate more on the words of the worship as well as to grow more easily in fellowship, two matters which may well be linked. This was again emphasized by the size of the congregation in that St Columba's building was large with a correspondingly sized congregation in which the elderly felt threatened, not by the age differences within the congregation but by the volume of physical space and the speed of movement of the younger people.

All those who received home communion missed participating as part of a community and they also longed for a formal worship space to create a more conducive atmosphere (Bogle, 2004, p. 41). Clearly, those unable to leave their beds or home surroundings accepted the attempts to create a focal point in their homes but this still detracted from the atmosphere created by a more formal worship space. However, these disadvantages clearly were outweighed by the advantages of extended communion in that it allowed spiritual nurture (Vickers, 2003, p. 13).

Threat of closure

All the satellite churches felt threatened by the small number of attendees and the prospect of closure was uppermost in most members' minds. This is hardly surprising since all three churches had experienced the possibility of closure in recent years (cf. Bowden, 1994, pp. 95–96). In addition, the congregations at St Jude's and St James' in particular are elderly and both congregations were aware that younger folk were not attending. There needs to be a sensitive perception of the needs of these elderly groups who know each other well and have bonded within the small groups of which they feel a part. For some, attending a church in close proximity to their homes gave them an independence which receiving lifts to the parish church would remove.

Conclusion

In general, the congregations studied have no perception of any differences between holy communion and extended communion. Most of the people have no problems with lay distribution of the elements and the majority would be happy with lay presidency. The worship space is more important than theological issues associated with either holy communion or extended communion and other issues such as possible closure are felt to be important. The isolation of the parish priest is an issue, but it is accepted within the constraints of finance, and in a sense it is seen in positive terms as allowing lay leadership to flourish. Finally, there was a real sense of grace within the parish as a whole, which confirms (perhaps subjectively from an academic viewpoint) that 'pastoral care ... is working properly' (Gledhill, 2003, p. 181).

Acknowledgements

The author would like to thank the ministry team at Overtown for its help and support during the data collection. It has been a privilege to work with such dedicated Christians.

References

Archbishops' Commission on Rural Areas. (1990). *Faith in the countryside.* Stoneleigh Park: Acora Publishing.
Bogle, J. (2004). Place, people, building, priest, and people: Some parochial history. In M. Torry (Ed.), *The parish: People, place and ministry* (pp. 38–48). Norwich: Canterbury Press.
Bowden, A. (1994). *Ministry in the countryside.* London: Mowbray.
Clinebell, H. (1984). *Basic types of pastoral care and counselling: Resources for the ministry of healing and growth.* London: SCM Press.
Davies, G. N. (2004). What's all the fuss about? *Church Times, 17 September 2004,* p. 11.
Dulles, A. C. (2002). *Models of the church* (expanded edition). New York: Doubleday.
Gledhill, J. (2003). *Leading a local church in the Age of the Spirit.* London: SPCK.
Hurtado, L. (1999). *At the origins of Christian worship.* Carlisle: Paternoster Press.
Littler, K., Francis, L. J., & Martineau, J. (2000). The acceptability of lay liturgical ministry: A survey among rural Anglican churchgoers. *Journal of Empirical Theology, 13,* 42–54.
Methodist Church. (2000). *A catechism for the use of the people called Methodists.* Peterborough: Methodist Publishing House.
Newbigin, L. (1996). Lay presidency at the eucharist. *Theology, 99,* 366–370.
Reader, J. (1987). The gardener: A symbol for rural ministry. In R. Lewis and A. Talbot-Ponsonby (Eds.), *The people, the land and the church: The second Hereford rural consultation* (pp. 184–188). Hereford: Diocesan Board of Finance.
Roloff, J. (2002). Eucharist and ministry in the NT. *Theology Digest, 49,* 128–138.
Russell, A. (1993). *The country parson.* London: SPCK.
Schweitzer, A. (1936). *The quest of the historical Jesus: A critical study of its progress from Reimarus to Wrede.* London: A&C Black Limited.

Smethurst, D. (1986). *Extended communion: An experiment in Cumbria*. Nottingham: Grove Books Limited.

Smithson, A. (1998). Lay presidency. *Theology, 101*, 3–13.

Tovey, P. (2001). *Public worship with communion by extension: A commentary*. Cambridge: Grove Books Limited.

Underhill, E. (1937). *Worship* (second edition). London: Nisbet and Co. Ltd.

Vickers, J. A. (2003). John Wesley: Pastor extraordinary. *Flame, January/February*, p 13.

Williams, J. A. (2004). Towards a people's church. *Modern Believing, 45*(2), 27–47.

Wilson, J. (2004). Solving the communion shortage. *The Methodist Recorder, 7652, August 19*, p. 7.

World Council of Churches. (1982). *Baptism, eucharist and ministry*. Geneva: World Council of Churches.

Part 7

LISTENING TO CHURCHGOERS

Chapter 21

ALL TYPES ARE CALLED, BUT SOME ARE MORE LIKELY TO RESPOND: THE PSYCHOLOGICAL TYPE PROFILE OF RURAL ANGLICAN CHURCHGOERS IN WALES

*Leslie J. Francis, Mandy Robbins, Angela Williams and Rhys Williams**

Abstract – In principle churches proclaim their invitation to worship to all sectors of the population. In practice some sectors appear more willing to respond. Alongside the more visible demographic bias in terms of sex and age, this article draws attention to the less visible bias in terms of psychological type. New data provided by 185 rural Anglican church-goers who completed the Francis Psychological Type Scales demonstrated that there were significantly higher proportions of individuals reporting ISFJ and ESFJ preferences in church congregations than in the population of men and women at large.

*   The Revd Canon Professor Leslie J. Francis is Professor of Religions and Education at the Warwick Religions and Education Research Unit. *Address for correspondence*: Warwick Religions and Education Research Unit, Institute of Education, The University of Warwick, Coventry, CV4 7AL.
    E-mail: leslie.francis@warwick.ac.uk
        Dr Mandy Robbins is Senior Lecturer in Psychology at Glyndŵr University. *Address for correspondence:* Division of Psychology, Institute for Health, Medical Science and Society, Glyndŵr University, Plas Coch Campus, Mold Road, Wrexham, LL11 2AW. E-mail: mandy.robbins@glyndwr.ac.uk
        The Revd Angela Williams is Incumbent of the Benefice of Llandegfan with Llandysilio (Menai Bridge). *Address for correspondence:* The Vicarage, Mona Road, Menai Bridge, Ynys Môn, LL59 5EA. E-mail: revangelawilliams@btinternet.com
        The Revd Rhys Williams serves as non-stipendiary priest in the Diocese of Bangor. *Address for correspondence:* Groeslon, Talybont, Bangor, Gwynedd, LL57 3YG. E-mail: mandy.williams1@virgin.net

Introduction

The invitation 'Everybody Welcome' remains a worthy and laudable theological aspiration for the notice board of rural Anglican churches. The inclusivity of the welcome is a proper reflection of the Great Commission recorded in Matthew 28:19-20. This inclusivity is also a proper reflection of the potential for the rural parish church to function as a community church rather than an associational church. On this account, a wide variety of people are likely to go to the rural parish church largely because they live in (belong to) the area rather than because they choose to associate with (belong to) a particular network of people.

This worthy and laudable theological aspiration, however, may be challenged by a range of empirical evidence. Analyses of the demographic profile of many congregations provide a highly visible challenge in terms of sex and age (see Francis, 1996). The breakdown by sex tends to demonstrate that there are two female churchgoers for every one male churchgoer. The proclamation is clearly made that men and women are equally welcome, but women are twice as likely to respond. Then it may become increasingly difficult for men to feel at home in an environment shaped largely by women for women. The breakdown by age tends to demonstrate that there are more post-retirement people in church congregations than pre-retirement people. The proclamation is clearly made that all ages are equally welcome, but the retired are more likely than younger people to respond. Then it may become increasingly difficult for younger people to feel at home in an environment shaped largely by retired people for retired people. These two points regarding the sex profile and the age profile of rural Anglican congregations are not voiced as a form of criticism. Rather, they serve simply to test theological aspiration against empirical realism.

While the demographic characteristics of church congregations may be relatively easy to recognize and to identify, other equally important characteristics of a psychological nature may be less easy to recognize and to identify. An appropriate lens through which to view this aspect of church life is offered by the model of psychological type, proposed originally by Carl Jung (1971) and developed and operationalized by instruments like the Myers-Briggs Type Indicator (Myers and McCaulley, 1985), the Keirsey Temperament Sorter (Keirsey and Bates, 1978) and the Francis Psychological Type Scales (Francis, 2005). Psychological type theory suggests that individuals differ in terms of four bipolar preferences: two orientations, two perceiving preferences, two judging preferences, and two attitudes toward the outer world.

The two orientations are defined as introversion (I) and extraversion (E). Introverts draw their energy from the inner world of ideas, while extraverts draw their energy from the outer world of people and things. Extraverts are energized by people and drained by too much solitude, while introverts are energized by solitude and drained by too many people.

The two perceiving processes are defined as sensing (S) and intuition (N). Sensers perceive their environment through their senses and focus on the details of the here and now, while intuitives perceive their environment by making use of the imagination and inspiration. Sensers are distrustful of jumping to conclusions and of envisioning the future, while intuitives are overloaded by too many details and long to try out new approaches.

The two judging processes are defined as thinking (T) and feeling (F). Thinkers reach their judgements by relying on objective logic, while feelers reach their judgements by relying on subjective appreciation of the personal and interpersonal factors involved. Thinkers strive for truth, fairness, and justice, while feelers strive for harmony, peace, and reconciliation.

The two attitudes toward the outer world are defined as judging (J) and perceiving (P). Judgers use their preferred judging process (either thinking or feeling) to deal with the outside world. Their outside world is organized, scheduled, and planned. Perceivers use their preferred perceiving process (either sensing or intuition) to deal with the outside world. Their outside world is flexible, spontaneous, and unplanned.

Taken together these four bipolar preferences generate 16 discrete psychological types. For example, the first author of the present article prefers introversion over extraversion, intuition over sensing, thinking over feeling, and judging over perceiving. In terms of the typology he is, therefore, described as INTJ. Reference to the population norms for the distribution of psychological types within the United Kingdom published by Kendall (1998) indicates that 2.5% of the male population fall into this type.

The Jungian-based model of psychological type belongs to the wider field of psychology concerned with personality and individual differences. Theologically speaking, it is important to be clear regarding the level of individual differences described by the notion of personality and regarding the ways in which personality needs to be distinguished from character. In the present study personality is used to describe a level of individual difference on a par with sex and with ethnicity. Personality describes the basic building blocks and is value-free. Character describes the way in which those building blocks are employed and is value-laden. The Christian call to repentance is concerned with a change of character but not with a change of personality, sex or ethnicity. Theologically speaking, there should be room in church congregations for all 16 psychological types, just as there should be room for all ages and for both sexes.

Against this background, the aim of the present article is to examine the extent to which rural Anglican church congregations reflect the psychological type profile of the United Kingdom as a whole as identified by Kendall (1998). Just two published studies have reported psychological type data relevant to understanding Anglican congregations. Although neither study reports these data alongside the population norms, taken together they suggest that there may be undue weighting toward preferences for sensing, feeling and judging (SFJ). In the first of these studies, Craig, Francis, Bailey and Robbins (2003) reported on the profile of a sample of 101 churchgoers (65% female and 35% male) from three rural benefices in the Church in Wales. Analysing the responses of men and women together, 55% of the total sample emerged with SFJ preferences (30% reporting ISFJ and 25% reporting ESFJ). In the second study, Francis, Duncan, Craig and Luffman (2004) reported on the profile of 327 churchgoers (65% female and 35% male) from five urban parishes in the Church of England. Analysing the responses of men and women separately, 39% of the women emerged with SFJ preferences (21% reporting ISFJ and 18% reporting ESFJ), and 24% of the men emerged with SFJ preferences (11% reporting ISFJ and 13% reporting ESFJ).

In order to test further the suggestion based on the data provided by Craig, Francis, Bailey and Robbins (2003) regarding the undue weighting toward SFJ in rural Anglican congregations, the present study aims to replicate their work among a larger sample, to analyse the responses of men and women separately, and to compare these responses with the population norms published by Kendall (1998).

Method

Measure

Psychological type was assessed by the 40-item Francis Psychological Type Scales (FPTS: Francis, 2005). This instrument uses a forced-choice format to indicate preferences between extraversion and introversion, between sensing and intuition, between thinking and feeling, and between judging and perceiving.

Procedure

Everyone who attended the services held in three benefices in the Church in Wales on a typical Sunday was invited to complete the questionnaire at the end of the service, or to return it the following Sunday. They were briefly informed of the nature of the study, and assured of confidentiality and anonymity. A total of 185 people returned their questionnaires, 133 women (72%) and 52 men (28%).

Participants

Of the participants, 9% were under the age of 40, 23% were in their forties or fifties, 52% were in their sixties or seventies, and 16% were aged eighty or over; 87% claimed to attend church every week, while 13% attended less frequently.

Results

Table 1 displays the 16 discrete psychological types comparing the profiles of male and female churchgoers with the United Kingdom population norms for men and for women provided by Kendall (1998). The selection ratio index (SRI), a development of chi square, is employed to check the statistical significance of differences between churchgoers and the general population. These data support the main hypothesis regarding the undue weighting toward SFJ in rural Anglican congregations.

Table 1: Psychological type of churchgoers compared with population norms

	Females				*Males*			
Type	*Norms* %	*Church* %	*SRI*	*p <*	*Norms* %	*Church* %	*SRI*	*p <*
Introverts								
ISTJ	8.6	6.8	0.79	NS	19.7	15.4	0.78	NS
INTJ	0.5	4.5	9.76	.001	2.5	5.8	2.27	NS
ISFJ	17.7	32.3	1.83	.001	7.0	19.2	2.77	.001
INFJ	1.7	3.0	1.73	NS	1.6	5.8	3.60	.05
ISTP	2.5	0.8	0.30	NS	10.8	0.0	0.00	.01
INTP	1.0	1.5	1.45	NS	4.1	3.8	0.93	NS
ISFP	7.9	1.5	0.19	.01	3.7	0.0	0.00	NS
INFP	2.8	0.8	0.27	NS	3.6	0.0	0.00	NS
Extraverts								
ESTJ	9.5	9.8	1.03	NS	11.6	9.6	0.83	NS
ENTJ	1.7	0.8	0.43	NS	4.3	0.0	0.00	NS
ESFJ	18.5	27.8	1.50	.01	6.0	26.9	4.48	.001
ENFJ	3.4	1.5	0.45	NS	2.0	7.7	3.84	.01
ESTP	2.1	0.0	0.00	.05	8.2	1.9	0.24	NS
ENTP	3.7	0.0	0.00	NS	3.6	0.0	0.00	NS
ESFP	11.0	4.5	0.41	.05	6.1	3.8	0.63	NS
ENFP	7.5	4.5	0.60	NS	5.1	0.0	0.00	NS

Among women ISFJ accounts for 32% of churchgoers, compared with 18% of the general population (P < .001), and ESFJ accounts for 28% of churchgoers, compared with 19% of the general population (P < .01). Among men ISFJ accounts for 19% of churchgoers, compared with 7% of the general population (P < .001), and ESFJ accounts for 27% of churchgoers, compared with 6% of the general population (P < .001). Over-representation of ISFJ and ESFJ among churchgoers leads to under-representation of other types.

Discussion and conclusion

Analysis of the more visible demographic characteristics of rural Anglican churchgoers (in terms of sex and age) suggested that, although the invitation and welcome may be issued indiscriminately to both sexes and to all ages, women are more likely to respond than men and the post-retired are more likely to respond than the pre-retired. Analysis of the less visible psychological characteristics of rural Anglican churchgoers (in terms of the 16 discrete types) has also suggested that, although the invitation and welcome may be issued to all psychological types, individuals with a type preference for SFJ are more likely to respond than individuals with other type preferences. According to the present survey, 60% of the 133 women and 46% of the 52 men reported an SFJ profile. In the earlier study by Craig, Francis, Bailey and Robbins (2003), 55% of the 101 men and women considered together reported an SFJ profile.

In her booklet, *Introduction to Type*, Myers (1998, p 7) provides insightful profiles of the two SFJ types: ISFJ and ESFJ. The ISFJ profile is as follows:

> Quiet, friendly, responsible and conscientious. Work devotedly to meet their obligations. Lend stability to any project or group. Thorough, painstaking, accurate. Their interests are usually not technical. Can be patient with necessary details. Loyal, considerate, perceptive, concerned with how other people feel.

The ESFJ profile is as follows:

> Warm-hearted, talkative, popular, conscientious, born co-operators, active committee members. Need harmony and may be good at creating it. Always doing something nice for someone. Work best with encouragement and praise. Main interest is in things that directly and visibly affect people's lives.

There are important ways in which these two profiles describe the kind of people we might expect to have responded to the indiscriminate call of welcome to the rural parish church. SFJ congregations possess a number of recognizable Christian strengths. The preference for feeling (F) characterizes a community concerned with human values, interpersonal relationships and with a loving and caring God. Here is a community concerned with peace and with harmony. The population norms show that feeling is a feminine preference *par excellence* (reported by 70% of women and by 35% of men). A community shaped by such a dominant preference for feeling may, however, be quite alien to individuals who view the world through the lens of thinking (including the majority of men). Thinkers, too, may desire to respond to the call of Christ, but this response may appear quite different from the response of the feeler.

The preference for sensing (S) characterizes a community concerned with continuity, tradition, stability, and with a God grounded in divine changelessness. Here is a community concerned with guarding what has been handed down by previous generations. The population norms show that sensing is the preferred mode of the British population (reported by 79% of women and by 73% of men). In this sense the church congregation is in step with wider society. A community shaped by such a dominant preference for sensing may, however, be quite alien to individuals who view the world through the lens of intuition. Intuitives, too, may desire to respond to the call of Christ, but this response may appear quite different from the response of the senser.

The preference for judging (J) characterizes a community concerned with organization, discipline, structure, and with a God who welcomes a regular pattern for worship (whatever that pattern may be). Here is a community concerned with valuing regular commitment, advanced planning and respect for the guidelines (implicit as well as explicit). The population norms show that judging is the preferred mode of the British population (reported by 62% of women and by 55% of men). In this sense the church congregation is once again in step with wider society. A community shaped by such a dominant preference for judging may, however, be quite alien to individuals who view the world through the lens of perceiving. Perceivers, too, may desire to respond to the call of Christ, but this response may appear quite different from the response of the judger.

Rural churches will go on displaying the invitation 'Everybody Welcome' and it is theologically appropriate that they should so do. There is a place, however, for empirical realism to stand alongside this theological idealism. Pragmatically speaking, churches which have established effective and sustainable ministry among women, among the retired, and among individuals with SFJ type preference may well be advised to work to their strengths and to nurture the spirituality and faith journey of these individuals who provide the backbone both of local church life and of life in the wider local rural community. It may, after all, be silly for churches to neglect those who have already responded to the invitation. Rather the challenge may be for those who are pioneering 'fresh expressions of church' (see Church of England, 2004) to issue the welcome in terms which may be understood more readily by those whose psychological type profiles currently remain so under-represented within the established and old expressions of church.

References

Church of England. (2004). *Mission-shaped church: Church planting and fresh expressions of church in a changing context.* London: Church House Publishing.

Craig, C., Francis, L. J., Bailey, J., & Robbins, M. (2003). Psychological types in Church in Wales congregations. *The Psychologist in Wales, 15,* 18–21.

Francis, L. J. (1996). *Church watch: Christianity in the countryside.* London: SPCK.

Francis, L. J. (2005). *Faith and psychology: Personality, religion and the individual.* London: Darton, Longman and Todd.

Francis, L. J., Duncan, B., Craig, C. L., & Luffman, G. (2004). Type patterns among Anglican congregations in England. *Journal of Adult Theological Education, 1,* 66–77.

Jung, C. G. (1971). *Psychological types: The collected works, volume 6.* London: Routledge and Kegan Paul.

Keirsey, D., & Bates, M. (1978). *Please understand me.* Del Mar, California: Prometheus Nemesis.

Kendall, E. (1998). *Myers-Briggs Type Indicator: Step 1 manual supplement.* Palo Alto, California: Consulting Psychologists Press.

Myers, I. B. (1998). *Introduction to Type: A guide to understanding your results on the Myers-Briggs Type Indicator* (fifth edition, European English version). Oxford: Oxford Psychologists Press.

Myers, I. B., & McCaulley, M. H. (1985). *Manual: A guide to the development and use of the Myers-Briggs Type Indicator.* Palo Alto, California: Consulting Psychologists Press.

Chapter 22

THE SOCIAL SIGNIFICANCE OF HARVEST FESTIVALS IN THE COUNTRYSIDE: AN EMPIRICAL ENQUIRY AMONG THOSE WHO ATTEND

David S. Walker*

Abstract – Many commentators have noted the diversification and fragmentation of village life. The present article draws on the conceptualization proposed by Walker (2006) to distinguish between ten identifiable groups of individuals visible in the rural landscape (including established residents, lifestyle shifters and tourists) and four ways in which individuals may experience or express their belonging to that rural community (through activities, events, people and places). In order to examine the extent to which Harvest Festivals enable rural Anglican churches to contact a broad cross section of the community, data were provided by 1,454 attendees at Harvest Festival services conducted within 27 rural churches in the Diocese of Worcester. The data suggest that, although demographically Harvest Festival and normal Sunday congregations are similar, Harvest services continue to reach out into the varied categories of rural inhabitants and attract significant numbers of non-residents, occasional churchgoers and those who belong by virtue of people, events or place rather than through activity based participation. As such it continues to provide an example of the public role and significance of religious practice in a twenty-first century setting.

Introduction

Many commentators have drawn attention in recent years to the increasing diversity and fragmentation of rural communities. Martineau,

* The Right Revd David S. Walker is Bishop of Dudley within the Diocese of Worcester. *Address for correspondence:* Bishop's House, Bishops Walk, Cradley Heath, B64 7RH. E-mail: bishopsofficedudley@cofe-worcester.org.uk

Francis and Francis (2004) in particular bring together contributions from a number of authors who cover (inter alia) governance, isolation, dynamics of community and the interplay between private property and public good. As the nature of country life has changed, rural Anglicanism itself has had many challenges to face (as set out in, for example, Francis, 1985, Russell, 1986 and more recently Bowden, 1994). Whilst some rural parish churches and the individuals associated with them have retained or even found a central role as the hub of a wide range of community activity and social provision, others have become marginal eclectic gatherings, the preserve of a particular section of the populace, or one among several agencies competing for the time and energies of local people.

In consequence of this fragmentation, the study of and engagement with contemporary rural issues, including church issues, will benefit from a categorization of the rural population along lines that enable diverse behaviours and responses to be understood and, to some extent, predicted.

The 'Walker' model

An earlier article (Walker, 2006) gave a qualitative description of 12 distinct types of people associated with present day rural areas. It was hypothesized that distinct patterns of behaviour were likely to be found where individuals had come to dwell in the countryside for different reasons, or where the nature of their ongoing engagement with the community and their surroundings differed. Such categories have the advantage of being fairly easy to define and indeed self-define. Examples were given as to how the varied groups relate in different ways to particular elements of the mission and ministry of the local parish church.

Ten of the categories developed in that article are relevant to the data presented here. Lifestyle shifters had been attracted out of urban areas by a (real or imagined) better way of living. Trophy owners had bought into rural living as a symbol of material success. Privacy seekers were looking for peace and quiet, often to re-balance lives lived largely at the hectic pace of the city. Established residents included those born locally as well as others who had lived many years there. Some were also commuters, especially where rural work had reduced. Travellers and gypsies were significant as the largest minority ethnic group in many areas of rural England. The arriving vulnerable had often come to live near family members, in order to receive support; the missing vulnerable were those forced to move away at times of (for example) illness, family breakdown or household formation. Absent friends were people who had strong connections with a community but were unable to live in it. Tourists and visitors had less formal connections but often identified strongly with the place.

The same article also developed a fourfold model of belonging which distinguished between belonging through activities, events, people and places. Those who belong through activities are most likely to join organizations and groups within the community and contribute to their maintenance by regular participation, including volunteering, sitting on committees and planning activities. Those who belong through events commit themselves one occasion at a time and may well withdraw if put under pressure to make an ongoing commitment. Belonging through places recognizes the powerful role that particular localities or buildings, and especially the historic rural parish church, have in many people's sense of rootedness, purpose and destiny. Belonging through people includes the importance of kinship and friendship relationships as well as identifying how particular 'public' individuals, such as the Church of England priest or school head teacher, may carry a wider iconic status.

The model recognized not only that the motivation for expressing and feeling belonging may differ from person to person, but that the same person is likely to operate in one dominant mode for belonging to bodies as varied as the local cricket club, village school and Women's Institute. By presenting 'place', 'event' and 'people' as three significant alternatives it opened the way for a critique of the 'activity' based model that underpins much present writing about and practice of church ministry and mission but which in some rural parishes has led to significant misunderstandings within congregations (as for example when weekly churchgoers doubt the commitment and faith of those responding to God in a different way) and to lost opportunities of engaging effectively with the wider community.

The 'special' case of Harvest Festival services

Harvest Festival services grew rapidly from an individual liturgy of thanksgiving devised and led by the Revd Robert Stephen Hawker in the Cornish parish of Morwenstow in 1843 (Baring-Gould, 2002). Within a generation they had become part of the furniture in Church of England parishes in both villages and towns. It is probably no coincidence that this growth came at just the moment when the nation was going through rapid urbanization: it emphasized a link with the land, and the produce of the land, that was no longer part of the daily experience of many people. But its popularity was not confined to the places to which rural people were being displaced by the need for work. This was no mere nostalgic ritual to commemorate a way of living they had left behind. In the countryside the Harvest Festival service no doubt served as an affirmation of the continued importance of food production, and hence of those engaged in it. It would be another century before England became substantially served by imported produce, but intriguingly Harvest has survived this transition too; even the most urban parishes are likely to feature it in their calendar, even if they seek to reinterpret some of its elements to meet their circumstances.

The distinctive element of most Harvest Festival services is that the church is richly decorated with a range of produce (see for example Francis, 1996). This may nowadays include processed foodstuffs (tinned goods for example) as well as flowers, vegetables, bread and fruit. In many parishes the service will have a deliberately 'accessible' style, keeping the structure simple, giving children an important part to play, and incorporating interactive rituals such as a procession where individual gifts of produce are brought forward to the altar steps. Two particular nineteenth century Harvest hymns remain very strongly associated with the festival, though supplemented by an increasingly wide range of other musical material. The service may be followed by a Harvest Supper, and the produce sold, auctioned, distributed to the elderly of the community or donated to charities serving the needy in nearby towns; but these are usually arranged at other times within a few days of the service itself rather than being incorporated into one event. Attempts in the late twentieth century to make the service more relevant in urban areas, by celebrating 'industrial Harvests' where the output of factories and mines was brought to church, did not catch on widely, and neither these nor yet further generalizations into the notion of a celebration of work (though the latter might in theory have more in common with the service economy of the present day) have impacted upon the rural areas that are the focus of this study.

By contrast with some other major festivals of the Church's year that continue to draw larger and potentially wider congregations, Harvest is dogmatically light. Whilst it refers to God as the one who creates and sustains life it carries none of the doctrinal weight of Christmas or Easter, and as such may speak to the implicit religiousness of many people who wish to participate in a communal ritual but are uneasy with the core credal elements of the Christian faith (see for example Bailey,

1997). It is distinguished from some other special services with limited doctrinal content, such as Mothering Sunday and Remembrance Sunday, by having no specific national day associated with it; hence it does not benefit from the wider secular publicity (and consequent sense of being part of a national commemoration) that those occasions receive. Whilst it has some similarities with Christingle, the latter is most often incorporated into the preparations for Christmas rather than standing alone.

As a free standing event Harvest carries no expectation of regular commitment; it speaks powerfully of the importance of land and hence place; it may well be an occasion on which personal invitation plays a role in bringing people into church and yet it remains part of the Sunday by Sunday routine to which regular churchgoers are attuned. For these reasons it is a good potential candidate for drawing people from across the diverse ways of belonging listed above.

The task of this present article is to use the tools developed in Walker (2006) to examine the data collected at Harvest 2007. It will look at what evidence this specific traditional church event provides as to how far the rural church is engaging with the pluriform pattern of belonging in modern rural society and whether it is reaching into the increasingly diverse community in which it is set; hence whether the methodology developed in the previous article provides implications for how Harvest fits into the mission and ministry of the rural English parish.

Method

Procedure

A total of 27 Church of England churches from across the Diocese of Worcester agreed to distribute questionnaires to adults attending Harvest Services in 2007. All had some claim to be rural, ranging from small isolated communities to villages bordering on the edges of urban areas. Some had resident incumbents, others not. Pencils were provided and those attending were asked to complete their questionnaires before leaving after the service. It was suggested to clergy that the forms would be best distributed as the congregation arrived and that some time might be allowed before the conclusion of the service, as well as over refreshments afterwards. The aim of seeking completion at the time of the service was to minimize any skew toward the most committed church members, these being considered disproportionately more likely to return completed questionnaires at a later date.

Sample

In response to the survey 1,454 valid questionnaires were returned, an average of 54 per church. There was a good range of sizes of returns from 9 to 143, with a high rate of response to each individual question.

Instrument

The themes explored were chosen in order to permit their analysis using the tools developed in the earlier article. The present article draws on the following aspects of the questionnaire.

The majority of questions analysed here sought factual information and accordingly offered 'yes/no' responses or a box to be ticked from a series. These covered: reasons why people had come to live in the community served by the church (13); connections with the community of those not resident (10); working/economic status (10); connections with the church in which the service was taking place (9); basic demographic information (6). An additional 25 questions about individuals' relationships with the church and the community were explored using a five-point Likert scale with the offered responses being: strongly agree; agree; not certain; disagree; disagree strongly.

Analysis

The numerical results to the Likert scale questions are presented below in tables with columns headed respectively: % Yes; % ?; % No. The first column aggregates those responding 'agree' and 'agree strongly', the second aggregates 'not certain' with those who left the question blank, the final column aggregates 'disagree' and 'disagree strongly' responses. The 'yes/no' and tick box questions are not aggregated in any way unless stated explicitly in the following discussion. In this case the percentages given exclude those who left the question blank.

Results and discussion

Demographic information

Francis (1996) found that for typical church attendance adult females outnumber males by a figure of 2 to 1. It might be thought that Harvest would attract more men, either because of its relationship to the world of agriculture where employment is not so heavily female or due to the impact of regular women attendees at services bringing their partners for this special occasion. However the respondents to the questionnaire were 66% women, indistinguishable from the normal Sunday pattern.

Unpublished figures from a survey in 2003 estimated (albeit on a small sample) an average age of 61 for adult church attendees in the Diocese of Worcester. The adult age distribution of the respondents showed a similar heavy skew toward the upper ends of the range with 2% in the 20–29 bracket; 6% aged 30–39; 10% aged 40–49; 15% aged 50–59; 27% aged 60–69 and 33% over 70.

Some 16% described themselves as visitors either from nearby or further afield. This is probably significantly higher than most rural churches would experience on an average Sunday. Harvest still reaches out beyond the locality of the congregation.

From this basic demographic analysis it can be concluded that to whatever extent Harvest services attract larger congregations than attend church on an ordinary Sunday, their catchment is 'more of the same'. Any distinctiveness will lie in the respondents' answers to more specific questions.

Harvest as an event

In terms of the model being used in this article, it might be hypothesized that Harvest constitutes an event; that is to say that attendance at it does not require or expect the participant to be committed to any habitual or frequent programme of activities; where by contrast attendance at a normal Sunday service or monthly Family Service might imply both in the mind of the individual and in the minds of others attending the same event that the attendee would come regularly.

The extent to which Harvest attendance is linked or not to regular Sunday churchgoing was explored by asking respondents to indicate their frequency of attendance at the church where they were completing the questionnaire: 56% reported attending church nearly every week; 20% at least once a month; 14% at least 6 times a year; 10% less than 6 times per year.

The significant finding here is that some 25% of those present claimed to attend the church less than monthly. It is supported by the fact that only 63% of respondents indicated that their names were entered on the church electoral roll. Comparisons of self-reported church attendance with congregation figures produced by ministers for denominational statistical returns invariably show that people claim more frequent church attendance than is actually the case. This all suggests that the true figure of occasional attendees in our sample would actually be greater than one in four. The size of these figures allows us to conclude that the reportedly larger congregations that churches enjoy at Harvest reflects something beyond the bunching effect that might be produced by a higher than normal proportion of the monthly or 'nearly every week' categories turning up on the same day.

In terms of the model being used here, those who attend monthly or more frequently could be said to express their belonging through participation in regular activities, those who come less often, especially those who have not chosen to be on the electoral roll, are 'event' attendees: people who make largely independent decisions to come to church on each separate occasion. Harvest is indeed an 'event'.

The importance to the respondents of other events, such as baptisms and weddings, was explored through a further series of questions. The results are set out in table 1 below.

Table 1: Occasional offices and related connections

	Yes %
I was baptized/christened here	11
I was married here	13
Family members were baptized/christened here	38
Family members were married here	29
I visit a grave in the churchyard	24

The question about graves was preferred to a more general one about funeral services as the former (including the burial of cremated remains) was felt to provide a better indicator of a strong connection. The high figures for positive responses to these questions are consonant with the experience of clergy that such events are an essential tool of mission.

Belonging and the place

In this section and some others, respondents were invited to signify agreement or disagreement on a five-point Likert scale as indicated earlier.

Table 2: Belonging with the church building

	Yes %	? %	No %
This church building is special to me	68	27	5
It wouldn't be the same to attend a service in another church	31	37	31
The people here are more important to me than the place	53	37	10
I have a strong sense of belonging to this church building	50	38	12
In this church I feel close to God	68	29	3

The significance of the building is illustrated powerfully by the fact that 31% of respondents felt it would not be the same to attend a service in another church. That less than a third of those considered the building more important than the people indicates that it is not easy to separate the venue from the congregation who populate it. Even if for over half of respondents the people matter more than the building, the scores for the building being 'special', inculcating belonging, and enabling the respondent to feel close to God reflect that place matters, and matters deeply. Further analysis of the data indicated that some 83% either reported agreement with at least one of those three statements or disagreed that the people are more important than the place. The conjecture in Walker (2006) that place is an important constituent of belonging for those who consider themselves as members of the rural church is borne out by these findings.

Belonging and activity in the community

The following group of questions was asked in order to explore the notion of activity as a major mode of rural belonging.

Table 3: Belonging with the wider community

	Yes %	? %	No %
There are people here I meet at other community activities	65	26	9
I am involved in other groups in the area	54	30	16
I enjoy community organizations	60	37	10
I have a strong sense of belonging to this church building	50	34	7
Being part of the church helps me to feel at home in this community	64	32	4

The substantial difference between the answers to the first two questions picks up the distinction between formal community groups and other less structured activities. These latter might include events such as coffee mornings that are informally arranged and school functions that are laid on by an institution rather than requiring involvement in group activities. Both figures are higher than the 46% who said they attended non-church functions in the locality but lower than the 73% who indicated that they attend other church functions in the local community and the 79% who claimed to be 'members of the congregation'.

That all of these questions provoked strongly positive responses, indicates both that church attendees are likely to be active in wider community events and that church membership has a significant role to play in inculcating a wider sense of belonging in the locality. Alongside the figures (above) of some three quarters of our sample who claimed monthly or more frequent church attendance, this would suggest both that activity is a main constituent of rural belonging and that those predisposed to belong to church in this way are also likely to belong to other community organizations.

We can conclude that activity is a model of belonging that is likely to lead to participating in the life of a range of distinct community organizations, of which the church is one. However, there remains a significant number whose only involvement in activities in the community is through the church.

Belonging with people

The next series of responses cover statements that investigate the role of relationships in rural belonging. For the sake of analysis they have been divided between pastoral support, congregational belonging and personal intimacy.

In terms of both personal intimacy and congregational belonging all statements received strongly positive responses. In an era when most rural incumbents have several parishes to cover it is significant that 51% of respondents felt that the vicar knew them well, and that this is not dependent on the traditional pattern of home visiting by the priest which was reported much less frequently (26%). This difference may indicate that the community role of the vicar, being visible at social events and elsewhere, remains significant. The level of reported friendship was extremely high at 81%, consistent both with the view that it is very hard to be an anonymous individual in a rural congregation and

Table 4: Belonging with people

	Yes %	? %	No %
Congregational belonging			
This is my 'family' church	66	24	9
I come to church to be with other people	48	34	17
I have a strong sense of belonging to this church community	62	30	8
Pastoral support			
There are people here who help me cope with things	48	38	13
There are people from this church who visit me at home	42	33	25
The vicar visits me at home	26	37	37
Another church leader visits me at home	14	44	43
Personal intimacy			
I have friends in this congregation	81	17	2
I feel that people here know me well	58	33	9
I feel that the vicar knows me well	51	36	13

with the contention that those who attend churches occasionally do so in the company of friends. Pastoral support does exist, but of a much less formal nature than the traditional model; some 48% of respondents felt there were people in the church who help them to cope; only a slightly lower figure (42%) are visited by someone at home.

The responses to one later question also shed light on the significance of relationships to the sample. 16% agreed or agreed strongly with the statement that they had come to the service because a friend had invited them.

These results confirm the hypothesis that relationships are an important factor in belonging to rural church communities.

Categories of rural Harvest attendees

The categories of rural 'belongers' described in Walker (2006) were here explored through a series of questions asking about their arrival in and connections with the community. Information about employment and economic status is also used. The data is analysed to test the hypothesis that Harvest services attract a diverse range of rural people.

Slightly over 80% of those responding indicated that they lived 'in the community served by this church'. Of these some 24% had always lived there (19% of the total sample). Those in this latter category fall within the definition of established residents from the previous article. They are clearly present in numbers in Harvest congregations; an indication that new arrivals with different liturgical styles and preferences have not alienated them.

For those who had moved to live in the community, a series of questions explored the relative draw factors of family, work, lifestyle choice and retreat. The ordering of the questions was mixed. Respondents were invited to give an answer to each question separately, in order to capture the multiplicity of reasons that might have led to their move.

The earlier article identified lifestyle shifters and trophy owners among the categories of rural inhabitants. The distinction between the two may be quite fine, and in terms of the types and levels of involvement in the community both were seen as likely participants. The large number of lifestyle responses suggests that attending such events is indeed part of the way of life that those moving to the countryside are adopting. The results clearly show that lifestyle factors considerably outweigh all others as reasons for moving into a rural parish among those who attend Harvest services.

Privacy seekers are a significant proportion of some rural communities; they are typically higher earners looking for peace and quiet. Some are second home owners escaping to the countryside after a demanding week. Whilst some 25% of respondents claimed to 'hold down a demanding job' only 7% of incomers (5% of total sample) cited privacy as a reason. This is consistent with the conjecture in the earlier article that this category would not be likely to participate in church events.

The presence of a significant number of commuters indicates that Harvest services do not exclude those whose work is outside the locality, notwithstanding the fact that rural commuting in Worcestershire is largely into the urban centres for employment with no natural rural link.

The arriving vulnerable are those moving into the countryside at a point of need; typically for reasons of health, accommodation or relationship breakdown. In each case only 2% of incomers responded positively to questions relating to these criteria. It is perhaps particularly notable that whilst breakdown of relationship is a very high factor in general household formation it features very low at 2% in this sample. Cultural attitudes have largely moved on from an era when divorcees felt unwelcome in Church of England congregations, reinforcing the view that this reflects the difficulty in affording rural accommodation in such circumstances and is part of the general push to the towns of those

Table 5: Reasons for moving to this community

	Yes %
Lifestyle factors	
To live in a good locality	33
For a better quality of life	29
For a desirable home	29
Family factors	
To be near to family	13
To marry/live with partner	13
Following breakdown of relationship	2
Work factors	
I work in the local community	17
To commute to work	16
For retirement	13
Other factors	
To find privacy	7
Because I could afford to rent	2
For health reasons	2

undergoing negative life experiences, where they form the category of missing vulnerable identified in the earlier article (Walker, 2006).

Travellers and gypsies are an important historical feature of Worcestershire: they still account for the largest minority ethnic group in the rural parts of the county. Only 11 respondents identified themselves as from this category, less than 1% of the sample, despite their longstanding connections with the agricultural trades and skills that are ostensibly being affirmed at Harvest services. This is consistent with the view that they do not feel welcomed at activities arranged other than by or for their own community.

The 283 (20%) respondents who indicated they were not local residents were asked what connections they had with the community. They were offered a range of responses covering work, family, lifestyle, church and historical factors. Their answers are set out in table 6 below.

Of note here is the range of factors that are cited by at least 20% of respondents. Personal history is unsurprisingly important as a factor; church allegiance is often not transferred unless the person moves a significant distance away. Friendships scored highly at almost 50%,

Table 6: Non-residents' connection with the locality

	Yes %
Personal factors	
I used to live here	25
My work brings me here	7
Relationship factors	
My parents live here	12
I have friends who live here	47
Lifestyle factors	
I like visiting this area	37
I would like to live here	14
Church factors	
I regard this as my main church	43
I only come here for church	20

indicating the importance to churches of sustaining such relationships if non-residents are to feel part of the church community. It is significant that a very large majority (80%) make some claim to coming into the community for something other than church attendance. Many of them would fall into the category of absent friends. For Harvest at least they are in church, and in church in numbers.

The remaining category from the earlier article explored here is that of tourists and visitors. These people are drawn to the countryside without necessarily having any immediate family or historic connections. It would appear from the responses to these questions that rural churches do reach out into this category at Harvest.

This section has demonstrated that Harvest services are not the preserve of any single category of the rural population, they attract long term residents, more recent arrivals and visitors with some connection to the community. They are frequented by those who have been drawn to identify with the rural community for a wide range of reasons.

Conclusion

Despite accusations of irrelevance to modern living, Harvest services continue to be a staple yet distinctive part of the rural English liturgical calendar. They draw congregations principally from their locality and demographically similar to their regular Sunday attendances but with significant numbers of occasional attendees, including visitors from outside the parish. Against any suggestion that Harvest is primarily of interest either to the agricultural community, or to some other subgroup of rural England, we have established that most categories of rural residents are present. Those who come include significant numbers who express their belonging to church and community by attachment to place and to people as well as being drawn by the 'event' nature of the festival. Harvest is an example of the enduring public significance of religious practice in rural England. Churches that understand the make-up of their Harvest congregations, and tailor their liturgies and pastoral ministries accordingly, will be best placed both to meet the needs of their congregations and to use the festival as a form of outreach into the wider community. What can be learned from the study of Harvest may have relevance to other occasions of celebratory activity and worship, both traditional and emerging.

References

Bailey, E. (1997). *Implicit Religion in Contemporary Society.* Kampen: Kok Pharos.

Baring-Gould, S. (2002). *The Vicar of Morwenstow.* New York: Adamant Media Corporation.

Bowden, A. (1994). *Ministry in the Countryside.* London: Mowbray.

Francis, L. J. (1985). *Rural Anglicanism: A future for young Christians?* London: Collins.

Francis, L. J. (1996). *Church Watch: Christianity in the countryside.* London: SPCK.

Martineau, J., Francis, L. J., & Francis, P. (Eds.). (2004). *Changing rural life: A Christian response to key rural issues.* Norwich: Canterbury Press.

Walker, D. S. (2006). Belonging to rural church and society: Theological and religious perspectives. *Rural Theology, 4,* 85–97.

Russell. A (1986). *The country parish.* London: SPCK.

Chapter 23

PSYCHOLOGICAL TYPE PROFILE OF VOLUNTEER WORKERS IN A RURAL CHRISTIAN CHARITY SHOP

Leslie J. Francis and Sue Pegg*

Abstract – Although over half of the United Kingdom population are extraverts, church congregations are generally weighted toward introverts. In this study 27 of the 30 volunteer workers in a rural Christian charity shop (who completed the Francis Psychological Type Scales) were extraverts. Other rural churches are encouraged to find similar opportunities for extraverts to express themselves.

Introduction

A series of recent studies has employed Jungian psychological type theory (Jung, 1971), as operationalized through the Myers Briggs Type Indicator (Myers and McCaulley, 1985), the Keirsey Temperament Sorter (Keirsey and Bates, 1978) and the Francis Psychological Type Scales (Francis, 2005), to profile those engaged in Christian ministry in the United Kingdom. These studies have generally revealed preferences for introversion, sensing, feeling and judging (ISFJ) as exemplified by Francis, Payne and Jones (2001) and Francis and Payne (2002) among male Anglican clergy in Wales. A more limited number of studies has

* The Revd Canon Professor Leslie J. Francis is Professor of Religions and Education at the Warwick Religions and Education Research Unit. A*ddress for correspondence*: Warwick Religions and Education Research Unit, Institute of Education, The University of Warwick, Coventry, CV4 7AL.
E-mail: leslie.francis@warwick.ac.uk
    The Revd Sue Pegg is Methodist minister in the Market Weighton section of the Pocklington and Market Weighton Methodist Circuit. *Address for correspondence*: Beverley Road, Market Weighton, YO43 3JN.
E-mail: revsuepegg@tiscali.co.uk

extended this research tradition to profile churchgoers in the United Kingdom. These studies have also generally revealed preferences for introversion, sensing, feeling and judging (ISFJ) as exemplified by Craig, Francis, Bailey and Robbins (2003), Francis, Duncan, Craig and Luffman (2004) and Craig (2005).

These main preferences for SFJ are explicable in terms of psychological type theory. Individuals who display both sensing and judging preferences tend to prefer the conventional and to be guardians of the traditional. Many Christian churches provide the ideal framework for such a perspective. Individuals who display a feeling preference tend to place a high priority on personal and interpersonal values. The Christian gospel, with its emphasis on personal and social values, is ideally placed to nurture such a perspective. The preference for introversion over extraversion within Christian ministries and Christian congregations may be somewhat more difficult to explain, especially in light of the observation that over half of the United Kingdom population (52%) are extraverts (Kendall, 1998). What is clear, however, is that churches which are shaped by and for introverts may fail to recruit and retain extraverts.

While many churches in the United Kingdom maintain a worship environment attractive to introverts, some churches also deliberately develop other activities which may be more attractive to extraverts. One such example is provided by the church-related charity shop in the rural town of Slaithwaite, Yorkshire, which draws volunteer workers from the neighbouring area. The aim of the present study is to test the hypothesis that these volunteers will display a more extraverted profile than the typical churchgoer, being attracted by the opportunities for extraverted behaviour promoted by the structure of working in small teams, by the interaction with customers, and by the environment of the 'coffee shop' located within the enterprise.

Method

All 40 volunteer workers associated with the Slaithwaite charity shop were invited to complete the Francis Psychological Type Scales (Francis, 2005). This instrument proposes four ten-item measures to distinguish between preferences for introversion or extraversion, for sensing or intuition, for thinking or feeling, and for judging or perceiving. Each item presents a forced choice between two personal descriptions. Completed responses were received from 30 of the volunteers, making a response rate of 75%. The majority of the respondents (27) were female, and 3 were male. The majority of the respondents (21) were in their sixties, 4 were in their fifties, 4 were aged 70 or over, and 1 was in her twenties. The majority of the respondents (21) were weekly church-goers, 4 attended church monthly, 4 attended church occasionally, and 1 never attended church.

Results

The data revealed clear preferences for extraversion (27) over introversion (3), for sensing (30) over intuition (0), for feeling (27) over thinking (3), and for judging (21) over perceiving (9). The predominant type was ESFJ (17), followed by ESFP (7).

Conclusion

Two main conclusions emerge from this study of the psychological type profile of volunteer workers in a rural Christian charity shop. The first conclusion concerns the difference between these volunteer workers and the profile of typical churchgoers. While church services seem to provide an environment preferred by introverts, volunteering opportunities within this Christian charity shop seem to provide an environment attractive to extraverts. From a strategic point of view the development of rural Christian charity shops may help not only to generate funding for local and national causes but also to extend the range of people in contact with the Christian gospel.

The second conclusion concerns the similarity between these volunteer workers and the profile of typical churchgoers. Both groups seem particularly to attract men and women with preferences for sensing, feeling and judging. Together the two types of ISFJ and ESFJ may constitute the backbone of the rural church and shape the contribution of the church to rural community life. It is the ESFJ, however, who is both motivated and equipped to engage with the wider community, to serve others, and to extend the outreach of local church life. Myers (1987, p. 7) ascribed the following characteristics to the ESFJ.

> Warm-hearted, talkative, popular, conscientious, born co-operators, active committee members. Need harmony and may be good at creating it. Always doing something nice for someone. Work best with encouragement and praise. Main interest in the things that directly and visibly affect people's lives.

It seems that Slaithwaite has discovered a way to harness the ESFJ. Other rural churches and rural communities may wish to learn from this example.

References

Craig, C. L. (2005). Psychological type profile of rural churchgoers. *Rural Theology, 3*, 123–131.

Craig, C. L., Francis, L. J., Bailey, J., & Robbins, M. (2003). Psychological types in Church in Wales congregations. *The Psychologist in Wales, 15*, 18–21.

Francis, L. J. (2005). *Faith and psychology: Personality, religion and the individual.* London: Darton, Longman and Todd.

Francis, L. J., Duncan, B., Craig, C. L., & Luffman, G. (2004) Type patterns among Anglican congregations in England. *Journal of Adult Theological Education, 1*(1), 65–77.

Francis, L. J., & Payne, V. J. (2002). The Payne Index of Ministry Styles (PIMS): Ministry styles and psychological type among male Anglican clergy in Wales. *Research in the Social Scientific Study of Religion, 13*, 125–141.

Francis, L. J., Payne, V. J., & Jones, S. H. (2001). Psychological types of male Anglican clergy in Wales. *Journal of Psychological Type, 56*, 19–23.

Jung, C. G. (1971). *Psychological types: The collected works, volume 6.* London: Routledge and Kegan Paul.

Keirsey, D., & Bates, M. (1978). *Please understand me.* Del Mar, California: Prometheus Nemesis.

Kendall, E. (1998). *Myers-Briggs Type Indicator: Step 1 manual supplement.* Palo Alto, California: Consulting Psychologists Press.

Myers, I. B. (1987). *Introduction to Type.* Oxford: Oxford Psychologists Press.

Myers, I. B., & McCaulley, M. H. (1985). *Manual: A guide to the development and use of the Myers-Briggs Type Indicator.* Palo Alto, California: Consulting Psychologists Press.

Part 8

LISTENING TO CHURCH LEADERS

Chapter 24

DEPLOYMENT OF THE CHURCHES' MINISTRY: ANGLICANS AND METHODISTS IN A RURAL DIOCESE

*Lewis Burton**

Abstract – Changes within society in recent years have created difficulties of various kinds for churches in England. Both the Church of England and the Methodist Church in Great Britain have found difficulty in staffing their churches as once they did. A survey of all the clergy in pastoral appointments in the Diocese of York and all similarly employed ministers in the York and Hull Methodist District seeks to document the differences in practice and contrasting provision of ministry to rural churches offered by these two denominations.

Introduction

Both Anglicans and Methodists tend to look back on their pasts with a certain nostalgia. For the Anglicans it was a time when each village or centre of population in the country had at its heart a parish church staffed by a clergyman whose duty it was to have the cure of souls for all those who lived within the parish boundary. This past has been well documented by Anthony Russell in *The Clerical Profession* (Russell, 1980) and *The Country Parish* (Russell, 1986). One element of nostalgia for Methodists in the countryside is when chapel and church existed side by side in the village, often perhaps in terms of social rivalry, and later in coexistence. Robert Moore's *Pitmen, Preachers, and Politics* (Moore, 1974), David Clark's *Between Pulpit and Pew: folk religion in a North Yorkshire fishing village* (Clark, 1982), and Clarke and Anderson's

* The Revd Dr Lewis Burton, a retired Methodist minister, is Honorary Research Fellow in the St Mary's Centre, Wales. *Address for correspondence*: 94 Sun Street, Haworth, Keighley, BD22 8AH. E-mail: lewisburton@blueyonder.co.uk

Methodism in the Countryside: the Horncastle Circuit, 1786–1986, (Clarke and Anderson, 1986) illustrate the situation of the Methodist chapel in County Durham, the East Yorkshire coast and Lincolnshire.

Nostalgia arises because what generally existed in the past has changed. Both the Church of England and the Methodist Church in recent times have had to grapple with the present reality of cultural, social and economic conditions. There has been a general erosion of belief under secular pressures. The institutional Church is no longer the force that it once was, and neither does membership confer the social benefits upon the believer that it once did. Church attendance and church membership have suffered serious decline, as shown by recent surveys of church life (Brierley, 1991). Alongside these sweeping changes, decline in vocations to ministry has created a shortage of clergy for parish and circuit work, and financial resources have been stretched to maintain a level of ministerial provision which was the norm in times past.

The Church of England addressed the problem in a number of commissions and reports in the latter part of the last century. The Paul Report, *The Payment and Deployment of the Clergy* (Paul, 1964), was followed in 1967 by the Morley Report (Morley, 1967) and later in 1974 by the Sheffield Report (Sheffield, 1974). The problem in the countryside was seen to be even more acute than in the towns, and so in the early 1990s the report, *Faith in the Countryside* (Archbishops' Commission on Rural Areas, 1990) was compiled by the Archbishops' Commission on Rural Areas. The fact finding exercise, The Rural Church Project, which provided data for the Archbishops' Commission on Rural Areas was written up and commented on by Davies, Watkins and Winter (1991) in *Church and Religion in Rural England.* Further suggestions regarding the development of ministry in the countryside have been offered by Andrew Bowden in *Ministry in the Countryside: a model for the future* (Bowden, 1994, 2003).

The Methodist Church has suffered from the same cultural, social and economic pressures as the Church of England, and triennial returns of membership, ministry, and churches have revealed much the same problems concerning shrinkage, and concerning ministerial deployment. Methodism, however, has not produced the bulk of reports on the subject which have been typical of Anglican concerns, although the Conference and official Methodism has not been unconcerned about recruitment to ministry and the difficulty of staffing country circuits (Conference, 2004; Howcroft, 2004). In practical terms both the Methodist Church and the Church of England have had to respond to clergy and ministerial shortage in different ways. Their response generally has been along the lines of the existing methods already employed in both their systems.

This superficial judgement of how both the Church of England and the Methodist Church in Great Britain possess diverging structures in the matter of ministerial deployment, especially in the way that such differences affect the provision of ministry in rural areas, needs to be tested empirically. The following are the results of a survey using the techniques of sociology to investigate the situation as it was during the summer of 2003 in East and North Yorkshire.

Method

Context

The main interest of the survey was in the deployment of clergy and ministers in the English countryside. The area chosen was the Diocese of York and the Methodist District of York and Hull, since both have few significant urban settlements and both have reasonably contiguous boundaries.

All the Anglican clergy, both incumbents and curates who were in pastoral care of parishes within the Diocese of York, and all Methodist ministers and probationers who had pastoral charge in the circuits in the York and Hull Methodist District were circulated with a questionnaire which sought responses to a number of questions relating to the location and the number of churches in their care. Responses indicated factors relating to policies of clergy and ministerial deployment and form the data for this survey.

Sample

The questionnaire was despatched to the sample of 318 by post in mid-May, 2003. The number of responses from 249 Anglican clergy was 126, a response rate of 50.6%. The number received from 69 Methodist ministers was 46, a response rate of 66.7%, making an overall response rate of 54.1%.

Of the Anglican respondents 26% were women, as against 43% of the Methodists. There was no one under the age of 26 in pastoral charge of churches in either denomination, but there was no one in the Methodist circuits aged 66 years or above, whereas the Anglicans had five clergy over that age. Both denominations had similar proportions in the middle age range of 56 to 65 years, around a quarter of their number.

The Methodist age distribution was a flatter curve with a shorter range, the Anglican being skewed toward the older age groups.

When considering years of experience in ministry the Methodists seemed much less experienced than the Anglicans: 50% of Methodists had served less than ten years in the circuits as against 31% of Anglicans who had served less than ten years in parishes and a few older Anglicans had over 40 years experience of ministry. Methodists could not match this record. Anglicans have also stayed longer in their present appointment than Methodists, although this fact is predictable when one takes into account the Methodist tradition of itinerant ministry. The proportions of those who had served less than four years in their present appointment were much the same, at just over one half. Taking age and length of service in pastoral ministry into account it can be inferred that in both churches late recruitment to ministry, after time spent in some other occupation, has become the norm.

Results

Strength on the ground

The first factor to note in relation to the deployment of these clergy and ministers over the geographical area of the diocese and the district relates not to relative proportions, but to absolute numbers. Anglican clergy in the parishes number 249 while Methodist ministers number 69. The boundaries of the two church administrations were not contiguous since in the north the Anglican Diocese extended to the Tees, but the extra 16 Methodist ministers in circuits south of the Tees (Minutes, 2003) still makes for a large imbalance in the pastoral care provided by the two denominations.

This imbalance becomes more obvious when the clergy workloads of this study are seen, not as proportions in a distribution, but as absolute numbers. Anglican respondents gave numbers baptized in 2002 as 2,161 whilst Methodists report only 425, despite the fact that the difference between the average number conducted by individual clergy and ministers is not significantly different. The data also show that the parish church is more popular than the chapel for weddings and funerals, as inferred from average scores, but absolute numbers again put this into the context of the Church of England being the greater provider. For weddings the figures are 845 as against 189, and for funerals 2,525 as against 742.

A number of questions could be posed regarding this imbalance. Are Anglicans stronger in this region only; are Anglicans not as short of clergy numbers as Methodists; has Methodism more churches in the care of each individual minister; or is it that Methodism is by no means as strong as the Church of England especially in a region of England which is mainly rural in composition?

Number of churches in pastoral care

Table 1 gives the number of churches in the pastoral care of one minister or one priest. The most typical number of churches in each of the distributions is two, but it will be readily noted that the Anglican distribution is very heavily weighted toward the smaller number of churches. 27% of the Anglicans have only one church in their care while only 9% of Methodists are in this situation. The highest number of churches in one person's care is eight for the Anglicans and seven for the Methodists. Proportions in the middle range are much the same for Anglican clergy and Methodist ministers but there are larger proportions of Methodists who have five or six churches in their care than the Anglicans. The whole distribution for the Methodists is more evenly spread, while that for the Anglicans is skewed. Larger proportions of Anglicans than Methodists have fewer churches in their care and larger proportions of Methodists have more churches in their care. The distributions were subjected to a statistical chi squared test to ascertain the level of difference between them and the result shows that the statistical difference is significant at a level of .001.

Table 1: Number of churches within the pastoral care of individual clergy and ministers

	Anglican		Methodist	
	N	%	N	%
One church	34	27	4	9
Two churches	40	32	13	28
Three churches	21	17	9	20
Four churches	10	8	4	9
Five churches	12	9	5	11
Six churches	4	3	7	15
Seven churches	1	1	4	9
Eight churches	2	2	0	0

Single church ministry

As the interest of the survey was on multiple ministry it was appropriate to ask where those with the care of only one church ministered. From table 1 it is observed that of the 125 Anglican respondents, 34, representing 27% had only one church in their care. Of the 45 Methodists only four, representing 9% of the total were in the same situation. It was possible to relate the incidence of single church ministry to the neighbourhood of ministry by analysing respondents' answers regarding the number of churches in their care to the type of area in which their churches were located. A scale of five categories of area type, namely inner city, council estate, suburban, country town and rural was used. One third of the Anglican singletons and one half of the Methodists were in suburbia, reflecting that both denominations promote ministerial concentration in this type of urban settlement, but proportions for Anglicans with only one church are also high in council housing estates and the inner city. The 21% of Anglicans found to have only one church in a rural area indicates that the practice of one village, one parish church and one parish priest in the Church of England is by no means dead, and that united benefices have not taken over completely.

By contrast, in the category of the country town there are only 2% of Anglican clergy with only one church to care for, which indicates that many who have charge of a parish church in a country town have also charge of a church or churches in the surrounding countryside. On the other hand, there are no ministers among the Methodists who have only one church in a country town and there are 39% of them stationed in that situation. The implication is that the deployment of Methodists in the English countryside follows the pattern of a minister in a country town having also charge of a church or a number of churches in the surrounding countryside. The conclusion is that although some Anglican clergy are based in a country town and have pastoral responsibility for rural churches, this particular pattern of ministry is much more typical of the Methodist situation.

Area of respondents' main church

The five areas of church location have been described above and consideration can now be given to the overall deployment of ministry by both Churches as distinct from single church ministry. Table 2 gives the five areas and indicates what proportions the 46 Methodists and the 125 Anglicans are in each category. In the urban part of the distribution there are greater proportions of Anglicans deployed in the inner city and the council estates than Methodists.

Methodists have the edge on ministry to suburban churches by 37% as against 27% which indicates the concentration of Methodist ministry in suburbia. The deployment of ministry in the countryside is very striking by contrast, with Methodists having 39% of their ministers with a main church in a country town but with only 15% having their main church in a rural area, Anglicans on the other hand have 18% with their main church in a country town and 40% with their main church in the rural situation. The reversal of these two proportions highlights the difference in deployment policy between the two denominations. The inference is that Anglicans minister to the countryside from the countryside but Methodists minister to the countryside largely by forays from the local country town. The distributions of area of main church were also subjected to a chi squared statistical test of difference and the result was a positive difference at the .0001 level.

Table 2: Type of area for the main church of individual clergy and ministers

	Anglican		*Methodist*	
	N	%	N	%
City centre	8	6	1	2
Council estate	11	9	3	7
Suburbia	34	27	17	37
Country town	22	18	18	39
Rural	50	40	7	15

Pastoral care of local rural churches

The data show that responsibility for multi-church pastoral oversight commonly straddled the boundaries between the different areas. The clergy and ministers in multi-church ministry in the urban situation were few and almost all straddled the divide between the city centre and the council estate, although some Methodists worked churches in council estates from their main church in suburbia. The most common link across the boundary of area type for both Methodists and Anglicans was to have multiple charge of local churches with a main church in suburbia or a country town with other churches in the countryside.

It was therefore clear from the data that much the larger proportions both of Anglican clergy in the Diocese of York and Methodist ministers in the Methodist District of York and Hull minister to churches in country areas. Analysis of the data for those who minister to churches in the countryside can then best be examined in three discrete cohorts; those whose main church is in suburbia, those whose main church is in a market town, and those whose main church is in a village centred among other villages.

Both Anglicans and Methodists with a main church in suburbia have also one other rural church in their care with the same proportion of 29%. The same proportion of Methodists have two rural churches in their care besides their main church in suburbia, but only 3% of Anglicans are similarly placed. This suggests that Methodists reach out in their ministry to a greater extent than the Anglicans to a rural fringe. No ministers or clergy in suburbia had more than two rural churches in their care, a fact which perhaps reflects on the work load of ministry in a suburban situation. When the number of those who have churches in a rural situation and their main church is in suburbia is contrasted with all those who have churches in suburbia without extra responsibility, the proportion for Methodists is 59% and for Anglicans 32%, which underlines the strategy of Methodist deployment to minister to the countryside from the suburban situation.

The striking factor relating to those who have care for churches in the countryside and are based in a country town is that every Methodist minister whose main church is in the country town also has one or more churches in the surrounding countryside, some having up to six churches in addition to their main charge. This is not the case with the Anglicans. Contrasting with the 100% of Methodist ministers in a country town, who in addition to their main church have churches in a rural setting, only 82% of Anglicans are similarly placed, and the maximum number of rural churches of which any one of them had pastoral responsibility is limited to a total of three.

Ministry to the rural church from a rural base is, however, the prerogative of the Anglican clergy. Of the 125 Anglicans, 50 had pastoral responsibility solely in the countryside, a proportion of 40%, whereas Methodism had only seven ministers who live and work solely in the countryside, representing 15% of Methodist respondents. The most typical number in a Methodist's care is five and the most typical in an Anglican's is two, which were in the care of ten of the clergy. However, nine of the Anglicans had three and another nine had five. The maximum number in a Methodist's care was six and in an Anglican's eight. The average number of rural churches in Methodist care is 4.0 and the average in Anglican care is 3.64. Anglicans on the whole had fewer churches in their care, although a few had rather more churches in their care than was typical of the Methodists.

In summary, from the analysis above, it can be seen that ministerial deployment to rural churches from a rural situation is clearly a mark of Anglican strategy and that ministry to churches in a rural situation from a main ministry in suburbia or a country town is the mark of Methodist strategy. In addition, however, further analysis of the data determined that there are 83% of Methodist ministers who have some rural churches in their pastoral responsibility as against 63% of the Anglicans. This difference was measured by a chi squared test and found to be significant at the .0001 level. In absolute numbers there are many more Anglican rural churches than Methodist, but in a consideration of proportions engaged in rural ministry Methodism lays a greater burden of the care of numbers of local churches on its ministers than Anglicanism.

It is possible to ascertain from the data the total number of rural churches within the care of respondents and so provide corroboration of the above statement. This calculation gives a total of 229 rural Anglican churches and 124 Methodist. This means that those Methodist respondents who care for rural churches have an average of 3.3 rural churches in their pastoral charge, and Anglican 2.9. If one extends this to calculate an average for all the respondents from the two administrations, including those with no ministry in rural churches, then it is 2.7 and 1.8 respectively. Using these averages it is possible to calculate a notional number of rural churches existing in the diocese and the district. This assumes that data from respondents are typical of the whole sample. This calculation shows that there are approximately 456 rural churches in the diocese and 186 in the district.

Discussion

All ministers who had churches in their pastoral care in the Methodist District of York and Hull were sampled in this survey, as were all the clergy in similar appointments in the Diocese of York. The response rate of over 50% represents, as near as it is practicably possible to ascertain by sociological survey technique, the situation which existed in mid 2003 regarding the deployment of ministers and clergy in East Yorkshire churches.

One of the first factors in the situation shown by the data is that the myth of one parish church in one village with one parish priest, and also that of a church and chapel in every village has not been superseded, only modified. Despite the overwhelming evidence of plurality of pastoral care which comes from the practice of united benefices in a contemporary Church of England situation there are still seven villages in East Yorkshire with their own parish priest who is not shared by other parishes. Anglican clergy also minister to an estimated total of 456 village churches, a calculation based upon the survey data, whilst Methodist ministers have an estimated 186 chapels in their care. The myth of a church and chapel in every village must therefore be modified.

Attention was drawn to the fact that over much the same area the Church of England has 249 clergy in pastoral work as opposed to 69 Methodist ministers. The discrepancy casts doubt upon the ostensible equal partner status of the two Churches nationally. However, the situation is rather altered in the rural situation when it is observed that there are 38 Methodists out of the 46 respondents, a percentage of 82%, as against the 79 Anglicans out of 125 respondents, a percentage of 63% who have village churches and chapels in their pastoral care. In considering the proportions of ministerial provision for rural areas, therefore, Methodism is not as overshadowed as much as it seems to be when compared with the proportions of all ministerial provision in the two administrations when treated as a whole. There is therefore a greater concentration of rural ministry by Methodism in the whole area than a simple comparison of the total numbers of clergy and ministers in pastoral care in the two church administrations show.

However, the data show clearly that Methodist ministers who have charge of rural churches do not live in the countryside. They live in suburbia, where their main church is situated, or in the country town. Only seven, or 18%, of the 38 Methodist respondents who have charge of churches in a rural situation live in the countryside, as against 50 Anglican respondents out of the 79 who minister in country situations, a proportion of 63%. Moreover seven of the 50 Anglicans in the rural situation are in charge of a single church and therefore 43 of them, a proportion of 86%, are in multi parish situations. By definition the 37% of Anglicans who minister in a rural situation, but who have their base in suburbia or a country town, are also probably in a united benefice. However, using the chi-square test, there is a significant difference of .0001 between the two sets of clergy which indicates clearly that Methodist provision for rural ministry comes from ministers who have their main church elsewhere rather than in a rural situation. Conversely

Anglican ministry to the countryside comes mainly from clergy who are based in the rural situation.

Other data show that distances of ten or fifteen miles between the nearest church in a minister's care and the furthest church, is by no means uncommon. This creates practical difficulties for both Anglicans and Methodists who do not live near to where they minister. Thus travelling cuts the time available for ministry, as well as adding to stress. The culture of suburbia is not that of the countryside and the country town is not quite the same as living in the country. There is therefore the danger of the minister being regarded as some sort of foreigner who does not understand country ways. Differences of outlook and understanding arise between the minister and the members of rural congregations. Time is taken up with ministry to a larger church elsewhere, and the migrant minister cannot build relationships with distant churches.

This study also brings into sharp contrast the differences by which church structures affect ministerial deployment, especially in the countryside. Being geographically based, the Church of England has some inflexibility in relation to ministerial deployment. The urban church, with parish populations of much greater number than in the countryside, gives rise to questions of priority and cost effectiveness regarding the overall deployment of clergy. Methodism has not the same limiting factors as its units are circuits, groups of local churches, not individual churches, and its structure is not geographically based. Circuit boundaries are notional and circuits can be reduced, extended, and merged. Deployment of ministry is centrally regulated every year through the traditional method of the itinerancy of the ministers. The annual Methodist Conference, through its Stationing Committee, has the responsibility for these changes and can re-deploy ministers at short notice. The whole system is therefore flexible and more open to changes in deployment to meet varying local needs. In relation to ministerial deployment in the rural church, the general response of the Church of England has been the creation of the united benefice or the multi-church parish. Methodist structures, however, allow comparatively short term withdrawal from rural localities and withdrawal of ministry through a diminution of numbers on the circuit staff. A key feature of rural Methodism has also been reliance on local lay people who share the ministerial task and church organization, and also offer pastoral care.

The Church of England, however, finds some benefit in its comparative inflexibility of structures, since there is also an inflexibility of attitudes and sentiments associated with its parish churches. The traditional attitudes of the village, where the parish church has a cherished place, and where the village rites of passage are carried through by the national Church, despite whether people belong or not, tend to make the local parish church inviolable. Not many weep over the closure of the local chapel, but the opposition to the closure of the local parish church would be intense. Even when sentiment is overcome the redundancy of a village parish church is difficult to carry through by virtue of church processes.

Thus the methods which both churches use in the deployment and the appointment of their clergy and ministers are very different, but both have advantages and disadvantages when assessed from different points of view: one achieves mobility of ministry and the other creates stability of the local church's presence. One of the problems for both denominations is whether their different systems are reconcilable.

Conclusion

The Diocese of York and the District of York and Hull are not the only rural dioceses and districts within the Church of England or within British Methodism. Every diocese and district has a similar structure, and policies of deployment generally are organized and implemented by their central governing bodies. The divergence of church structures in the two church administrations in East Yorkshire reflects the differences in the deployment of Anglican clergy and Methodist ministers typical of both national churches. Such differences have implications for progress in the Covenant which now exists between them. The matter of restructuring their presence on the ground will be an important part of the ongoing discussions, especially toward the deployment of a possibly unified ministry. Such a diverse pattern of ministerial provision, such as that which exists between the two churches in East Yorkshire, would inhibit any common ministry which the two Churches could evolve, and lead to overlap of responsibility and inefficiency of pastoral provision. As has been demonstrated in this survey the structures of both the churches have something to commend them as well as other factors which inhibit good service to local church communities. These should be recognized and included in any further discussion about ministry in the progress toward unity.

References

Archbishops' Commission on Rural Areas. (1990). *Faith in the countryside*. London: Churchman.

Bowden, A. (1994 and 2003). *Ministry in the countryside: a model for the future*. London: Continuum.

Brierley, P. (1991). *Christian England*. London: MARC.

Burton, L. (2004). Blackshawhead: A local case history in rural church categorisation. *Rural Theology*, 2, 41–51.

Clark, D. (1982). *Between pulpit and pew: Folk religion in a North Yorkshire fishing village*. London: Cambridge University Press.

Clarke, J. N., & Anderson, C. L. (1986). *Methodism in the Countryside*. Horncastle: Clarke and Anderson.

Conference. (2004). *The Agenda of the Methodist Conference*. Peterborough: Methodist Publishing House.

Davies, D., Watkins, C., & Winter, M. (1991). *Church and Religion in Rural England*. Edinburgh: T&T Clark.

Howcroft, K. (Ed.). (2004). *Presence: A workbook to help and sustain an effective Christian presence in villages*. Peterborough: Methodist Publishing House.

Minutes. (2003), *The Methodist Church: Minutes of Conference and Directory*, Peterborough, Methodist Publishing House.

Moore, R. (1974). *Pit-men, preachers, and politics*. London: Cambridge University Press.

Morley, F. (1967). *Partners in ministry: Report on the commission and deployment of the clergy*. London: CIO.

Paul, L. (1964). *The payment and deployment of the clergy*. London: CIO.

Russell, A. (1980). *The clerical profession*. London: SPCK.

Russell. A. (1986). *The country parish*. London: SPCK.

Sheffield Report. (1974). *The deployment of the clergy: The report of the House of Bishops' working group*. London: CIO.

Chapter 25

VIEWS ON BAPTISM AND CONFIRMATION IN THE CHURCH IN WALES: ARE RURAL CLERGY DIFFERENT?

*Keith Littler**

Abstract – A survey of all Church in Wales stipendiary parochial clergy sought clerics' views on various aspects of baptism and confirmation. A 65% response produced data to suggest that 58% of the respondents serve in urban parishes and 42% in rural parishes. The views of urban and rural clerics were found to show statistically significant differences in respect of eleven key items on baptism and confirmation. These data support other research suggesting that rural clergy are more community orientated and probably more sensitive to the conservative views of parishioners.

Introduction

The difficulties of attempting to divide Anglican clergy into two clear categories according to whether they minister in a rural or an urban parish are well documented. Factors designed to identify 'rurality' were presented by Francis (1985) and further developed by Lankshear (2001). Littler (2005) has presented a working definition of the 'rurality' of each Church in Wales diocese using figures for population per parish and the number of parishes per diocese. It remains, however, that no official theory or figures are available for the designation of either Church of England or Church in Wales parishes according to whether they may be deemed rural or urban and it has to be accepted that the distinction between 'rural' and 'urban' remains imprecise (Burton, 2004).

* The Revd Dr Keith Littler is Research Fellow at St Mary's Centre, Wales. *Address for correspondence:* Myrtle Hill Cottage, Broadway, Laugharne, Carmarthenshire, SA33 4NS. E-mail: ktlittler@btinternet.com

Despite these difficulties there is considerable evidence, both anecdotal and empirical, to suggest that the experience of Anglican clergy in rural parishes differs from the experience of clergy in urban parishes. Osborne (2004), for example, argues that while all Anglican clergy, urban or rural, have to face a clash of myth and reality concerning their role in the community, this is probably more pronounced in respect of the country vicar. In his contribution to the collection of essays on rural ministry by Anglican Bishops edited by Martineau, Francis and Francis (2004) Rowan Williams concluded that the ministry of the parish priest in a rural parish is different from that of the parish priest in an urban setting and that the problems of the former 'cannot be resolved by importing styles and structures formed in other settings' (p. 255).

Empirical evidence lends weight to the notion that the rural church is different in a number of ways, including the experience and personality of clergy and congregations (Roberts, 2005). For example, Francis and Rutledge (2000) have considered how far rural clergy may experience more stress than their urban counterparts. Reporting on a sample of over 1,000 full-time stipendiary parochial Anglican clergy, they found that rural clergy have a lower sense of personal accomplishment than comparable clergy working in other types of parishes but that they suffer no higher levels of emotional exhaustion. A series of recent studies by Francis and Lankshear (1998), Francis and Littler (2001), Francis and Rutledge (2004) and Francis, Smith and Robbins (2004) employed the Eysenck Personality Questionnaire to compare the personality profile of Anglican clergy engaged in rural ministry with Anglican clergy engaged in ministry in non-rural parishes. A key conclusion from this group of studies is that rural clergy tend to be more socially conformist than clergy serving in non-rural areas.

Other studies have looked at the difference between the urban and rural congregations. Craig (2005), for example, utilized the Francis Psychological Type Scales in a study of 2,658 people attending church services in 95 congregations across the United Kingdom. The results indicated that rural churchgoers display a personality profile conducive to a more conservative approach to issues of faith and belief.

Michael Langrish, writing from extensive personal experience of rural parish ministry, identifies one core characteristic of the different perspective modelled by rural ministry in terms of 'community'. He writes as follows:

> The rural community is seen as the essence of the English good life, a collection of people well integrated into their local society and living productive and rewarding lives. (Langrish, 2004, p. 22)

In his classical work entitled *The Little Community*, Redfield (1967) identified the dimensions and attributes which make up a rural community, including small size, high social homogeneity, face-to-face relationships and perhaps a certain isolation and a natural resource-based economy. Many of these characteristics reflect the distinction between *Gemeinschaft* and *Gesellshaft* introduced by Ferdinand Tönnies (Tönnies and Harris, 2001). *Gemeinschaft* is broadly characterized by strong personal ties and relationships. In such communities religious beliefs tend to be intertwined with the folkways and mores of society and with 'family spirit'. There is seldom need to enforce external control on *Gemeinschaft*. Unlike *Gemeinschaft*, *Gesellschaft* emphasizes secondary relationships and there is generally less evidence of individual loyalty to society. It is necessary for control to be imposed externally if social cohesion is to be maintained in such societies. *Gesellschaften* tend to be more loosely-knit associations of people, of which urban parishes are typical. *Gemeinschaften* tend to be more closely-knit communities, of which rural parishes are typical.

Despite the obvious limitations of applying such complex concepts to contemporary British parish life, Tönnies nevertheless points us to a recognition both that the population of a parish may have properties of its own that are more than the sum of its members, and also that these properties can influence the functioning of that population and the functioning of individuals. Jean (2006) makes use of the distinction between *Gemeinschaft* and *Gesellschaft* in a recent study of Canadian communities and reminds us of the practical value of these theoretical concepts for the study of what he calls 'the rural-urban dichotomy' (p. 62).

Against this background, the aim of the present study is to examine whether rural clergy are more inclined than urban clergy to identify with *Gemeinschaft*, in respect of their understanding of Christian initiation.

Method

As part of a wide-ranging survey Littler (2005) mailed questionnaires to all 593 stipendiary parochial Church in Wales clergy and 384 fully completed questionnaires were returned, making a response rate of 65%. The clergy were asked to assess whether their parish was best described as city centre, urban, suburban, market town, or rural. The data showed that 58% described themselves as ministering in city centre, urban, suburban or market town parishes, while 42% described themselves as ministering in rural parishes. The questionnaire included a set of questions designed to distinguish between approaches to Christian initiation based on *Gemeinschaft* and on *Gesellschaft*. Each item was arranged for response on a five-point scale: agree strongly, agree, not certain, disagree, and disagree strongly.

Results

Eleven of the questions showed a statistically significant difference at the one per cent level of probability between the responses of clergy serving in rural and urban areas. These statistically significant responses are displayed in table 1. In this table the agree strongly and the agree responses have been combined into a single category 'yes'.

Discussion

The data presented in table 1 support the view that the community model of the church in rural areas not only survives but remains strong. While the data in table 1 are specific to a small number of aspects of baptism and confirmation, they nevertheless show important differences between rural clergy and urban clergy in respect of key areas of ministry and these differences may be explained in terms of the ministers' community involvement. In rural surroundings clergy are given greater opportunities to experience a *Gemeinschaft* model of ministry through contact with local schools and other local functions and activities. Church-based festivals, funerals, weddings and baptisms are essentially community centred. One could imagine, in such circumstances, that it is more difficult for the cleric in a rural parish to deny baptism to all but regular churchgoers, given that they may see the parents of children presented for baptism in a whole range of contexts outside the church congregation. Similarly, it is understandable, for the same reason, that clerics in rural parishes would be more inclined than clerics in urban parishes to baptize a baby if the parents confessed no faith but the grandparents were regular communicant members at that cleric's church; and again, that they should support the suggestion that churches should baptize all babies whose parents request it.

Table 1: Views of clergy in urban parishes and clergy in rural parishes

	Urban %	Rural %	χ2	p <
Churches should only baptize babies of regular churchgoers	15	5	8.7	.01
Baptism preparation courses should be run by members of the congregation	62	48	7.2	.01
Generally requests for baptism outside the main services should be granted	64	51	6.7	.01
I would baptize a baby if the parents confessed no faith but the grandparents were regular communicants of my church	57	73	9.0	.01
Churches should baptize all babies whose parents request it	48	64	9.2	.01
Churches have a responsibility for the continuing Christian education of babies they baptize	94	86	6.9	.01
Infant baptism may lull people into a state of false security about their position before God	54	34	14.6	.001
In infant baptism the naming of the baby is important	61	74	7.0	.01
Confirming young people helps them to find their way back into church in later life	61	77	10.4	.01
Churches should not confirm anyone under the age of 13 years	16	6	8.1	.01
Churches should only confirm young people if they come to church regularly	66	51	8.3	.01

Indeed, the argument that clerics in rural parishes are more generally 'community orientated', than are clerics in urban parishes, would seem to explain much of the statistically significant difference in the views of rural and urban clergy, as shown in table 1.

Conclusion

This study has tested the thesis that clergy serving in rural ministry are shaped by theology and practice based more on *Gemeinschaft* and less on *Gesellschaft* than is the case among clergy serving in urban ministry. Taking understanding of Christian initiation as reflecting differences in these perspectives, the data clearly support the thesis. It may, then, be important for bishops to take such fundamental differences in clergy attitudes toward matters of Christian initiation into account when appointing to rural parishes.

References

Burton, L. (2004). Blackshawhead: A local case history in rural church categorization. *Rural Theology, 2*, 41–51

Craig, C. L. (2005). Psychological type preference of rural churchgoers. *Rural Theology, 3*, 123–131.

Francis, L. J. (1985). *Rural Anglicanism*. London: Collins.

Francis, L. J., & Lankshear, D. W. (1998). Personality and preference for rural ministry among male Anglican clergy. *Pastoral Psychology, 46*, 163–166.

Francis, L. J., & Littler, K. (2001). Personality and preference for rural ministry among Church in Wales clergy. *Psychologist in Wales, 11*, 3–5.

Francis, L. J., & Rutledge, C. F. J. (2000). Are rural clergy in the Church of England under greater stress? A study in empirical theology. *Research in the Social Scientific Study of Religion, 11*, 173–191.

Francis, L. J., & Rutledge, C. F. J. (2004). Personality and preference for rural ministry: replication and reconsideration. *Pastoral Psychology, 53*, 43–48.

Francis, L. J., Smith, G., & Robbins, M. (2004). Do introverted clergy prefer rural ministry? *Rural Theology, 2*, 127–134.

Jean, B. (2006). The study of rural communities in Quebec: from the 'folk society' monographic approach to the recent revival of community as place-based rural development. *Journal of Rural and Community Development, 1*, 56–68.

Langrish, M. L. (2004). Dynamics of community. In J. Martineau, L. J. Francis and P. Francis (Eds.), *Changing rural life: A Christian response to key rural issues* (pp. 21–43). Norwich: Canterbury Press.

Lankshear, D. W. (2001). *One church or three? Using statistics as a tool for mission.* Unpublished Ph.D. dissertation. University of Wales: Lampeter.

Littler, K. (2005). *The views of Church in Wales clergy on Christian initiation: 1993–2003.* Unpublished D.Min dissertation. University of Wales: Bangor.

Martineau, J., Francis, L. J., & Francis, P. (2004). *Changing rural life: A Christian response to key rural issues.* Norwich: Canterbury Press.

Osborne, D. (2004). *The country vicar: Shaping rural ministry.* London: Darton, Longman and Todd.

Redfield, R. (1967). *The little community and peasant society and culture.* Chicago: University of Chicago Press.

Roberts, C. (2005). Rural Anglicanism: One face or many? *Rural Theology, 3*(1), 25–39.

Tönnies, F., & Harris, J. (2001). *Tönnies: Community and civil society.* Translated from Tönnies original work of 1887 by M. Hollis and edited by J. Harris. Cambridge: Cambridge University Press.

Chapter 26

CHILDREN AND COMMUNION: LISTENING TO CHURCHWARDENS IN RURAL AND URBAN WALES

*Ann Howells and Keith Littler**

Abstract — A survey of Church in Wales churchwardens undertaken during 2003 in the dioceses of Bangor and Llandaff included twelve questions central to the idea of children receiving communion before confirmation. Analyses of the responses to these questions show few differences in the views of churchwardens from rural parishes compared with the views of church-wardens from urban parishes. More significantly, when compared with studies concerning the views of Church in Wales clergy on children receiving communion before confirmation, churchwardens emerge as notably less supportive than clergy. It is argued that clergy and church-wardens need to work closely together to ensure that parishes move forward in an agreed way.

Introduction

The New Testament is not particularly helpful in providing information about children and communion. Certainly there is evidence that children were present at worship from the earliest times and this may well have included the Eucharist. Strange (1996) has suggested that if the earliest Christians saw some similarities between the Eucharist which commemorated the sacrifice of Christ, whom Paul described as 'our

* The Revd Ann Howells (formerly Smitham) is Vicar of the Parish of Llandybïe in the Diocese of St Davids. *Address for correspondence*: The Vicarage, 77 Kings Road, Llandybïe, Ammanford, Carmarthenshire, SA18 2TL.
E-mail: ann.howells1@tesco.net
  The Revd Dr Keith Littler is Research Fellow at St Mary's Centre, Wales. *Address for correspondence:* Myrtle Hill Cottage, Broadway, Laugharne, Carmarthenshire, SA33 4NS. E-mail: ktlittler@btinternet.com

Passover lamb' (1 Corinthians 5:7), and the Passover celebration already familiar to them, then we might expect that children would partake of the Christian meal as they had done of the Jewish one (Exodus 12:21-27). It is a fair point but lacks the support of solid evidence.

More revealing is the effect that another New Testament reference (John 6:53) would seem to have had on St Augustine. This key text in John's Gospel, 'unless you eat the flesh of the Son of Man and drink his blood you can have no life in you', appears to have persuaded St Augustine that there could be no halfway house between the unbaptized and the communicant. From this axiom St Augustine built a powerful case for the admission of children to communion (Strange, 1996). The admission of children to communion in the Eastern Church became defined from this time onwards and remains so. In the West, however, the situation has been less straightforward and, despite Augustine's weighty support, a combination of custom and theology have worked together against the acceptance of child communion.

By the late Middle Ages, a growing reverence for the sacrament of holy communion meant that the Eucharist had become virtually a privilege for the priesthood. It is hardly surprising, therefore, that children were debarred from participation in the sacrament. Indeed, the place of children in the scheme of things was prescribed in a detailed way when in AD1215 the Fourth Lateran Council linked the taking of holy communion with the child's arrival at years of discretion (Lowther Clarke, 1932). Thus the Council ruled that children should not be admitted to communion until they had arrived at an age which would allow them to distinguish clearly the elements of the communion from ordinary food. The appropriate age was initially thought to be around seven years, but was later pushed back to between ten and fourteen years. This was the first time that a specific age was set on receiving communion.

Despite a good deal of subsequent repudiation of the theology of the Fourth Lateran Council, and despite sporadic efforts since to revive the primitive practice of child communion, described by Holeton (1981), the resulting pattern which has emerged for the Anglican Church remains one of baptism in infancy and confirmation in adolescence, followed by communion (Fisher and Yarnold, 1989). Binfield (1994), through his persuasive summary of an experiment in the involvement of children at the Eucharist, asked why, if children are baptized, they should be refused communion. It was a question to which the Anglican Church was obliged to respond.

In March 1997, the Church of England House of Bishops issued *Guidelines on the Admission of Baptized Persons to Holy Communion before Confirmation* (Church of England, 1997) which had previously been approved by General Synod in November 1996. Prior to these guidelines, only the dioceses of Peterborough, Southwark and Manchester were officially admitting the unconfirmed to holy communion, having been given permission as an experiment in 1991. In 1993, the then National Children's Advisers' Panel discovered that unconfirmed children were receiving communion in every Church of England diocese, from either their parents or officiating clergy. There was also a recognition that children who were not receiving communion were sometimes given alternatives, such as sweets. It was reported that the practice in one church was to give children their Sunday school stamp at the altar rail and that a visiting child consumed his (Gay and Williams, 1995).

It is against this backcloth that it was felt necessary to issue the 1997 guidelines (Church of England, 1997). These guidelines made it clear that, since communion before confirmation is a departure from the inherited norm, it requires special permission and that, after consultation, every diocesan bishop would have the discretion to make a general policy whether or not to entertain new applications for communion before confirmation.

In November 2000, the Church of England General Synod debated a motion from the diocese of Bristol requesting the House to initiate a change in Canon Law so that Synod could decide whether communion before confirmation should be the nationally agreed common practice, rather than leaving the decision to individual dioceses and parishes. The motion was amended to read:

> That this Synod request the House of Bishops to continue to monitor the implementation in dioceses of its 1997 guidelines on Communion before confirmation and to report back to Synod by 2005, with a recommendation as to whether any changes in Canon Law are required as a result of developing practice and understanding in the Church (Church of England, 2001).

The report to Synod in 2005 (Church of England, 2005a) indicated that 1,650 churches, roughly 10% of all Church of England churches, were admitting the non-confirmed to communion. The report goes on to recommend that children who have been baptized but who have not yet been confirmed and are not yet ready or desirous to be confirmed, as required by paragraph 1(a) of Canon B15A, may be admitted to holy communion, subject to regulations which essentially require the approval of the diocesan bishop. At its meeting in July 2005, Synod took note of the report with a view to its return to Synod for final approval in 2006 (Church of England, 2005b). It is unlikely that the Church in Wales will remain unaffected by these decisions for long.

Jackson (2004) suggests that children will not accept the discrimination of exclusion from communion and sees the continuation of such actions as one reason why young people leave the Church before they are old enough for confirmation. It is unlikely that the reason young people leave the Church is this simple, as Kay and Francis (1996) point out. Even so, it would seem that this was a line of thinking inherent within the Ely Report (1971) and which was in turn to influence the *Report of the Doctrinal Commission of the Church in Wales on Christian Initiation* (Church in Wales, 1971) and also much subsequent thinking within the Church in Wales.

In the same year as the Church in Wales *Book of Common Prayer* became available, a questionnaire concerning the issue of children and communion was distributed to clerics throughout the Church in Wales (Church in Wales, 1984a). Following the circulation of this questionnaire, one Cardiff parish was persuaded to seek permission for the admission of children to communion prior to confirmation. A pilot scheme for admitting baptized children to communion before confirmation was launched in the Cardiff parish of Gabalfa in 1991 and the Church in Wales established a working group to consider the question of the admission of baptized children to communion prior to confirmation.

It is within this general context that Thomas (1994) surveyed Church in Wales clergy to seek their views on a range of aspects of initiation into the Church in Wales. Among his findings he presented data that showed Church in Wales clergy to be clearly in favour of admitting baptized children to communion without previous confirmation or a desire for confirmation. Littler, Francis and Thomas (2002) have assessed Thomas' research and draw attention to a number of important conclusions relating to Church in Wales clergy's views on confirmation. Younger clergy are even more in favour of children taking communion before confirmation than older clergy. Clergy of all ages believe that children who are to be given communion should also be encouraged to attend nurture groups, but they are not in favour of children having to learn the catechism as a specific requirement of entry to communion. Thomas apparently found no significant difference between the views of clergy in rural ministries and the views of clergy in urban parishes.

In spite of the support of clergy for the admission of children to communion prior to confirmation as indicated by Thomas' survey, this practice still seems to be the exception rather than the general practice within the Church in Wales. Official Church in Wales statistics of pre-confirmation communicants show that in all dioceses of the Church in Wales a number of people are granted access to communion without previous confirmation, but this practice seems as established among adults as among young people. From 2001 the Representative Body of the Church in Wales has collected total figures for pre-confirmation communicants and from 2003 has collated these figures separately for persons under eighteen years of age and eighteen years and over, in respect of each diocese. The figures provided by the Representative Body show that in 2003 a total of 702 non-confirmed persons were reported to have been welcomed to communion, of whom 356 were under the age of eighteen years.

The admission of children to communion before confirmation in the Anglican Church represents a very significant departure from established practice. To know that clergy are largely in favour of this change provides only half the picture. The views of lay people are also of crucial importance. The aim of the present study, therefore, is to listen to the views on this matter held by key lay people within the local parishes of the Church in Wales. Because of the formal legal status that they hold within church structure, churchwardens were selected for this study.

Method

A bilingual questionnaire was distributed by post to churchwardens in all Church in Wales parishes in the dioceses of Bangor and Llandaff, a total of 574 churchwardens. All told, 400 questionnaires were returned, making a response rate of 70%. The two dioceses were selected to provide a contrast between north and south Wales, between a rural and an urban diocese, and between a predominantly Welsh-speaking and a predominantly English-speaking diocese.

A question was included in the questionnaire requesting church-wardens to indicate whether the area around their church could best be described as city centre, urban, suburban or rural. Two fifths of the respondents (40%) described the area around their church as either city centre, suburban or urban and the remainder (60%) described their parish as rural.

Part three of the questionnaire consisted of 39 questions used by Thomas (1994) in his 1993 survey of Church in Wales clergy about their attitude to children receiving communion before confirmation and about the importance that they placed on communion. Each of these questions utilized a five-point Likert scale, anchored in agree strongly, agree, not sure, disagree, and disagree strongly.

Table 1 compares the responses of the churchwardens in urban and rural parishes to the twelve questions included in the survey specifically about children receiving communion before confirmation. For this purpose, those respondents who indicated that they agree strongly are combined with those who agree, in order to produce a single category. The statistical significance of any differences between rural and urban churchwardens has been tested by the chi-square statistic.

The most notable feature of the table is the fact that there are only two instances where the difference in the viewpoint of churchwardens in rural parishes and churchwardens in urban parishes is statistically significant. Indeed, it is evident from the table that in response to the statement, 'Children cannot take a full part in communion services unless they receive communion', 39% of rural respondents agree and also 39% of urban respondents agree. It would seem that rural churchwardens and urban churchwardens are in agreement with each other but only a minority of each group (39%) support the statement. When Thomas (1994) conducted his survey of the views of Church in Wales clergy in 1993, he found that 50% of clergy supported this particular statement.

The table shows that when respondents were presented with the statement, 'Infants who have been baptized should be welcome to receive communion', 13% of rural churchwardens agree while 15% of urban churchwardens agree. By way of comparison, Thomas (1994) found that 34% of Church in Wales clergy were in favour of admitting baptized children to communion prior to confirmation.

The table shows three statements concerned with the question of the appropriate age at which young people should be welcome to receive communion. It is evident that 20% of rural respondents and 18% of urban respondents deem the age of seven years to be appropriate. Rather more respondents deem nine years to be the appropriate age (25% of rural and 24% of urban respondents) and rather more again deem eleven years to be the appropriate age (34% of rural and 31% of urban respondents). By way of comparison, Thomas (1994) found that 54% of Church in Wales clergy were in favour of welcoming children to receive communion at

Table 1: Responses of rural and urban churchwardens compared

	Urban % agree	Rural % agree	χ^2	$p <$
Children cannot take a full part in communion services unless they receive communion	9	9	0.01	NS
Infants who have been baptized should be welcome to receive communion	15	13	0.19	NS
Churchgoing seven-year-olds who have been baptized should be welcome to receive communion	18	20	0.22	NS
Churchgoing nine-year-olds who have been baptized should be welcome to receive communion	24	25	0.09	NS
Churchgoing eleven-year-olds who have been baptized should be welcome to receive communion	31	34	0.52	NS
Churches should not give communion to children until they have been confirmed	68	59	3.04	NS
Churches should not give communion to children until they are desirous of being confirmed	59	54	0.96	NS
Churches should not give communion to children until they are old enough to understand what is happening	83	76	2.46	NS
Churches should not give communion to children until they have committed themselves to the Lord Jesus	55	47	2.11	NS
Churches should not give communion to children until they know the catechism	51	43	2.47	NS
Churches should not give communion to children unless they are part of a Christian nurture group	39	26	5.88	.01
Churches which admit children to communion should also encourage them to attend nurture groups	72	53	13.31	.001

the age of seven years, 56% at the age of nine years, and 60% at the age of eleven years.

The next two statements in the table read as follows: 'Churches should not give communion to children until they have been confirmed', and 'Churches should not give communion to children until they are desirous of being confirmed'. These statements reflect the ruling in the Church in Wales Book of Common Prayer (Church in Wales, 1984b), and in the absence of the permission of the diocesan bishop to do otherwise, remain the official position of the Church in Wales. The former statement is supported by 59% of rural churchwardens and 68% of urban churchwardens, while the latter statement is supported by 54% of rural churchwardens and 59% of urban churchwardens. The difference in viewpoint of rural and urban churchwardens is not significant. However, Thomas (1994) found that 31% of Church in Wales clergy maintained that churches should not give communion to children until they have been confirmed and 38% of clergy maintained that churches should not give communion to children until they are desirous of being confirmed.

A high proportion of churchwardens agree with the statement, 'Churches should not give communion to children until they are old enough to know what is happening' (76% of rural and 83% of urban). Again, the difference is not significant. Just under half of the rural churchwardens (47%) and just over half of the urban churchwardens (55%) agree that churches should not give communion to children until they have committed themselves to the Lord Jesus. Again the difference is not significant. By contrast, Thomas (1994) showed Church in Wales clergy to hold a different viewpoint since only 43% of clergy agreed with the first statement and even fewer (34%) agreed with the second point.

The table shows that when the respondents were presented with the statement, 'Churches should not give communion to children until they know the catechism', 43% of rural respondents agree and 51% of urban respondents agree. The Church in Wales service of baptism includes the statement, 'you must see that he or she is instructed in the catechism' (Church in Wales, 1984b). While specific reference to the catechism is excluded from the Alternative Order (Church in Wales, 1990), it is included in the popular confirmation preparation material (Church in Wales, 2002) and certainly at the time of confirmation the bishop requires to be advised that the candidate has been properly prepared. That less than half of rural churchwardens (43%) and only just over half of urban churchwardens (51%) deem knowledge of the catechism to be important is interesting. It is also interesting that Thomas (1994) shows that only 18% of clergy believe this to be important.

The final two questions in the table both deal with the provision of nurture groups. It is here that significant differences emerge between the perceptions of churchwardens in rural areas and churchwardens in urban areas. While 39% of churchwardens in urban areas maintain that churches should not give communion to children unless they are part of a Christian nurture group, the proportion falls to 26% among church-wardens in rural areas. While 72% of churchwardens in urban areas maintain that churches which admit children to communion should also encourage them to attend nurture groups, the proportion falls to 53% among churchwardens in rural areas. The truth of the matter may well be that rural churches would find it so much more difficult to maintain the provision of nurture groups in the first place.

Conclusion

Two main conclusions emerge from this new study. First, the survey of Church in Wales clergy carried out by Thomas in 1993 (Thomas, 1994) showed that the majority of clergy were in favour of admitting children to communion before confirmation. The fact that the majority of church-wardens who responded to the present survey were opposed to the idea of children being admitted to communion before confirmation, may explain why the practice is not more widespread in the Church in Wales.

Second, the study has shown that there are few significant differences in attitudes of churchwardens in rural and in urban areas toward the admission of children to communion. Although other studies, like those reported by Francis and Lankshear (1997), Roberts (2003), Lankshear (2004), Francis and Rutledge (2004) and Craig (2005), point to significant differences between certain aspects of the rural and the urban church, such differences clearly do not extend to the attitudes of churchwardens concerning the admission of children to communion.

The practical implication to emerge from this study concerns the importance for clergy and churchwardens in both rural and urban areas working closely together to ensure that parishes move forward in an agreed way. The data show that clergy and churchwardens differ in their views on the access of children to communion. The underlying reasons for such differences must be addressed with sympathetic care and understanding.

References

Binfield, C. (1994). The Purley Way for children. In D. Wood (Ed.), *The Church and childhood* (pp. 461–476). Studies in Church History 31. Oxford: Blackwell.

Church in Wales. (1971). *Christian initiation: A report of the doctrinal commission of the Church in Wales.* Cardiff: Church in Wales Publications.

Church in Wales. (1984a). *Members of One Body: a questionnaire circulated to clergy.* Representative Body of the Church in Wales, Cardiff: Church in Wales Publications.

Church in Wales. (1984b). *Book of Common Prayer.* Cardiff: Church in Wales Publications.

Church in Wales. (1990). *Alternative Service of Baptism.* Cardiff: Church in Wales Publications.

Church in Wales. (2002). *Eighteen module confirmation course.* Cardiff: Church in Wales Publications.

Church of England. (1997). *Admission of Baptized Persons to Holy Communion before Confirmation.* GS 488. London, General Synod of the Church of England.

Church of England. (2001). *Report of Proceedings of General Synod, Vol.31, No.3:* Motion by the diocese of Bristol to change Canon Law B15A relating to Communion before confirmation. London: Church House Publishing.

Church of England. (2005a). *Children and Holy Communion: A review. GS1576.* London: General Synod of the Church of England.

Church of England. (2005b). *Resourcing Mission of the Church of England: Interim report. GS1580B.* London: General Synod of the Church of England.

Craig, C. L. (2005). Psychological type preferences of rural churchgoers. *Rural Theology, 3,* 123–131.

Ely Report. (1971). *Christian initiation: Birth and growth in Christian society.* London: Church of England Information Office.

Fisher, J. D. C., & Yarnold, E. J. (1989). The west from about AD500 to the reformation. In C. Jones, G. Wainwright and E. J. Arnold (Eds.), *The Study of the Liturgy* (9th impression) (pp. 110–117). London: SPCK.

Francis, L. J., & Lankshear, D. W. (1997). The rural church is different. *Journal of Empirical Theology, 10*(1), 5–20.

Francis, L. J., & Rutledge, C. J. F. (2004). Personality and preference for rural ministry: Replication and reconsideration. *Pastoral Psychology, 53,* 43–48.

Gay, J., & Williams, V. (1995). *Communion before Confirmation: A report on the survey conducted by Culham College for the Church of England National Children's Advisers' Panel.* Oxford: Culham College Print Resources.

Holeton, D. R. (1981). *Infant Communion: Then and now.* Nottingham: Grove.

Jackson, H. (2004). Children at the font and altar. *Church Times, No 7394,* p 10.

Kay, W. K., & Francis, L. J. (1996). *Drift from the churches: Attitude toward Christianity during childhood and adolescence.* Cardiff: University of Wales Press.

Lankshear, D. W. (2004). Is the rural church different? The special case of confirmation. *Rural Theology, 2,* 105–117.

Littler, K., Francis, L. J., & Thomas, T. H. (2002). The admission of children to communion before confirmation: A survey among Church in Wales clerics. *Contact: International Journal of Pastoral Studies, 139,* 24–38.

Lowther Clarke, W. K. (1932). Confirmation. In W. K. Lowther Clarke assisted by C. Harris (Eds.), *Liturgy and Worship* (pp. 443–457). London: SPCK.

Roberts, C. (2003). Is the rural church different? A comparison of historical membership statistics between an urban and a rural diocese in the Church of England. *Rural Theology, 1,* 25–39.

Strange, W. A. (1996). *Children in the Early Church: Children in the ancient world, the New Testament and the Early Church.* Carlisle: Paternoster.

Thomas, T. H. (1994). *An examination of the attitudes of the clerics in the Church in Wales to Christian initiation.* Unpublished MTh dissertation.University of Oxford.

Part 9

SATISFACTION AND STRESS IN MINISTRY

Chapter 27

BURNOUT AND THE PRACTICE OF MINISTRY AMONG RURAL CLERGY: LOOKING FOR THE HIDDEN SIGNS

Christopher J. F. Rutledge*

Abstract – A sample of 318 stipendiary male clergy in the Church of England who held responsibility for rural parishes completed a modified form of the Maslach Burnout Inventory together with a questionnaire designed to assess their practice of ministry. The data suggest that an unacceptably high number of rural clergy show signs of emotional exhaustion from their ministry and that burnout is reflected in many subtle ways in the practice of ministry.

Introduction

Clergy working in the rural ministry have been seen as an occupational group under stress. Russell (1993) noted that the demands placed upon clergy in multiparish benefices (with a lack of clarity about their roles, and no easily definable boundaries) created an increasingly stressful 'work environment'. The Archbishops' Commission on Rural Areas (1990), *Faith in the Countryside,* also identified the additional pressures which rural living placed upon the clergy in comparison with their urban and suburban colleagues. Further analyses published by the Church in Wales (1992) and Bowden (1994) also reached the conclusion that clergy working in rural parishes were subjected to factors which resulted in increased stress and burnout.

A study conducted by Francis and Rutledge (2000) used a modified measure of the three dimensional model of burnout proposed by Maslach and Jackson (1986). The first aspect of this model of burnout

*   The Revd Canon Dr Christopher J. F. Rutledge served as vicar of St Mark's, Talbot Village. *Address for correspondence*: 48 Wollaton Road, Ferndown, BH22 8QY. E-mail: christopher.rutledge@talktalk.net

relates to emotional exhaustion, where workers find that they can no longer continue to give at an emotional level. Emotional exhaustion is often associated with such expressions as 'I don't care any more', and 'I don't have any feelings left'. The second aspect relates to depersonalization. This refers to a negative, cynical and dehumanized attitude toward clients, which will include certain types of language expressing compartmentalism, intellectualism and other withdrawal techniques. Clients are often viewed as somehow deserving of their problems, and are often blamed for their own victimization. The third aspect is a tendency for workers to feel reduced personal accomplishment and for them to evaluate themselves negatively.

Francis and Rutledge (2000) found that problems associated with the lack of personal accomplishment may be felt more acutely among clergy who are working in rural parishes. The aim of the present study is to extend previous research by focusing on the following questions: To what extent is burnout in general, and feelings of a lack of personal accomplishment in particular, experienced amongst the rural clergy? How does this manifest itself in the fulfilling of their parochial role?

Method

Procedure

As part of a wider survey, a questionnaire was sent to male clergy working in rural ministry. The overall response rate was 73%, producing 318 completed questionnaires from stipendiary male clergy in the Church of England who considered that the benefice in which they worked would be classed as 'rural'. Included in the questionnaire were three areas of enquiry: the first area was concerned with the sociography of the clergy, the second area examined the practice of parochial ministry, and the third area assessed the degree to which clergy suffered from burnout.

Measures

Burnout was assessed by the modified form of the Maslach Burnout Inventory adapted by Rutledge and Francis (2004) from Maslach and Jackson (1986). This instrument proposes three ten-item scales of emotional exhaustion, depersonalization and lack of personal accomplishment. Each item is assessed on a five point scale: agree strongly, agree, not certain, disagree, and disagree strongly.

Practice of ministry was assessed by inviting the clergy to rate 55 areas of ministry, including their role in the church and the wider community, in worship, and in their personal life. Each item is assessed on a five point scale.

Results

Who are the rural clergy?

Three fifths of the clergy working in rural benefices (61%) were 50 years of age or older, with only 7% of the clergy under the age of 40 years. Over half the clergy (52%) had been in their present position for less than 5 years, while 10% had been in their present role for 15 years or more. The overwhelming majority of the clergy were married (88%), leaving 10% single and 2% widowed. In terms of churchmanship, 29% of the rural clergy considered that they were 'Catholic' in contrast with the 21% of the clergy who were 'Evangelical.' The remaining 50% were committed to neither of the two party wings. A similar split was found in terms of the 'Conservative–Liberal' continuum: 22% of the clergy considered that they were Liberal, compared with 26% who considered that they were Conservative. The remaining 52% considered that they occupied the middle territory between the two wings.

Many benefices consisted of more than one worship centre. The existence of mission churches, the formation of teams, and the creation of united benefices, together with a number of other factors, often mean that clergy are responsible for looking after more than one place of worship. While 19% of the rural clergy had responsibility for just one church, 28% had two, 22% had three, and 31% had four or more churches.

In terms of appointments, the majority of clergy (78%) held incumbent status which would generally entitle them to freehold of their livings. Only 5% of the clergy were members of teams: team rectors consisted of 2% of all appointments and team vicars 3%. Priests-in-Charge made up 15% of the clergy, and the remaining 2% were assistant curates.

The size of the benefices varied considerably, although half the rural benefices (50%) had a total population of fewer than 2,000. Indeed, 12% had a population of fewer than 1,000.

The relatively small population size of the benefices is reflected in the number of occasional offices in which the clergy are involved. Nearly half the rural clergy (47%) officiated at fewer than 10 baptisms during the year, and some 70% of the clergy officiated at fewer than ten weddings during the year. In terms of funerals and cremations, nearly three quarters (74%) of the clergy officiated at 19 or fewer funerals or cremations during the year.

How burned out are the rural clergy?

The scores from the modified form of the Maslach Burnout Inventory have produced some interesting results. In terms of scores on the items of the emotional exhaustion subscale, the majority of the clergy are in good heart. Thus the majority (74%) do not feel at the end of their tether, nor do they feel burned out in their ministry (70%). They do not find that working with people is a real strain (62%), nor do they feel fatigued when they awake in the morning (71%). The majority of the rural clergy do not consider that they would be better off if they got out of the parochial ministry (82%). They feel neither that people generally create too much stress for them (80%), nor that they are emotionally drained (62%).

Looked at from the opposite perspective, however, an unacceptably high number of clergy show signs of emotional exhaustion. Too many of the rural parochial clergy consider that they are working too hard (25%), that they feel frustrated in their ministry (26%), and that at the end of the day they feel 'used up' (31%). Added to this are the facts that 9% of the rural clergy feel that they are very much at the end of their tether, that 10% feel burned out with their parish ministry, and that 12% find working with other people is a real strain. A number of clergy feel tired out when waking in the morning (12%), emotionally drained (16%), and under stress from those with whom they are ministering (6%). Indeed, 7% believe that they would feel a lot better if they could get out of parochial ministry.

On the basis of these statistics, it would be incorrect to say that the majority of rural parochial clergy are generally suffering a high degree of emotional exhaustion. Nevertheless, there are significant indications that too many rural clergy are clearly under emotional pressure, experiencing frustration in their ministry, working unduly hard and experiencing a feeling of being 'used up' at the end of the day.

The scores on the depersonalization subscale indicate that, with the passage of time, the majority of the clergy are not any the less patient with their parishioners than previously (65%), that they have not become increasingly callous toward those to whom they minister (87%) and that they are still concerned to understand how others feel about things (90%). They clearly do not feel that they are so bothered by their parishioners that they want to be left alone (81%), nor have they reached the stage where they are treating people as if they were impersonal 'objects' (88%). The majority of the clergy are willing to listen to what their parishioners are saying to them (70%), and they clearly do not feel that they are in danger of becoming emotionally hardened by their parochial experience (78%). The rural parochial clergy are clearly concerned about their parishioners and what happens to them (88%) and they believe that the majority of their parishioners can be helped with their problems (70%). The majority of the clergy do not operate under the belief that they are the object of blame for things which may go wrong with their parishioners (63%).

Looked at from the opposite perspective, however, the number of rural clergy who show some tendencies of depersonalization is not insignificant. There are 16% of the clergy who feel that parishioners blame them to some extent for the things which go wrong, and 10% of the clergy feel less patient with their parishioners than they once did. However, the rest of the items on this scale record low levels of depersonalization. Of the rural clergy 3% believe that they have become more callous toward their parishioners, and 4% feel strongly that they would like their parishioners to leave them alone. While only 1% of the clergy feel that they have become so insensitive that they are no longer bothered to be concerned with how others feel, there are still 7% of the rural clergy who find it difficult to listen to what others are saying. Some 1% of the clergy experience that depersonalized state where they believe they are treating their parishioners as objects, while 3% of the clergy have reached the state of not really caring what happens to their parishioners. A number of the rural clergy (4%) feel that most people cannot be helped with their problems, and 8% of the clergy feel that they have become more 'hardened' as a consequence of their time in the ministry. Certainly, on the above findings, it would be difficult to say that rural clergy in general are experiencing burnout as measured on the depersonalization subscale, although it would be a mistake not to take seriously the warning signs among the minority.

Scores on the personal accomplishment subscale indicate that rural clergy do not feel that they are necessarily achieving a great deal in terms of personal accomplishment. Only 37% feel that they have accomplished many worthwhile things in their ministry, and while a number feel exhilarated after working with parishioners (47%) and gain a lot of satisfaction from working with them (76%), only 36% of the clergy feel that they are positively influencing the lives of others. Only 16% of the clergy feel that they are effective in dealing with the problems of their parishioners, even though 60% feel that they can create a relaxed atmosphere with them, deal with emotional problems calmly (51%), and believe that they understand how their parishioners feel about things (38%). Only

19% of the clergy feel very energetic, but in spite of that, if the clergy were to have their time over again, 76% of them would still go into parish ministry.

On the negative side, 12% of the rural clergy believe that they have accomplished very little of worth in their ministry; 17% believe that they have no positive influence over the lives of others, and 13% find that they gain no exhilaration from working with others, even though only 4% admit to gaining no satisfaction from working with other people. To some extent there is a feeling of inadequacy amongst the rural clergy. A large percentage of the clergy (20%) do not believe that they deal effectively with the problems of their parishioners; 4% of the clergy find it difficult to understand just what their parishioners feel about things, and 5% of the clergy consider themselves far from calm in dealing with emotional problems. Some 5% of the clergy do not believe they create a relaxed atmosphere with those about them, and in part this might be explained by the fact that 33% of the rural clergy feel very tired and far from energetic.

In some ways the findings of this dimension of personal accomplishment is the most disconcerting and supports the conclusions reached by Francis and Rutledge (2000). In a profession where the vocational element is strong, if not paramount, a feeling of 'not achieving' can be very disheartening. The fact that nearly one rural clergyman in eight feels that he has accomplished little of worth in his ministry is certainly a matter of concern, and clearly an issue which needs to be addressed.

How does burnout impact the practice of ministry?

Given that there is a significant group of clergy working in rural ministry who are experiencing burnout in one form or another, does this affect the way in which they view their role and carry out their work? In the following analyses particular attention will be given to the four roles of pastor, counsellor, church administrator and educator.

In terms of the role as pastor, those rural clergy who recorded high scores on the emotional exhaustion subscale are less likely to attempt a visit to every home in the benefice ($r = -0.37, p < .001$), to visit church members who were hospitalized ($r = -0.19, p < .001$) and also other members of the benefice who may be in hospital ($r = -0.22, p < .001$).

Those who are suffering from depersonalization are less likely to be involved in visiting all those homes in their benefices ($r = -0.35, p < .001$), engaging in local community life ($r = -0.19, p < .001$), visiting church members who are in hospital ($r = -0.20, p < .001$), visiting other parishioners who are in hospital (r = -0.20, p <.001) or being available to parishioners at all times (r = -0.16, p <.01).

Those rural clergy who perceive that they are achieving little in terms of personal accomplishment are less likely to be visiting all homes in their benefice (r = -0.32, p <.001), engaging in church social events (r = -0.23, p <.001), involving themselves in community life (r = -0.17, p <.01), visiting church members ill in hospital (r = -0.16, p <.01), visiting other parishioners who may be in hospital (r = -0.23, p <.001), or being available to their parishioners at all times (r = -0.19, p <.001).

In terms of the role as counsellor, rural clergy who achieve high scores on the emotional exhaustion subscale are less likely to be involved in counselling people with spiritual problems (r = -0.15, p <.01). Again, those clergy who score high on the depersonalization subscale are less likely to be involved in counselling people with spiritual problems (r = -0.19, p <.001). Those clergy who consider they are not achieving in terms of personal accomplishment are less likely to be counselling people with marital problems (r = -0.32, p <.001), psychological problems (r = -0.21, p <.001), and spiritual problems (r = -0.31, p <.001).

What is of note about these aspects of the role of pastor and counsellor is that all these activities are ones in which clergy can clearly decide to involve themselves or not. They are all relatively easy to avoid, and clearly those clergy who are experiencing perceived burnout, are likely to do just that. What appears to be the case, in this instance, is not that those rural clergy who are actively engaged in people-related activity are experiencing burnout, but rather that those who are experiencing burnout do not appear to be so involved with people-related activities.

In terms of the role as general church administrator, with functions ranging from chairing church committees, dealing with church administration, encouraging lay chairmanship, writing own business letters, the one area where those suffering from burnout appear to be less engaged is editing the parish magazine. Those suffering from emotional exhaustion (r = -0.22, p <.001), depersonalization (r = -0.21, p <.001) or lack of feelings of personal accomplishment (r = -0.20, p <.001) are significantly less involved in editing the parish magazine. In terms of those administrative roles which may best be described as 'church maintenance' (taking an active part in raising church funds, organizing church fetes and fairs and the such like) experiencing burnout does not appear to have a direct bearing on the degree of engagement in these activities.

In terms of the role as educator, those rural clergy suffering from depersonalization are less likely to be involved in Sunday school activities

(r = -0.23, p <.001) and taking an active part in youth activity (r = -0.15, p <.01), while those scoring low on the personal accomplishment scales are again less likely to be involved in Sunday school activities (r = -0.19, p <.001), or in running confirmation classes (r = -0.15, p <.01).

In terms of their personal life, those rural clergy who are experiencing emotional exhaustion are less likely to say the daily office (r = -0.16, p <.005), or to set time aside to pray (r = -0.26, p <.001). This latter trend is one also likely to be experienced by those suffering from feelings of depersonalization (r = -0.26, p <.001) or from a lack of personal accomplishment (r = -0.20, p <.001).

Conclusion

The present study indicates that there are a significant number of clergy working in rural ministry, who are suffering symptoms associated with emotional exhaustion and feelings of lack of personal accomplishment. In practical terms those clergy experiencing symptoms of burnout are more likely to show a subtle disengagement with those traditional roles associated with rural parochial clergy. In a situation where the majority of rural clergy are responsible for three or more parishes in their benefices it can come as no surprise that many of the clergy feel over-worked, frustrated in their ministry and 'used up' at the end of the day.

There is clearly a need for further research in this area. However desirable the community model of parochial ministry may be within rural Anglican structures, it has to be asked whether it is sustainable in its present form, given the malaise experienced by a significant number of rural clergy.

In addition, given the duty of care which the Church of England has for its clergy, it has to be asked what strategies are in place to support those who are suffering from ministerial burnout. As at December 2001, the Provinces of Canterbury and York (excluding Europe) consisted of 16,220 churches, 12,951 parishes and 8,308 benefices (Church of England, 2001a). These benefices are served by a declining number of stipendiary parochial clergy. In 1961 there were 13,429 parochial stipendiary clergy (Church of England, 1987). By 2001 the number engaged in stipendiary ministry in the parishes had fallen to 8,538 (Church of England, 2001b). Rural clergy are working under increasing pressures. Over half of the benefices have three or more places of worship in each, and over 91% of the clergy are working alone as the only stipendiary minister in the benefice. Those experiencing one form of burnout or another display signs of withdrawal, not wanting outside clerics to enter their domain. They will do all that has to be done, providing the 'rites of passage' and looking after the 'plant'. But they will avoid the one to one engagement that pastoral care, visiting, counselling, and youth work generate. In their personal life the saying of the daily office and setting aside time for prayer is not a high priority. All of these trends exhibited by those experiencing burnout are a real cause of concern in a professional group which is fundamentally a vocation, underpinned by a spiritual foundation.

In the introduction to *Mission-Shaped Church* (Church of England, 2004) the Bishop of Maidstone wrote: 'It is clear to us that the parochial system remains an essential and central part of the national Church's strategy to deliver incarnational mission'. Whilst it may well be desirable and pragmatic to support the present parochial structures, the real question that has to be asked is whether the present parochial model is any longer sustainable within the context of rural ministry. What will be the toll of burnout among those clergy working within rural ministry, and if the symptoms of burnout amongst the rural clergy remain largely hidden, will their needs be properly addressed by those who have a duty of care?

References

Archbishops' Commission on Rural Areas. (1990). *Faith in the countryside*. Stoneleigh Park: Acora Publishing.

Bowden, A. (1994). *Ministry in the countryside*. London: Mowbray.

Church in Wales. (1992). *The Church in the Welsh countryside: A programme for action by the Church in Wales*. Penarth: Church in Wales Board of Mission.

Church of England. (1987). *Church statistics*. London: The Central Board of Finance.

Church of England. (2001a). *Church statistics*. London: Church House Publishing.

Church of England. (2001b). *Statistics of Licensed Ministers*. London: Church House Publishing.

Church of England (2004). *Mission-shaped church*. London: Church House Publishing.

Francis, L. J., & Rutledge, C. J. F. (2000). Are rural clergy in the Church of England under greater stress? A study in empirical theology. *Research in the Social Scientific Study of Religion, 11*, 173–191.

Maslach, C., & Jackson, S. E. (1986). *Maslach Burnout Inventory* (second edition). Palo Alto, California: Consulting Psychologists Press.

Rutledge, C. J. F., & Francis, L. J. (2004). Burnout among male Anglican parochial clergy in England: Testing a modified form of the Maslach burnout inventory. *Research in the Social Scientific Study of Religion, 15*, 71–93.

Russell, A. (1993). *The country parson*. London: SPCK.

Chapter 28

HOW HAPPY ARE RURAL ANGLICAN CLERGY?

Christine E. Brewster*

Abstract – A sample of 722 Church of England clergy who are responsible for three or more rural churches (excluding those who work in team ministries) completed the Oxford Happiness Questionnaire. The data produced are considered in the context of work-related psychological health, whereby the 'happiness' of rural clergy is seen as part of a broader picture which presents 'positive affect' as a counter-balance to 'negative affect'. These data suggest that while the majority of rural clergy do experience moderately high levels of 'happiness' in their work environments, the benefits of this positive affect are often diminished by the presence of the enormous demands placed upon them in rural multi-parish benefices at the beginning of the twenty-first century.

Introduction

The decline in the number of stipendiary parochial clergy in the Church of England from 15,446 in 1993 to 8,764 in 2005 (Church Society, 2007) has resulted in the amalgamation of many rural parishes, which has caused widespread 'overextension' amongst rural clergy. This article, which looks at 'subjective wellbeing' amongst rural clergy in the context of work-related psychological health, makes the assumption that the happiness of rural clergy is best assessed as part of a broader picture which presents 'positive affect' as a counter balance to 'negative affect'. In order to present 'happiness' among rural clergy in context, therefore, this article will first look at some of the factors which cause negative affect

* The Revd Dr Christine Brewster serves as a priest in mid-Wales and as Senior Tutor at the St Seiriol's Centre. *Address for correspondence*: The Vicarage, Llanwnog, Caersws, Powys, SY17 5JG. E-mail: cbholly@btinternet.com

(in the form of 'overextension', 'stress' and 'emotional exhaustion') within this group of people. Definitions of 'happiness' and 'subjective wellbeing' will then be offered; the Oxford Happiness Questionnaire (OHQ: Hills and Argyle, 2002), which has been used in the present study, will be outlined and previous research which has looked at subjective wellbeing among the clergy will be reviewed.

'Overextension' among rural clergy

There are enormous drains associated with being a clergyperson at the beginning of the twenty-first century, particularly concerning the pervasiveness of the clergy role, in which expectations, both from other people and from the clergy themselves, are ever-present. Ministry in the church is the only profession in which personal identity, professional identity and religious faith are all encapsulated in the same individuals. Clergypersons are often considered to be role models for members of their congregations and for local communities; they are aware that preaching does not come from the pulpit only, but also from the examples they give by the way they live their lives, and these factors place a tremendous burden upon them. Gilbert (1987), in the opening chapter of *Who Ministers to Ministers?*, suggests that clergypersons have problems with expectations as follows:

> I am appalled at what is required of me. I am supposed to move from sick bed to administrative meeting, to planning, to supervising, to counselling, to praying, to trouble- shooting, to budgeting, to audio systems, to meditation, to worship preparation, to newsletter, to staff problems, to mission projects, to conflict management, to community leadership, to study, to funerals, to weddings, to preaching. And, I am expected to be superior, or at least first rate, in all of them. What I am not supposed to be is depressed, discouraged, cynical, angry, hurt. I am supposed to be up-beat, positive, strong, willing, available. (Gilbert, 1987, p. 2)

The expectations listed by Gilbert (1987) are relevant to clergypersons ministering in both rural and urban areas. Rural ministry, however, also encompasses the frustrations which relate to multi-church parish work which involves several different communities.

Clergy stressors have been classified into the four categories of 'parish conflicts', 'difficulties involving parish commitment and development', 'emotional difficulties' and 'time-related overextension' by Dewe (1987), as cited by Fletcher (1990, pp. 16–17). In the parish conflict category, the research of Brewster (2007) indicates that more than half of rural clergy (56%) find 'managing tensions and conflicts between different people and different churches' to be stressful. Brewster (2007) also found that, in the 'difficulties involving parish commitment and development' category, more than two thirds (68%) of rural clergy are frustrated by 'having a limited number of people to take on church responsibilities'. In the 'emotional difficulties' category, well over half of rural clergy (59%) find 'keeping spirituality alive and well' to be a cause of stress, and in the 'time-related over-extension' category, the most frequently positively endorsed item was 'having too many demands on my time' (60%), which was followed closely by the item 'being unable to respond to the needs of everyone' (59%). The findings from Brewster's (2007) study highlight very clearly that the professional life of rural clergy today is frequently found to be stressful and exhausting. This profile is very different from Sir Francis Galton's classic nineteenth century characterization of country clergy as a group of people who enjoyed an 'easy country life and family repose' (Galton, 1872, p/ 129); the 'easy country life and family repose' would seem to have been replaced by a profession in which rural clergy too often find themselves to be under unacceptable levels of pressure.

Happiness and subjective wellbeing

Early researchers in the field of happiness and wellbeing acted on the supposition that positive affect and negative affect are best assessed at opposite ends of a single continuum. This view was, however, radically criticized by Bradburn's (1969) theory of balanced affect, which suggests that positive and negative affect are best assessed on two separate continua and not at opposite ends of a single continuum. This allows for the fact that people can and do experience moderately high levels of positive affect in the form of happiness and subjective wellbeing at the same time as they are experiencing negative affect in the form of emotional exhaustion.

From 1974 to 1991 psychological 'abstracts' included seventeen times as many articles on 'anger', 'anxiety' and 'depression' than on 'joy', 'life satisfaction' and 'happiness' (Myers, 1995), but in recent years, as psychologists have sought to understand the causes and explanations of happiness as well as people's evaluations of their own lives, research in the area of 'happiness', 'subjective wellbeing', 'quality of life' and 'life satisfaction' has increased dramatically. However, as Gullone and Cummins (2002) point out, in view of the fact that research in this field is still in its infancy, researchers find it difficult to agree on the precise character of this construct, and there is, therefore, a general lack of clarity concerning its definition, measurement and conceptual structure. This has resulted in the terms 'happiness', 'wellbeing' and 'quality of life' being used inconsistently within the human sciences. It has, however, been widely acknowledged since the research of Campbell, Converse and Rodgers (1976) that perceived wellbeing, or 'subjective wellbeing', with which this article is concerned, comprises both affect and cognition. Other terms in use describe a focus on either affect or cognition, but not on both. The most general term in use is 'happiness', which focuses on affect, whereas 'life satisfaction' is concerned with cognitive processes. The Oxford Happiness Questionnaire, which is being used in the present study, in spite of its title, is actually a measure of subjective wellbeing, which focuses on both positive affect (happiness) and on a cognitive component which involves some form of internal comparison process which can be measured through questions of satisfaction.

Cummins, Gullone and Lau (2002) believe that most people experience a moderately positive level of wellbeing, with the population average being at about 75% of maximum. They propose that subjective wellbeing is under the influence of a 'homeostatic' system consisting of a person's personality, a set of cognitive buffers and a person's needs, which is designed to hold its value within a narrow, positive, set-point-range for each individual. Cummins, Gullone and Lau (2002) suggest that a set of cognitive buffers acts to absorb the impact of a person's changing need states, which in the case of rural clergy include the need to 'manage' stressors such as 'overextension', and that these buffers combine with an individual's personality in order to control a person's level of subjective wellbeing. The importance of personality in this process has been highlighted by Kobasa (1982) who, in his research on 'hardiness' drew attention to the fact that individuals who are high on the personality variable of 'internal control' frequently interpret stressful events as challenging and believe that they can cope with them, whereas those with lower levels of 'internal control' often succumb to depression.

This study concerns measures of subjective wellbeing levels as influenced by extrinsic conditions in the work-related lives of rural clergy.

The Oxford Happiness Questionnaire

The Oxford Happiness Questionnaire (OHQ: Hills and Argyle, 2002) which has been used in this study, was derived from the Oxford Happiness

Inventory (OHI: Argyle, Martin and Crossland, 1989) and is described by its authors as 'an improved scale' (Hills and Argyle, 2002). It focuses on both positive affect (happiness) and global life satisfaction (subjective wellbeing) and no two items are so alike that they are measuring the same facet of happiness/subjective wellbeing.

The Oxford Happiness Questionnaire consists of twenty-nine single items which (in its original form) were answered on a six-point Likert scale (1932) ranging from 'strongly agree' to 'strongly disagree'. The present study, however, uses a five-point Likert scale in the belief that a 'midpoint' prompts a more accurate self-assessment. Hills and Argyle (2002) point out that about half of the items have been reversed in an attempt to reduce the probability of contextual and compliant answering.

The major strength of using this instrument concerns the clear definition and contextualization of wellbeing within broader theoretical frameworks. The major weakness of this tool is that this new and robust development from the Oxford Happiness Inventory has not yet received sufficient use to have established norms against which the experiences of rural clergy can be compared.

Although no previous study has explored the Oxford Happiness Questionnaire among the clergy, Randall and Francis (2002) examined the findings from employing the earlier Oxford Happiness Inventory among a sample of stipendiary Anglican clergy in England and Wales. They drew two main conclusions from their data. First, they demonstrated that individual differences in happiness were strongly related to the personality dimensions of extraversion, neuroticism and psychoticism, as defined and measured by the Eysenckian dimensional model of personality (Eysenck and Eysenck, 1985). Scores on the Oxford Happiness Inventory were correlated positively with extraversion, were correlated negatively with neuroticism and were independent of psychoticism. Second, they demonstrated that individual differences in happiness were also related to churchmanship. Overall Evangelical clergy were less happy than Anglo-Catholic clergy.

The present study builds on the pioneering work of Randall and Francis (2002) by undertaking a new survey using the Oxford Happiness Questionnaire amongst Anglican clergy working in multi-parish rural benefices in England.

Method

Procedure

The data collected for use in the present study was obtained by means of a mailing list designed to capture all Church of England clergy responsible for three or more rural churches, excluding those who work in team ministries. The number of clergy invited to take part in the survey was 1,959 of whom 722 accepted the invitation. This produced a response rate of 47% (excluding the 434 clergy who indicated that they were not currently responsible for three or more rural churches), which is sufficiently high to allow considerable confidence to be placed in the findings.

Sample

Three quarters (75%) of the sample was male while one quarter (25%) was female. A small number (4%) of the rural clergy were in their thirties, 22% were in their forties, 41% were in their fifties, 31% were in their sixties and 1% was aged seventy or over. Over half of the clergy (54%) had been in their present positions for at least five years, while 7% had been in their current positions for 15 years or more. The majority of the clergy (85%) were married, while 7% were single, 3% were widowed and 4% were separated or divorced. In terms of churchmanship, 47% considered themselves to be 'Catholic', while 30% indicated that they were of 'Evangelical' persuasion, and 23% were committed to neither of these persuasions. Similar splits were found in terms of 'liberal – conservative' (50% 'liberal'; 30% 'conservative'; 20% committed to neither of these), and 'charismatic – non-charismatic' (28% 'charismatic'; 49% 'non-charismatic'; 23% committed to neither of these positions).

Over one third of the rural clergy (37%) served three churches, while those caring for four or five churches totalled 42%, and one fifth (20%) of the sample cared for six or more churches. More than a quarter (27%) of the sample had to travel at least seven miles to their farthest churches and almost two out of every three (64%) of the participants indicated that it was not easy for their churches to pay their parish shares (quotas).

Measure

Happiness was assessed by means of the Oxford Happiness Questionnaire (Hills and Argyle, 2002). This instrument comprises 29 items, each assessed in the present study on a five-point Likert scale, which was designed to indicate whether participants 'agree strongly', 'agree', are 'not certain', 'disagree' or 'strongly disagree' with each item. Higher scores indicate greater levels of happiness.

Results and discussion

Table 1 provides insight into the happiness levels of this sample of rural clergy by presenting the percentage figures for those clergy who 'agree' and 'disagree' with each statement in the questionnaire as well as for those who are 'not certain'. The column headed 'yes' is the product of the 'agree' and 'agree strongly' responses; the column headed 'no' is the product of the 'disagree' and 'disagree strongly' responses; the column headed '?' is the 'uncertain' response.

How happy are the rural Anglican clergy?

The scores from the Oxford Happiness Questionnaire show that the majority of the rural clergy consider themselves to be reasonably content. They feel happy with the way they are (66%); they are intensely interested in other people (75%); they feel that life is very rewarding (76%), and they have warm feelings toward almost everybody (58%). The majority of the rural clergy indicate that they wake up feeling rested (53%), that they are optimistic about the future (58%), that they feel they are always committed and involved (57%), and that they sense that life is good (78%). They believe that the world is a good place (67%); they laugh a lot (63%); they consider themselves to be very happy (51%), and they find beauty in some things (94%). In addition, they often experience joy and elation (56%); they find it easy to make decisions (59%); they have a sense of meaning and purpose in their lives (81%), and they consider that they usually have a good influence on events (64%). They also consider that they have fun with other people (84%); they feel healthy (62%), and they have happy memories of the past (68%).

Looked at from the opposite perspective, however, many of the rural clergy express discontent in some areas of life; the data produced by the Oxford Happiness Questionnaire in this study draws attention to several major areas of vulnerability. Of particular significance are the items which indicate that 70% of the rural clergy feel they cannot fit in everything that they want to do; that 75% consider that there is a gap between what they would like to do and what they have done; that 53%

do not feel able to take anything on, and that 40% feel that they do not have a great deal of energy. Too many of the rural clergy do not feel particularly happy with the way they are (23%); too many do not have very warm feelings toward other people (19%), and too many rarely wake up feeling rested (32%). Many are not particularly optimistic about the future (23%); they do not find most things amusing (26%); they are not always committed and involved (17%), and they do not think that the world is a good place (18%). Too many do not laugh a lot (15%), are not well satisfied about everything in life (27%), do not think they look attractive (24%), and do not consider themselves to be very happy (17%). An unacceptable proportion of the rural clergy also feel that they are not especially in control of their lives (34%), that they do not feel fully mentally alert (30%), and that they do not often experience joy and elation (18%). The percentage figure for those who do not find it easy to make decisions (24%), who do not feel particularly healthy (21%) and who do not have particularly happy memories of the past (18%), are also too high.

On the basis of these statistics it would be wrong to say that the majority of rural clergy experience very high levels of happiness. Many of these clergy do experience fairly high levels of happiness, but rather too many are clearly under the pressures of 'overextension', 'stress' and 'emotional exhaustion'. These pressures cause them to experience lower levels of happiness which, as noted by Rutledge (2006, p. 64), lead to 'a subtle disengagement with those traditional roles associated with rural parochial clergy', which include the pastoral, counselling, administrative and managerial roles referred to by Gilbert (1987) above. These data provide evidence concerning both the sources and levels of 'happiness' and 'stress' which depict rural clergy as being happy in many aspects of their work, whilst at the same time being subject to distinctive sources of stress. Galton's (1872) characterization of country clergy as a group of people who enjoyed an 'easy country life and family repose' seems to have been eroded beyond recognition.

Table 1: Item endorsement for the Oxford Happiness Questionnaire

	Yes %	? %	No %
I don't feel particularly happy with the way I am*	23	11	66
I am intensely interested in other people	75	16	9
I feel that life is very rewarding	76	15	9
I have very warm feelings toward almost everybody	58	23	19
I rarely wake up feeling rested*	32	15	53
I am not particularly optimistic about the future*	23	19	58
I find most things amusing	41	32	26
I am always committed and involved	57	26	17
Life is good	78	15	7
I do not think that the world is a good place*	18	16	67
I laugh a lot	63	22	15
I am well satisfied about everything in life	27	37	37
I don't think I look attractive*	24	39	37
There is a gap between what I would like to do and what I have done*	75	10	15
I am very happy	51	32	17
I find beauty in some things	94	2	4
I always have a cheerful effect on others	49	42	9
I can fit in everything I want to	17	13	70
I feel that I am not especially in control of my life*	34	24	42
I feel able to take anything on	19	28	53
I feel fully mentally alert	44	27	30
I often experience joy and elation	56	26	18
I do not find it easy to make decisions*	24	18	59
I do not have a particular sense of meaning and purpose in my life*	9	10	81
I feel I have a great deal of energy	33	27	40
I usually have a good influence on events	64	32	5
I do not have fun with other people*	7	9	84
I don't feel particularly healthy*	21	18	62
I do not have particularly happy memories of my past*	18	14	68

*These items have been reverse coded

Conclusion

Analysis of the rural clergy responses to the Oxford Happiness Questionnaire draws attention to both the positive features of the work-related psychological health of rural clergy and also to major areas of vulnerability. While 78% of the rural clergy consider that 'life is good' and 76% feel that life is very rewarding, only 33% feel that they 'have a great deal of energy', and only 17% feel that they can 'fit in everything they want to do'.

These discrepancies between endorsement levels apportioned to different items of the Oxford Happiness Questionnaire suggest that, among rural clergy today, moderately high levels of positive affect in the form of happiness and satisfaction in ministry can, and do, exist alongside moderately high levels of negative affect in the form of overextension, stress and emotional exhaustion. As a result of the severely declining number of stipendiary parochial clergy, many are working under increasing pressures in order to serve 'amalgamated' parishes, and while the happiness levels of many rural clergy are sufficiently high to enable them to cope adequately (or in many cases, well) with the demands of three or more rural parishes, the data presented suggest that a significant number of these clergy are 'overstretched'. The happiness of rural clergy can only be fully appreciated when it is seen against the broader picture, and it is only when the buffers of the Cummins, Gallone and Lau (2002) 'homeostatic' system are able to deal with negative affect that rural clergy are prevented from experiencing levels of negative affect which may be detrimental to their work-related psychological health.

A consideration of happiness among rural Anglican clergy would not be complete without some suggestions as to how the happiness of this group of professionals might be regulated. In this respect, the Church of England might seek to put in place effective support strategies for those rural clergy whose work-related psychological health is being compromised. Those who have the wellbeing of rural Anglican clergy in their care might also implement regular training in order to encourage rural clergy in the implementation of work strategies which might lead to the enhancement of their work-related psychological health. It may be that much of this encouragement could take place during annual performance reviews or appraisals.

Finally, it must be noted that the experience among the clergy of moderately high levels of positive affect in the form of happiness and subjective wellbeing, alongside moderately high levels of negative affect in the form of emotional exhaustion, has also been demonstrated by the research of Francis, Kaldor, Robbins and Castle (2005). The findings of these researchers, through the implementation of the 'Francis Burnout Inventory' (FBI: Francis, Kaldor, Robbins and Castle, 2005), support Bradburn's (1969) view that positive affect and negative affect are not opposite ends of a single continuum, but two separate continua. The profiling of rural clergy in terms of the unidimensional model of subjective wellbeing proposed by the Oxford Happiness Questionnaire communicates a somewhat mixed message of high levels of positive feeling mixed with some serious questions about levels of satisfaction. It is likely, however, that the two-dimensional model, as presented by Francis, Kaldor, Robbins and Castle (2005) in the 'Francis Burnout Inventory' more accurately detects the warning signs of poor work-related psychological health, which occurs when high levels of negative affect (emotional exhaustion) coincide with low levels of positive affect.

This article makes the assumption that the happiness of rural clergy is best assessed not in isolation, but as part of a broader picture which presents 'positive affect' as a balance of 'negative affect'. The responses to the Oxford Happiness Questionnaire draw attention to both positive features of their work-related psychological health and to major areas of vulnerability. Analysis of the results shows that the majority of rural clergy experience fairly high levels of happiness, but that this is tempered by unacceptable levels of negative affect. Research in the area of 'happiness' among rural clergy is in its infancy, and there is clearly a need for further studies in this field.

References

Argyle, M., Martin, M., & Crossland, J. (1989). Happiness as a function of personality and social encounters. In J. P. Forgas and J. M. Innes (Eds.), *Recent Advances in Social Psychology: an international perspective* (pp. 189–203). North Holland: Elsevier.

Bradburn, N. M. (1969). *The structure of psychological well-being.* Chicago, Illinois: Aldine.

Brewster, C. E. (2007). *Rural clergy today: A survey of personality, coping strategies and work-related psychological health amongst Church of England clergy in multi-church parishes.* Unpublished PhD dissertation. University of Wales, Bangor.

Campbell, A., Converse, P. E., & Rodgers, W. L. (1976). *The quality of American life.* New York: Sage.

Church Society. (2007). Ministry, captive creative. Retrieved from www.churchsociety.org/issues. Date accessed: 8 March 2007.

Cummins, R. A., Gullone, E., & Lau, L. D. (2002). A model of subjective well-being homeostasis: The role of personality. In E. Gullone and R. A. Cummins (Eds.), *The Universality of Subjective Wellbeing Indicators* (pp. 7–46). Dordrecht: Kluwer Academic.

Dewe, P. J. (1987), New Zealand ministers of religion: Identifying sources of stress and coping processes. *Work and Stress, 1*, 351–364.

Eysenck, H. J., & Eysenck, M. W. (1985). *Personality and individual differences: A natural science approach.* New York: Plenum Press.

Fletcher, B. (1990). *Clergy under stress: A study of homosexual and heterosexual clergy.* London: Mowbray.

Francis, L. J., Kaldor, P., Robbins, M., & Castle, K. (2005). Happy but exhausted? Work-related psychological health among clergy. *Pastoral Sciences, 24*, 101–120.

Galton, F. (1872). Statistical inquiries into the efficacy of prayer. *Fortnightly Review, 12*, 125–135.

Gilbert, B. G. (1987). *Who ministers to ministers?* Washington, DC: Alban Institute.

Gullone, E., & Cummins, R. A. (2002). The universality of subjective wellbeing. In E. Gullone and R.A. Cummins (Eds.), *The universality of subjective wellbeing indicators* (pp. 5–6). Dordrecht: Kluwer Academic.

Hills, P., & Argyle, M. (2002). The Oxford Happiness Questionnaire: A compact scale for the measurement of psychological well-being. *Personality and Individual Differences, 33*, 1073–1082.

Kobasa, S. C. (1982). The hardy personality: towards a social psychology of stress and health. In G. S. Sanders and J. Suls (Eds.), *Social psychology of health and illness* (pp. 3–32). Hillsdale, New Jersey: Lawrence Erlbaum Associates Inc.

Likert, R. (1932). A technique for the measurement of attitudes. *Archives of Psychology, 140*, 1–55.

Myers, D. G. (1995). *Psychology* (fourth edition). New York: Worth.

Randall, K. J., & Francis, L. J. (2002). Are evangelical Anglican clergy as happy as they could be? A quantitative perspective in empirical theology. *British Journal of Theological Education, 13*(1), 57–73.

Rutledge, C. J. F. (2006). Burnout and the practice of ministry among rural clergy: Looking for the hidden signs. *Rural Theology, 4*, 57–65.

Chapter 29

PERCEPTIONS OF STRESS ON THOSE IN RURAL MINISTRY: LISTENING TO CHURCH LEADERS

*Paul Rolph and Jenny Rolph**

Abstract — This article examines the perceptions of eleven senior church leaders on the nature and extent of stress among rural clergy. Analysis of the interview data from these church leaders reveals five key themes: first, the unreasonable expectations laid on ordained rural ministers; second, their difficulty in maintaining a work/life balance; third, the need to share the responsibility for stress management between the individual minister and the wider church; fourth, the particular insights of church leaders who had recently worked in a rural setting; and fifth, the need for further research, especially into the effective deployment of limited specialist resources to support ordained rural ministers when in stressful situations. The senior church leaders differed in their 'location of responsibility' for managing stress and the enhancement of psychological health in ordained rural ministers. The recommendation is then made for an integrated approach in which the responsibility is shared between the individual minister and the wider church. The article concludes with the need for a large-scale survey of senior church leaders in several denominations into the management of stress and the enhancement of the psychological health of ordained rural ministers.

Introduction

The study of clergy stress and burnout has become well established. An earlier study by Sanford (1982), writing from the perspective of an

* Dr Paul Rolph is Research Fellow at Glyndŵr University, Wales. *Address for corre-spondence:* 71 Andover Road, Winchester, SO22 6AU. E-mail: paul.rolph@o2.co.uk
  Jenny Rolph is Director of The Olive Branch Christian Counselling Service, Winchester. *Address for correspondence*: 71 Andover Road, Winchester, SO22 6AU. E-mail: paul.rolph@o2.co.uk

Anglican priest and Jungian analyst, identified eight characteristics of ministry that could generate burnout. These were as follows: ministerial tasks are never finished; the work can be repetitive; clergy work with the same people year in and year out; it is often difficult to see the results of ministry; clergy are constantly faced with other people's expectations; constantly dealing with people in need is emotionally draining; people often come to church for a 'quick fix' and not solid spiritual food; clergy often have to adopt a persona which is emotionally exhausting to maintain.

A further study by Coate (1989), a former member of a religious community, was written from a psychotherapeutic perspective. She argues that although everyone is likely to experience stress at times, what can exacerbate the situation for ordained ministers is the difficulty they often have in admitting to stress in their work. She found that they felt that they should somehow cope better than their non-clerical counterparts. She saw four main areas of stress for clergy: the strain of caring; the strain of relating to God; the strain of proclaiming; and the strain of being.

Although Kirk and Leary's (1994) study was specifically concerned with clergy marriage they include a chapter in their book on clergy stress. They identify several key factors which cause clergy stress. These are: marginality; alienation; social isolation; lack of leisure time and financial constraints; and illness in the family. They saw all these factors as having a heavy toll on the physical, mental, emotional and spiritual health of the clergy household. Subsequently, Davey (1995), an Anglican priest and psychologist, identified four main areas of stress for clergy. These were: the ministerial role; career development; lack of appropriate support; and recognition and home/work balance.

Although these studies of ministerial stress vary in their emphases, it is possible to identify certain general areas of concern, both from these studies and others such as Fletcher (1990) and Warren (2002). There is the nature of the work itself. It is challenging, never finished, difficult to evaluate, isolating and often carried out in a context of conflict and constant change. Ordained ministers are subject to wide variations in attitudes toward them and to their work. They feel discounted and marginalized by some parishioners, while expected to be accessible at all times and possess an enhanced spirituality by others. Living on the job makes the work/life/family balance particularly difficult and the demands of pastoral ministry can have adverse effects on the psychological and physical health of the ministers and their families. This is not helped by the relatively low income that goes with the job. There are also the expectations that the ministers have of themselves. They can suffer from the belief that, because of their role, they should be able to cope, should have a special spirituality and be accessible to people at all times. If these expectations are not met, ministers can experience a strong sense of failure.

Whilst acknowledging that all ordained ministers are subject to a variety of stressors, Bowden (1994) emphasized the additional pressures which a rural living may place on them. He also claimed that many rural clergy feel that those who run the diocese do not appreciate how different and demanding rural ministry can be. Russell (1993), in his book *The Country Parson*, saw the stress experienced by rural clergy as rooted in an over-busy job with no easily definable boundaries. He argued that the demands of looking after multi-parish benefices, combined with a lack of clarity about the role of the clergy in a rapidly changing society and church, and a feeling of being unsupported by bishops and archdeacons can lead to considerable stress.

Francis and Rutledge's (2000) study, based on 1,071 returned question-naires from a sample of male parochial clergy, provided further evidence for believing that clergy working in rural settings were more stressed than their urban and suburban colleagues. They used a permitted adaptation of the Maslach Burnout Inventory with a random sample of full-time stipendiary male parochial Anglican clergy. Using this three-component model of burnout (emotional exhaustion, depersonalization and personal accomplishment) they found that although rural clergy had a similar level of emotional exhaustion and depersonalization, they had a lower sense of personal accomplishment when compared with their urban and suburban colleagues.

In a follow-up study, Rutledge (2006) went on to investigate the effect on their ministry of rural clergy experiencing burnout. He found that many rural clergy felt overworked, frustrated in their ministry and 'used up' at the end of the day. This resulted in them being more likely to disengage from the traditional roles associated with work in rural parishes. He goes on to question what strategies are in place to support those suffering from ministerial burnout.

In *The Cracked Pot*, Warren (2002) reported on the state of today's Anglican parish clergy. Using a psychodynamic approach, she interviewed 64 incumbents, 37 in a northern diocese and 27 in a southern diocese. Her aim was to explore the dynamic relationship between the institution of the Church of England and the life of its ordained clergy by investigating six pertinent areas of their lives: why they were ordained; their view of authority; what it means to be a priest; personal relationships; working within the parish; and emotional and spiritual health. Warren identified five themes in her interview data from the 64 clergy: first, their feeling of being irrelevant; second, their feeling of being isolated; third, their need to understand that physical, spiritual and emotional health are deeply interwoven; fourth, their feeling of guilt resulting from 'never quite doing enough'; and fifth, their feeling of low self-worth from constant denigration by disaffected laity and the press.

In this insightful and groundbreaking study, Warren found a clear cry from the clergy to be heard, and listened to, by their bishops and other senior church leaders. However Warren felt that this criticism by clergy of their senior church leaders needed to be balanced by an acknowledgement of the enormous workloads experienced by church leaders themselves. As a result, she interviewed two bishops from the dioceses where her research was carried out and two other senior church leaders. All four senior church leaders stated that the needs of clergy should be met by care at the local level through shared ministry with lay and ordained colleagues; by an easy access to the bishop and his advisors when there are problems; and by ready access to specialist help, psychotherapy, spiritual direction or medical advice. In addition, they identified the need for clergy to be helped in the effective management of the boundaries needed in their relationships with people. All four senior church leaders recommended regular interviews with clergy to review their work and to explore the possibilities for future ministry. Warren's interviews afforded valuable insight into how church leaders perceive clergy stress and their work-related psychological health but her study is limited, for understandable reasons, to the perceptions of four church leaders only.

Hence the new empirical research, on which this article is based, sought to discover the perceptions of a larger group of senior church leaders on the stress experienced by and the work-related psychological health of clergy specifically engaged in rural ministry.

Method

Fifteen senior church leaders were invited to be interviewed on their perceptions of the stress experienced by ordained ministers working in rural settings and on ways of enhancing their work-related psychological health. All were willing to be interviewed although, in the event, arrangements could be made to complete only eleven of the interviews. Five church leaders were in the Church of England; two came from the Methodist Connexion, two from the United Reformed Church and two from the Roman Catholic Church. All church leaders interviewed were male; four were in their forties, five in their fifties and two in their sixties. The aim of each interview was to listen carefully to each church leader on the work-related psychological health of, and the stresses experienced by, those in ordained rural ministry. Semi-structured interviews were employed so that a conversational style between interviewer and interviewee could be used. Careful notes were taken during the interview but not in a way that interfered with the conversational style that was sought.

The church leaders interviewed may be divided into two groups: one group is designated in this study as 'episcopal church leaders' and the other as 'ecclesial church leaders'. The five 'episcopal church leaders' carried pastoral oversight (episcope) responsibilities in their diocese, district or designated region; for example, as bishop, chairman of a Methodist District, or moderator in the United Reformed Church. On the other hand, each of the six 'ecclesial church leaders' was a 'designated officer with specialist responsibilities' across their diocese, district or designated region; for example, a priest with ecumenical responsibilities across the diocese, an academic with ministerial training responsibilities across the district or a minister with counselling responsibilities for other ministers across the designated region.

The issues covered during the interviews were prompted by questions such as: What is particularly challenging and stressful for those in ordained rural ministry? What are the causes of stress in ordained rural ministry? What use do ordained rural ministers make of the specialist counselling support available to them? How might the work-related psychological health of ordained rural ministers be enhanced? Does the nature of stress vary according to the type of ministry, for example, in non-stipendiary and stipendiary ordained rural ministers? What can initial and in-service ministerial programmes offer to enhance the work-related psychological health of ordained rural ministers? Do you want to see more research in this field and, if so, what would you like to see attempted?

Results and discussion

Grounded theory was used to analyse the interview data from the senior church leaders. Each narrative account of the eleven interviews was read and re-read several times. Selected text of each narrative account was highlighted and coded in order to identify key recurrent themes. This analysis of the interview data revealed five key themes. These five themes will now be explored. The themes are best characterized as: first, unreasonable expectations; second, work/life balance; third, responsibility for stress management and enhancing work-related psychological health; fourth, the particular perspectives of church leaders who had recently worked in a rural setting; and fifth, the need for further research.

Unreasonable expectations

The eleven church leaders spoke of those in rural ministry feeling marginalized by the communities that they serve and feeling pressurized by the unrelentingly high expectations of those who attended their churches. Even people who rarely attended church saw their 'vicar' as a significant person in their village and expected him/her to be constantly available for village events. There was also a constant demand for clergy to operate in liminal areas, where issues of life and death were being faced.

Four episcopal church leaders were concerned to report that those in rural ministry were seldom affirmed or given positive feedback by members of their churches or communities. They often have to put up with carping and nit-picking criticism. One ecclesial church leader spoke of those in ordained ministry, and particularly those in rural settings, feeling the need to live up to what he called 'the myth of enhanced spirituality' where church members put their ministers 'on a spiritual pedestal', rarely allowing them to show human frailty and doubt. This church leader reported that the disparity between how ministers saw themselves spiritually and what their church members expected of them often led to considerable stress and damage to their work-related psychological health. The five episcopal church leaders saw the heavy demands of rural ministry leading to many ministers having difficulty in finding time and space to nurture their own spiritual lives.

All eleven church leaders stated that clustering churches and/or parishes in rural areas and bringing them under the responsibility of fewer clergy made the burden of high expectations even worse. One church leader highlighted the link between the reduction in the number of rural clergy and the weakening of particular village communities where there is now no resident member of the clergy.

Work/life balance

Four ecclesial and four episcopal church leaders drew attention to the particular problems faced by those in ordained rural ministry when attempting to maintain a healthy balance between work, personal life and family commitments. The stress arising from these demands too often had a negative effect on ministers' family life and, where the breakdown of ministerial marriages occurred, this was said to be a major contributing factor. Five ecclesial church leaders highlighted the difficulty for those in ordained rural ministry maintaining what were often an old house and a large garden on a relatively low income. The lack of rural transport meant that many rural ministers had to maintain two cars and spend too much time driving. The need to have their office in their home was not seen by these church leaders as conducive to a healthy work/life balance.

Responsibility for stress management

A difference in perspective between those who should carry the main responsibility for stress management and for enhancing work-related psychological health in rural ministers was noted between the ecclesial and episcopal church leaders. Although all five episcopal church leaders agreed that there was a clear need for specialist counselling, nevertheless these five church leaders saw the prime responsibility for managing his or her stress as resting with each individual minister. They spoke of their own heavy workloads and the limited specialist resources available for supporting ministers experiencing stressful situations. One episcopal church leader talked at some length about the church encouraging 'a dependency culture' among its ministers, which, in his view, discouraged them from taking responsibility for managing their own stress and looking after their own work-related psychological health.

The six ecclesial church leaders, including one with expertise in the counselling of ordained ministers, reported that bishops and archdeacons were too often seen by their fellow Anglican clergy as lacking empathy. This was said to derive from tension between the support roles carried by bishops and archdeacons and their responsibilities for 'hiring and firing'. Three ecclesial church leaders said that many ordained ministers saw their senior church leaders as sending the message, 'I survived, and therefore you must survive.' All six ecclesial church leaders emphasized the value of confidential counselling services but they felt that this provision was under too much pressure and needed to be further resourced and extended so that waiting lists would not develop or could be shortened. They also claimed that the churchmanship of ministers seemed to influence their willingness to seek specialist counselling support. They said that there was evidence that liberal Catholic clergy go for counselling whereas Evangelical ministers tend not to go. Evangelical ministers appeared to think that admitting their work was stressful indicated that there was something wrong with their relationship with God.

It was, however, the one ecclesial church leader with specialist responsibility for ministerial training who provided the valuable insight that it was not a matter of where the prime responsibility lay for stress management in ordained rural ministers. We should not, he said, be arguing about whether the church's provision for dealing with ministerial stress was more or less important than the need for individual ministers to manage their own stress and to look after their own work-related psychological health. Instead, he argued for an integrated approach, in other words, one where individual ministers fully accepted responsibility for looking after their own work-related psychological health, but in the full knowledge that there was an effective and confidential support system which could be accessed by a minister who needed such help. This church leader said that he felt so strongly about this that he included 'an integrated approach to stress management and the need to look after one's psychological health' within his courses for ordinands.

Another church leader spoke of this being furthered through 'a written covenant' between each ordained minister and their senior church leader(s), with a section that should be given to the needs of ordained rural ministers.

Insights of church leaders with recent rural experience

Two episcopal church leaders and one ecclesial church leader had recently moved from ministering in urban settings to working in mainly rural ones. This personal and recent experience had, they said, given them a particular sensitivity to stresses in ordained rural ministry. They emphasized what they had said earlier in their interview, namely that meeting the cost of heating what were often large and/or 'run-down' rural vicarages and manses, the need to run two cars because of poor rural transport and the constant pressure of fund-raising for rural churches with small congregations were major stressors for those in rural ministry. All three church leaders observed how the problems particularly felt in rural communities, such as the foot-and-mouth pandemic and the floods, had led to even more pressure on already pressurized ministers. The responsibility for clusters of churches was also likely to result in ministers spending more time travelling when visiting their church members and attending a greater number of meetings than was likely for their urban and suburban colleagues.

One episcopal church leader said that he had recently moved from being a lead minister in a large inner city church to an oversight responsibility covering several mainly rural counties. He highlighted problems that partners, sons and daughters of rural ministers faced when seeking employment. Opportunities for employment in rural settings were restricted and wages tended to be low. This put even more pressure on the salary of the rural minister, especially if the main breadwinner.

Need for further research

All eleven church leaders were aware that research had been conducted into the causes of clergy stress and the enhancement of their work-related psychological health; and some referred to particular books or other publications they had read. However, there was a general consensus that more research needed to be conducted especially into the best ways of deploying limited resources.

Two of the senior church leaders made the point that much of the research in this field was based on full-time, paid clergy in the Anglican Communion. This neither reflected the variety of ordained rural ministries in the Anglican Communion, nor the fact that ordained ministers from other denominations worked in rural settings. This observation offers implications for the design of future research in this field.

Conclusions

The major limitation of this study was that only eleven church leaders could be interviewed. However, the study highlighted the need for further research particularly into the location of responsibility for stress management and the enhancement of psychological health in ordained rural ministers, especially the effective deployment of limited resources, including those of specialist support.

All church leaders in this survey agreed that, if these issues were to be researched, a large-scale survey of senior church leaders is needed. It was further observed that the nature and size of the sample should reflect that, although the Anglican Church is the largest provider of rural ministry in England and Wales, there are other denominations providing rural ministry. It was the general hope of all those interviewed that such research would take place and that the funding could be found to do this much-needed work.

References

Bowden, A. (1994). *Ministry in the countryside.* London: Mowbray.

Coate, M. A. (1989). *Clergy stress: The hidden conflicts in ministry.* London: SPCK.

Davey, J. (1995). *Burnout: Stress in ministry.* Leominster: Gracewing.

Fletcher, B. (1990). *Clergy under stress: A study of homosexual and heterosexual clergy.* London: Mowbray.

Francis, L. J., & Rutledge, C. J. F. (2000). Are rural clergy in the Church of England under greater stress? *Research in the Social Scientific Study of Religion, 11,* 173–191.

Kirk, M., & Leary, T. (1994). *Holy matrimony? An exploration of marriage and ministry.* Oxford: Lynx.

Russell, A. (1993). *The country parson.* London: SPCK.

Rutledge, C. J. F. (2006). Burnout and the practice of ministry among rural clergy. *Rural Theology, 4,* 57–65.

Sanford, J. A. (1982). *Ministry burnout.* London: Arthur James.

Warren, Y. (2002). *The cracked pot: The state of today's Anglican parish clergy.* Buxhall, Suffolk: Kevin Mayhew.

CONTRIBUTORS

The Revd Dr Jennie Annis is Honorary Research Fellow at the St Mary's Centre, Wales, UK.

Dr Tania ap Siôn is Executive Director of the St Mary's Centre, Wales and Senior Research Fellow, Warwick Religions and Education Research Unit, University of Warwick, UK.

The Revd Professor Jeff Astley is Director of the North of England Institute for Christian Education, Durham, UK.

The Revd Dr Christine E. Brewster is a priest in mid-Wales, Visiting Research Fellow at Glyndŵr University, and Senior Tutor at the St Seiriol's Centre, Wales, UK.

The Revd Dr Lewis Burton, a retired Methodist minister, Visiting Research Fellow at Glyndŵr University, and Honorary Research Fellow at the St Mary's Centre, Wales, UK.

The Revd Dr John Drane is a freelance researcher and theological consultant, a Fellow of St John's College, Durham and Adjunct Professor of Practical Theology at Fuller Seminary, Pasadena, CA, USA.

The Revd Canon Dr Richard T. France is an Anglican clergyman, and a former Principal of Wycliffe Hall, Oxford, UK.

The Revd Canon Professor Leslie J. Francis is Professor of Religions and Education at the Warwick Religions and Education Research Unit, University of Warwick, UK.

The Revd Ann Howells (formerly Smitham) is Vicar of the Parish of Llandybïe in the Diocese of St Davids, UK.

Canon Keith Ineson is Agricultural Chaplain for Churches Together in Cheshire, and Coordinator for Cheshire Farm Crisis Network, UK.

The Revd Professor William K. Kay is Professor of Theology at Glyndŵr University, Wales, UK.

Professor Trevor Kerry is Professor Emeritus at the University of Lincoln, UK.

The Revd Dr Michael Keulemans served as chaplain of Liverpool Nautical Sixth Form, UK.

Dr David W. Lankshear is Research Fellow at the Warwick Religions and Education Research Unit, University of Warwick, UK.

The Revd Dr Keith Littler is Research Fellow at the St Mary's Centre, Wales, UK.

The Revd Professor Gareth Lloyd Jones is Professor Emeritus of Theology and Religious Studies at the University of Wales, Bangor, UK.

The Revd Canon Jeremy Martineau OBE is Director of the Centre for Studies in Rural Ministry, Wales, UK.

Professor Stella Mills is Professor of Multimedia Technology at Staffordshire University, and Methodist Local Preacher in the Dove Valley Circuit, Stafford, UK.

The Revd Norman Morris is Rector of Wentnor with Ratlinghope, Myndtown, Norbury, More, Lydham and Snead, UK.

The Revd Sue Pegg is Methodist minister in the Market Weighton section of the Pocklington and Market Weighton Methodist Circuit, UK.

Dr Mandy Robbins is Senior Lecturer in Psychology at Glyndŵr University, UK.

The Revd Dr Carol Roberts is Assistant Curate in the Parish of Bangor, Gwynedd, UK.

Jenny Rolph is Director of The Olive Branch Christian Counselling Service, Winchester, and Visiting Research Fellow at Glyndŵr University, UK.

Dr Paul Rolph is Visiting Research Fellow at Glyndŵr University, Wales, UK.

The Revd Canon Dr Christopher J. F. Rutledge served as vicar of St Mark's, Talbot Village, Ferndown, UK.

The Rt Revd Mark Rylands is Bishop of Shrewsbury, within the Diocese of Lichfield, Shrewsbury, UK.

The Ven. Dr William A. Strange is Archdeacon of Cardigan, Diocese of St David's, UK.

The Rt Revd David S. Walker is Bishop of Dudley within the Diocese of Worcester, Cradley Heath, and Visiting Research Fellow of Glyndŵr University, UK.

The Revd Angela Williams is Incumbent of the Benefice of Llandegfan with Llandysilio (Menai Bridge), Anglesey, UK.

Dr Emyr Williams is a Lecturer in Psychology at Glyndŵr University, UK.

The Revd Rhys Williams serves as non-stipendiary priest in the Diocese of Bangor, Gwynedd, UK.

SOURCES

Chapter 2, Israelite wisdom and pastoral theology in the rural church, was first published in *Rural Theology*, 2, 75–87, 2004.

Chapter 3, The invisible countryside of the New Testament, was first published in *Rural Theology*, 4, 75–84, 2006.

Chapter 4, Sheep and goats: pastoral imagery in the Bible and today, was first published in *Rural Theology*, 6, 3–10, 2008.

Chapter 5, Ordinary theology for rural theology and rural ministry, was first published in *Rural Theology*, 1, 3–12, 2003.

Chapter 6, The kneelers are most impressive: reflections on reading a visitors' book, was first published in *Rural Theology*, 6, 97–100, 2008.

Chapter 7, Ordinary prayer and the rural church: an empirical study of prayer cards, was first published in *Rural Theology*, 7, 17–31, 2009.

Chapter 8, Encountering New Age spirituality: opportunities and challenges for the rural church, was first published in *Rural Theology*, 2, 3–14, 2004.

Chapter 9, God in creation: a reflection on Jürgen Moltmann's theology, was first published in *Rural Theology*, 3, 74–84, 2005.

Chapter 10, Belonging to rural church and society: theological and sociological perspectives, was first published in *Rural Theology*, 4, 85–97, 2005.

Chapter 11, Blackshawhead: a local case history in rural church categorization, was first published in *Rural Theology*, 2, 41–51, 2004.

Chapter 12, Is the rural church different? The special case of confirmation, was first published in *Rural Theology*, 2, 106–117, 2004.

Chapter 13, Rural Anglicanism: one face or many?, was first published in *Rural Theology*, 3, 25–29, 2005.

Chapter 14, Pastoral fragments: discovered remnants of a rural past, was first published in *Rural Theology*, 5, 85–110, 2007.

Chapter 15, I was glad: listening to visitors to country churches, was first published in *Rural Theology*, 2, 53–60, 2004.

Chapter 16, Sacred place and pilgrimage: modern visitors to the shrine of St Melangell, was first published in *Rural Theology*, 4, 99–110, 2006.

Chapter 17, Visitor experiences of St Davids Cathedral: the two worlds of pilgrims and secular tourists, was first published in *Rural Theology*, 5, 111–123, 2007.

Chapter 18, Social capital generated by two rural churches: the role of individual believers, was first published in *Rural Theology*, 3, 85–97, 2005.

Chapter 19, Local festivals in two Pennine villages: the reactions of the local Methodist church congregations, was first published in *Rural Theology*, 4, 11–22, 2006.

Chapter 20, Extended communion: a second best option for rural Anglicanism?, was first published in *Rural Theology*, 4, 23–35, 2006.

Chapter 21, All types are called, but some are more likely to respond: the psychological type profile of rural Anglican churchgoers in Wales, was first published in *Rural Theology*, 5, 23–30, 2007.

Chapter 22, The social significance of Harvest Festivals in the countryside: an empirical enquiry among those who attend, was first published in *Rural Theology*, 7, 3–16, 2009.

Chapter 23, Psychological type profile of volunteer workers in a rural Christian charity shop, was first published in *Rural Theology*, 5, 53–56, 2007.

Chapter 24, Deployment of the churches' ministry: Anglicans and Methodists in a rural diocese, was first published in *Rural Theology*, 3, 13–24, 2005.

Chapter 25, Views on baptism and confirmation in the Church in Wales: are rural clergy different?, was first published in *Rural Theology*, 4, 127–132, 2006.

Chapter 26, Children and communion: listening to churchwardens in rural and urban Wales, was first published in *Rural Theology*, 5, 13–22, 2007.

Chapter 27, Burnout and the practice of ministry among rural clergy: looking for the hidden signs, was first published in *Rural Theology*, 4, 57–65, 2006.

Chapter 28, How happy are rural Anglican clergy?, was first published in *Rural Theology*, 6, 43–53, 2008.

Chapter 29, Perceptions of stress on those in rural ministry: listening to church leaders, was first published in *Rural Theology*, 6, 55–63, 2008.

SUBJECT INDEX

Abraham 9, 34, 110
Achaia 24
Acts 22–25, 27, 30–31, 34, 37, 98
affiliation 106, 111–112, 203, 206, 216, 227
Africa 75
Age Concern 223
agrarian, agriculture 3, 22, 26–27, 29–31, 47, 107, 172, 278, 280
All Saints' Day 163
alternative spirituality(ies) 83–85
Amos 11
Anglican Church 139, 181, 221, 245, 259, 261, 267, 294, 306, 309, 346
Anglican(s) 2, 35, 66, 231, 258, 286, 288–296
Anglo-Catholic 251, 329
Antioch 24
apocalyptic 39, 170
Apocrypha 8
apologetics 49, 65
Apostle 24, 37
arable 26, 28
Archbishop's Licence(s) 115
Archbishops' Commission on Cathedrals 202–203, 214
Archbishops' Commission on Rural Areas 6, 121, 166, 197, 284, 287, 316
architecture 57, 184, 203, 208, 211, 213
Ark of the Covenant 229
Arthur Rank Centre 6, 53, 173
Articles of Religion 243
Asia Minor 23, 37
astrology 88
atheism 16

Athenian(s) 98
atonement 99
Augustine (Saint) 100, 306
autumn 19

Bangor 305, 309
baptism(s) 5, 55, 57, 60, 111, 113, 115, 146–147, 151, 153–154, 158, 237, 273, 299, 302–303, 306, 312, 319
Bardsey Island 188
Belgium 96
belong(ers)/belong(ing) 3–4, 105, 107–118, 139, 153, 165, 168, 206, 247, 249–259, 266, 268, 270, 273–276, 280, 297
Ben Sira (Wisdom of) 9
benefice(s) 5–6, 123, 130, 261, 291, 295–296, 316–318, 321–323, 325, 329, 339
Bethlehem 28, 34–35
Bible, biblical 1, 3, 20, 33, 90, 96, 111, 164, 214, 225, 229
Birmingham 132–133
bishop(s) 11, 164, 168, 190, 307–308, 311–312, 324, 340–341
black theology 1
Board of Mission 166, 197
Board of Mission Rural Commission 197
Book of Common Prayer 137, 168–169, 244, 308, 311
British 86, 96, 105, 108–109, 163, 203, 222, 264, 301
British Social Attitudes Survey 113
Bronze Age 189, 195–196
Buddhist(s) 13, 206

burnout 5–6, 316–317, 319–324, 335, 338–339

Cadfan 189
Canaan 13, 195
Canon Law 251, 307
Canterbury 133, 323
career 108, 163, 166, 338
Carlisle 133, 147–149, 152, 154, 156–159
carnival(s) 229–230
catechism 223, 243, 308, 311–312
cathedral(s) 4, 163, 182, 188, 190–191, 201–214
Catholic 318, 330, 344, see also Roman Catholic(s)
celebrant 244, 251
Celtic 90, 191, 195–196
Cenchreae 24
census 86, 113, 121–122, 135, 151, 157
Centre for Studies in Rural Ministry 6
chapel 61, 68, 122–129, 168, 246, 288–289, 295, 297
charismatic 126–127, 330
charity shop 5, 281–283
Chelmsford 133
Chichester 133
child 28, 162, 166, 171, 173, 223, 306–307
childhood 125, 172
children 5, 11, 17, 55, 69, 108, 111, 126, 162, 164, 166, 170, 172–173, 198, 223, 230, 232, 269, 302, 305–313
Christ 23, 37, 97, 99–100, 102–103, 196, 224–225, 243, 245, 250, 264, 305
Christian Aid 221, 223
Christian education 49, 65, 303
Christian Scientists 84
Christingle 127, 270
Christmas 33, 55, 113–114, 127, 147, 152, 154, 221, 223, 235, 269–270
Christmas communicants 152, 154, 159
christology(ies) 66
Chronicles 229
church council 113, 127, 146, 153
Church in Wales 5, 180, 197, 261, 299, 301, 305, 308–313, 316

church leaders 1, 5–6, 47, 87, 337, 340–346
church musician(s) 236
Church of England 4, 52, 95, 121–122, 131–140, 146, 148, 150, 152, 154, 163, 165–166, 197, 203, 242, 244, 261, 265, 268, 270, 277, 286–291, 295–297, 299, 307–308, 316, 318, 323–325, 330, 334, 339, 341
Church of England Year Book(s) 141, 136, 147
Church Society 325
Church Tourism Association 182
church visitor(s) 234–235
churchgoers 1, 5, 43–44, 49, 53, 61, 66, 193–196, 205, 207, 209, 212, 219, 224, 226, 235, 259, 261–263, 265, 268, 270, 282–283, 300, 302–303
churchwarden(s) 5, 114, 305, 309–313
churchyard 55, 107–108, 116–117, 183, 185, 189–190, 193, 273
citizenship 17
city (cities/city centre) 14, 22–27, 29–31, 49, 85, 90, 103, 108, 197, 204, 214, 230, 267, 291–292, 302, 309, 345
club(s) 173, 222, 231
communicants 132–134, 137–139, 143, 147, 151–153, 159, 303, 309
communion 5, 111, 137–138, 152, 221, 242–254, 305–313, 345
community 1, 4–5, 14–17, 23, 53–54, 65, 82, 86, 91–92, 97, 100, 103, 105–111, 113–118, 122, 124–125, 127–130, 139, 162, 167, 174–175, 181–182, 216–227, 231, 233, 237, 239–240, 244–245, 248, 250–253, 259, 264–271, 274–280, 283, 299–303, 317, 321–323, 338
commuter(s) 106, 108, 113–114, 117, 232, 267, 277
concert(s) 113–114, 231
confirmation 5, 131–134, 138–140, 154, 151, 154, 299, 302, 305–310, 312–131, 323
confirmation candidates 4, 132–140, 142–144, 147, 151, 153–154, 159
congregation(s) (al) 5, 24, 49–50, 68, 91, 116, 125–128, 130, 167, 181, 198,

219, 229, 233, 238–239, 242–243,
    245–248, 250–251, 253, 258–259,
    261–262, 264, 267–270, 272–277,
    279–282, 296, 300, 302–303, 326, 345
consecration 250–251
conservative 5, 127, 166, 239, 299–300,
    318, 330
Constantine, Emperor 91
Corinth/Corinthians 22, 24–25, 29–30,
    244, 306
counsellor 18, 321–322
countryside 3, 5, 22–32, 42, 48–49,
    52–53, 56–57, 61–62, 83, 85, 90,
    95, 105–110, 112, 121–122, 129,
    167, 170, 173–175, 191, 197, 267,
    269, 277, 279, 286–288, 291–293,
    295–296
Countryside Alliance 109
Countryside Commission 182
Coventry 133, 203
creation 3, 59, 94–95, 97–103, 164,
    175, 186
Cuddesdon 163
curates 288, 318

Dales 120
Damascus 24
Darwin (Darwinian/Darwinism)
    164–165
David (King) 13, 16, 35, 164, 229
David (Saint) 188
deacon(s) 111, 162
denomination(s) 5, 33, 87, 111, 122,
    139, 206, 217, 224, 226–227, 245,
    272, 286, 288, 291–292, 297, 337,
    345–346
Derby 133
Derbyshire 91, 115, 220
Deuteronomy 9, 29, 195
Diana, Princess of Wales 86
Diocesan Advisory Committee 116
Diocesan Tourism Officer(s) 52
diocese(s)/diocesan 4–5, 52, 121, 123,
    131–138, 140–141, 145–159, 181,
    266, 270, 272, 287–289, 292, 294,
    297, 299, 305, 307, 309, 339–341
divine 9–11, 39–40, 44, 95, 97–103,
    111, 195, 242–243, 264

doctrinally 92
dogmatic(s) 17, 44, 53, 269
Dorset 161–162, 166

early church 111–112
Easter 31, 55, 137, 152, 191, 230, 235,
    244, 269
Easter day communicants 131,
    133–134, 137–139, 143, 147,
    151–152, 159
Eastern Church 306
Ecclesiastes 8
Ecclesiastical 45, 198
ecclesiastical theology 3, 42
ecological/ecology 20, 98
ecotheology 175
ecumenical 2, 13, 341
Egypt 13
elder(s) 34, 37
elderly 223, 228, 235, 247, 253, 269
electoral roll 131, 133–137, 139,
    142–143, 147, 150, 153–154, 158,
    272–273
Ely 203, 308
empirical theology 4, 145
English Cathedrals and Tourism 202
English Tourist Board 202, 212
enlightenment 83–84, 191
Ephesus 24
Esalen Institute 85
Esau 195
eschatology 96
established resident(s) 107, 113,
    266–267, 277
Eucharist 305
eucharistic prayer 243
European 75, 203
European Union 109
Evangelical 127, 174, 250–251, 318,
    329–330, 344
evangelism 49, 65, 103, 112, 132, 225
evangelistic 36, 92, 240
evolution 100
Exeter 147–148, 150, 156–159
exile 16–17, 108, 114
Exodus 9, 15, 29, 306
extended communion 5, 242–243,
    245–254

extraversion 260–261, 282–283, 329
Eysenck Personality Questionnaire
  (EPQ) 300
Ezekiel 35
Ezra 17

faith 10, 16, 44–45, 47–49, 52, 58, 67,
  86, 112, 116, 139, 165–166, 169, 175,
  192, 194, 196, 198, 221, 223, 234,
  240, 244, 252, 268–269, 300, 302, 326
faith development 71, 76, 154
faith groups 117–118
faith journey 265
faithful(ness) 30, 47, 97, 240, 424–244,
  250, 252
family 12, 17, 26–28, 34, 38, 46, 54,
  57, 70–73, 107–109, 116–118, 123,
  125–127, 139, 161–167, 169–170,
  175, 193, 203, 223, 235–237, 239,
  245, 247, 267–268, 277–279, 327,
  332, 338, 343
family research 184, 186
family service 272
farm(ing)(s) 25, 28, 30, 38, 40, 45, 54,
  121, 123–125, 127
Farm Payment Scheme 109
farmer(s) 19, 109
farmers' market 173
feeling (F) 260–261, 264, 281–283
feminist theology 1, 43
festivals 5, 114, 222, 229–230,
  233–240, 269, 301
fete 127
fig tree 29
Findhorn Foundation 85, 89–90
fisherman 37
flock 35–39
Flower Festival 55–56
folk tradition(s) 91
foot-and-mouth 34, 56, 173, 345
Forces Chaplain 219
Fourth Lateran Council 306
Francis Burnout Inventory (FBI) 335
Francis of Assisi (Saint) 90
Francis Psychological Type Scales
  (FPTS) 258–259, 261, 281–282, 300
French Revolution 84
friend(s/ship) 13, 72, 276

funeral(s) 35, 117, 248, 273

Galatia/Galatians 24
Galilee 25–28
garden(ing) 48, 102–103, 107, 115,
  166, 220, 343
General Synod 173, 307
Genesis 9, 98, 101, 195
Gentile(s) 22–23
Germany 67, 96
Gifford lectures 94–96
gift shop 183, 185–186
Girl Guide(s) 163
globalization 82
Gloucester 133
Gloucestershire 162
Gnosticism 83
God-talk 2, 43–44, 46, 48, 52–53, 65
Good Shepherd 31, 33, 35–36, 39
Gospel(s) 3, 22, 24–31, 91, 175,
  282–283
government 110, 117, 173
grandparent(s) 302–303
grass roots 45
graveyard 57, 117
Grounded theory 342
gypsy(ies) 107, 267, 278

hamlet(s) 25, 123, 162
happiness 325–332, 334–335
harvest 19, 36, 55, 114, 127, 235, 265,
  269–273, 276–280
Harvest Festival(s) 5, 266, 268–269
heaven 15, 60, 72, 75, 100, 103, 195
hell 15
Hellenistic 31
Hereford 132–133
hermeneutical 20, 84
Hidden Britain 53
holiness 53–54, 66, 168, 189, 198, 245
holy 10, 53, 59, 116, 168, 189, 190
Holy Communion 221, 242–245, 248,
  250–251, 253–254, 306–308
holy place(s) 59, 195–196
Holy Spirit (also see Spirit) 37, 97–98,
  103
Holywell 188
House of Bishops 307

Huddersfield 85, 120, 232, 238–239
human rights 12
hymn(s) 14, 59, 170, 192, 194

ideology 11, 85, 88
implicit religion 91
incumbents 270, 275, 288, 339
Inner Wheel 221, 224
intercessory prayer 61, 64, 66, 68
interview 66, 73, 128, 194, 203, 219,
    247, 337, 340–342, 344
introversion (I) 163, 260–261, 281–283
intuition (N) 260–261, 264, 282–283
Iona 190
Isaac 110
Isaiah 244
Israel 10–13, 16, 27, 35, 111–112, 195,
    229–230
Israelite 3, 8–11, 13, 16

Jacob 34, 110, 195
jazz 5, 231, 233–234, 236–240
Jerusalem 13, 24, 34, 112, 229
Jesus 12, 22, 24–31, 34–37, 39, 67,
    76, 91, 97, 111, 164, 195, 230, 243,
    311–312
Jew(s) 13, 22, 206
Jewish Law 111
Job 8
John (Gospel of) 25–27, 31, 36–37, 98,
    111, 306
John the Baptist 25–26
Jubilee laws 112
Judeo-Christian 59
judging (J) 259–261, 264, 281–283
Jungian 260, 281, 338
justice 35, 75, 111, 260

Keirsey Temperament Sorter (KTS)
    259, 281
kneeling theology 46
Korea 95

laity 145, 153, 222, 243, 245, 340
Lancashire 85, 91, 121, 323
law(s) 9, 12, 17, 87, 164
lay leader(s) 127, 218, 243, 245–246,
    251–252, 254

lay people 130, 243, 248, 252, 296, 309
lay presidency 242–243, 249–251, 254
Leeds 85, 128, 232
Leicester 133
Leviticus 112
liberal 318, 330, 344
liberation theology 1, 16, 43
licensed readers (lay readers) 114,
    147, 150, 158, 220, 223, 245–248,
    250–252
Lichfield 133, 203
lifestyle(s) 85, 90, 107, 277–279
lifestyle shifter(s) 107, 113, 266–267
Likert (scale(s)) 191–192, 206, 233,
    271, 273, 310, 329, 331
Lincoln 133, 147–149, 152, 154,
    156–159, 162–164, 168, 181, 204
Lincoln Theological College 162
Lincolnshire 162, 172–173, 287
Lindisfarne 190
liturgical 16, 43, 146, 277, 279
Liverpool 133
Llandaff 305, 309
Lleyn Peninsula 188
Local Ecumenical Partnership (LEP)
    219, 238
local non-stipendiary ministry (LNSM)
    242–243
local preachers 124
London 108, 133, 192
Lord's Supper 243–244
Lourdes 190
Luke (Gospel of) 22–31, 34–36, 225

Magdalene, Mary 186
Malta 24
Malvern College 162
Manchester 128, 133, 132, 307
manses 344
Mark (Gospel of) 25–29
market town 246, 293, 302
marriage 70, 73, 105, 115–116, 338
Marxist 98–99
Maslach Burnout Inventory (MBI) 5,
    316–317, 319, 339
Matthew (Gospel of) 12, 23–25,
    27–29, 4–36, 225, 243, 259
Mazdaznan 85

meditation 186, 193, 197, 248, 326
memorial(s) 116, 195
memorial chapel 68
Messiah/messianic 26, 35, 37, 97, 99,
    102–103, 244, 286
Methodism/Methodists/Methodist
    Church 122–124, 126, 218–221, 223,
    230–232, 235, 237–238, 243–244,
    284–297, 341
Methodist chapel 122–123, 126
    224–225, 227, 287
Methodist circuit(s) 122, 124, 130, 238,
    287–289, 296
Methodist Conference 296
Methodist district(s) (also see
    Methodist circuit) 5, 286, 288,
    293–294, 341
Methodist minister(s) 288–290,
    292–295, 297
Micah 35
Middle Ages 190, 193, 196, 306
Middle East 75
ministry team 114
mission 22, 24, 53, 145–146, 153, 203,
    214, 217, 225, 228, 240, 267–268,
    270, 273, 318, 324
Mission-Shaped Church 105, 324
Moonraker Festival 5, 231–233, 237,
    239–240
Mormons 84
Moses 17, 195
Mothers' Union 113
multi-parish 325, 329, 339
Muslim(s) 13, 89, 206
Myers-Briggs Type Indicator (MBI) 259

National Census 113
National Children's Advisers 307
National Church Tourism Group 182
National Rural Officer 173
natural theology 94–95, 102
nature 95, 97–100, 102
Nazareth 26
New Age 3, 82–83, 86, 88–92
New Religious Movement(s) 83–84
New Testament 3, 9, 22, 25, 30–33, 35,
    96, 111–112, 175, 195, 230, 243–245,
    305–306

Newcastle 133
Nicene Creed 98
non-charismatic 330
non-churchgoers 43, 49, 53, 194–196,
    209
non-stipendiary (NSM) 43, 49, 53,
    193–196, 209
Northern Ireland 221
Norwich 133, 147–148, 150–152,
    156–159
numinous 58, 168

occasional office(s) 114–115, 273, 318
occult 88–89
Old Testament 3, 8–10, 13, 15, 33,
    35–36, 110–112, 175, 195, 339,
    337–345
ordained 2, 114, 148, 164, 242,
    244–245, 248–249, 252
ordained local ministry (OLM) 147,
    149–150, 157
Order of the Golden Dawn 84–85
ordinary prayer 64, 66, 77
ordinary theology 1, 3, 42, 50, 52–54,
    56, 61–66, 78, 175
ordination 33, 243–245, 248, 250–252
organist 169, 221, 236
Oxford Happiness Inventory (OHI) 6,
    329
Oxford Happiness Questionnaire
    (OHQ) 325–326, 328–331, 333–335

pagan(s) 10–11, 88, 91, 196, 239
Palestine/Palestinian 26–28, 30–31
Palm Sunday 230
panentheism/pantheism 95
parent(s) 109, 126, 198, 226, 279,
    302–303, 307
parish church(es) 4, 54, 67, 105,
    108–109, 116, 164, 171, 194, 213,
    220–221, 246–248, 253, 259,
    264, 267–268, 286, 289, 291, 294,
    296–297
Parish Workbook 146
parishioner(s) 5, 49–50, 66, 173, 299,
    319–322, 338
Parochial Church Council (PCC) 133,
    146, 153

parson 38–39, 161, 163, 339
parsonage 117
Passover/Passover Lamb 34, 306
pastoral care 49, 65, 248–249,
    251–152, 254, 288–290, 292,
    294–296, 324
Pastoral Epistles 111
pastoral theology 3, 8
Paul/Pauline 22–23, 25, 29–31, 34, 94,
    98, 111, 244, 305
peace 12, 54, 57–62, 67, 70–76, 90,
    107, 168–169, 184, 193–194, 196,
    203, 208, 210, 213, 260, 264, 267,
    277
Pennine(s)/Pennine hills 5, 122, 124,
    129, 229, 231–232, 238, 240
Pentateuch 9, 17
Pentecostal 218
perceiving (P) 259–261, 264, 282–283
personality 260, 300, 328, 329
pet 74–75
Peter (Saint) 37, 39, 250
Peterborough 307
Pharisees 26
Philippi 24
philosophical 10, 66, 84
pilgrimage 4, 14, 59–60, 188–190, 193,
    195–197
population norms 260–262, 264
post-Christian 202
practical theology 3, 65, 145
prayer/prayer board/prayer cards/
    prayer requests/prayer tree 3, 46,
    52–54, 59–64, 66–78, 117, 126, 137,
    165, 168–169, 183–184, 186, 189,
    193, 197, 205–206, 208–209, 220,
    243–244, 250–251, 308, 311, 324
preaching 20, 49, 65, 219, 326
presbyter(s) 111
Presbyterian 92
priest 17, 33–34, 68, 111, 146, 195,
    222, 225–226, 242–245, 248,
    250–252, 254, 268, 275, 290–291,
    294–295, 300, 338, 340–341
priesthood 13, 250, 306
priest-in-charge 318
privacy seeker(s) 106, 110, 113, 115,
    267, 277

probationer(s) 288
prodigal son 27
prophet(s) 9, 17, 111, 195
prophetic 10, 14, 88, 146, 195
Protestant 95, 98
Proverbs 8–10, 12–14, 16–20
Psalm(s) 35, 40, 95–96, 98, 169, 230
psychological health 326, 334–335,
    338, 340–345
Psychological Type 5, 258–263, 265,
    281–283, 300
pulpits 3, 8–9, 286, 326

questionnaire 6, 132, 183, 184, 186,
    188, 191, 194, 202–202, 206, 212,
    231, 233–234, 237, 246–247,
    249–250, 261–262, 270–272, 288,
    300–302, 308–310, 316–317,
    325–326, 328–331, 333–335, 339

rabbinic 25
rating scale(s) 180
reincarnation 88
Renewing Faith in the Countryside 166
Representative Body of the Church in
    Wales 309
retire(d) 73, 108, 130, 172–173, 192,
    220–223, 226, 251–252, 259, 263,
    265, 278
Revelation (Book of) 39, 103, 112
Ridley Hall 163
Ripon College 133
rites 111, 115
rites of passage 108, 112, 116, 294, 324
Rochester 133
Rogation Sunday 165
Roman Catholic 67, 190, 218–219,
    221–222, 224–227, 230, 244, 250,
    341
Roman Empire 23
Rome 24, 27
Rotary Club 221, 224
Rural Church Project 121, 146, 287
rural life 32, 42, 90, 107, 115, 117, 163
rural ministry 3–4, 6, 8, 42–43, 49, 64,
    66, 68, 162, 240, 294–295, 300, 303,
    316–317, 321, 323–324, 326, 337,
    339–346

rural parishes 153, 162–163, 168, 268, 299–303, 305, 310, 316–317, 325, 334, 339
Rural Strategy Group 173
rural theology 1–4, 6, 31, 42–43, 47–48, 94, 120, 161, 175
Rural Theology Association 2, 6
Rural Wales Consultative Document 181
rurality 121–122, 133, 146, 299

Sabbath 29, 101
sacred 4, 11, 46, 189, 196, 214, 244–245, 253
sacred place 54, 58, 61, 117, 188–189, 191, 193–196
sacred space 207
Salisbury 133, 147–151, 156–159, 163
salvation 2, 4, 15, 91, 97, 164
salvation-history 9, 15–16, 20
Samuel (Book of) 9, 35
school(s) 54, 73, 77, 110, 146, 163, 166, 171–172, 174, 220, 222, 268, 275
scripture 3, 16, 31, 46, 96
secular 4, 10–11, 14, 59–60, 96, 101, 111, 115, 127–128, 174, 196, 214, 230, 238, 240, 245, 270, 287
secular tourists 201, 207, 213–214
secularization 11, 165, 227
Seeds in Holy Ground 173
sensing (S) 260–261, 264, 281–283
Sepphoris 25–26
sermon 98, 126, 163–164, 248
Sharing of Church Buildings Act 219
Sheffield 133, 287
shepherd 31, 33–40
shop 125, 183, 185–186, 194, 206, 208, 211, 213–214, 219, 281–283
shrine 4, 54, 188–191, 193, 196–197, 199
Shrove Tuesday 230
sin 16, 99
social capital 5, 106, 128, 216–217, 219, 224–228
social network(s) 216, 218, 227
social-scientific 66
Solomon (Wisdom of) 8
Somerset 162

Son of Man 36, 306
Song of Songs 110
soteriology 66
South America 95
Southwark 133, 307
Spirit (The, also see Holy Spirit) 25, 83, 96–99
spirit guide 88
spirit world 84
spiritual 3, 15, 17, 44, 52–54, 56–62, 66, 82, 84–92, 100, 111, 116, 124, 126–129, 189, 191–194, 196–198, 203–210, 212–213, 224–225, 228, 233, 235, 244–245, 253, 322, 324, 338, 342
spiritual health 197, 338
spirituality 15, 62, 82–83, 85–86, 88–92, 210, 212, 215, 227, 236, 265, 327, 338–339, 342
spring 23
St Davids Cathedral 4, 202, 206
St Edmundsbury and Ipswich 133, 147–148, 151, 156–159
St Vincent de Paul Society 219, 222, 225–226
statistical significance 207, 262, 310
Statistical Supplements 141, 147
statutory community agencies 227
stewardship 175
stipendiary 5, 38, 147–150, 153, 157, 299–301, 316–317, 323, 325, 329, 334, 339, 341
stoic 98
stress 1, 5–6, 146, 198, 296, 300, 316, 326–327, 332, 334, 337–345
stressors 326, 328–339, 345
subjective wellbeing 325–329, 334–335
suburban/suburbia 48–49, 128, 132, 146, 192–196, 302, 309, 316, 339, 345
summer 56, 90, 127, 191, 288
Sunday School 171, 221, 233, 235, 307, 322–323
survey 5, 66, 113, 122, 132, 146, 180, 182–183, 186, 196–198, 202–205, 212, 233, 263, 271–272, 286, 288, 291, 294–295, 297, 299, 301, 305, 309–310, 313, 317, 329–330, 337, 346

Swami Vivekananda 84
Synoptic gospels 3, 22, 25, 27, 29–30

tarot cards 84, 88
temple 9, 13, 17, 34, 111
thanksgiving 59, 61, 67–68, 243, 250, 268
theologian 30, 44, 46, 50
theological college 162
theological listening 50
theology 3–4, 6, 8–10, 13, 15–17, 20, 31, 42–50, 52–54, 56, 61–66, 78, 86, 91, 94–98, 101–102, 120, 145, 161, 164, 175, 195, 224, 226, 243, 245, 251, 303, 306
Thessalonians 24
thinking (T) 260–261, 264, 282–283
Tiberias (sea of) 25–27
Torah 10
tourism/tourists 52–53, 56, 124, 181–182, 186–187, 193, 202, 212, 214, 232
town(s) 28, 49, 122–125, 127, 130, 188, 192, 221, 246, 282, 291–296, 302
transcendence 100, 214
traveller(s) 23, 127
Trinitarian 95, 97–98, 240
Trinity 97, 101, 103, 240
Troas 24
trophy owner(s) 107, 110, 113, 267, 277
Truro 133, 147–149, 151–152, 154, 156–159

United Kingdom 86–87, 260–262, 281–282, 300
United Reformed Church 238, 341
United States of America (USA) 83–84, 203
urban 22, 24–27, 30–32, 34, 38, 40, 48–49, 52, 66, 85, 88, 90, 92, 106–109, 117, 120–122, 124, 128–144, 146, 155–156, 162, 165, 167, 174, 197–198, 267, 269–270, 277, 288, 291–292, 296, 300–303, 306, 309–314, 316, 326, 339, 344–345, 352

urban parishes 146, 155, 261, 269, 299–303, 308, 310
urban shadow 122, 129

vicar 166, 176, 275–276, 280, 300, 304, 342
vicarage 184
Victorian (era) 14, 163, 170, 197
village(s) 5, 53–54, 61, 90, 95, 103, 109–110, 116, 121–130, 140, 156, 162, 168–172, 177, 184, 192, 216, 218–219, 221, 227, 229, 231–234, 236–240, 266, 286, 291, 293–295, 297–298, 342–343
visiting 26, 54, 61, 114, 168, 173, 181–182, 186, 196–197, 203–207, 210, 213–214, 223, 234, 275, 279, 307, 321–322, 324, 345
visitor(s) 4, 53, 55, 181–182, 184, 186, 190, 201–202, 204–205, 212, 234
visitors' book(s) 55, 109
vocation 43, 65, 324
voluntary 130, 190, 202, 218, 227, 247
volunteer(s) 5, 281, 282–283
vulnerability 109, 171, 331, 334–335

wage(s) 39, 345
Wakefield 123, 133
Wales 4, 6, 40, 54, 130, 141, 180, 188, 192, 201, 206, 212, 258, 281, 299, 301, 305, 309, 329, 346
Walsingham 190
website 116, 206, 208, 211–212
wedding(s) 55, 57, 60, 117, 273, 289, 302, 318, 326
wellbeing 12, 15, 67, 217, 325–329, 334–336
Wells 163, 203
Welsh culture 208, 211
Westcott House 163
winter 29, 123, 138, 191
wisdom 85–86, 88
Wisdom tradition 3, 8–16, 18–21
Wolds 120
Worcester 266, 270, 272
work/life balance 337–338, 342–343
workload(s) 293

World Council of Churches 245, 250, 252, 255

World War, First 84, 124, 165, 167, 172

World War, Second 96, 125, 166, 172, 219

Worldview 11, 89, 91, 207, 214

worship 9, 16–17, 43–44, 49, 59–60, 65, 97, 113, 117, 126–127, 146, 152, 173, 175, 181, 183–184, 202, 207–208, 218–220, 224–226, 233–237, 240, 242–244, 247–255, 258, 264, 280, 282, 305, 314, 318, 323, 326

Yahweh 13

YMCA 96

Yorkshire 4, 85, 120–122, 130, 168, 235–236, 282, 286–288, 294–295, 297–298

young people 140, 146, 154–155, 203, 226–227, 236, 247, 280, 303, 308–310

Youth Hostel 54, 56

youth work 324

Zechariah 35

NAME INDEX

Adams, S. 182, 187
Alexander, K. 84–85, 92
Allchin, A. M. 189, 199
Anderson, C. L. 286–287, 298
Anderson, G. W. 21
Annis, J. 4
ap Siôn, T. 3, 61–64, 67–68, 77–79
Applebaum, S. 25, 27, 32
Aquinas, T. 95
Argyle, M. 326, 328–330, 335
Armstrong, R. 163, 175–176
Arweck, E. 83, 92
Astley, J. 3, 45, 47–48, 51, 53, 58, 63, 65–66, 78–79, 175–176
Avis, P. 225, 228

Bailey, E. 91–92, 269, 280
Bailey, J. 261, 263, 265, 282, 284
Bailey, K. E. 28, 32
Baring-Gould, S. 268, 280
Barker, E. 83, 92
Barr, L. J. T. 163, 176
Barth, K. 44, 51, 96, 97
Bates, M. 259, 265, 281, 284
Bauckham, R. 102–103
Benson, J. 172, 176
Binfield, C. 306, 313
Bishop of St Asaph 190
Blathwayt, B. 162
Blathwayt, F. L. 4, 161–163, 165, 168, 175–177
Blathwayt, J. 4, 161–162, 165–166, 176
Blathwayt, L. D. 163, 165
Blavatsky, H. 84
Bogle, J. 252–254
Booth, W. 15

Bowden, A. 253–254, 267, 280, 287, 298, 316, 324, 339, 346
Bowden, J. 51
Bowen, K. 40
Bradburn, N. M. 335
Bradley, I. 191, 199
Brewster, C. E. 6, 326–327, 335
Brierley, P. W. 113, 118, 226, 228, 287, 298
Britnell, W. J. 189, 199
Bromley, C. 118
Brown, A. 54, 61, 63, 67, 78–79
Brown, C. G. 169, 174, 176, 202, 214
Brueggemann, W. 16, 21, 112, 118
Bultmann, R. 96, 103
Bunton, P. 95, 103
Burke, C. 40
Burton, L. 3–5, 54, 58, 61, 63, 67, 78–79, 298–299, 304

Calvin, J. 90
Campbell, A. 328, 335
Canaan, T. 28, 32
Canary, R. 177
Carmichael, D. 58, 63, 189, 199
Casson, L. 23, 32
Castle, K. 335–336
Chadwick, O. 164, 176
Chapman, M. L. 190, 199
Chaucer, G. 196
Christie, A. 66, 79
Clark, D. 286, 298
Clarke, J. 236, 240
Clarke, J. N. 287, 298
Clifford, R. 84, 91–93
Clinebell, H. 252, 254

Cloke, P. 121, 129–130
Coate, M. A. 338, 346
Coats, G. W. 21
Converse, P. E. 328, 335
Cox, H. 11, 21
Craig, C. L. 166, 176, 261, 263, 265,
　　282, 284, 300, 304, 313–314
Crossland, J. 329, 335
Cumbey, C. 88, 92
Cummins, R. A. 327–328, 334, 336
Cunliffe, B. 189, 199
Curtice, J. 118
Cush, D. 88, 92

Davey, J. 338, 346
Davids, P. H. 37, 40
Davie, G. 86, 92, 106, 111, 118, 139,
　　141, 227–228
Davies, D. 121, 129–130, 146, 155, 287,
　　298
Davies, G. N. 251, 254
Davies, P. 190
De Graff, N. D. 113, 118
Dell, K. 12, 21
Dennen, L. 181, 187
Descartes, R. 98, 100
Dewe, P. J. 326, 336
Drane, J. 3, 83–84, 86, 89, 92–93, 236,
　　240
Dulles, A.C. 244–245, 254
Duncan, B. 261, 265, 282, 284
Durbar, S. 230
Durston, D. 187

Edwards, G. 121, 129–130
Edwards, L. M. 190
Edwards, N. 195, 199
Eichrodt, W. 10–11, 21
Eliot, T. S. 174, 176
Ellwood, R. 83, 93
Emerton, J. 10, 21
Eysenck, H. J. 300, 329, 336
Eysenck, M. W. 329, 336

Fanstone, M. J. 237, 241
Farley, E. 44, 51, 65
Fisher, J. D. C. 306, 314
Fletcher, B. 326, 336, 338, 346

Fletcher, P. 92–93
Ford, D. F. 44, 51, 103
Forgas, J. P. 335
Fowler, J. W. 49, 51
Fox, K. 84
Fox, Margaret 84
Fox, Matthew 89, 93
France, R. T. 3, 36, 40
Francis, L. J. 4–5, 53, 63, 66, 79, 106,
　　111, 118, 132–133, 140–141, 146,
　　149, 155–156, 163, 168, 176–177,
　　182–183, 187, 197–199, 204–205,
　　214, 234–235, 241, 244, 251, 254,
　　258–259, 261, 263, 265, 267, 269,
　　271, 280–282, 284, 299–300, 304,
　　308, 313–314, 316–317, 321, 324,
　　329, 335–336, 339, 346
Francis, P. 118

Galton, F. 327, 336
Gasson, R. 203, 212, 214
Gay, J. 307, 314
Gaze, S. 173, 176
Gilbert, B. G. 326, 332, 336
Gledhill, J. 252, 254
Green, M. 95, 104
Gribbin, B. 186, 187
Griffiths, A. 192, 194, 197
Groothuis, D. 88, 93
Grossoehme, D. H. 67, 79
Guijarro, S. 27–28, 32
Gullone, E. 327–328, 336

Haase, W. 32
Hall, P. A. 216, 228
Hancocks, G. 67, 79
Hanifan, L. J. 216–217, 228
Hardman, C. 91, 93
Harris, C. 314
Harris, J. 167, 176, 301, 304
Harrod, H. L. 88, 93
Harvey, G. 91, 93
Hay, D. 86, 93
Heaton, R. B. 189, 199
Heelas, P. 86, 88, 93
Hemp, W. J. 189, 199
Herbert, J. 58, 63, 189–190, 199
Herbert, M. 190, 199

Hills, P. 326, 328–330, 336
Hobson, T. 181, 187
Hoggart, K. 121, 130
Holeton, D. R. 306, 314
Holmer, P. L. 50–51
Hopkinson, J. 173, 176
Horn, P. 173, 176
Howard, R. 88, 90, 93
Howcroft, K. 287, 298
Howells, A. 5
Hudman, L. 203–204, 212, 214
Hunt, K. 86, 93
Hurtado, L. 250, 254
Hybels, B. 181, 187

Ineson, K. 4
Inge, J. 195, 199
Innes, J. M. 335

Jackson, H. 308, 314
Jackson, R. H. 203–204, 212, 214
Jackson, S. E. 316–317, 324
Jantzen, G. 91, 93
Jarvis, L. 118
Jean, B. 301, 304
Jennings, B. 123, 130
John, T. 196, 199
Johns, C. 175–176
Johnson, P. 84, 91–93
Jones, A. 188, 197, 199
Jones, C. 314
Jones, S. H. 146, 155, 281, 284
Jowell, R. 118
Jung, C. G. 259, 265, 281, 284

Kaldor, P. 335–336
Kawanami, H. 92–93
Kay, W. K. 3, 308, 314
Keirsey, D. 259, 265, 281, 284
Kendall, E. 260–262, 265, 282, 284
Kerry, T. 4, 161–168, 172, 176–177
Keulemans, M. 4, 54, 58, 63
Kightly, C. 168, 172, 177
King-Smith, D. 38, 40
Kirk, M. 338, 346
Kobasa, S. C. 328, 336

Lane, B. B. 58, 63

Lane, B. C. 189, 199
Langrish, M. L. 300–301, 304
Lankshear, D. W. 4, 132–133, 137,
    140–141, 146, 154–156, 198–199,
    300, 304, 313–314
Lardner, M. 67, 79
Lau, L. D. 328, 334, 336
Lawrence, D. H. 169
Le Guin, U. K. 46, 51
Leary, T. 346
Lee, J. M. 48, 51
Leibnitz, G. W. 99
Lessing, G. E. 96
Lewis, J. R. 92–93
Lewis, R. 202, 214, 254
Likert, R. 336
Littler, K. 4–5, 53, 63, 66, 79, 146, 156,
    168, 177, 204, 214, 244, 251, 254,
    299–301, 304, 308, 314
Lloyd Jones, G. 3
Long, B. O. 21
Lowerson, J. 166, 177
Lowther Clarke, W. K. 306, 314
Luffman, G. 261, 265, 282, 284

MacKenzie, I. M. 214
Macquarrie, J. 44, 51
Marshall, I. H. 37, 40
Martin, M. 329, 335
Martineau, J. 4, 53, 63, 118, 146, 156,
    182–183, 187, 197, 199, 204–205,
    214, 234, 240–241, 244, 251, 254,
    266, 280, 300, 304
Marx, K. 99
Maslach, C. 316–317, 324
Maslow, A. 84, 93
McCaulley, M. H. 259, 265, 282, 284
McDermott, T. 95, 104
McFague, S. 47, 51
McGrath, A. E. 95, 104
Mee, A. 177
Melton, J. G. 84, 92–93
Mills, S. 5
Mink, L. 174, 177
Moltmann, J. 94–104
Moore, G. E. 42
Moore, R. 286, 298
Morgan, D. 163, 177

Morgan, K. O. 165, 177
Morley, F. 287, 298
Morris, N. 3
Morrison, A. 88, 93
Morrison, R. 180, 187
Murphy R. E. 12, 21
Myers, D. G. 263, 265
Myers, I. B. 259, 265, 282, 284

Need, A. 113, 118
Newbigin, L. 244, 254
Newton, I. 99
Nietzsche, F. W. 96

Obelkevich, J. 164, 169, 177
Osborne, D. 300, 304
Otto, R. 58, 63

Pack, S. 146, 155
Pahl, R. E. 121, 130
Paley, W. 95, 104
Park, A. 118
Paul, L. 287, 298
Pearson, J. 88, 93
Pegg, S. 5
Percy, M. 227–228
Phillips, D. Z. 50–51
Poole, C. 163, 177
Postman, N. 88, 93
Price, H. 189–190, 199
Pugh, M. 165, 177
Putnam, R. D. 106, 118, 217, 227–228

Radford, C. A. R. 189, 199
Randall, K. J. 329, 336
Reader, J. 245, 254
Redfield, R. 301, 304
Rees, N. 196, 199
Reeves, B. 58, 63, 189, 199
Reventlow, H. G. 9, 21
Richards, A. 226–228
Richardson, A. 51
Riddell, C. 85, 89–90, 93
Robbins, M. 4–5, 63, 79, 106, 111, 118,
   163, 176, 261, 263, 265, 282, 284,
   300, 304, 335–336
Roberts, C. 4, 131–133, 135–136, 141,
   146, 156, 300, 304, 313–314

Rodgers, W. L. 328, 335
Roloff, J. 244–245, 254
Rolph, J. 6
Rolph, P. 6
Russell, A. 122, 129–130, 175, 177,
   243, 253–254, 267, 280, 286, 298,
   316, 324, 339, 346
Rutledge, C. F. J. 146, 156, 300, 304,
   313–314, 316–317, 321, 324, 332,
   336, 339, 346

Saliba, J. A. 83, 93
Sanders, G. S. 336
Sanford, J. A. 337, 346
Sardar, Z. 89, 93
Scharf, B. 169, 177
Schenk, A. 58, 63
Schenke, A. 189, 199
Schmied, G. 67, 78–79
Schweitzer, A. 96, 104, 244, 254
Sexson, S. W. 46, 51
Seymour, S. 146, 155
Sharpe, R. 199
Short, B. 177
Short, C. 146, 155
Smethurst, D. 243, 255
Smith, D. 92–93
Smith, G. 163, 176, 300, 304
Smithson, A. 244–245, 255
Starhawk 89, 93
Stibbe, M. 198, 200
Strange, W. A. 3, 34, 40, 175, 177, 306,
   314
Stratfords, S. 118
Strong, R. 170, 175, 177
Suls, J. 336
Sutcliffe, S. J. 83–85, 93

Talbot-Ponsonby, A. 254
Tannen, D. 46, 51
Temporini, H. 32
Thacker, A. 199
Theissen, G. 30, 32
Thomas, R. 112, 118
Thomas, T. H. 308–310, 312–314
Thompson, F. M. L. 176–177
Thomson, K. 118
Thwaites, J. 181, 187

Tönnies, F. 301, 304
Torry, M. 254
Tovey, P. 243, 250–251, 255
Towner, W. S. 13, 21
Toynbee, J. 195, 200
Trueman, C. 88, 93

Underhill, E. 244, 255

van der Ven, J. A. 49, 51, 145, 156
Vickers, J. A. 252–253, 255
Voase, R. 204, 212, 214
von Balthasar, H. U. 46, 51
von Goethe, J. W. 96
von Rad, G. 12, 19–21

Wainwright, G. 314
Waite, A. 84
Walker, A. 95, 104
Walker, D. S. 3, 5, 109, 118, 168, 177, 266–267, 270, 274, 276, 278, 280
Walton, J. 230, 241
Walvin, J. 230, 241
Ward, P. 181, 187
Ward-Perkins, J. B. 195, 200
Warren, Y. 338–340, 346

Watkins, C. 121, 129–130, 146, 155, 287, 298
Weber, K. 36, 40
Wibberley, G. P. 121, 129–130
Wiles, M. 10–11, 21
Williams, A. 5
Williams, J. A. 245, 255
Williams, Rowan 46, 51, 197, 200, 300
Williams, R. 5
Williams, V. 307, 314
Wilson, B. R. 217, 227
Wilson, J. 251, 255
Winter, M. 121, 129–130, 146, 155, 287, 298
Wittgenstein, L. J. J. 50–51
Wood, D. 313
Woodhead, L. 92–93
Wright, G. E. 9–10, 21

Yarnold, E. J. 306, 314
Yeats, W. B. 84
York, M. 91, 93

Zar-Adusht Ha'nish, O. 85
Ziebertz, H. G. 79
Zozicki, H. 177